The Game Audio Tutorial

The Game Audio Tutorial

A Practical Guide to Sound and Music for Interactive Games

Richard Stevens

Dave Raybould

AMSTERDAM • BOSTON • HEIDELBERG • LONDON • NEW YORK • OXFORD • PARIS
SAN DIEGO • SAN FRANCISCO • SINGAPORE • SYDNEY • TOKYO
Focal Press is an imprint of Elsevier

Focal Press is an imprint of Elsevier
30 Corporate Drive, Suite 400, Burlington, MA 01803, USA
The Boulevard, Langford Lane, Kidlington, Oxford, OX5 1GB, UK

Cover Photography by Tom Jackson, SummerSound Photography (www.summersound.co.uk)
Cover 3D Illustration by Darren Wall (www.toastedpixels.com)

Game Art by Chris Forde (CJ.GameStudios@live.co.uk)

The contents of this book are not endorsed by Epic games.
Unreal Development Kit (UDK) © 2009–2011, Epic Games, Inc. Epic, Epic Games, Gears of War, Gears of War 2, Unreal, AnimSet Viewer, AnimTree Editor, Unreal Cascade, Unreal Content Browser, Unreal Development Kit, UDK, Unreal Editor, Unreal Engine, UE3, Unreal Kismet, Unreal Lightmass, Unreal Matinee, Unreal PhAT, UnrealScript and Unreal Tournament are trademarks or registered trademarks of Epic Games, Inc. in the United States of America and elsewhere. Audacity(R) software is copyright © 1999–2011 Audacity Team. The name Audacity(R) is a registered trademark of Dominic Mazzoni. All other trademarks are the property of their respective owners.

Notices
Knowledge and best practice in this field are constantly changing. As new research and experience broaden our understanding, changes in research methods, professional practices, or medical treatment may become necessary.

Practitioners and researchers must always rely on their own experience and knowledge in evaluating and using any information, methods, compounds, or experiments described herein. In using such information or methods they should be mindful of their own safety and the safety of others, including parties for whom they have a professional responsibility.

To the fullest extent of the law, neither the Publisher nor the authors, contributors, or editors, assume any liability for any injury and/or damage to persons or property as a matter of products liability, negligence or otherwise, or from any use or operation of any methods, products, instructions, or ideas contained in the material herein.

Library of Congress Cataloging-in-Publication Data
Application submitted

British Library Cataloguing-in-Publication Data
A catalogue record for this book is available from the British Library.

ISBN: 978-0-240-81726-2

For information on all Focal Press publications
visit our website at www.elsevierdirect.com

11 12 13 14 15   5 4 3 2 1

Printed in the United States of America

Working together to grow
libraries in developing countries

www.elsevier.com | www.bookaid.org | www.sabre.org

ELSEVIER   BOOK AID International   Sabre Foundation

This book is dedicated to JP.
(42 - 1)

Contents

Contents

Contents

Contents

Contents

Contents

Contents

Contents

**Additional appendices available on the website
(www.thegameaudiotutorial.com) include:**

Acknowledgements

Thanks must go firstly to the Game Audio community for being an inspiring, helpful and supportive bunch of people. To everyone who has ever done a presentation at GDC, Develop or the AES, or who has ever offered advice on a forum, joined a working group, done an interview, or written a magazine article on Games Audio. This book is particularly indebted to two people who have led the way in bringing a critical eye to the theory of what we do, Karen Collins and Rob Bridgett (read their books too!). Our gratitude must also go to Andrew Quinn for his contribution to this book and supporting materials – thanks for picking up the slack! Thanks to all our colleagues and students at Leeds Metropolitan University and to the members of the IASIG and the EDU-WG for their always challenging and interesting discussions.

Other people we'd like to specifically thank are Mark Kilborn, Nathan Rausch, Peter Drescher, Jeff Essex, Ben Mosley, JP Lipscomb-Stevens, Tobias Brogaard, Tom White, Tom Bowers, Chris Forde, Chris Latham, Evangelos Chouvardas, Michael Ward and all the team at Focal Press.

Finally thanks to Andrea Watson, Maria Allen, Polly Stevens, our respective parents, and our wider families for their love and support.

Introduction

We wrote this book because we love games. We also love sound and music, and we love what they can bring to games to make them thrilling, involving, and moving. We want you to be able to try out your sound and your music in a real game. For a book whose examples are based exclusively around one piece of software, it may appear contradictory to say that actually the tools are not important. Once you've had experience with any game editor or audio middleware package, the concepts you learn are easily transferable to others. We chose the Unreal Development Kit (UDK) for this book, as it's a serious game development tool, it's used for lots of games, it's free, and it's fun. In terms of sound and music there are easier tools to use, but unless you're already working for a games developer, you can't get them to work in an actual game. Putting your sound and music into a real game environment = cool. Having to be already working for a games developer to get access to the tools to get them in game = not cool.

We want to put control into the hands of sound designers and composers and to show what you can do, and how far you can go, with the standard tools that come with a typical game editor. As a sound designer, composer, or game designer (we hope there are a few of you reading too!), you have to be an advocate for audio. The good thing about audio is that it tends not to be noticed that much. This means we can affect the player on a powerful subconscious level. The bad thing about audio is, well, that it tends not to be noticed much. You will have to constantly convince people of the importance of investing in sound and music. You'll have to be able to make your case, explain and persuade people that better use of audio makes a better game. You can do this by talking, but you can do it better by showing. We've tried to give you not only the sound and music systems themselves but also an introduction to a number of gameplay systems. By having the means of production, you won't just be the passive provider of assets but can understand the game design process, experiment, and get involved in building systems to demonstrate your ideas effectively. If you want to create great sounds or music and then hand them over for someone else to put into the game, then this book isn't for you (and P.S., your days are numbered). Game audio is about a system of sound or music elements that interact in real time with game events. If you want to be part of the future of game audio you need to learn how to produce interactive audio, not just one-shot sound effects or music loops. You can't separate asset creation from implementation.

A note on genre. There are many genres of games appealing to many different people. Although we've tried to mention several, we have not exhaustively explored the particular aspects of implementing sound for each one, as the principles here are intended to be applicable to many. The biggest-selling, highest-grossing games are undoubtedly first- and third-person shooters. As this is the case, they also tend to be the areas where the most investment is being made in taking the technology of games, and game audio, further. If this is not your preferred genre we can only apologize for the amount of gunfire, death, and explosions in this book, but we hope you understand our reasoning. (We also just like blowing stuff up.)

The Structure of the Book and Tutorial

We have called this book *The Game Audio Tutorial,* as that is what it's intended to be—a practical, hands-on tutorial to introduce the subject of sound and music in games. To find out what's going on at the cutting edge, visit www.thegameaudiotutorial.com for links to some great articles and further research into the subject.

This book does not stand alone. While you're reading this introduction, go to the website and download the tutorial game level and exercises. These are practical demonstrations and exercises built in UDK for you to learn from as you work your way through the book. You'll also find more than 20 video tutorials on the website that you can download and watch to reinforce key techniques. We're very pleased to say that sound designer Andrew Quinn has also put together a fantastic resource of sound effects on the site for you to download and use. These can be found on the Sound Library page.

This book is roughly chronological in terms of skills development, so it's intended that you'll read through from the start. After Chapter 2 you should have enough of a basic understanding to be able to dip in and out, but you won't necessarily be able to skip straight to Chapter 7 without understanding all of what has come before. The text will discuss transferable principles, and their implementation in the accompanying tutorial level, before going on to suggest an exercise that you should do in order to embed this knowledge. This hands-on experience will equip you with the skills and knowledge to apply this learning to other games engines and platforms you may encounter or wish to use in the future. Each chapter will follow this approach with the exception of Chapter 8: Next Steps, which is by its nature more discursive.

We hope you find this book useful,

Richard and Dave.

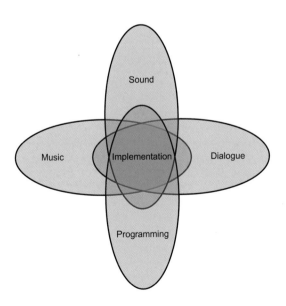

1

Basic Training

In this chapter you'll be introduced to the chosen platform for demonstrating the principles within the book, Epic Game's Unreal Development Kit (UDK, available to all readers for free at www.udk.com). We will also begin to look at the importance of ambient sound in adding character and immersion to game environments.

Opening the Tutorial Level

The first step is to download and install UDK. While you're waiting, go to the companion site www.thegameaudiotutorial.com and download the tutorial files. Once downloaded, unzip the package by right-clicking and selecting "Unzip to" (Choose a folder). See the README file in the zip package for full instructions on how to get everything up and running.

You will need to remember the UDK install folder. This is typically C:\UDK\UDK-(*Date of current version*).

As the precise location may change depending on which version you are using we will simply refer to C:\UDK\(***) in the text.

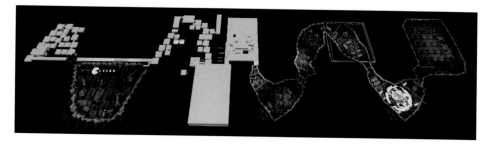

The Game Audio Tutorial Level.

Before you start the tutorial level, we recommend that you play some of the levels that come with the UDK. From the Start menu, select Unreal Development Kit/Game–Unreal Development Kit. If you're not used to this first-person-shooter style environment, then use the mouse to look around and to shoot and use the WASD keys to move.

When you're done, exit the game and then from your Programs menu choose Unreal Development Kit/Editor–Unreal Development Kit. When this has started up, choose Open from the File menu and open the level GAT_V01_000. To play the tutorial level now, click on the Start this level on PC icon from the top menu bar.

Start this level on PC.

Spend some time exploring the level, and when you're ready to move on press the Esc key on your computer keyboard then choose Exit Game to return to the Editor window. Before we start looking at the level, you should save it under a different filename. That way if you start playing around with it (which we would encourage you to do), you can always go back to the original version. Do this now from the File/Save menu in the main window.

It's a good idea to get into good habits straight away, so start by having useful information in the filename, like today's date and the version number: MyGame_1901_01_01_V01.

Then after making any significant changes, you can save it again, this time calling it MyGame_1901_01_01_V02. You'll notice that we've used underscores (_) instead of spaces. You should do this with all your files including sound or music files. The general rule is that games software doesn't like spaces!

Explore the Level: Navigation

If you haven't used a game editor before, then simply navigating your way around is probably going to be your steepest learning curve. Most editors use a combination of mouse buttons to enable you (sometimes referred to as "the camera") to move around in the 3D space. Some (like UDK) also allow you to also use the WASD keys that are typical of first-person shooter navigation.

In the tutorial level, we've put in some basic navigation points. Try jumping between these points by pressing the keys 1, 2, 3, 4, 5, 6, and 7 on your keyboard. These correlate to the start room for each of the chapters of the book. (You can override these or create your own by pressing Ctrl + the number key to set them up.)

You can see within the tutorial level that we have numbered all the rooms. These correspond with the room numbers in the text below. To help you navigate your way around the level, we've also added colored doorframes. Green is a room that moves forward in the order of the book, Red goes back. For annex rooms that come off the main rooms Blue takes you forward, and Yellow takes you back. We hope you don't get lost!

Go back to navigation point 1 by pressing "1" and you should find yourself in the first room.

Views

You'll see that you have four different viewports of the map: Front, Side, Top, and Perspective. (If the editor has started with one full screen view then click on Maximize Viewport—the square icon on the Viewport toolbar—to change to the view below.)

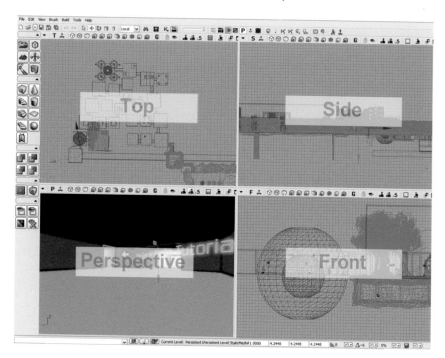

You can change these using the Viewport Options menu (the drop-down arrow on the left of each viewport) and choosing Viewport Type.

You can also cycle through the viewports by clicking on the button currently marked "P."

Try changing the viewports for the bottom-left screen and then return to Perspective view "P."

Navigation

Now try using your left mouse button, your right mouse button, your mouse wheel, and both mouse buttons together to start seeing how you can move around the level.

> Left mouse button (LMB): Pan the camera left/right, Move forward/back
> Right mouse button (RMB): Mouse look
> LMB + RMB: Move left/right, Move up/down

If you hold down your right mouse button, you can also "fly" through the level by using the keyboard keys W,A,S,D and using Q and E to move up or down. It's often easiest to use a combination of "flying" in the Perspective viewport and clicking and dragging in the Top viewport to navigate your way around.

If at any time you want to just start playing the game from a particular spot, then right-click on the floor and select "Play from here." (Press the Esc key to return to the editor.) Or you can play the whole level from the beginning in the Editor window by clicking on the aptly titled "Play this level in an editor window" button.

Building

As you work your way through the book we'd encourage you to learn by playing around with items in the tutorial level and exercise rooms. As you do so you'll quickly become aware that when you make a significant change to a level you need to "Build" it again. You can do this from the Build menu or the shortcut icons on the top toolbar. See Appendix C: Building for some specific guidance on this.

Actors

100 Start Room

Go back to the first room (Press 1 on your keyboard) and turn around using the left mouse button until you are looking behind you. If you press the G key a few times, you should see the small switch icon disappear and reappear. The G key hides everything that's not actually visible in the game itself. These objects are what control the events in the game; they are called Actors.

This particular Actor is called a **[Trigger]** and we will be seeing a lot more of it as we move forward. If you look up you'll also see a *Light* Actor and the button is a *Static Mesh* Actor.

It's possible that you might not be seeing these at all. The interface can get very complicated with many Actors and other objects on the screen, so you have the ability to *Show* and *UnShow* certain types of objects (you will also find that the number and types of things you display can have a significant impact on the smoothness of the system as well). This is again controlled from the Viewport Options menu (from the *Show* submenus). For the moment, select Use Defaults.

You can move the Actors in a couple of ways, either by clicking and dragging their arrows or by holding Ctrl and using the usual mouse combinations.

    Ctrl + LMB = Moves on the X axis
    Ctrl + RMB = Moves on the Y axis
    Ctrl and LMB + RMB = Moves on the Z axis

Grab the **[Trigger]** or light and move it around. Notice how its movement has a different appearance in the different viewports because of their different perspectives. Now try selecting any random Actor in one of the viewports. Right-click and choose Go to Actor from the menu that appears (or press the keyboard shortcut Home key). You'll see that all the viewports snap immediately to focus on the Actor that you have selected.

Using the Home key to make all the viewports focus on the Actor you have selected is very useful, particularly when used in combination with clicking and dragging to move around in the Top viewport. You can quickly move across your whole level, find an Actor in roughly the place you want to go, and then press the Home key to jump to that position.

You can select multiple items at once by holding down Ctrl while you click to select with the LMB or use Ctrl + Alt in any of the views (apart from the Perspective view) for a marquee selection (this creates a box and selects anything within that box). Try this in the Top viewport.

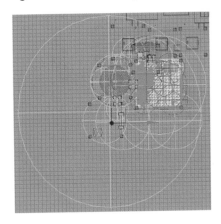

The Content Browser: Finding Actors

It's easy to find Actors in the restaurants of most major cities (they're the ones serving you the food), and in UDK it's equally straightforward. You may already have seen a floating window that you haven't used yet. If not, then either click on the icon indicated in the following figure or press the keyboard shortcut Ctrl + Shift + F to open it. This is the Content Browser that you will come to know and love.

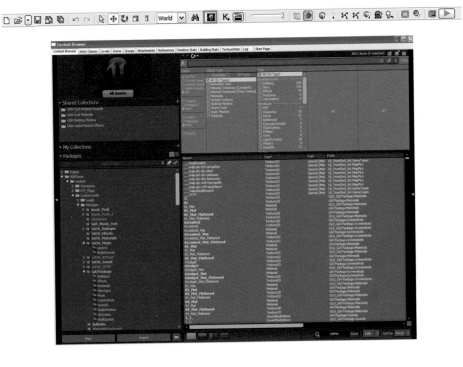

You'll notice that this browser has several different pages as shown by the tabs at the top. You can see these pages by clicking on the tab, but you may find it more convenient later to select them directly from the menu that comes up if your press the Ctrl key and the Tab key simultaneously on your keyboard.

It's from this browser that you can select the Actors you need to place in the level, and it's also from here that you can open the packages that contain all of the assets that go into making a game (such as materials, meshes, and, of course, sound and music files). Select the tab called Scene.

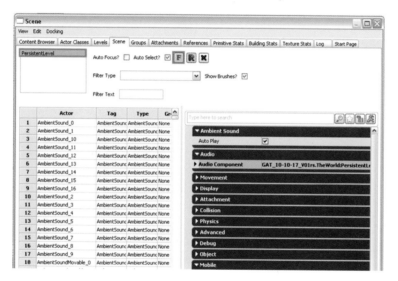

In the top-left box, select Persistent level. This will now show you a list of all the Actors in the level. At the top of the list, you should see some **[AmbientSoundSimple]** Actors listed. Select one of them by clicking on it, and the press the F (Focus) button.

> So you can identify them more easily within the text, we will be placing the names of all the Actors or Objects we refer to within square brackets, such as **[Actor]**.

Your viewports should then jump to focus on this Actor. Try this with a few other items from the list. You can also check (tick) the Auto Focus box to jump to any Actor you select automatically. When you've finished, press "1" to return to the first room, then follow the arrow pointing left into Room 101.

Every Room Has a Tone: Ambience

101 Room Tone

In the real world, there's no such thing as silence (even in an anechoic chamber you can hear your blood and heart beat). In most buildings (or spaceships!), there will be some electrical or mechanical sound sources. These electric or mechanical sounds will often be either constant or repeating. We can replicate them by using looping sound files. These *room tones* not only make an environment feel more real, but they can also be used to set the mood of a particular place. Never use complete silence in an environment in your game unless it's for an explicit aesthetic purpose (and even then, don't).

[AmbientSoundSimple] for Looping Sounds

In Room 101, you should see the **[AmbientSoundSimple]** icon in the center of the room.

If you can already hear it, you will notice that this type of sound loops around to play continuously. In this case it's a room-tone hum. If you can't hear it, you need to try a couple of things.

To hear things live in the Editor windows, you need to enable Toggle Real Time Audio. This is the speaker icon in the top toolbar.

If it's not already on you'll also want to enable the Real Time option for the Perspective viewport using the joystick icon.

With the **[AmbientSoundSimple]** icon selected, press "F4" on your keyboard (or right-click and select Properties) to open its properties. (You can also double-click with the left mouse button). Now click on the AmbientSoundSimple menu bar to fully expand it. (You can also choose to right click to fully expand all the submenus).

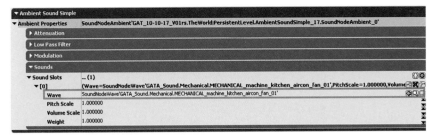

You can see in the Sounds section that at the moment this **[AmbientSoundSimple]** is playing the sound file MECHANICAL_machine_kitchen_aircon_fan_01. Before we can change this or add our own, we need to look at how these sound assets are stored in UDK.

Changing your First Sound

We're going to try changing the sound of an existing **[AmbientSoundSimple]** to get used to some of the basic principles involved in using assets in UDK. When you import a sound file into UDK, it is referred to as a SoundNodeWave. We'll be using the terms *sounds*, *wavs*, and *SoundNodeWaves* interchangeably.

Packages

All of the assets in UDK are contained in the Packages section. You'll note that the **[AmbientSoundSimple]** you just looked at referenced GATA_Sound.Mechanical.MECHANICAL_ Machine_Kitchen_aircon_Fan_01. The part of the name before the first full stop/period is the name of the package that holds that sound file.

Open the Content Browser (Ctrl + Shift + F).

In the bottom-left window, you can navigate your folder structure (the package tree). The sounds in the tutorial level are in the GATA_Sound package within the UTGame/Content/CustomLevels/ Packages Folder.

If you select this package (as in the preceding screenshot), you can see that we've sorted the assets into different groups within this package so it's easier to find things. If you select the Ambience group, then you can double-click on the names of the sounds in the right-hand window to hear them. Try this now. You'll see that at the bottom of this browser window you can also choose to view your assets using List view, Split views, or Thumbnail view.

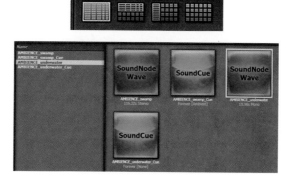

Vertical Split view for packages.

The top right-hand window serves as the search bar where you can search directly for named assets or filter the selections by specifying the type of asset you want, using either the Object Type or the Tags. For instance, you may only want to see Sounds, or Animation sets, or Fonts. You can do this by checking or unchecking the relevant boxes. Select the All Types tab initially, then try filtering the objects by different types to see how this works.

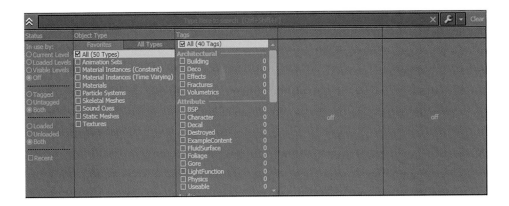

You can see that the UDK packages also have some sounds that come with them. In the bottom-left Packages window, expand the UTGame folder/Content/Sounds/A_Ambient_Loops/Interiors.

Then from the Search filter, choose to see only Sound Wave Data.

Preview these sounds by double-clicking on the name of the sound and settle on one you like. You can use this sound in your first exercise.

Exercise 101_00 Changing an [AmbientSoundSimple]

From the File menu, open Exercise_101_00.udk from the exercise folder.

Tips

1. Select the sound you want in the Content Browser (try one from UTGame/Content/Sounds/A_Ambient_Loops/ Interiors).
2. Select the **[AmbientSoundSimple]** in the center of the exercise room and bring up its properties (right-click and select Properties, or choose Select and press F4, or just double-click).
3. In the AmbientSoundSimple/Sounds section of the properties, you should see the sound that's already assigned to it, where it says "Wave."

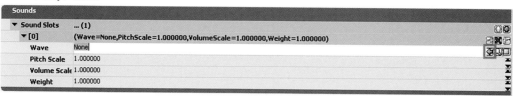

4. Click on the green arrow, and UDK will replace this sound with the one that you currently have selected in the Content Browser. (If it doesn't work, then go back to the Content Browser and make sure the sound is still selected.)
5. You should now hear your sound from the Perspective viewport.
6. Now select "Play this level in an editor window" from the top toolbar (the Play icon) and walk around the room to see how your new sound works. (To jump into any room and play you can also right-click on the floor in the Perspective viewport and choose "Play from here.")
7. Try changing to some other sounds like ones from the Fire, Machines, or Water groups.

Adding your First Sound

Exercise 101_01 Adding an [AmbientSoundSimple]

Open the Exercise file 101_01 and look at the first room that is empty. You'll notice that actually there's no ambient sound in this room. This makes it sound lifeless and unreal (pun intended). It needs a room tone. Add a bit of life by introducing an **[AmbientSoundSimple]** to the room.

Tips

1. In the Content Browser, select the sound file you want. (Try A_Ambient_Loops.Interiors.stereo_interior15; use the search bar.)
2. Now right-click on the floor of the room in your Perspective viewport.
3. Select Add Actor/Add AmbientSoundSimple: Stereo_Interior15.
4. Now play the level in the Editor window (right-click on the floor and select "Play from here").
5. Sit back in smug satisfaction.
6. This was a shortcut. Later on you'll need to know how to add different sorts of Actors; not all of these are available from the right-click menu. Go to the Content Browser (Ctrl + Shift + F), and select the Actor Classes tab. This is where all the Actor types hang out. Expand the Sounds menu and the AmbientSound menu, and select **[AmbientSoundSimple]**. Now in your Perspective viewport, right-click and choose "Add AmbientSoundSimple Here." If you still had a sound selected in the Content Browser, then it will have been automatically selected to fill this **[AmbientSoundSimple]**; if not, then you'll have to go back to the Content Browser and add one to your new **[AmbientSoundSimple]** using the green arrow (within its properties) as shown in Ex101.

Importing your First Sound

Exercise 101_02 Importing Your Own Sound

By now you'll probably want to know how to start adding your own sounds to a level instead of using the ones that come with UDK or this tutorial. So you're going to have to make your own package and import your sounds into it. You can download wavs from the Sound Library on the website, but also try this out with your own sounds as soon as you can.

Tips

1. Your sound files can be any mono or stereo 16-bit wavs (or waves) at any sample rate. Mono files will be spatialized in the game (pan around); stereo files will not.
2. First, make sure that in the Content Browser (Ctrl + Shift + F) window you have selected the Packages folder within the Custom Levels folder. We're going to import the new sounds into this folder. Click Import at the bottom of the screen.
3. Browse to your Wavs folder and select the file you want. Remember, with your own sounds (or any other assets) you must not have any spaces in the filenames, so try to get into the habit of replacing these with an underscore (_).

4. You'll now need to name your new package. UDK tends to call its audio packages by names starting with A_, so let's adopt that convention. Name your package for example A_TutorialTestpackage. (Here's where you also have the opportunity to create subgroups for your assets as well if you wish.)

5. You'll see that your package appears at the very bottom of the packages list under New Packages until you right-click and save it. Then it should appear within the Custom Levels/Packages folder where we want it.
6. When you import any new sounds, you should save the package (right-click/Save or Ctrl + S) before using them.
7. Now try adding this to an **[AmbientSoundSimple]** in a room like you did in Exercise 101_00.

(See Appendix C: UDK Tips, "Importing Sounds," for some more very useful advice.)

Looping Sounds

Once you've imported some of your own sounds and added them to your level using an **[AmbientSoundSimple]**, you may find that they sound a bit clunky, particularly at the point at which they end then go back and start at the beginning. Getting these *loop points* right can be tricky.

We've put tips related to audio editing, such as looping, in Appendix D on the website so if you're familiar with this then you can just carry on with the book. If you want to look a bit more at how to get your sounds to loop nicely in game, then now's the time to have a look at Appendix D at www.thegameaudiotutorial.com. We'll refer to audio editing software and sequencer packages by the catch-all title of digital audio workstations (DAWs) from now on to keep things simple.

Exercise 101_03 Looping Machinery

Open Exercise room EX101_03. You'll see that there are various pieces of machinery here. Using **[Ambient SoundSimple]**s, bring this room to life. Use existing UDK sounds or import your own.

Tips

1. Remember to make a new package and import your sounds into it. Use the Import button at the bottom of the Content Browser.
2. Save your package after you import anything new. (You'll notice that unsaved packages are marked by an asterisk (*).)
3. You will probably want to adjust the volume of each sound to create an effective mix. Use the Volume Scale adjustment to do this, using the value 1.0 as the maximum volume.

Sounds		
▼ **Sound Slots**	... (1)	
▼ **[0]**	(Wave=SoundNodeWave'A_Ambient_Loops.Machines.machine_engine01'	
Wave	SoundNodeWave'A_Ambient_Loops.Machines.machine_engine01'	
Pitch Scale	1.000000	
Volume Scale	1.000000	
Weight	1.000000	

Ambient Sounds Case Study

To be good at designing sound and music for games, your most important skill is your ability to listen. Even a relatively simple game audio (or real) environment is made from layers of sounds. Paying close attention to sounds in the real world will allow you to develop the attention to detail you're going to need if you're going to get it right in the game world.

102 Ambient Sounds Case Study

In Yorkshire there are 24 different words for types of rain. This room demonstrates some of these types. You may be thinking this whole **[AmbientSoundSimple]** thing is pretty easy. Adding them to your level is easy, getting them right isn't. This room is a simple demonstration using just rain sounds. If you look at it, you'll perhaps begin to think about the thorough approach you need to re-create a convincing world.

There is not just one big rain sound for this area. In fact, there are six different types of rain because rain sounds different according to the surface it's falling on.

1. General rain
2. Rain on trees
3. Rain on water
4. Rain on metal roof
5. Rain on hollow metal barrels
6. Rain on plants

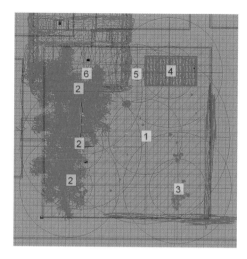

You can see from the diagram that these have had to be carefully arranged to make sure they cover the correct areas.

Attenuation and Radius Min/Radius Max

Attenuation refers to how sound gets quieter, in this case over distance. We can't replicate the range of volume or the physics of the real world in games (for reasons explained later); therefore, we have to cheat. Most game editors deal with this by giving each sound a Min and Max radius. The sound is not attenuated (i.e., not made quieter) when the player is within the Min radius, but it gradually gets quieter until you reach silence at the Max radius.

In Room 102, you'll notice that the blue circles around each **[AmbientSoundSimple]** are of different sizes. These represent the radius within which you can hear a sound and how the sound attenuates (gets quieter) over distance. Think of these as defining the size of two spheres surrounding the **[AmbientSoundSimple]**. Within the Radius Min sphere, the sound is at its loudest. The volume then drops as we travel out to silence at the Radius Max sphere.

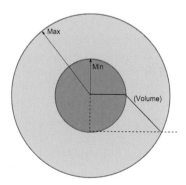

Within the Min area, the volume is at its highest. It then drops off to a volume of zero at the Max radius.

You can adjust the Radius Min and Radius Max settings from the AmbientSoundSimple/Attenuation menu in the **[AmbientSoundSimple]** properties (Press F4). You can either enter figures directly or use the arrows on the right-hand side.

The other way to adjust them is to use the Scaling widget. When you have an Actor selected, the space bar on your keyboard will cycle through three functions: Move, Scale, and Rotate. For an **[AmbientSoundSimple]**, the Scale mode allows you to click and drag the square blocks to adjust the Radius Max size. (For more on scaling Actors, see Appendix C: UDK Tips.)

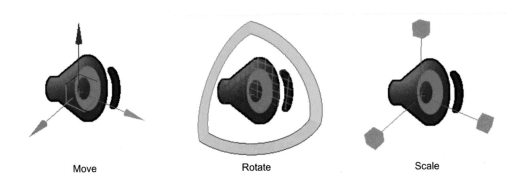

Move   Rotate   Scale

A Word About Distances in UDK

When you are resizing the Radius Min and Radius Max values for your **[AmbientSoundSimple]**s, the numbers you are dealing with are the units of distance that UDK uses. (As a very general rule of thumb, you may typically be looking at a player height of 96 units, average room dimensions of 1024 × 1024 × 256, and a door height of 128.) The documentation states that 1 unreal unit is equal to 2 cm, but that's not really the whole story. You may have noticed in the past that for a variety of reasons distances in games are not the same as distances in the real world. To measure a distance in the viewports, it's easiest to use the Top view. By holding down the middle mouse button and dragging the mouse, you will get a distance readout. You can use these values to help you judge your Radius Min and Radius Max sizes.

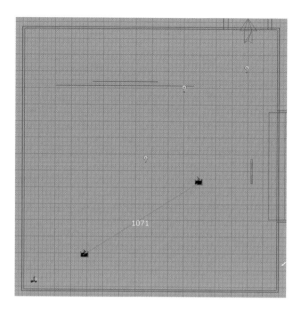

A Word About Numbers in UDK

In computing terms, you have two types of number, integers and floating point numbers. Integers are whole numbers, and floating point numbers (or floats) are numbers with decimal points.

$$Integer = 1$$
$$Float = 1.0$$

So the previous distances are integers, but the volume and radius numbers we've been looking at are floats. It's important to get the type right in UDK, as objects are usually set to use one type or the other. Use the wrong type, and they will not work.

Exercise 102_00 Ambient Sound Radii

This room is a slightly different arrangement of the objects in the Tutorial Room 102. Using either the sounds provided in the GATA_Sounds/Weather group, or the Sound Library, add appropriate sounds to this level. You could also try adding your own rain sounds. (If you live in Wales or Seattle you'll have a distinct advantage.)

Tips

1. Remember, for **[AmbientSoundSimple]**s just select the SoundNodeWave in the Content Browser then right-click in your level to add one with the sound already attached. (Make sure the package is fully loaded, Right Click/Fully Load).

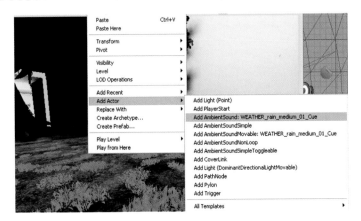

2. Think carefully about the Radius Min/Radius Max distances of your **[AmbientSoundSimple]**s so that the sound is only heard around the objects you want, not across the whole area. To alter these settings, press F4 to access the selected **[AmbientSoundSimple]**s properties.

3. Within the AmbientSoundSimple section of the properties, expand the Attenuation settings by clicking on "Attenuation."

4. Adjust the Min and Max numbers and note the change in size of the blue radius indicators in the Top viewport. You can adjust these values either by typing numbers directly into the boxes or by using the arrows on the right to scroll the values up or down.

5. Test your changes by right-clicking in the Perspective viewport and selecting "Play from here."

6. Don't forget to also use the volume settings of the **[AmbientSoundSimple]** in combination with your radii settings.

Toggle a Looping Sound

103 Toggle Sounds On/Off

If you take shelter from the rain of Room 102 in the small building hut (Room 103), you'll see that there is an array of buttons on the right-hand side controlling a fictitious generator. Walk up to this panel and "use" it (E on your keyboard). To interact with things in UDK, the default is the E key. When we refer to "using" things from now on, what we mean is to walk up to them and press the E key. By "using" this, you "toggle" the generator sound on. "Use" it again to toggle it off.

As we are now interacting with sounds, we need to look at UDK's visual scripting system, called Kismet.

Kismet 101

The more you know about how actions are triggered within your game engine, the more understanding and control you have. It is essential that you can manipulate these triggering systems so that you are not just a passive sound designer handing over assets. Time to get your hands dirty.

Kismet uses a graphical object orientated programming paradigm. In other words, you have a bunch of objects that do stuff and by connecting these up with wires in the right way, you can build systems that do more interesting stuff. This is an increasingly common approach to many software packages, so even if you don't anticipate using UDK in your next project, the concepts you will learn by using Kismet will be useful. If you press K on your keyboard, you will see all of the Actors in the game that are linked into a Kismet system. Now press K again to toggle them off.

Click the K button on the top menu bar to open Kismet.

(If you have an Actor selected in the viewport that is referenced by Kismet, you can also press Ctrl + K to open Kismet and jump straight to the system where it's referenced. You will find this extremely useful.)

In Kismet you can have *actions, conditions, variables,* and *events* to create systems to perform certain functions in your level.

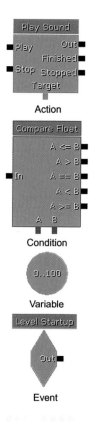

(Note that there are two types of number variable, integers and floats. These whole numbers or decimal numbers were described earlier. This is just a reminder to make sure you use the right type for the right object.)

As you can see, right-clicking in an empty space within Kismet reveals that there are many of these objects to choose from, so the potential for creating your own systems is huge. (See Appendix C: UDK Tips for more on Kismet.) We'll highlight the use of these objects in the text using **[Action/ Condition/Events]**, and we'll highlight the variables by using *italics.*

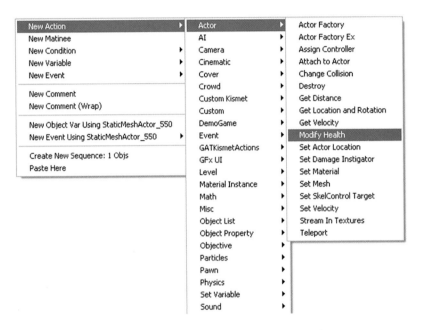

In the Kismet window for the tutorial level, you'll see several boxes. These are *sequences* where the systems have been packaged up to keep the screen from getting too cluttered. For the moment, choose the sequence named Room 103, and double-click to open it.

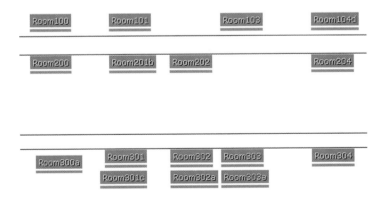

[AmbientSoundSimpleToggleable] for Toggleable Looping Sounds

The electrical unit on the wall in Room 103 is just a graphic, or to be more precise, a *Static Mesh,* and is not involved in the system. The switch icon represents a **[Trigger]** Actor. It is this **[Trigger]** that the player "uses" (by pressing E within a given proximity of it) to **[Toggle]** an **[AmbientSoundSimpleToggleable]** on or off.

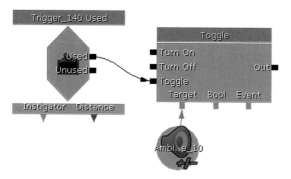

The **[AmbientSoundSimpleToggleable]** is from the Sounds/AmbientSound menu within the Actor Class tab of the Content Browser (the same place as the **[AmbientSoundSimple]**s we've already been using).

After it has been added to the level (Right-click, Add Actor/Add AmbientSoundSimpleToggleable) sounds are added to this by opening its properties (F4), selecting the sound in the Content Browser, and using the green arrow in the same way we did when we selected a sound for an **[AmbientSoundSimple]**.

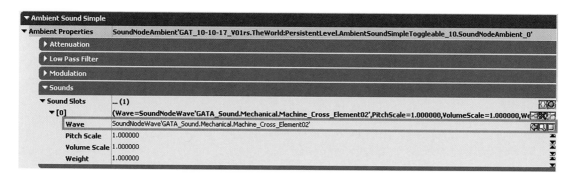

You see that a cylinder appears around the **[Trigger]** when it is selected. This is its *collision radius*. It's only when within this radius that the player can interact. The collision radius is set within the properties of the **[Trigger]** (F4) from the Trigger/Cylinder component using the Collision Height and Collision Radius featues. It can also be adjusted using the Scaling widget in the same way that we adjusted the Attenuation properties of the **[AmbientSoundSimple]** earlier. You may also want to use the Scaling widget (or the **[AmbientSoundSimple Toggleable]** properties) to set the Radius Min/Radius Max attenuation for the sound (shown now with yellow spheres).

Work through the following tutorial to get a better understanding of how to implement this simple Kismet system.

Exercise 103_00 Kismet [Trigger] "Used" to Toggle Sound

In this exercise, you should make a switch that turns the machine on and off. Create a Kismet system with a **[Trigger]** and an **[AmbientSoundSimpleToggleable]** to do this.

Tips

1. Right-click in your Perspective viewport and choose Add Actor/Add Trigger.
2. Select your chosen sound in the Content Browser then Right Click in the Perspective viewport and select Add Actor/All Templates/Add AmbientSoundSimpleToggleable : (***)
3. Open Kismet, and with your **[Trigger]** selected in the Perspective viewport, right-click in the Kismet window and select New Event Using (***)/Used.

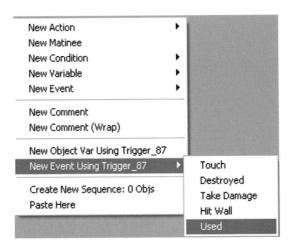

4. Now create a **[Toggle]** object (right-click in the Kismet window and choose New Action/Toggle/Toggle). Connect the Used output of the **[Trigger]** to the Toggle input of the **[Toggle]** object by clicking on the input, holding down the left mouse button, and dragging a wire from one to the other.

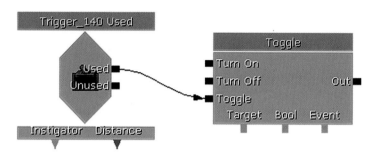

5. The **[Toggle]** object is going to toggle your **[AmbientSoundSimple Toggleable]** on and off, so select the **[AmbientSoundSimpleToggleable]** in your Perspective viewport, then right-click on the Target output of the **[Toggle]** object in Kismet and choose New Object Var using AmbientSoundSimpleToggleable_1.

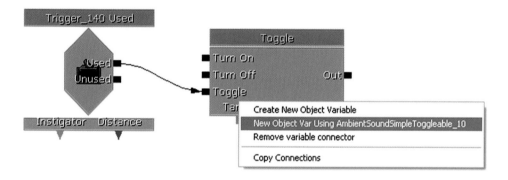

6. There's just a couple more things to do before you test it in the level. By default, **[Trigger]**s are invisible within the game, so in order for you to test this action, you need to see where your **[Trigger]** is. Select your **[Trigger]**, go to its Properties (F4), and uncheck the Hidden box. You should now be able to see the **[Trigger]** in your level for testing purposes.

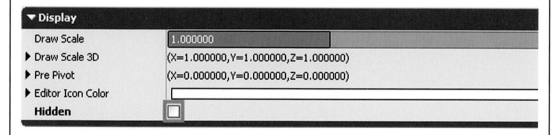

7. With your **[Trigger Used]** event selected in Kismet, look at its properties, shown in the section at the bottom of the Kismet window. You will probably want to uncheck the Aim to Interact option, as this can make it tricky to interact. While you're there, you should also change the Max Trigger Count to 0. This effectively sets it to be able to be triggered an infinite number of times.

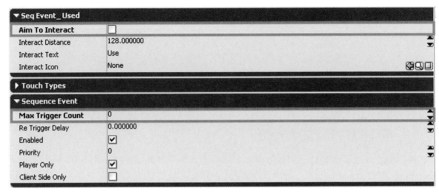

▼ Seq Event_ Used		
Aim To Interact	☐	
Interact Distance	128.000000	
Interact Text	Use	
Interact Icon	None	
▶ **Touch Types**		
▼ **Sequence Event**		
Max Trigger Count	0	
Re Trigger Delay	0.000000	
Enabled	☑	
Priority	0	
Player Only	☑	
Client Side Only	☐	

8. Now select Play from Here, walk up to your **[Trigger]**, and press E on the keyboard to use it. You should now be able to Toggle this ambient loop on or off.

Exercise 103_01 Kismet [Trigger] "Touch" to Toggle Sounds

Open Exercise 103_00. You can see here that there is a precious energy crystal in the center of the room. However, it is protected by laser sensors. Create a "touch" **[Trigger]** so that when the player enters this area an alarm goes off. Then adapt it so that it stops when the player leaves the area. Extend your system so that the player is able to press the red button in the room to switch off the alarm.

Tips

1. Add a **[Trigger]** to the level. In the Perspective viewport, right-click and choose Add Actor/Add Trigger.
2. Adjust its collision to be the correct size (either via Properties (F4) or by using the space bar to select the resize widget).
3. Open Kismet using the K icon from the top menu bar.
4. With your **[Trigger]** still selected in the viewport, right-click in an empty space and select New Event using Trigger (***)/Touch.
5. Change its Max Trigger Count (from the Properties/Sequence Event menu at the bottom) to 0. This means it is able to be retriggered indefinitely.
6. Create a **[Toggle]** object in Kismet (New Action/Toggle/Toggle) and connect the Touched output of the Trigger Touch event to the Toggle input.
7. Back in your Perspective viewport, right-click to Add Actor/Add **[AmbientSoundSimpleToggleable]**.
8. Choose an alarm sound from within the GAT_A_Alarm package.
9. Add this sound to the **[AmbientSoundSimpleToggleable]** by selecting the Sound wave in the Content Browser and using the green arrow within the properties of the **[AmbientSoundSimple Toggleable]**.
10. With your **[AmbientSoundSimpleToggleable]** selected in the map go to Kismet and Right Click on the Target of the **[Toggle]** object. Choose "New Object Var using AmbientSoundSimpleToggleable_0".
11. Play your level. When the player collides with the invisible **[Trigger]**, the alarm should sound. When the player moves away, it should stop.
12. You could now extend this system by putting a **[Trigger]** around the button and creating a 'Used' action in Kismet to toggle off the alarm.

Ambient Loops and "Phasing Loops"

Looping sounds are good for things that produce sounds that are by their nature constant or repetitive. If you have a problem loop that sounds unnatural, you can break up the looping feel by having another sound of a slightly different length playing at the same time. These two loops will drift out of time with one another, so the resulting combination of the two sounds will be different each time.

104 "Phasing" Ambient Loops

We've discussed how room tones and mechanical/electrical sources are often repetitive or constant in nature, and most of the time this is why the **[AmbientSoundSimple]** loops are appropriate. You may feel under certain circumstances that these loops are too repetitive. This is a particular problem when creating an ambient environment for more natural sounds. We'll deal with other solutions later, but at this stage you'll note that you can actually play more than one sound at once with an **[AmbientSoundSimple]** by adding another *sound slot* (using the + sign). It will then loop both (or more) of your sounds.

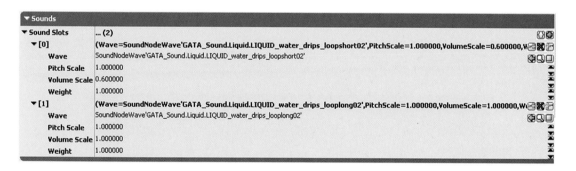

You can help to beat the sense of repetition by making these looped sounds different lengths. This means they will "phase" in and out of time with each other. As each sound loops around, it does so at a different time to the other loop, so you will get a new combination of the two sounds. In the tutorial-level example, there are two short loops of water dripping in a cave. As the two sounds loop around, they will be out of time with each other; this will create new rhythms and combinations of their drip sounds, which would otherwise be repetitive. In the following illustration you can see that the combination of the two sounds will not actually become the same as it was in the beginning (with the beginning of both sounds heard at the same time) for quite some time.

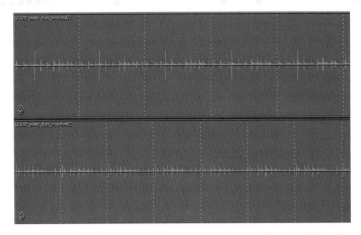

These are sometimes referred to as "phasing loops" as the two loops "phase" in and out of time with each other. This useful technique is not to be confused with "phasing," which is actually a problem to avoid that we'll be dealing with later. In the next chapter, we'll also be looking in more detail at methods for dealing with the problems of repetition in game audio.

The "Walls" Problem

Accurately calculating and re-creating the physics of sound in the real world still remains out of the reach of modern consoles because of their current processing capabilities. In many games editors we still need to fudge things a little to make them sound right—little things, like the existence of walls!

105 Ambient Sounds "Walls" Problem

In Room 105, you can see that we have put an **[AmbientSoundSimple]** on the machine inside the smaller room. If you wander around the room in-game, then you will quickly notice the problem. When on the outside of this room (around the back) you can still clearly hear the machine that's on the inside, despite the fact that there's actually a wall in the way.

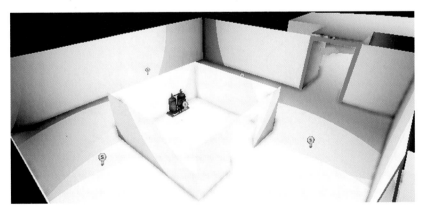

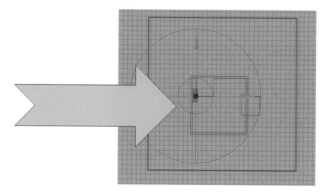

When standing here, you can still hear the machine on the other side of the wall.

For the machine to sound natural in the room itself, the Min/Max attenuation needs to be as it is, but the walls do not automatically block the sound as they would do in the real world. Trying to stop this overlap means moving the sound's center of origin away from the object itself. This is not satisfactory. There are other solutions to this problem, but in some editors it is common for you to need to create several instances of the ambient sound so that it fills the room space but does not overlap the wall.

Multiple Sounds Solution to the Walls Problem

105a Multiple Sounds Solution

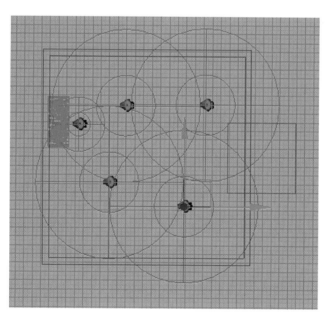

In Room 105a, you can hear that several smaller **[AmbientSoundSimple]**s have been used to give the impression of the room being filled with the sound of the machine. We no longer perceive the machine as a point source, but instead its sound fills the room. This approach requires care with the Radius Min and Max settings, as overlapping sources effectively double the volume. We can see that this is a partial solution but remains less than ideal. Fortunately, UDK offers another solution that we will look at in Chapter 3 (see the section titled "Ambient Zones"), but in some other editors you may need to continue to use this approach. If you do, then you should be conscious of some additional issues that may arise.

The Number-of-Voices Problem

We will discuss the numbers of simultaneous sounds you can have playing in your games later (Chapter 6, in the section titled "Voice Instance Limiting and Prioritization"), but be aware that it is a finite resource. Using multiple versions of the same sound will use up multiple voices.

Panning Problem

105b Panning

You'll notice in Room 105b that each copy of the sound is spatialized. In other words, it pans from speaker to speaker as you move around. This will sound very strange, as you want to give the impression of one sound source, not many. If your editor supports it, then you can turn of panning/ spatialization for these sounds. In UDK, you can do this in the **[AmbientSoundSimple]** properties by unchecking the spatialize box.

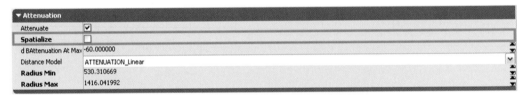

This has been done for Room 104b.

Phasing Problems

105c Phasing problem of overlapping sounds

When sounds are played simultaneously, their waveforms interfere with each other. If the same sound is played very slightly out of time with itself (anywhere between approximately 1 to 35 milliseconds), you get an artifact known as phasing. (This does not refer to the more useful Phasing loops techniques explored earlier.) If we have multiple versions of the same sound overlapping each other in order to fill a space, then the chances of producing phasing are significant. Listen to the effect on the sounds of running water in Room 105c. Sounds with greater high-frequency content are more susceptible to this problem, so avoid overlapping these sounds. If you have no other choice, then you can use the Pitch property of the **[AmbientSoundSimple]** to slightly detune them from each other to help alleviate this effect.

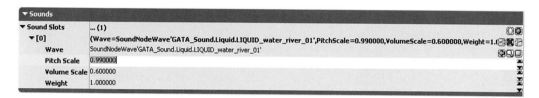

Exercise 105c_00 [AmbientSoundSimple] Test Area

Open the Exercise 105c_00 level. You will notice that there are a number of problem areas where the existing ambient sounds are appearing where they shouldn't be. Edit their Radius Min/Radius Max settings or try re-creating the space using several more **[AmbientSoundSimple]**s to overcome these problems.

Tips

1. Try using multiple versions of the sound to fill the space.
2. Experiment with the Radius Min/Radius Max settings.
3. Switch off Spatialization if the panning of sounds is too distracting.
4. Slightly detune multiple instances of overlapping sounds to avoid phasing problems.

[Trigger Volume] Switching Solution to the Walls Problem
105d Inside/Outside Toggle

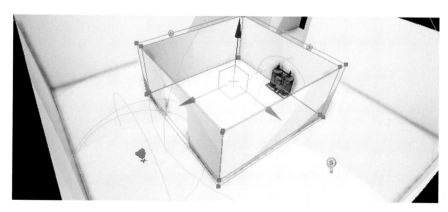

In 105d we can see the problem illustrated again as we have the machine tone inside the inner room and a general room tone for outside of this room. You can also see a green box surrounding the inner room. This is a **[Trigger Volume]**, and it is going to help us avoid the issues that arise from the "multiple sounds" solution identified earlier. This time the sounds are using **[AmbientSoundSimpleToggleable]** Actors.

What the **[Trigger Volume]** is going to do is to toggle off the outside sound and toggle on the inside sound when the player is inside, and vice versa.

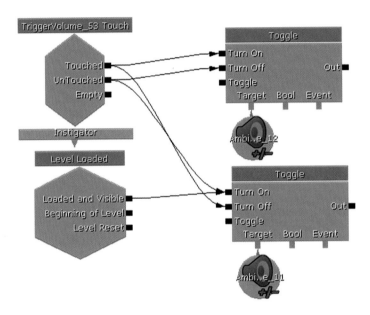

The **[AmbientSoundSimple Toggleable]** Actor has additional settings that can give it a more subtle fade in/out as we cross the threshold from inside to outside. In this case, the distance is so small it takes place over one second.

To create **[Trigger Volume]**s, we use an approach that is similar to that used for making level geometry. As this is a slight tangent to our main topic, we have put these level building tips and techniques into Appendix C: UDK Tips. Please read the section on the Builder Brush before attempting the next exercise.

Exercise 105d_00 Kismet [Trigger Volume] "Touch" Switching for Occlusion

In this exercise there is a city street and a cafe. Using sounds from the Sound Library (Cafe ambience // City ambience), or your own, implement a simple switching occlusion for this environment.

Tips

1. Use two **[AmbientSoundSimple]** toggleables one for the outside area and one for the inside. (Remember, these are found in the Actor Classes tab of the Content Browser). Select this Actor Class, then right-click in your Perspective viewport to add.
2. Add your sound waves to the **[AmbientSoundSimple Toggleable]**s in the usual way, by selecting them in the Content Browser then using the green arrow within the properties of the Actor.
3. Select the green **[Trigger Volume]** around the Cafe area we have provided for you then right-click in Kismet to create a New Event using Trigger Volume (***) Touch. Then use the Touched and Untouched outputs of this to toggle your inside and outside ambiences on and off. (Remember to set the Max Trigger Count within the Sequence Event properties of the Touch event to 0 so that it can be retriggered multiple times).

Exercise 105d_01 [Trigger Volume]s Exercise

Use **[Trigger Volume]**s to trigger the dialogue cues as described in the exercise README to help your players find their way through this maze.

Tips

1. Use the builder brush (select F2/then the Home key to find it) to make **[Trigger Volume]**s (see Appendix C: UDK Tips/Builder Brush).
2. Use the scale and rotate tools (space bar) to alter the Builder Brush's size and rotation before right-clicking on the Volumes button to create the **[Trigger Volume]**.
3. With the **[Trigger Volume]** selected in the Perspective viewport, right-click in Kismet to select New Event using Trigger Volume (***) Touch.
4. Link the Touch output to your **[PlaySound]** objects (right-click New Action/Sound/Playsound).

Ambience: A Painterly Approach

Much of this chapter has focused on creating background ambience to make your game world seem alive and real. A useful analogy when considering ambience is that of an oil painting. When you look at a finished oil painting, you get the impression of a complete and convincing picture. However, not one area of the painting is the result of a single brushstroke but instead is made up of layer upon layer of paint to achieve the final effect. You should think of you ambience in the same way. The final effect will need to be built of many different layers of sound, such as layers of distant, middle distance, and close.

Exercise 105d_02 Listen

There is no exercise room for this task. You will simply need a pen, a piece of paper, and some ears (preferably, but not exclusively, two). Listen to what's around you right now and write down everything you can hear. Absolutely everything. Try this alongside someone else, then compare your findings. The hope is that you'll be surprised by your findings (unless you happen to be sitting in an anechoic chamber, and even then ....).

Tips

1. Listen and write down what you hear.
2. Now draw a diagram of all the sounds around you. Put them in the location from which you hear them, and use different circles of different sizes to represent their relative volumes.

3. Now grab your audio recorder and record them. Get one of the previous exercise rooms, delete everything, and make a game level called "MyPlace."

How Big is the Truck?

This chapter deals with the issues of memory when developing audio for games. A number of solutions to nonrepetitive design are discussed and illustrated. These techniques and principles are particularly applicable to platforms where the memory or download size is a significant restriction, such as the Nintendo DS, Playstation Portable, iPhone/iOS, Android, or other mobile devices, but they are also equally important for other consoles such as the Wii, Xbox 360, and Playstation 3 albeit on a different scale.

How Big is the Truck?

> When designing and implementing sound or music for games, obviously your uppermost thought should be "making it sound good" (see Chapter 6). However, unless your sound is going to actually work on whatever console or platform you're using, this consideration is rather immaterial.

When starting a project, you should have this question in the back of your mind: "How big is the truck?" RS Writes:

> *When I went to university, I was fortunate enough to be surrounded not only by lots of musicians but also by Actors and "drama" people (although sometimes they were perhaps a little too dramatic). Every year they would take a play out on tour. This involved packing the set and costumes into a large truck and setting off across Wales. When designing the set, there were two important thought processes going on. The first was obviously how do we make this good? How do we use the set to tell the story and make it a more involving experience for the audience, etc., etc. The second, and equally important question was "How big is the truck?" You could design the most fantastic set in the world, but if you didn't design it such that it could actually fit into the truck, then the whole exercise would be a waste of time.*

> *The parallel I'm trying to make is this. On any games platform there will be limitations, usually chiefly in terms of the RAM [random access memory] available. Some of your sounds will play off disk, where they still have to compete for space with all the graphics assets, but many will need to be loaded up into RAM to be able to play instantaneously when needed. RAM costs money. RAM is limited. One of the chief differences between designing sound for film—where you can have practically unlimited channels and the highest quality sounds—and games is that in games the sounds you want available to play instantaneously (most of them) have to fit into the RAM available. On some consoles, particularly portable ones, this can be frighteningly small.*

RAM Budgets and Streaming

Before starting work, you need to talk to your programmers to be fully informed as to the capabilities of the system they are using for your chosen platform. Understanding the way the system's audio playback works in terms of its capabilities when playing back from RAM or streaming sound and music from disk will be fundamental to the approach you decide to take.

Unless you are a licensed developer, the actual specifications of some gaming systems can be shrouded in mystery, as much information is covered by the infamous nondisclosure agreement (NDA). There is fierce competition between gaming platforms, so information that might portray one as being somehow better or weaker than another is often a closely guarded secret, particularly early on in the console's life cycle. If you haven't got access to the specific information, then some careful reading of audio postmortems or articles (or this chapter) can give you some basic guidelines.

The current generation of portable consoles can be seen as pretty much the equivalent of previous generations of home consoles. For example, the PlayStation Portable is roughly equivalent to the PlayStation 2. This had 2 MB of RAM available for sound. You could also stream sound from the DVD disk itself, but this method required the use of some of your RAM as a buffer, so realistically you were looking at around 1.8 MB. This would get you about 10 seconds of audio at CD quality—for your entire level (CD quality audio taking up around 176 kB of memory per second). The good news was that compression was available that reduced your files to about 3.5 times smaller. (If this all sounds like complete babble to you, then it's time to go to the website and read Appendix G: Digital Audio.)

$$\text{Memory:} \quad 1\,\text{kB} = 1{,}024 \text{ bytes}$$
$$1\,\text{MB} = 1{,}024{,}000 \text{ bytes}$$
$$1\,\text{GB} = 1{,}000{,}000{,}000 \text{ bytes}$$

The most popular portable platform, the Nintendo DS, is rather more limited, typically having no more than 500 kB of memory available for sound (although, again, you can "stream" a 10- to 30-second piece of stereo music or ambience from the "cart"). Games for mobile phones or web-based games are often even tighter.

In terms of home console systems, it's very common for games to be developed for multiple platforms, so to save time you are often working within the lowest specs available. The Wii sits somewhat below the capabilities of the PlayStation 3 and Xbox 360, typically at around 8 MB of RAM, so the sounds will need to be rethought specifically for that system. Generally PS3 and 360 versions are developed with the same assets, which means that they have anywhere between 15 and 25 MB of RAM and three to six stereo streams available from the disk. PC games tend to be more generous but can be restricted both by the increased use of downloadable content (DLC) and by simultaneous development for consoles. These are ballpark figures, and this isn't the whole story as sound and music can be streamed in and out of memory for specific areas of a game (see Appendix B, the section titled "Audio Optimization"). The specifics will very much depend on the priorities of the game (e.g., it might be a music-orientated game) and may need to be negotiated along with the rest of the assets competing for this precious resource. The point is that you need to know your RAM budget and how to get the best out of the system you're working with, or else!

If you are more used to your audio sessions being measured in gigabytes rather than megabytes (or even kilobytes), then you may be having palpitations at this point.

Don't panic!

The rest of this chapter is dedicated to offering some solutions.

A Lifetime's Work

> The greater the interactivity there is in your game, then the greater the number of possible outcomes and therefore the greater the number of possible sounds. Nothing breaks immersion in a game more than hearing exactly the same sounds/sample being used repeatedly, as few sounds in the natural world repeat in this way.

At this point, some Smart Alec will usually pipe up to say, "Yes, maybe repetition is a problem on the NDS or in a mobile phone game, but I play on a PS3 and a PC. We've got loads of RAM, so we can just add more sounds. It's not a problem!"

First, let's put stereo music, speech, stereo ambience, and all of the "big moments" that you can anticipate onto the DVD or Blu-ray so they can stream straight off of the disk. There's a small time delay in getting the data off the disk before you actually hear it, but for these types of sounds this isn't usually a problem.

That step got rid of a bunch of stuff to free up our RAM. Now find a nearby object. In my case, I have a pen on my desk. So this pen is going to be an interactive pen in a game. Here's a list of what I might want to do with it and the subsequent sound files I will need to record and load into RAM:

Pick up pen from desk, put pen down on desk:
penup.wav, pendown.wav
Drop pen onto desk:
pendrop.wav
Drop pen from different heights onto desk:
pendrop01.wav, pendrop02.wav, pendrop03.wav, pendrop04.wav
Scrape pen along desk:
Penscrape01.wav, Penscrape02.wav
Tap pen on desk:
Pentapsoft01, pentapsoft02, pentaphard01, pentaphard02

So far we have 13 wavs. Now for the interesting bit. Look around where you are sitting and see how many different surfaces there are. From my desk I can see the following:

Paper, diary, speakers, monitor, keyboard, plastic wallet, kettle, book, cardboard folder, carpet, wooden desk, metal shelf, big sack of cash, pony, Aston Martin DB9

So for each of these surfaces I'd need all of the preceding sounds:

$$13 \text{ sound types} \times 15 \text{ surfaces} = 195$$

So we have 195 sound samples sitting in RAM for my pen. Now look around you and find the next object. See the problem?

To record the sound of every possible interaction of my pen with its immediate environment, my office, would probably be a lifetime's of work. As the pen example shows, simply adding more sounds is not always the solution because (1) you will never have enough RAM (or disk space) to store them all, and (2) life's too short. (PS: If anyone is interested in developing an interactive pen game, then go and see your psychiatrist.)

The Triangle of Compromise or "Triangle of Pain!"

To begin to look at some solutions to this quandary, let's examine a useful concept from the industrial world. Imagine that you owned a factory that produced a revolutionary new gaming peripheral (a pair of "Reacto-Sound" glasses that automatically turn completely black whenever you get to an exciting part of the game—so that players can concentrate on how good it sounds). You're talking to the distributor that's hoping to get them into every corner shop in the country. Here's what you might say.

- "You can have it fast and cheap, but it won't be good because I'll have to rush it and the quality will go down."
- "You can have it made good and fast, but it won't be cheap because I'll have to employ extra labor to get it done quickly while maintaining quality."
- "You can have it cheap and good, but it won't be fast. I can maintain the quality standards without hiring extra people, but this will limit the speed of production."

This can be represented by a triangle of the words "Good", "Fast" and "Cheap". The compromise is that you can only have two corners of the triangle simultaneously.

In terms of games audio, a similar triangle of compromise could be seen to apply. What we want is good-quality sounds, lots of variation in those sounds so that the game feels natural and we don't get bored with the repetition, and that they fit into the truck. Sorry RAM.

- "You can have lots of variation with good-quality sounds, but this will take up lots of memory."
- "You can have good quality sounds that will fit into memory, but there won't be much variation as we can't fit many of them in."
- "You can have lots of variation within a small amount of memory, but the quality of our sounds would have to go down."

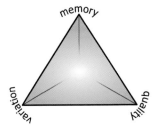

To look at some solutions that might make this compromise less painful, we're going to first need some understanding of digital audio. If you're happy with digital audio, then please read on. It's an important topic for game audio, so if you are not familiar with the principles of digital audio and sampling, or if you just want a quick reminder, then please turn to the online Appendix G: Digital Audio.

Squaring the Triangle: Basic Memory Saving Techniques

> Before considering putting your sounds or music into the game, get the files in the best format and condition for doing so. Appropriate editing and sample rate choices for your sound files need to become second nature to you.

Here are the basics of keeping your sound files small. Before we even open their game level, we can tell quickly which of our students "get" game audio, and which don't, just by looking at the sounds themselves. If you don't demonstrate an awareness of these three basic concepts before you even put your sounds into the game, then you are guilty of schoolboy errors and will bring shame and humiliation upon yourself and your family for generations to come.

The Importance of Editing

> Silence takes up the same amount of memory as sound. Get rid of what you can.

Look at the waveform of the two wav files shown here. They represent two different edits of the same sound.

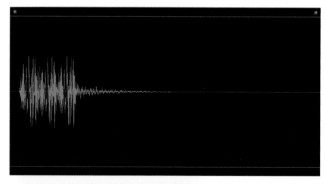

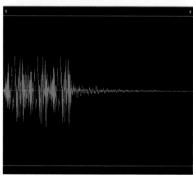

The first, the "schoolboy," version is 34,688 bytes in size; the second, the "pro" version, is 17,576 bytes in size. They sound exactly the same. The only difference is that the first version has been lazily edited, leaving lots of silence in the file. Silence takes up the same amount of memory as sound. By trimming off the silence we've made a saving of nearly half. A saving of 17,112 bytes may not sound much to you, sitting there on your home PC with 6 GB of RAM and a 3-TB hard disk, but if you're making a game for a mobile phone, it's a different story.

If you've not done much audio editing before, then have a look at the online Appendix D: Audio Editing for Games for a quick introduction.

File Compression

The MP3 format has become synonymous with the ability to share small files over the Internet. In games audio, we want our files to be small too. There are some issues with MP3s in games, but there are plenty of alternatives that can save space while still sounding good.

We have looked at why CD-quality audio takes up about 10 MB of memory per minute (or at least we did if you did what you were told and read Appendix G). One way to help alleviate the compromises inherent in the "triangle of pain" is to make the files themselves smaller. Although in theory we need this memory to store this quantity of numbers, there are various methods by which we can actually make the file size smaller. These fall into two categories: "lossless," in which no attribute of the sound is affected by the process, and "lossy," in which the process does compromise the sound in some way.

The best known of these audio file compression methods, of course, is the MP3. This lossy format works on the principle of perceptual redundancy, using knowledge of psycho-acoustic principles to remove sounds (and therefore data) that are hard to hear, such as high-frequency sounds or sounds that are masked by other, louder, simultaneous sounds. The problem with many audio file compression formats, MP3 included, is that they take processing time and power to decode and are therefore rarely suitable for the kind of instantaneous playback required in games.

The good news is that both Microsoft (Xbox 360) and Sony (PlayStation 3) can use compression formats (XMA and Vorbis) that are appropriate for games and can achieve compression of up to 10:1.

In the Unreal Development Kit (UDK), right-clicking a wav from your package in the Content Browser will enable you to select Edit using Sound Previewer. Looking at the Vorbis Data Size column will give you an indication of the file savings possible.

Audio file compression can occasionally produce some unpredictable results or artifacts, so you should always check to see the impact on the final sounds in the game. After you've opened the Sound Previewer, you will see that it takes a moment to convert the files. Double-clicking on one of the sound quality settings in the Vorbis Data Size column will allow you to preview what it will sound like at this setting. Once you've decided on an appropriate setting, click OK to apply it to the SoundNodeWave. (In the current build, you will only be able to preview Vorbis compression). Warning: This quality setting defaults to 40 for all SoundNodeWaves. Even at this setting it can have noticeable effects on your audio, so don't forget to check this setting for all your sounds.

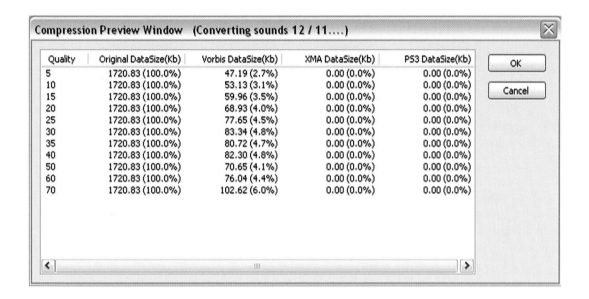

Quality	Original DataSize(Kb)	Vorbis DataSize(Kb)	XMA DataSize(Kb)	PS3 DataSize(Kb)
5	1720.83 (100.0%)	47.19 (2.7%)	0.00 (0.0%)	0.00 (0.0%)
10	1720.83 (100.0%)	53.13 (3.1%)	0.00 (0.0%)	0.00 (0.0%)
15	1720.83 (100.0%)	59.96 (3.5%)	0.00 (0.0%)	0.00 (0.0%)
20	1720.83 (100.0%)	68.93 (4.0%)	0.00 (0.0%)	0.00 (0.0%)
25	1720.83 (100.0%)	77.65 (4.5%)	0.00 (0.0%)	0.00 (0.0%)
30	1720.83 (100.0%)	83.34 (4.8%)	0.00 (0.0%)	0.00 (0.0%)
35	1720.83 (100.0%)	80.72 (4.7%)	0.00 (0.0%)	0.00 (0.0%)
40	1720.83 (100.0%)	82.30 (4.8%)	0.00 (0.0%)	0.00 (0.0%)
50	1720.83 (100.0%)	70.65 (4.1%)	0.00 (0.0%)	0.00 (0.0%)
60	1720.83 (100.0%)	76.04 (4.4%)	0.00 (0.0%)	0.00 (0.0%)
70	1720.83 (100.0%)	102.62 (6.0%)	0.00 (0.0%)	0.00 (0.0%)

Sample Rates

Lowering the sample rate of a sound can save huge amounts of memory. It can also ruin the sound. Learning to make the right choice of sample rate is a fundamental technique of producing game audio.

200 Triangle Room

Another way of making our sound files smaller is to reduce their *sample rate*.

In Room 200, go and "use" button A (key E to "use").

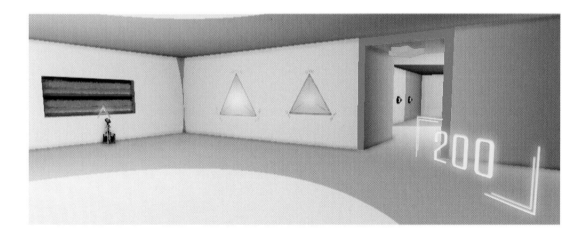

You should hear some crickets chirping along nicely. When you press the button again, you can hear another version of the crickets. This file is smaller because it has been *downsampled*. Press the button again and listen to the other versions. You can hear that the sound quality gets worse and worse.

Now walk up to button B; here is another sound, again followed by different versions and lower sample rates. This time, however, you will notice that although the sample rate goes down and the file gets smaller, the actual quality of the sound is not affected. What magic is this? Is there a way out of the triangle?

When discussing digital audio (Appendix G), we noted how we need to capture, or "sample," a sound at twice its frequency in order to accurately reproduce it (as explained by the Nyquist-Shannon sampling theorem). In other words, to reproduce a sound containing frequencies up to 12 kHz you would need to sample it at 24 kHz. However, if your sound does not actually contain any frequency components at 12 kHz, then you can sample it at a lower rate (and therefore reduce the file size) without losing any quality.

Say we had 3 MB of memory to use (16 bit sounds):

    A 44 kHz sample, taking up 88.2 kB per second, gives us 34 seconds
    A 22 kHz sample, taking up 44.1 kB per second, gives us 68 seconds
    A 11 kHz sample, taking up 22.05 kB per second, gives us 136 seconds
    A 8 kHz sample, taking up 16 kB per second, gives us 187.5 seconds

So lower sample rates allow us to fit more sound into memory. You will, however, have heard the devastating effect that the wrong sample rate can have on the sound quality with the Crickets samples in Room 200, so you must carefully choose a sample rate that is appropriate to the frequency content of the sound itself.

Let's look more closely at sound A (the crickets) and sound B from this room. You can see that although the energy in the Crickets sample is focused around 6 kHz, it covers the full frequency range up to 22 kHz.

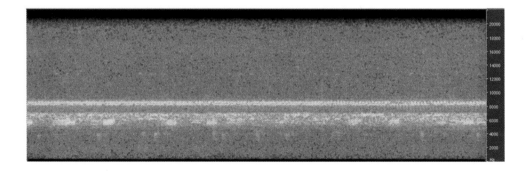

Downsampling to 22 kHz would indeed save half the memory (going from 369 kB to 186 kB) but would entirely remove the higher frequencies of the sound.

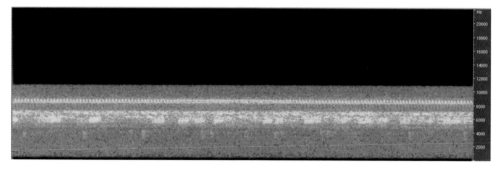

If we look at a frequency display of sound B (LowRumble01), we can see that most of its frequency content lies beneath 2 kHz. Therefore, this sound does not need to be sampled at a rate any higher that 4 kHz to be reproduced entirely accurately.

So the LowRumble01 sample will sound exactly the same at any of the sample rates we've chosen, and we will make significant savings in terms of the file size:

Sample Rate	File Size
44 kHz	2,101 kB
22 kHz	1,050 kB
11 kHz	525 kB
6 kHz	285 kB

(See online Appendix G: Digital Audio for more practical tips.)

Sample Rate Choices

Exercise 200_00 Sample Rate Room

In this exercise, there are two identical rooms. The first room is filled with **[AmbientSoundSimple]**s, but the overall file size for this room is too large. Using your knowledge of sample rates and file size, take the files provided in the exercise folder, downsample them appropriately (they are all at 44.1 kHz at the moment), then import them into the second room. Try to re-create the ambience of the first room as closely as possible but with as small a file size as possible.

Tips

1. Remember that to preserve the highest frequencies in the sound, the sample rate needs to be twice that of these frequencies.
2. Having said that, in a limited memory situation you can usually afford to lose a bit off the top end without affecting the nature of the sound too drastically.
3. Use your ears.

Speakers for portable consoles do not have a great frequency range, so there would be no point

You should consider the playback medium that you're developing for to inform your decisions on what sample rates to use. Also think carefully about the relative importance of the sounds in your game. Which sound will the player hear most often? Which sounds need to be at the highest quality? Sample rate choices are not always based solely on the frequency content of the sound. You might also decide on some specific rules regarding sample rates for different categories of sound.

in using some sample rates for your audio (even the Wii is limited to 32 kHz output). If you get the opportunity, try running some white noise through the speakers of your platform and looking at the results. You may be unpleasantly surprised. These decisions are, of course, complicated by the fact that people can also switch to headphones, but when you look at the frequency response of most consumer headphones they're not great either. (See online Appendix G: Digital Audio for some utilities that can help you to visualize the frequency spectrum of a sound.)

In addition to using a frequency spectrum view (and your ears) to decide on the most appropriate sample rate for your sounds, you should also consider each particular sound's importance within the game or how often the player will hear it. For example, the sound of glass smashing during each of 10 climactic boss fights might be preserved at a high sample rate. To achieve this effect, you may choose to lower the sample rate, and thus sacrifice the quality, of the distant background sound you hear only once in level 17d.

You might adopt a broad strategy such as the following:

> 44 kHz—High-frequency sounds of key importance to the game
> 22 kHz—Player weapon sounds
> 18 kHz—Dialogue
> 11 kHz—Distant ambience or room tones

Non-repetitive Design

Caveat—Sometimes repetition is OK

Our aim for most sounds in a game is that they are convincingly real (i.e., they respond in the way that we'd expect them to in the real world). This is a problem for many sounds, which in reality vary and change in subtle ways, but this does not necessarily apply to the same extent for all sounds. Sounds created by mechanical systems (for example, a weapon firing) are inherently similar each time they occur, as the mechanism producing them is the same, but we are also forgiving of repetition in sounds that carry meaning or convey information.

The chief criticism of game audio over the years has been its repetitive nature (this is not entirely our fault, as one of the fundamental traits of games is to make repeated use of a few basic mechanics). Sound sources that are varied in the real world can appear in games with one wav repeated over and over. Although we will devote a significant part of this chapter to avoiding this consequence, you should invest your time wisely by only applying these techniques to sounds that need it.

Repetition in Mechanical Systems

The first category of sounds that is less problematic when used repeatedly comprises sounds that are naturally repetitive, such as those created by mechanical systems. The majority of mechanical sounds will typically only have very small variations in their sound in the physical world, so overdoing the variation on these in games is (1) unrealistic (2) wasteful.

Repetition in Symbolic Sounds

The second category of sounds that you may wish to allow to be repetitive is made up of sounds that convey information in the game. This might be a pickup sound that tells you that you received an additional health or a bonus star powerup. The majority of the time these are symbolic sounds. Players need to be aware that the sound has occurred so that they can interpret its meaning. The nature of the sound itself does not provide any inherent information. We don't want players to have to listen closely to the sound itself, we merely want them to be able to quickly acknowledge its meaning. Having variation in the sounds would be both confusing and distracting. See Chapter 6 for more discussion on this topic.

Reuse of Sounds: The Power of Pitch

Multiple Use Using Pitch Shift

> When memory is important (and it's always important), then try to use the same sound in different ways by changing the pitch at which it plays back within the game engine. The most obvious method is to use different pitched versions of a sound for different sizes of the same object, but you'll also be surprised by how radically different things can sound when they are pitched up much higher or pitched down much lower. To reuse sounds and preserve memory, pitch shift is probably your greatest ally.

201 Pitch Shift 01: Multiple Use of the Same Sound: Size

In the physical production of sound, pitch is related to the size of the object. The larger or longer the pipe, the longer the string, the bigger the surface, then the deeper the pitch of the sound it produces. Given this fact, the most obvious application of using pitch shift to vary your sound file is when you have different sized versions of the same object.

Take a look at Room 201. You can see that the same sound (NewYorkAirCon.wav) has been used for each fan. The pitch of this sound has been changed by using the Pitch Scale parameter of the **[AmbientSoundSimple]** properties.

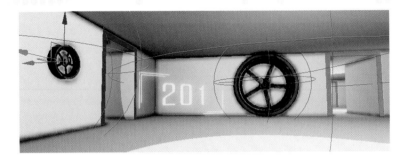

Small fan: Pitch scale = 1.8
Medium fan: Pitch scale = 1.0
Large fan: Pitch scale = 0.5

Sounds		
▼ Sound Slots	... (1)	
▼ [0]	(Wave=SoundNodeWave'GATPackage.Sounds.NewYorkAirCon01',	
Wave	SoundNodeWave'GATPackage.Sounds.NewYorkAirCon01'	
Pitch Scale	0.500000	
Volume Scale	1.000000	
Weight	1.000000	

RS Writes:

The wonderful sounds you are hearing actually come from a recording I made of the air conditioning unit across the alleyway from a hotel room in New York. When I complained about the noise, the helpful manager suggested I try turning my own air conditioning unit on. "Why would I want to do that?" I naively asked. "To cover the noise of the other one," he replied.

201a Pitch Shift 02: Multiple Use of the Same Sound: Character

In addition to changing the pitch for similar objects of a different size, sometimes a change in pitch can alter the sound's character more significantly. If you've ever tried extreme changes of pitch in your audio editor, you know what a huge impact this can have on the nature of the sound itself. (The pitch shift in UDK works by playing back the sample faster or slower. Your digital audio workstation [DAW] may have other options.) Although the pitch shift range in UDK is relatively limited (one octave higher, at a pitch scale 2.0, to over half as low, at a pitch scale of 0.4), we can apply this method to reuse the same sample for different purposes.

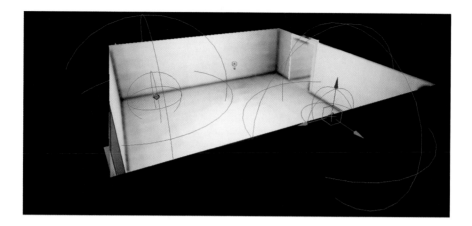

In one corner of this room there is a group of chickens. In the other there is a group of rats. These are played back via two **[AmbientSoundSimple]**s, but both actually reference the same sound sample.

The original recording is of chickens. Because of the relatively restricted pitch shift available within UDK, it's already been slightly pitched up in the DAW then played back at a pitch multiplier = 0.7 to get it back to its original pitch.

▼ Ambient Sound Simple	
▼ Ambient Properties	SoundNodeAmbient'GAT_10-10-29_V04.TheWorld:PersistentLevel.AmbientSoundS
▶ Attenuation	
▶ Low Pass Filter	
▼ Modulation	
Pitch Min	0.700000
Pitch Max	0.700000
Volume Min	0.700000
Volume Max	0.700000
▶ Sounds	

The Rats reference the same sound wav, but it is now played back with a pitch multiplier of 1.5.

▼ Ambient Sound Simple	
▼ Ambient Properties	SoundNodeAmbient'GAT_10-10-29_V04.TheWorld:PersistentLevel.AmbientSoundS
▶ Attenuation	
▶ Low Pass Filter	
▼ Modulation	
Pitch Min	1.500000
Pitch Max	1.500000
Volume Min	0.700000
Volume Max	0.700000

If you're working on a platform with relatively restricted embedded memory, or restrictions on the size of the download, then the ability to use pitch shift to change the character of a sound so it can be reused in different ways is a vital tool.

Exercise 201a_00 Multiple Use through Pitch Change

In this room you have several objects. Using only the sounds in the Exercise 201a_00 folder, ensure that each object has an appropriate sound. You will want to use pitch shifted versions of the sounds for large/small versions of the same object and also some more extreme pitch ranges to completely change the character of the sounds you've been given.

Tips

1. Use the Pitch Scale parameter within your **[AmbientSoundSimple]**s properties (F4).
2. Try to reuse the same samples so that you are keeping your memory footprint low.

Pitch Up/Play Down

To reduce the size of your sound file by half, you can pitch it up an octave in your audio editor (see Online Appendix D) before you bring it into the game editor. You can then use the editor tool to pitch it back down again. You will lose some quality, but it may be worth it if you're really tight for memory space.

201b Pitch Shift 03: Pitch Up/Play Down

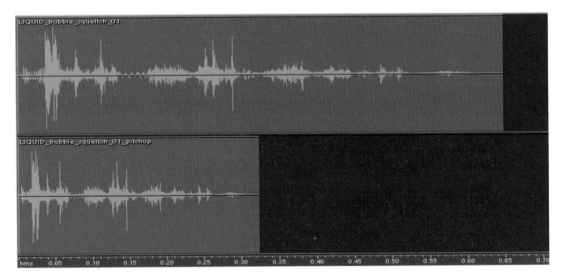

In addition to using pitch shift to change the character of a sound (making it sound smaller/larger or changing its character completely), you can also use it for a neat little trick to halve the file size of the sound you need to store in memory.

By pressing the button in Room 201b, you will hear three sounds:

1. The original sound (56 kB)

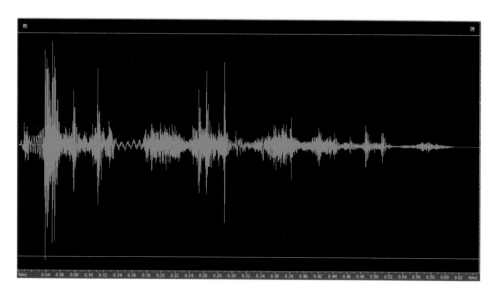

2. This sound after having been pitched up one octave in an audio editor (28 kB)

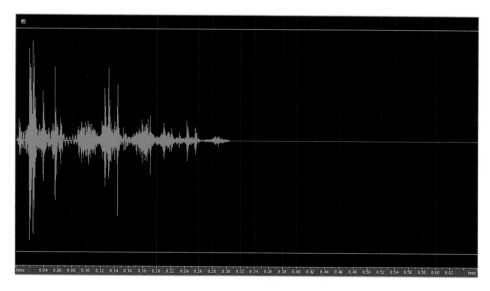

3. Sound number 2 again, but this time it uses the pitch change function within UDK to play it back down an octave, therefore re-creating the sound of the original (28 kB) (this example uses a SoundCue, which we'll be coming to a little later).

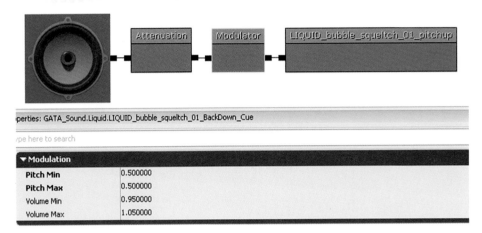

If working on a game for a portable console or a downloadable game for a smartphone, these kinds of savings can be critical. The (nonscientific) diagrams that follow give you an idea of the losses. First is our original sample.

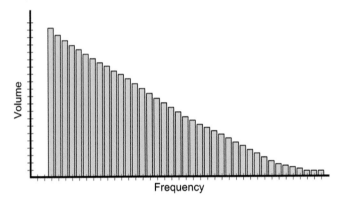

By taking it up an octave, we have a good chance of losing some frequencies at the top end.

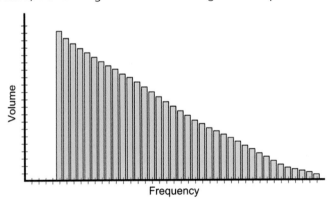

But if we were to halve the file size by downsampling it to half the sample rate, the effects would be much worse.

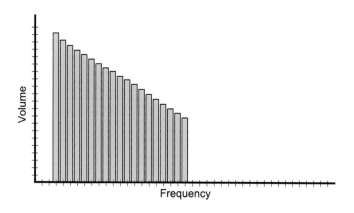

Reuse of Sounds: Using Filters

> Try using any DSP process your editor may include to change the sounds you hold in memory. For example applying filters to your sounds can change them significantly. This way you can make more use of the sounds that you hold in memory, perhaps using them multiple times in different ways.

202 Ambience + Filter

You'll see that Room 202 uses **[AmbientSoundSimple]**s, but the sounds in the corners of the room appear to be different than that in the middle. As you have learned, the amount of memory you have to store sounds for games is always a problem, so here we have actually reused the same sound in all the **[AmbientSoundSimple]** Actors. You can see this by selecting their properties (F4), expanding the *AmbientSoundSimple* menu by clicking on it, and looking at the wave chosen in the SoundSlot. You'll see that they all refer to the sound GATA_Sound.Mechanical.Aircon01.

The reason they sound different is that the central sound has had a low-pass filter applied to it. This means that the higher frequencies are removed, making the sound duller in tone (the low-pass filter allows the lower frequencies to pass through the filter unaffected). This gives us a low rumble room tone in the center of the room as well as the air conditioning sounds in the corners, all from one sound stored in memory.

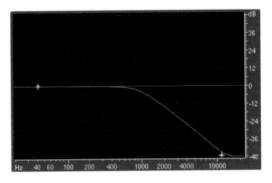

Function of a low-pass filter.

AmbientSoundSimple	
▼ Ambient Properties	SoundNodeAmbient'GAT_10-10-10_V02.TheWorld:PersistentLevel.Am
Attenuation	
LowPassFilter	
Attenuate With LPI ☑	
LPFRadius Min	0.000000
LPFRadius Max	50.000000

This property of the **[AmbientSoundSimple]** applies a low-pass filter fully at the given LPFRadius Max, gradually returning to an unfiltered version of the sound at the LPFRadius Min. In this instance, we have had to be slightly cunning and place the sound under the floor of the room so that the player never actually experiences the sound at the Min distance; therefore, the player never actually experiences the unfiltered version in the middle of the room.

Exercise 202_00 Multiple Use through Filters

In this exercise room, you'll see that several dangerous gases are escaping from the pipes. Using only the sound Steamtest01.wav from the exercise folder, see if you can create a convincing ambience for the room and sounds for the different sized pipes.

Tips

1. Import and select the Steamtest01.wav file in the Content Browser, then right-click in the Perspective viewport and select Add Actor/Add AmbientSoundSimple (***).wav.
2. Edit the properties of the **[AmbientSoundSimple]**s you used (F4), and adjust the Low Pass Filter settings.
3. Remember to tick the check box Attenuate with Low Pass Filter.
4. Use a combination of filter, volume, pitch, and attenuation settings to derive variation from this one sound file.

Randomization in Time, Pitch, and Volume

Looping sounds are useful for room tones or machinery that is by nature repetitive. When we try to create in-game ambiences that are based on more naturally occurring sounds, the use of loops becomes a problem as we quickly spot them as feeling false and unnatural. We should save the disk space used by long loops for something better or more important. By re-creating ambiences through the random recombination of individual elements, we not only save on memory and avoid repetition but we also have more control over them.

203 Randomization: Pitch/Volume/Time

Apart from the obvious reuse of the same sample the main thing that will stop a game environment from feeling immersive and natural is any repetition of a series or sequence of sounds. These immediately jump out as being artificial. Imagine this scenario in the real world. A dog barks a few times, then a car door slams, somebody shouts, a helicopter flies overhead. If any of those sounds were to repeat but actually sounded pretty much the same (i.e., the same sample), then it might be unusual but you'd probably accept it. If they sounded again but with exactly the same timing in exactly the same order, then the next sound you might expect to hear would be from the big white van belonging to the men in white coats.

[AmbientSoundNonLoop] for Randomized Sounds

In Room 203 you can see that (finally) we have a new type of sound Actor. This is the imaginatively titled **[AmbientSoundNonLoop]** (and it's friend the **[AmbientSoundNonLoopingToggleable]**).

The **[AmbientSoundNonLoop]** allows us to construct our ambience out of individual elements and adds aspects of randomization that give a more natural feel. These are much better at generating non-repetitive ambience, as they have a list of sounds that are played in a random order, at random time intervals (and can have random pitch and volume changes applied).

The Radius settings are the same as for the **[AmbientSoundSimple]** (shown now with red spheres), and at the bottom of the Actors properties is a list of SoundSlots. Here is where you can add a list of sounds to be randomly chosen.

If you listen in the area of the blue square floor tile, you can hear how the old **[Ambient SoundSimple]** would create this ambience. You can hear it looping around and around, and this repetition of the same sequence of sounds feels wrong and artificial. The red area creates the same ambience but this time it is randomized and so feels more natural.

In the red area, select one of the **[AmbientSoundNonLoop]** Actors. Go to its properties, expand the **[AmbientSoundSimple]** menu, and you can see that here the overall sound is created by the random playback of several individual sounds.

The Delay Min and Delay Max values control when the sounds are triggered. A random number between the Min and Max settings is chosen and used as a delay time between playing back the next sound from the SoundSlots. That is, if the Delay Min were 3 and Delay Max were 8, the sounds would not be triggered any more often than every 3 seconds, but you would also not have to wait any longer than 8 seconds. When this sound has played, a new random delay time is chosen and a new random SoundSlot selected.

The Weight component for each sound is important because you can use it to make certain sounds play more (or less) often than others. Currently they are all set to a weight of 1, so they all have an equal chance of playing.

Now is also a good time to experiment with randomizing the volume and pitch of these sounds each time they play using the Modulation menu within the **[AmbientSoundNonLoop]** Actor.

▼ Modulation	
Pitch Min	0.800000
Pitch Max	1.100000
Volume Min	0.500000
Volume Max	0.700000

Randomizing the time, pitch, and volume of sounds is a crucial method for building up non-repetitive ambient environments in games without the need for very long sounds in memory. Instead of taking up lots of memory with a long looping sound, we can re-create a more natural sense of random variation in the ambience by splitting it into individual elements and randomizing these. (Warning: Make sure you are only pitch-shifting in a subtle way sounds that would naturally have this kind of variation in them. Be particularly aware that this will not sound good if applied to voices!)

Exercise 203_00 [AmbientSoundNonLoop]: Wooded Area

Open the level Exercise 203_00. Here we are aiming for a more natural-sounding environment. Using **[AmbientSoundNonLoop]**s and the sounds from the Animal and Weather folders of the Sound Library, create a convincing audio environment for this location.

Tips

1. To add your own randomized **[AmbientSoundNonLoop]** Actor, go to the Content Browser and select the Actor classes tab.
2. Now select Sounds/AmbientSound/AmbientSoundSimple/AmbientSoundNonLoop.

    ⊟ **Sounds**
       ⊟ AmbientSound
          ⊟ AmbientSoundSimple
             ⊞ AmbientSoundSimpleToggleable
             ⋯⋯ AmbientSoundNonLoop
          ⋯ AmbientSoundMovable

3. With this Actor still selected, right-click in your viewport to add it (Add AmbientSoundNonLoop here).
4. You will probably want to add several sound slots. In the Sounds menu you do this by clicking on the green plus sign.
5. Once you have added several slots, you can then select your sounds in the Content Browser and add them to the sound slots (using the green arrow in the normal way).
6. Now adjust the **[AmbientSoundNonLoop]**'s Delay Min and Delay Max settings to control how often the sounds are triggered.
7. You might also want to experiment with *weighting* (within the Sound Slots menu) if you want some sounds to appear more frequently than others. In addition to the **[AmbientSoundNonLoop]**s for randomized animal calls, have some **[AmbientSoundSimple]** loops for a background texture (wind etc.).
8. As well as setting the frequency with which the sounds play by using the Delay Min and Delay Max settings, try randomizing their pitch and volume levels a little using the Modulation settings. This will pick random values between whatever you set as the possible Min and Max values.
9. The most effective way to modulate pitch and volume for animal-type sounds is to have only small variations in pitch but larger variations in volume so that the sounds are varied but not too unnatural.

The related **[AmbientSoundNonLoopingToggleable]** Actor has additional controls to Fade in or Fade out to a given volume level. This can be useful in making your ambiences more dynamic or in fading them back a little once the location has been established (see the discussion in Chapter 06/Subjective Sound States).

Randomization in Time, Pitch, and Volume Using [SoundCue]s

In the immortal words of Brian Schmidt, "Anyone who still thinks there is a one-to-one relationship between a game event and a wav file just doesn't understand game audio." (Chris Grigg Project BBQ report 2001, http://www.project barbq.com/bbq01/bbq0185.htm). Most game editors will have a more abstracted layer for sound events. Rather than simply playing back one wav file, you are triggering a system that contains wav files. In UDK, this system is called the **[SoundCue]**.

Most of the interactive sounds we'll be dealing with from now on do not simply play wav files like the **[AmbientSound]** Actors. They play **[SoundCue]**s, which you can think of as a system of playback, rather than the playing back of a single sound.

You may find it useful at this point to use the search bar in the Content Browser. To see what **[SoundCue]**s already exist, select the Content folder within the Content Browser Packages menu.

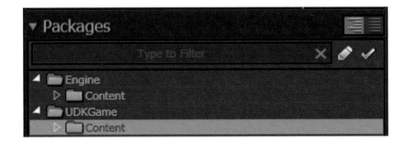

You can now use the check boxes in the Search Filter section (shown next) to define the type of asset that you are looking for so that only those are visible. You can also type your search words into the top box.

Search for the **[SoundCue]** A_Character_Footstep_DefaultCue using the text search box at the top. If you repeatedly double-click on the **[SoundCue]**, you can hear that it actually swaps between three different footstep wavs.

You can take a look inside this **[SoundCue]** by right-clicking and selecting Edit Using SoundCue Editor. Inside your SoundCue editor you will see the Audio Node Graph, which is where the different objects, or *nodes*, can be linked together to form systems.

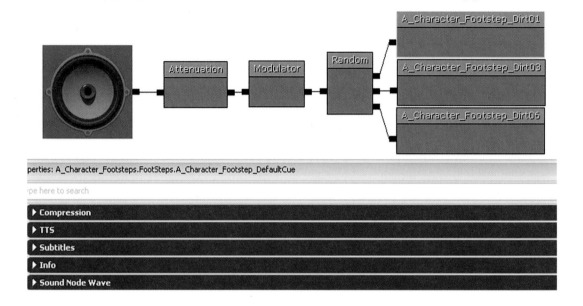

perties: A_Character_Footsteps.FootSteps.A_Character_Footstep_DefaultCue

pe here to search

▶ Compression

▶ TTS

▶ Subtitles

▶ Info

▶ Sound Node Wave

Like the systems in Kismet, **[SoundCue]**s are constructed by adding objects, and then chaining them together with wires. The systems operate from right to left and the objects within the **[SoundCue]** are referred to as *nodes.* In this case, the **[Random]** node is randomly selecting one of the sounds to play; this then has some slight variations in pitch and volume introduced by the **[Modulation]** node; finally the sound is attenuated and spatialized using the **[Attenuation]** node before going to the **[Speaker]** node, which contains the overall pitch and volume multipliers. This is useful for non-repetitive design. Instead of playing the same sample each time, we can randomly pick from a few and we can also modulate them in pitch and volume to create variation without necessarily needing many sounds in memory.

To add any of the various nodes available to your **[SoundCue]**, right-click and choose them from the menu that appears. You can then drag the objects/nodes around the screen by clicking on them while holding down the Ctrl key. Try this in the A_Character_Footstep_DefaultCue you just opened.

Try adding a few nodes now (from the Right-Click menu) and linking them together by dragging wires to link their inputs and outputs. You can also break or change these wires by right-clicking on an input or output and choosing Break Link, or by Alt-clicking on them.

Delete any nodes you added to reset any changes you made to the A_Character_Footstep_ DefaultCue **[Soundcue]** before exiting. Now open some others to get an idea of how they work. To preview the **[SoundCue]** with the SoundCue editor, you can use the Play SoundCue button at the top of the screen.

You can also choose to preview a particular section or node of the **[SoundCue]** by choosing the Play Selected Node option.

Advantages of Using [SoundCue]s

Using multiple references to one sound system is a good time-saving strategy. If all of the trees in your level reference the same Birds_and_wind_Sound_System, then by making small adjustments to the one system or cue, all of the instances are updated. This is better than having to go around the level for hours tweaking each individual instance by hand.

The advantage of using **[SoundCue]**s is that we can use these multiple times throughout our level, and if we don't feel it's quite right we can adjust or change the **[SoundCue]** rather than having to go around and individually adjust each **[AmbientSound]** or **[AmbientSoundNonLoop]**. Any changes you make to the **[SoundCue]** will be applied to all instances.

[AmbientSound] Actor for Noninteractive [SoundCue]s

204 Reuse of Sound Cues

Room 204 is a good example of where you might want to use multiple instances of the same **[SoundCue]**. There are several trees in this area, so we can use the same sound cue for each. We could of course do this with an **[AmbientSoundNonLoop]** and copy it for each tree, but if we then wanted to adjust the timings or weightings, we would have to do this for each instance. By using a single **[SoundCue]**, any adjustments made to this cue will be instigated wherever it is used.

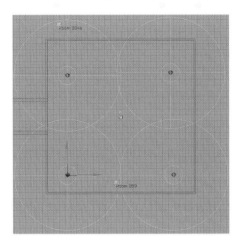

In this room you can see that a new **[AmbientSound]** Actor has been used to play back the **[SoundCue]**s. As long as they include an **[Attenuation]** node and reference mono sound files **[SoundCue]**s played back via an **[AmbientSound]** will emit from the position of this Actor in the level. The sounds from this object will be either one shot or looping depending on the contents of the **[SoundCue]** selected.

Note that the **[SoundCue]** for the bird sounds in the trees is not simply playing a looping wav of bird sounds but instead is made up of individualized elements. These are played back using the principles for simple non-repetitive design outlined earlier (i.e., single wav elements are played back at random time intervals with randomized pitch and volume adjustments).

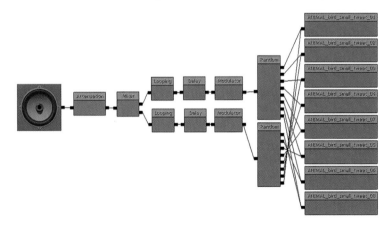

Exercise 204_00 Adding a SoundCue

Here is a simple outdoor area with some trees. Add a **[SoundCue]** directly to this level using an **[AmbientSound]** Actor and then reuse the same one for the other trees.

Tips

1. Navigate to the **[SoundCue]** GATA_Sound.Animal.Bird_Tweets_Reusable. (Either find it via the path given in the name or use the search toolbar of the Content Browser).
2. With this **[SoundCue]** selected in the Content Browser, right-click in the Perspective viewport and select Add Actor/ Add AmbientSound: Bird_Tweets_Reusable.
3. You can copy this item by making sure the Move widget is selected (cycle through them with the space bar until the Move widget with arrows appears). Now hold down the Alt key while you select one of the arrows and drag with the mouse. This way you will make a copy and retain the correct references to sound files and settings.
4. Out of interest now try changing the **[SoundCue]** that this **[AmbientSound]** references.
5. Open the **[AmbientSound]** properties (F4) and use the green arrow within its Audio menu to attach whatever **[SoundCue]** you currently have selected in the Content Browser.
6. Note that unless the **[SoundCue]** you have chosen has a Looping object, then it will play once and stop.

Nodes and Functions within a [SoundCue]

We'll be dealing with each of these elements in the following exercises, but for the moment here's a list of the nodes available within the **[SoundCue]** and a brief description of what they do.

[Speaker]

This isn't strictly a node because it contains the global properties of the **[SoundCue]** itself. Here you can set the overall volume and pitch multipliers together with the max concurrent play count (see the section titled "Voice Instance Limiting and Prioritization" in Chapter 6) and information relating to facial animations.

Sound Class	Ambient
Volume Multiplier	0.750000
Pitch Multiplier	1.000000
Face FXAnim Set Ref	None
Face FXGroup Name	
Face FXAnim Name	
Max Concurrent Play Count	16

[Attenuation]

This node determines how the sound will attenuate over distance and spatialize. If your **[SoundCue]** has an **[Attenuation]** node, then you can also access these settings from the properties (right-click) of the **[SoundCue]** in the Content Browser.

[Concatenator]

This node will chain together a series of sounds attached to its input. As soon as the first has finished playing, it will play the next input and so on.

[Delay]
This node produces a time delay that can be randomized between min and max settings.

[Distance Crossfade]
Two or more sounds can have volume envelopes applied depending on their distance from the sound source.

[Looping]
This node will loop whatever enters its input a fixed, random, or indefinite number of times.

[Sound Node Mature]
This node designates the sound as belonging to the "Mature" category for age-appropriate reasons.

[Mixer]
The volume level of two or more inputs can be set using this node.

[Modulator]
This node can vary the volume or pitch of a sound with fixed or randomized settings.

[Continuous Modulator]
This node can be used to vary the pitch or volume of a sound in response to game variables such as the velocity of vehicles (see Chapter 7).

[Oscillator]
This oscillator can be applied to the pitch or volume of a sound.

[Randomized]
This node will randomly choose between two or more inputs to play.

[SoundnodeWaveParam]
This parameter refers to the sound sample or wave itself and uses the name of the SoundNodeWave when you add it to a **[SoundCue]**.

[SoundCue]: [Attenuation]

You may have noticed that the **[AmbientSound]**s in the trees in Room 204 have their attenuation Radius Max marked by an orange circle, rather that the usual blue **[AmbientSoundSimple]** or red **[AmbientSoundNonLoop]**. Unlike these two Actors the **[AmbientSound]** attenuation and spatialization is set within the **[SoundCue]** it references, not within the Actor itself.

The **[Attenuation]** node within the **[SoundCue]** works in the same way that you've come across in the **[AmbientSoundSimple]**s.

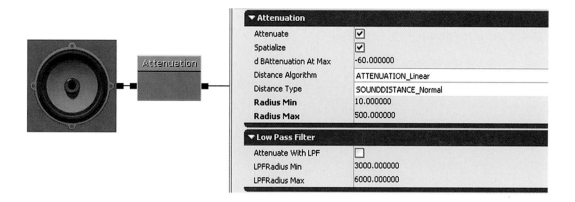

When a **[SoundCue]** is placed directly into a level via an **[AmbientSound]** Actor, you can see its attenuation marked as orange circles. These are not adjustable in the level and do not always immediately update when you make changes within the **[SoundCue]**. It's useful with these to use the middle mouse button technique for measuring distances in the level mentioned earlier.

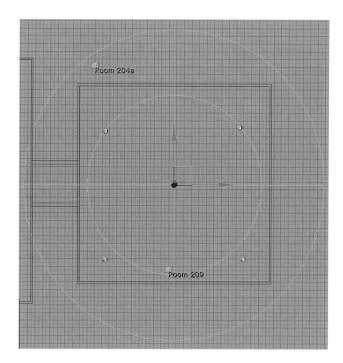

Another reason we need **[SoundCue]**s is that these are the only types of sound that can be triggered by Kismet's **[PlaySound]** object in response to game actions and systems.

[SoundCue]: [Random]

204a Soundcues O1

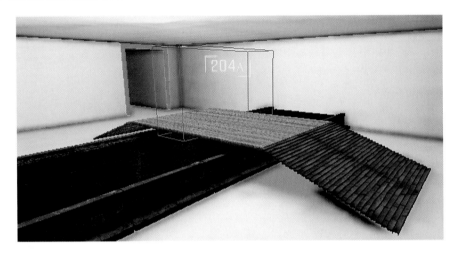

As you cross over the dangerous-looking liquid in this room, you should hear the creak of the wooden bridge. You will note that this does not always play the same creak sound. Navigate to the GATA_Sound.Collision package to find the **[SoundCue]**COLLISION_wood_creak_cue.

If you right-click the COLLISION_wood_creak_cue **[SoundCue]** and select Edit using SoundCue editor, you can see how it works.

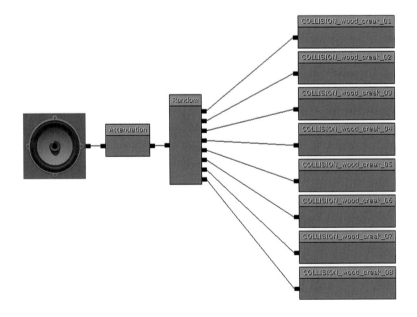

Within the **[SoundCue]** you can select the nodes, and their properties will appear in the window below. Select the **[Random]** node. When the **[SoundCue]** is triggered, the *Random* node chooses randomly from any sound that is connected to one of its inputs. (You can create additional inputs by right-clicking the **[Random]** node and choosing Add Input.) The sounds can also be weighted to increase or decrease the chances of a particular one being chosen.

SoundNodeRandom	
▼ Weights	... (8)
[0]	1.000000
[1]	1.000000
[2]	1.000000
[3]	1.000000
[4]	1.000000
[5]	1.000000
[6]	1.000000
[7]	1.000000
Randomize Without Replacer ☑	

The "Randomize without replacement" option is a particularly useful one. This will keep track of which sounds have been played and randomly choose between only the sounds that have not been played recently. This is useful not only for avoiding the distraction of the same sound being played twice in succession but also for spacing out the repetition of sounds. For example:

1. The **[Soundcue]** is triggered and sound 3 (out of a possible 1, 2, 3, 4) is chosen and plays.
2. The **[Soundcue]** is triggered again, but this time the **[Random]** node will only choose from sounds 1, 2 and 4. Sound 1 is chosen and plays.
3. The **[Soundcue]** is triggered again. This time the **[Random]** node will only choose from sounds 2 and 4. Sound 4 is chosen and plays.
4. The **[Soundcue]** is triggered again and sound 2 is chosen to play. The **[Random]** node then resets itself so that all sounds are once again available.

This system is sometimes referred to as *random cycle down* in other engines to describe the random choice cycling down each time through the samples left available. Using this randomize without replacement technique is another key principle in non-repetitive design.

This **[SoundCue]** is called from a **[PlaySound]** action in Kismet (right-click/New Action/Sound/PlaySound). As one of the fundamental sound playback mechanisms in UDK, you can imagine that we will be seeing considerably more of this object as we go on. This **[PlaySound]** is triggered in Kismet from a **[TriggerVolume]** in the center of the bridge. At the moment the **[PlaySound]**s target is the player (right-click/New Variable/Player/Player), but as we will find out later, you can actually target any Actor in the level to be the point of origin of a sound in the level.

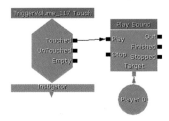

While using **[Random]** is good for avoiding repetition and creating variation and **[Attenuation]** is necessary for spatializing the sound correctly, they do not directly address our outstanding concern, which is to produce a nonrepetitive design within a given memory constraint. Fortunately, there are other nodes that do help in this regard, the most fundamental being the **[Modulator]**.

[SoundCue]: [Modulator] for Variation

Like the settings in the **[AmbientSoundNonLoop]**, the **[Modulator]** node within a **[SoundCue]** can add randomized variation to the sound files by altering their pitch or volume.

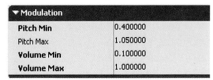

▼ Modulation	
Pitch Min	0.400000
Pitch Max	1.050000
Volume Min	0.100000
Volume Max	1.000000

Each time the **[Modulator]** is called, it will pick a randomized value between the values you set for the minimum and maximum. In this instance, the pitch will not go further than the 0.4 to 1.05 range, and volume will vary between 0.1 and 1.0 of the full volume.

Exercise 204a_01 Randomized Spooky Ambience

Exercise 204a_01 is a replica of Exercise 204a_00. This time, however, you're going to create a nonrepetitive spooky atmosphere rather than just a one shot sound.

Tips

1. Open the **[SoundCue]** you made earlier.
2. This time add a **[Looping]** and a **[Delay]** object.

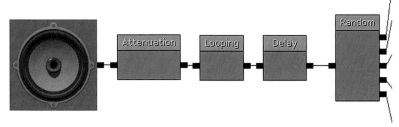

3. Try swapping your current sounds for some others. A useful shortcut for adding sounds is to select them all in the Content Browser, right-click in the SoundCue Editor, and select *Random:* (your filename). This will actually insert all the sounds you have selected already pre-wired into a **[Random]** object.
4. For the moment, set the **[Delay]** object's properties to 5 seconds for both Min and Max.
5. When you're done, save your package.
6. Now use an **[AmbientSound]** Actor to play the **[SoundCue]**.
   With your SoundCue selected in the Content browser right-click in the level and select Add Actor/Add Ambient Sound: (***). (Or you can add an **[AmbientSound]** from the Actor Classes, then add your **[SoundCue]** to this.)
7. If it's Auto Play is enabled (it is set by default) then it will begin immediately on the start of the level and be heard over whatever distance you apply in the **[Attenuation]** settings of the **[SoundCue]**. As you have a **[Loop]** in your **[SoundCue]**, it will continue to play sounds at intervals designated by the **[Delay]** node.

Exercise 204a_02: Reuse of Randomized [SoundCue]s

For this exercise we're going to re-use the natural ambience area of exercise 203_00. Try re-creating the ambience of animal noises that you created using **[AmbientSoundSimple]**s and **[AmbientSoundNonLoop]**s, only this time do it with a **[SoundCue]**. You'll find that now you can use the same **[SoundCue]** around each tree, rather than having to re-create a new **[AmbientSoundNonLoop]** for each.

Tips

1. Import your own sounds or use some from the Sound Library/Animals folder.
2. Don't forget the shortcut to add multiple selected waves to a **[SoundCue]** at once (with or without being attached to a **[Random]** object). Select multiple sounds in the browser, then right-click in the **[SoundCue]**. You have a choice to "add" or "add with attachment to random object," and this will add all of the SoundNodeWaves you have currently selected.

(There is also a function available from the Batch Process menu (right-click on a package or group) that does something similar. Cluster Sounds or Cluster Sounds with Attenuation will auto-create a **[SoundCue]** from consecutively named SoundNodeWaves (Sparkle01.wav, Sparkle02.wav, etc.) within a package or group (attached to either a **[Random]** or a **[Random]** and **[Attenuation]** node). We mention this just out of completeness as the preceding method (of just selecting multiple wavs, then right-clicking in your **[SoundCue]** to add them all) is actually quicker in the majority of cases.

You can automatically create **[SoundCue]**s when importing sounds. (See Appendix C: UDK Tips, "Importing Sounds.")

The Combinatorial Explosion: Vertical Combinations

You don't need thousands of sounds in memory to get thousands of different sounds out of your system. By combining sounds in randomized ways, you can create new combinations and therefore new sounds.

So far we've looked at using pitch, simple filters, volume, and time variations to create variety in our sounds without increasing their memory footprint. Another productive method is to use **[SoundCue]**s to randomly combine the sound elements we have. This will produce new combinations and therefore new sounds.

For example, if you had three sounds in memory you could hear the following:

Sound 1
Sound 2
Sound 3
Sound 1+Sound 2
Sound 1+Sound 3
Sound 2+Sound 3
Sound 1+Sound 2+Sound 3

This will give us seven different combinations and seven different sound possibilities.

Suppose we had five sounds in memory:

1, 2, 3, 4, 5
1+2, 1+3, 1+4, 1+5
2+3, 2+4, 2+5
3+4, 3+5, 4+5
1+2+3, 1+3+4, 1+3+5,1+4+5, 2+3+4, 2+3+5,2+4+5, 3+4+5, 5+1+2, 5+1+3
1+2+3+4, 1+3+4+5, 2+3+4+5, 4+5+1+2, 5+1+2+3
1+2+3+4+5

This would give us 31 different combinations. Seven sounds would give us 127, Ten would result in a possible 1,023 combinations.

(To find out the number of possible permutations, use 2 to the power of your number, then take away 1 [because playing 0 is not useful when it comes to sound]. On your scientific calculator, press 2, press the x^y button, then enter the number of sounds you have. Then take away 1. Then dazzle everyone with how clever you are.)

Layering for Variations (Explosion/Debris)

205 Explosion/Debris

As you enter this bunker, an enemy artillery attack starts on your position. This consists of four explosion sounds, and three falling debris sounds. The explosion sounds can be layered in any combination with each other so, combined with the random debris sounds, this gives us 127 possible combinations (i.e., 127 possible sounds).

The combination of these sounds is taking place inside the **[SoundCue]** ExpDebris01 from the GATA_Sounds/Explosion package. If you open this in the SoundCue Editor (use the search box in the Content Browser then right-click the **[SoundCue]**), you can see that the **[Mixer]** node has been used to mix these randomly chosen sounds. This node allows you to control the relative volume levels of its inputs (right-click the node to add further inputs).

▼ Sound Node Mixer	
▼ Input Volume	... (4)
[0]	1.000000
[1]	0.700000
[2]	1.000000
[3]	1.000000

You can also see that there is a **[Delay]** node for the debris sounds so that they happen after the main explosion. The **[Delay]** node is generating a randomized delay amount, thereby further varying the combination of sounds. Finally, a **[Modulator]** node varies the pitch and volume slightly for further variation and an **[Attenuation]** node controls how the sound is heard over distance.

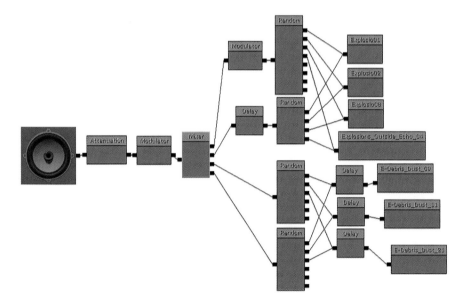

You could extend this system by having a **[Modulator]** for each individual sound element for greater variation. If this system were replicated within Kismet using separate **[SoundCue]**s, you could also have specific control over the volume of each element. This might be useful if you wanted a basic explosion system that could be varied by recombining individual elements according to what size the explosion was or what materials were involved.

You can also see how such a system of recombining elements could also be applicable to melee weapon impacts—creating a lot of variation in what are very repetitive motions (for your typical boxing or hack-and-slash game) without needing the large memory resources of dozens of sounds.

Exercise 205_00 Layering for Variation

You are working on a fighting game where players can enjoy fruitless hand-to-hand combat. Create a **[SoundCue]** that plays new variations for each punch.

Tips

1. **[Trigger]** your **[SoundCue]** so that when you walk up to the robot and press "Use," it fires off a punch sound **[PlaySound]**. Create a **[Trigger]** around the bot (right-click/New Actor/Trigger), then right-click in Kismet and choose New Event Using Trigger *(***)*/Used. (Also link this to the existing bot animation we've already put in the exercise.)
2. Use your own sounds or sounds from the Collision folder in the Sound Library.
3. Create a **[SoundCue]** and use a **[Mixer]** to combine the outputs of several **[Random]** objects.
4. Experiment with adding **[Modulators]** and short **[Delays]** (with random Min/Max) to add further variation to your sounds.

The Combinatorial Explosion: Horizontal Concatenation

The process of recombining sounds to generate new variations can also be done in a horizontal way by changing the order in which segments of sounds are chained together.

Concatenation: Radio Crackle

206 Concatenation Room: Radio Chatter

Every time you press the button in this room you can hear some radio crackles and a speech sample advising you to "Try again." Every time you do this you will likely notice that the radio crackles are slightly different. Instead of having 30-plus different sounds for this operation held in memory, this process is actually generated from 10 sounds of less than 0.4 seconds long to create new variations on the fly. The total file size is 139 kB.

The chaining together of events, one after another, is referred to as concatenation. You can see from the radio crackle **[SoundCue]** that a **[Concatenator]** node is used within the **[SoundCue]** to chain up the different pieces of the radio crackle in a randomized order. You can add as many inputs as you like to the **[Concatenator]** (right-click/add input), and when the first has finished playing it will play the next and so on. (The **[Concatenator]** also has a volume control for each input).

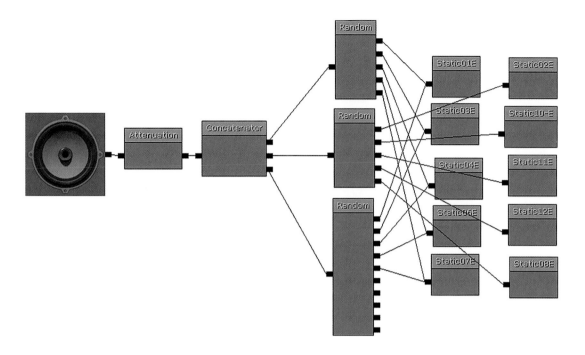

The image below represents the original recording of the radio crackles.

This recording was then edited into smaller sound files. (See Appendix D for editing tips.)

These small chunks are then reordered on the fly using the **[Concatenator]** node. For example:

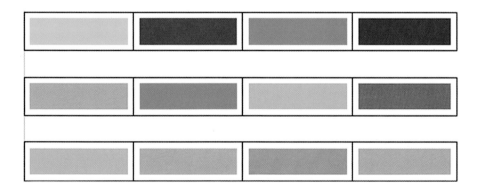

206 Concatenation Room: Fire

In Room 208 you can see a similar method adopted for a variable fire sound. Again, this is produced by randomly ordering five samples of less than a second long. You'll note that one of the fire crackle samples also has some slight modulation on it to vary the pitch.

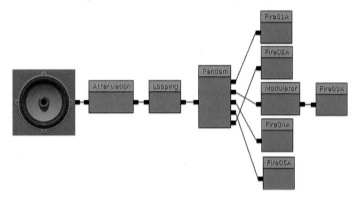

Concatenation: Footsteps

206a Concatenate Footsteps

One of the sounds that players will hear most in many games is the sound of their own footsteps. Although arguments rage (at least among game sound designers) about why these remain a particular problem (see the discussion presented later in the "Footsteps" section), we can increase the variation of these sounds by adopting the concatenate method just described.

Most footsteps when walking consist of two parts: part a, when your heel touches the ground, and part b, when your toes or the flat of your foot at the front touch the ground. With careful editing you can separate these two elements so that we have more possible sound combinations without increasing the memory required.

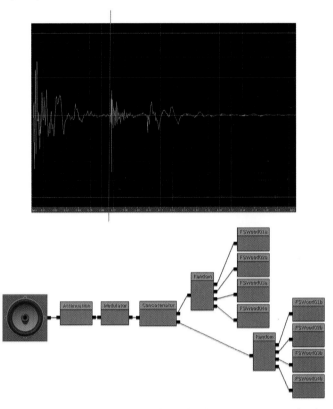

In this illustration, there were four original samples of a footstep on wood. These were edited into Heel/Toe sections (a and b). Each time the **[SoundCue]** is called, it will randomly choose one of the heel sounds, then randomly choose one of the toe sounds. Instead of playing back the four original heel + toe sounds, this system will give us more variation.

Original sounds:

    1 (a + b), 2 (a + b), 3 (a + b), 4 (a + b)
    = 4 possible footstep sounds

After concatenation:

    1a − 1b, 1a − 2b, 1a − 3b, 1a − 4b
    2a − 1b, 2a − 2b, 2a − 3b, 2a − 4b
    3a − 1b, 3a − 2b, 3a − 3b, 3a − 4b
    4a − 1b, 4a − 2b, 4a − 3b, 4a − 4b
    = 16 possible footstep sounds

Exercise 206a_00 Broken TV Robot

In this game scenario the player is dealing with a recalcitrant robot. Unfortunately, it doesn't speak English, just a series of beeps and bloops. So that it doesn't reply in the same way each time you need to randomize it's sounds. The wav you have been supplied with in the exercise folder is BrokenTVRobot.wav.

Tips

1. Open the BrokenTVRobot.wav in your sound editor (see Appendix D for tips on editing). You'll see that it consists of a number of individual peaks with gaps in between. This makes it ripe for a concatenated approach.

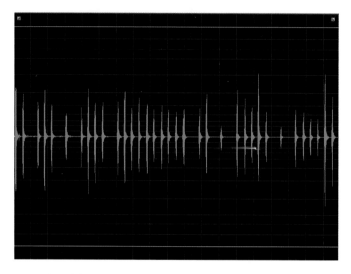

2. Mark out the separate sounds and then save each as a separate file.

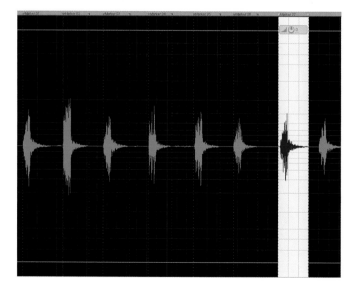

3. Create a **[SoundCue]** that concatenates these individual elements in a random order.
4. Create a **[Trigger]** "used" around the robot in the level to trigger your **[SoundCue]**.
5. Perhaps extend the variation by trying **[Modulation]** or **[Delay]** objects in your **[SoundCue]**.

Concatenation: Multiple Sample Rates

206b Concatenation: Gunshots

We have discussed how it is possible to save memory by resampling our sounds at an appropriate rate given their frequency content. When looking at certain sounds in detail (in this example, a gunshot), it is clear that their frequency content varies considerably over time.

Here you can see that the part of the sound containing high frequencies is isolated to the first 400 milliseconds. After that, the remaining tail is mostly composed of low-frequency content. If we could chain these two together, then we could actually save the files at different sample rates because the latter part does not need to be anywhere near the same sample rate as the first.

The original weapon sample was at 44 kHz and was 397 kB. The initial part of the sound (referred to as the transient) is kept at 44 kHz (now 77 kB). The tail is resampled to 15 kHz (as it has little frequency content above 7.5 kHz) and is now 108 kB. The final file size for both combined is 185 kB—less than half the size of the original (397 kB) yet with little significant audible difference.

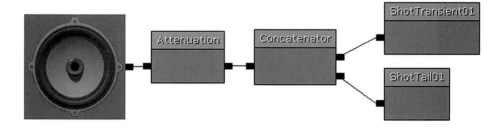

By pressing the switch you can compare the sounds:

1. The original 44 kHz sound file
2. The transient only
3. The tail resampled to 15 kHz
4. The new transient and tail recombined using a concatenated **[SoundCue]**

In circumstances where the memory is tight, this can be a very effective way to reduce file sizes. (For advice on visualizing the frequency content of your sounds, like in the preceding diagrams, see Appendix G.)

Exercise 206b_00 Concatenation of Multiple Sample Rates

Your producer has added the sound of her favorite dog whining to the game sound track as one of the creature sounds for your latest PSP game. The producer insists that it "works really well," and because the deadline for the game beta is tomorrow morning, you should "try to find savings elsewhere." Look in folder 206b_00. You will see several samples. Open these in your audio editor and examine the frequency over time of each sample. Is there a way to save some file space here?

Tips

1. Look at the frequency content of these files. Many of these files could be edited into two or more separate files, saved at different sample rates, and then concatenated back together in the game.
2. Make two **[SoundCue]**s for each, one with the original sound, and then a copy with a downsampled and concatenated version. Make a note of the memory you've saved.
3. Add a series of **[Triggers]** (used) to exercise room 206b_00 to illustrate the original then smaller sounds. You could use a multi output switch like the one in the tutorial room 206b. Add a button static mesh in the center of each **[Trigger]** to see where they are in game.
4. Punch a wall, not your producer.

Multiple Start Points

In some engines you can set markers within the wave file itself to have multiple possible start points—a little like what you could do with a concatenation system but without the hard work of chopping them up!

The sample that follows (of rocks falling) could be played all the way through. It could also be played starting at Marker 01, or Marker 02, Marker 03, or Marker 04. Each would have a different sound. If your audio programmer is very friendly, you might even be able to designate "end" markers as well; or if you have an envelope control, you could make the playback fade out before the end.

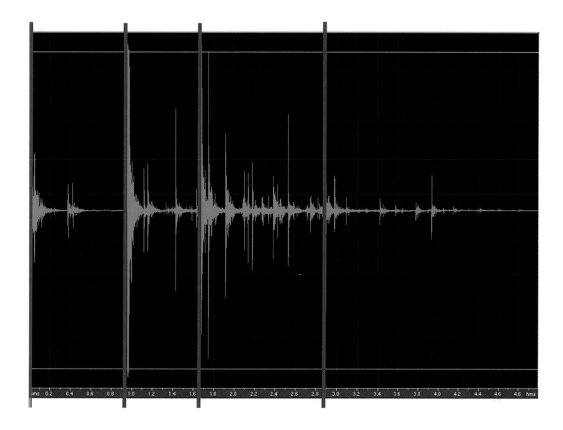

If you have a system like this available to you, then you will usually be asked to add the markers to your audio files in your audio editor. Wav files contain a *header,* which holds this information so that your programmer can access it. Talk to your programmer about their particular requirements for this.

Some DSP

As we mentioned earlier when discussing filters, you should use whatever digital signal processing (DSP) is available to create variations on the sounds you have rather than simply putting more sounds in memory.

Envelopes

207 Waves Envelope

In this room you should hear the gentle rise and fall of waves at the seaside (plus some randomized gulls). The waves vary in length and intensity but are all actually produced from the same sound source—a burst of brown noise (like white noise but with a 6 dB per octave low-pass filter roll-off).

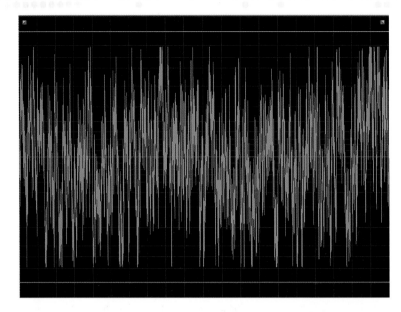

This source is varied by using the Fade In and Fade Out values of the **[PlaySound]** object.

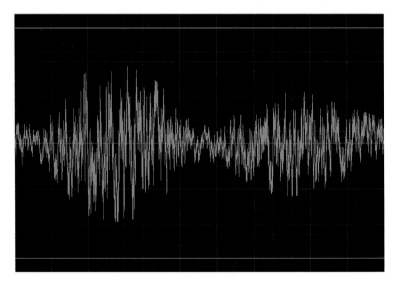

Many objects in Kismet have variables available that are not immediately apparent from the default outputs on the object itself. A variable is basically a number (or other parameter) that can be changed. If you right-click an object in Kismet, you get a list of the other variables it's possible to expose.

By default the **[PlaySound]** object only has its Target variable (where the sound will emit from) exposed. Right-clicking will show you the others that it is possible to access.

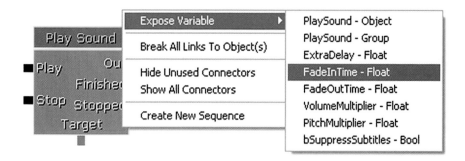

In the Kismet system for Room 207, you can see that the "Fade In Time" and the "Fade Out Time" are exposed. The system uses a **[Random Float]** variable to alter these (right-click in Kismet: New Variable/Float/Random Float) to play the sound with a randomly generated fade-in length. As this happens, a **[Delay]** node (lasting the same length) is started. When the fade-in time has been counted, the **[Delay]** sends out a signal to stop the **[PlaySound]** object. When a **[PlaySound]** object receives the command to stop, it will start fading out (according to its fade-out value).

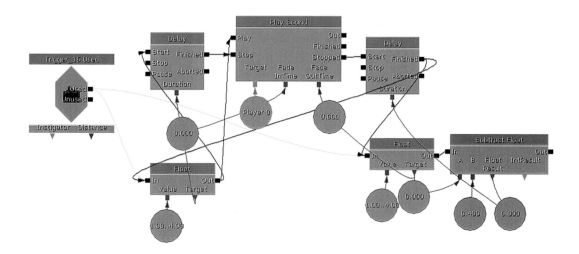

When the Stopped message leaves the **[PlaySound]** object, a new random variable is calculated to determine the fade-out length. This number also powers the delay that waits until the fade out is complete (−0.4 seconds so the sounds doesn't drop to complete silence before starting again) before restarting the whole system for the next wave.

This system is also aided and abetted by the **[SoundCue]**'s pitch and volume variation. The use of randomized fade-in and fade-out lengths for a **[PlaySound]** allow you to alter the volume envelope of a sound to get a huge range of variation from one sound file in memory.

Oscillators: Volume for Wind

208 Wind Oscillator

In Room 208 you can hear some wind that gradually sweeps up and down. In fact, the original sound itself is simply white noise. The variation in its volume is produced by using the **[Oscillator]** node within the **[SoundCue]**.

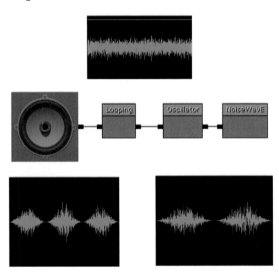

An **[Oscillator]** produces a continuously changing variable around a central value. In this case the oscillator uses a sine wave curve to determine the change in values over time. The **[Oscillator]** node in the **[SoundCue]** has a variable frequency (how often the oscillator cycles around), and so you can get a changing variation in the volume (or pitch) of the sound over time.

Because of the way our ears respond to frequencies and the volume of a sound, this not only has the effect of making the volume of the noise go up and down but there also appears (to our ears) to be a change in the spectral content on the sound. This is useful for noise-based sources such as wind and waves.

Oscillator		
Modulate Volume	☑	
Modulate Pitch	☐	
Amplitude Min	0.400000	
Amplitude Max	0.400000	
Frequency Min	0.200000	
Frequency Max	0.500000	
Offset Min	0.000000	
Offset Max	0.000000	
Center Min	1.000000	
Center Max	1.000000	

Modulate Volume/Modulate Pitch. Choose to modulate either or both.

Amplitude Min/Max. This is the amplitude of the oscillator's modulation (following a sine wave pattern).

The wave is centered by default at around 1.0, so if this amplitude were set to 0.5 you would get a range of values from 0.5 to 1.5. There is both a min and max setting so you can also randomize this parameter between those two values.

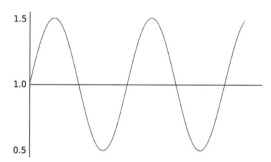

Center Min/Max: You can offset the center of the modulation so that, for example, the sound does or does not drop to complete silence when at the lowest point of its cycle.

Frequency Min/Max: This value is twice the frequency of the sine wave's modulation in Hertz. Again, the Min/Max designation is for the randomization of this value.

Offset Min/Max: Where the sine wave starts in its cycle is referred to as "phase." This offset value allows you to shift the phase of the cycle. This value is multiplied by 2*Pi. Min/Max fields are for randomization.

In the case of the wind example, the amplitude will cycle from between 0.6 (center value 1.0 − 0.4) and 1.4 (center value 1.0 + 0.4). The frequency varies each time it is triggered from between 0.2 (0.125 Hz) and 0.4 (0.2 Hz) to give us different length wind sounds.

Applying an **[Oscillator]** to the volume of a looping sound is a good way to add some movement, variability, and life to it.

Oscillators: Pitch for Flies

208a The Flies

Shooting the glass box in this room (as you inevitably will) releases a number of flies. A short buzzing sound is looped, and the pitch and volume variation over time is produced by the **[Oscillator]** node.

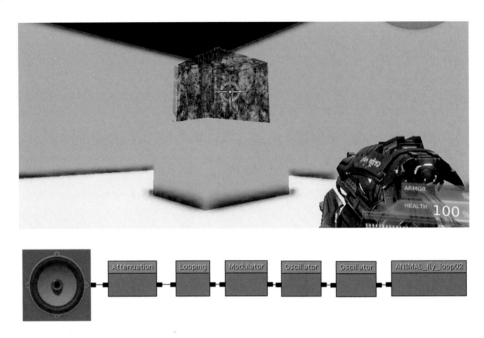

As you can see, this **[SoundCue]** uses a separate **[Oscillator]** for its pitch and for its volume. This enables them to modulate independently rather than both following the same cycle. The volume oscillator has varying frequency and the amplitude varies around a changing center point.

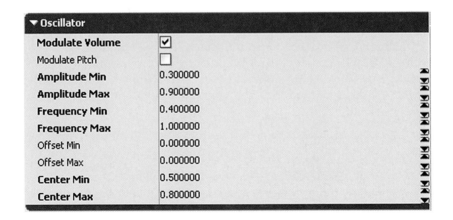

The pitch oscillates with varying frequency around a fixed center point with some slight changes in the amplitude of the oscillator.

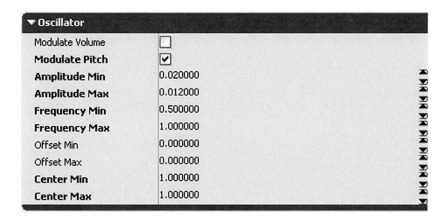

The trigger system uses the **[InterpActor]**s (the glass) Take Damage event within Kismet to play the flies **[SoundCue]**. (This is created in the same way that you created a Touch event for a **[Trigger Volume]**.) For more on **[InterpActor]**s and Take Damage events, see Appendix C: UDK Tips.

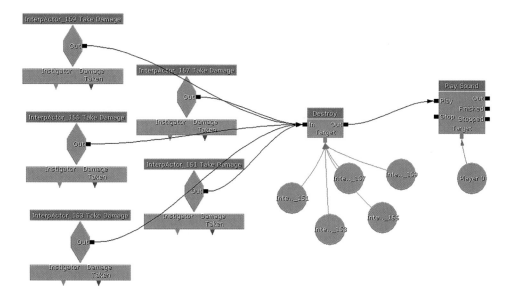

The old glass box in the level itself is actually made of two layers of **[InterpActor]**s representing broken and unbroken glass. These layers are shown here for illustration. When the unbroken **[InterpActor]** takes damage, these **[InterpActor]**s are destroyed, leaving the broken glass **[InterpActor]**s behind.

Exercise 208a_00 Kismet [Trigger Volume] Take Damage and [Oscillator]

The player has to shoot the three generators in this room so that the security door will overload and the player can escape. Each generator will *take damage* and needs to be shot 10 times. In response to this damage, each has an alarm sound (of increasing intensity). You have to create these alarm effects using the one-second triangle wav sample you have been supplied with.

Tips

1. Create three or more **[SoundCue]**s that all reference the same wav, but use the wav in different ways. (Use the Triangle.wav supplied).

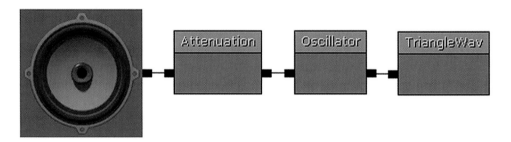

2. Use the **[Oscillator]** to produce an alarm sound that changes in pitch from the triangle.wav tone.
3. For the frequencies of the three different **[SoundCue]**s, you could initially start with values of 0.2, 0.1, and 0.05.
4. The Take damage system has been already created for you using **[DynamicTriggerVolume]**s. Simply add your **[SoundCue]**s to the three **[PlaySound]** objects.

"Back to the Old Skool"

209 Wavetables

Taking memory-saving techniques to their (il)logical extreme, this room plays a couple of well-known tunes (badly). The total file size required to play these tunes (or any other you can think of) is little bigger than the size of the wave file used to produce it, 3.9 kB (which, as you will appreciative by now, is tiny).

We've included this example as a slightly perverse homage to the history of game audio when all of the sounds and music in a game might have been produced from a few very small samples (and a bit of FM synthesis if you were lucky). Although such lengths would not be necessary today, the principles behind this method will never be obsolete with regard to interactive music; we'll be returning to this discussion in the Chapter 4.

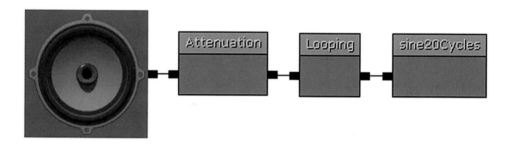

The method here is analogous to wavetable synthesis. The sound source is just 10 cycles of a sine wave (45 milliseconds of sample memory). The looping sine wave produces a tone (as any repeating wave cycle would). By using different **[SoundCue]**s playing the same tone with different pitch multipliers (playing the sample back at different rates), we can get all of the different notes we need.

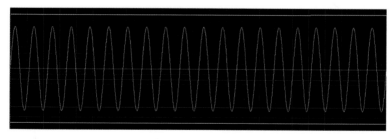

Pitch Multiplier	0.749200	
Play Sound	SoundCue'GATPackage.Sounds.sineWave'	

Pitch Multiplier	0.594600	
Play Sound	SoundCue'GATPackage.Sounds.sineWave'	

In this instance, a **[Matinee]** object is used like a musical sequencer to start (and stop) each note at the appropriate time. We'll be looking at the **[Matinee]** object in more detail later on in Chapter 3.

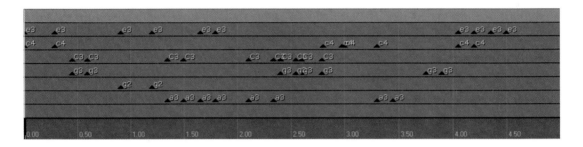

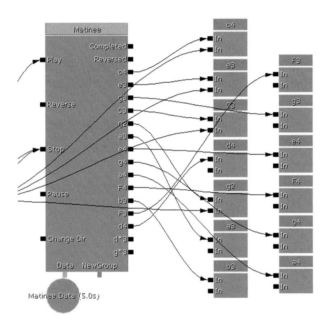

The original sample tone was generated at 220 Hz (pitch A3). To get the other notes, their pitch multipliers were scaled accordingly:

A4 (440 Hz): the pitch multiplier would be 440/220 = 2.0
C3 (130 Hz): the pitch multiplier would be 130.81/220 = 0.595
E3 (164 Hz): the pitch multiplier would be 164/220 = 0.74

If this kind of retro geekery floats your boat (like it does ours), then check out the bibliography for further reading and the MIDI+DLS tutorial on the GameAudioTutorial.com website.

Recap of Sound Actors

[AmbientSoundSimple]: Loops waves (or loops multiple waves).

[AmbientSoundSimpleToggleable]: Loops waves + toggle on/off via Kismet toggle.

[AmbientSoundNonLoop] and **[AmbientSoundNonLoopingToggleable]:** Random sounds chosen at randomized times (+pitch and volume variation).

[AmbientSound]: Plays a **[SoundCue],** either once on collision or looping if the **[Soundcue]** has a loop in it.

And coming up in Chapter 3, **[AmbientSoundMoveable]:** Plays a **[SoundCue]** and attaches to a matinee to move it around.

Conclusions

The nature of interactivity means that there will be a balance between what you can do to represent that interactivity in sound, and what you have in terms of resources to collect and hold in memory. Get as much variation out of as little material as possible and understand your tool in depth in order to fully exploit its potential. You may feel that this is a strange way to start a book, by immediately talking about problems rather than all the exciting things we can do with sound and music in games. However, by tackling these issues early, their importance will become embedded in your normal practice so that you are automatically making sensible decisions. That way you can concentrate on the real tasks at hand.

Firstly, making it sound real.

Making it Sound Real

Many game environments are imitations or at least hyper-real versions of environments that might be found in the real world. Therefore, a player will have pretty clear expectations of what they will sound like, having experienced these environments in some form before. Even if the game is set in a fantasy world, the player will still have expectations about the way sound will behave that has been developed through a lifetime of experience in the physical world. Although we shouldn't always necessarily focus on realism (see Chapter 6), the way things sound needs to be consistent and believable if the player is going to become immersed in the game world.

For a long time, game audio has sought to accurately represent real-world sound to support the verisimilitude (the appearance or semblance of truth or reality) of the experience. To do this, games developers need some understanding of the physics of sound in the real world.

Sound Propagation

Sound emanates from a source and travels through matter in waves. Your ears either receive the sound directly (dry) or indirectly (wet) after it has passed through, or bounced off, the various materials it comes into contact with. Typically you'd receive both these types of sound, and this gives you important information about the environment you are in.

Reverb

300 Sewer Pipe

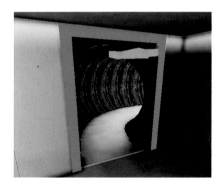

As you descend into the sewer pipe in Room 300 you should hear that your footsteps have more echo to their sound. This is because we have applied a **[ReverbVolume]**. Reverb is short for "reverberation," and it refers to the way that sound reflects and bounces around the surfaces with which it comes into contact. People tend to use the word "echo" to describe this effect, but unlike an echo, which is a distinct separate version of the sound being reflected, reverberation is a much more dense collection of reflections.

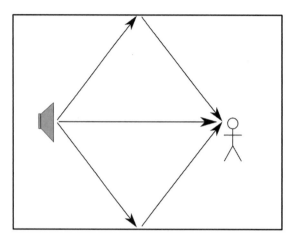

Direct and reflected versions of a sound source.

The character of reverberation can change dramatically depending on the nature of the space. If there are lots of distinct echoes, then this might be an outdoor space, with the sound perhaps reflecting off distant mountains or buildings. If there are lots of reflections within a short time, then this might be a confined space, like a bathroom or tunnel. Fewer reflections over a longer time might represent a large room, and lots of reflections over a long time would be typical of a large cave or hall.

Reverb for a typical room might look something like this.

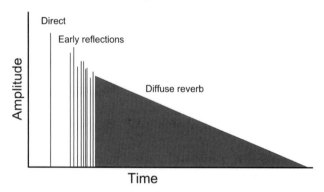

Constructing a reverb that sounds good is a hugely complex task in itself. Trying to model the way sound would actually reflect around a specific space in a game would require a significant amount of computing power, so in games you usually have some precalculated reverb effects available to choose from. You define the area within which your reverb will be applied and then choose the specific type of reverb that's appropriate to the space.

Reverbs are applied in the Unreal Development Kit (UDK) using a **[ReverbVolume]**. This is much like the **[TriggerVolume]** you have come across already. The *Builder Brush* is used to define a rectangle of the appropriate size around the area you want the reverb to apply in. Then you right-click on the AddVolume button and select **[ReverbVolume]** from the list. (For more on building volumes with the **Builder Brush** feature, see Appendix C: UDK Tips).

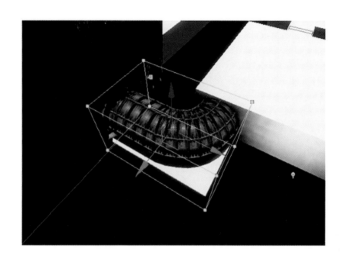

Adding a reverb volume.

By clicking on a **[ReverbVolume]** in the editor and selecting its properties (F4), you can choose which reverb type to apply. For the first pipe, we have chosen the appropriately named Sewer Pipe reverb.

▼ Reverb Volume	
Priority	0.000000
▼ Settings	(bApplyReverb=True,ReverbType=REVERB_SewerPipe,Volume=1.000000,FadeTime=0.100000)
Apply Reverb	☑
Reverb Type	REVERB_SewerPipe
Volume	1.000000
Fade Time	0.100000
▶ Ambient Zone Settings	(bIsWorldInfo=False,ExteriorVolume=1.000000,ExteriorTime=0.500000,ExteriorLPF=1.000000,ExteriorLPFTime=0.500000,InteriorVolume=1.0000

In many editors you will have access to the reverb parameters themselves to adjust them in detail, but within UDK we have a collection of presets.

```
REVERB_Default
REVERB_Bathroom
REVERB_StoneRoom
REVERB_Auditorium
REVERB_ConcertHall
REVERB_Cave
REVERB_Hallway
REVERB_StoneCorridor
REVERB_Alley
REVERB_Forest
REVERB_City
REVERB_Mountains
REVERB_Quarry
REVERB_Plain
REVERB_ParkingLot
REVERB_SewerPipe
REVERB_Underwater
REVERB_SmallRoom
REVERB_MediumRoom
REVERB_LargeRoom
REVERB_MediumHall
REVERB_LargeHall
REVERB_Plate
```

A sudden change between the reverb of two rooms can sound unnatural and jarring, so a fade time is provided for you to bring the reverb gradually into effect if you wish, and the volume controls how much of the effect you hear.

Reverb Prioritization

300a Cave

In the main room with the waterfall the **[ReverbVolume]** has been set to *Cave*. In this room you can hear clearly how any ambient sounds playing back within the **[ReverbVolume]** also have the reverb applied to them. In many circumstances you will have awkwardly shaped rooms that make your **[ReverbVolume]**s overlap, or as in this case a room within a room.

300b A Cave Within a Cave

Behind the waterfall is another cave area. This is obviously smaller than the large chamber, so we want a different reverb for it, in this case it's set to StoneCorridor. Although this **[ReverbVolume]** actually falls within the larger **[ReverbVolume]**, we can tell the system to override the reverb settings of the larger volume by using the Priority setting. The priority for this **[ReverbVolume]** is set as 5.0, and the priority for the larger volume is set as 0.0; therefore, this smaller cave's reverb settings will take precedence because its priority value is greater than the other.

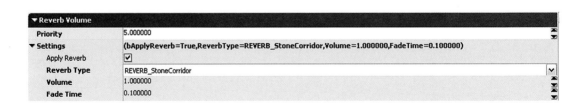

Exercise 300b_00 Reverb

This exercise "room" has a series of spaces of different character. Use **[ReverbVolume]**s with appropriate reverb types to make them feel more authentic.

Tips

1. In the same way as you might use a Builder Brush to create a **[TriggerVolume]**, you can also create **[ReverbVolume]**s.
2. To make the **[ReverbVolume]** exactly the same size as the geometry brush for a room, select the geometry (shown in blue in the Top Down view) and press Ctrl + P; the Builder Brush will mould to exactly the same size. It's then advisable to make your Builder Brush a little bigger than your room using the Scaling widget, so that when you create the **[ReverbVolume]** you can see it and select it more easily.

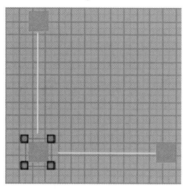

3. If you do leave the Builder Brush, and hence the **[ReverbVolume]**, the same size as your room, you may find it hard to select; use Q to hide BSP (the level geometry) to see it.
4. Now that your Builder Brush is the right size, go to the left-hand panel and right-click on the Add Volumes icon like you did when creating **[TriggerVolume]**s.

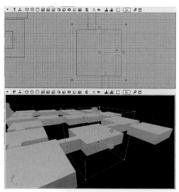

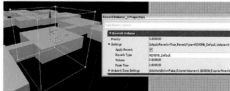

5. Move the Builder Brush out of the way, and then you can then select the **[ReverbVolume]** itself. Press F4 to enter its properties. Under Reverb Type, you can select lots of different types of rooms or spaces. Try different options to hear their effect.

6. If you have smaller rooms within larger areas, you can have a large **[ReverbVolume]** for the whole area and then put the smaller ones within it. Change the Priority settings so that the smaller rooms take priority over the large one.

Sound Sources and Spatialization

Sound spatialization in games is literally a matter of life and death. The field of view for a typical first-person shooter is between 65 and 85 degrees, so most things in the world are actually off-screen. Sound plays a vital role in describing this off-screen space for the player and providing vital information about the direction and source of other characters or objects in the game. Sound sources might be stereo, mono, or three-dimensional (3D). They might originate from a single point source or actually come from a large area. Deciding what is appropriate for each sound and "faking" the physics of how sound behaves in the natural world is an important task in building a convincing and effective audio environment.

Types of Sound Source

Stereo Sources
301 Stereo Sources

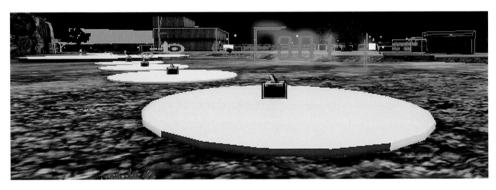

In Chapter 2, we saw some examples where a **[SoundCue]** was set to be played back to the Player variable (i.e., directly to the player's ears). This gives us a normal stereo image that does not pan as the player rotates but remains constant. This is an appropriate method to use for game music that is *not* coming from a specific object, such as a radio, and also for distant stereo ambiences.

If you stand on the first disc in area 301, you will hear some music. As you look and rotate around, you should hear that the music remains consistently still in the stereo field. As you enter the disc, a **[Trigger]** touch is used to trigger a **[PlaySound]**; this targets the player (Right-Click/New Variable/Player/Player). The properties of this variable have also been edited so that it does not play back to All Players but only the player. As it is played back to the player's ears, you will hear it as a two-dimensional (2D; in this case a stereo sound file) stereo sound.

Playing Back Sounds from Objects
301a Stereo Attenuation Only

If you now walk over to the next disc (301a), you can see that this music emanates from the static mesh in the center. The **[SoundCue]** has an **[Attenuation]** node with Radius Min/Radius

Max settings as usual, so you can hear the music attenuate over distance from the sound source. Whether or not the Spatialize option within the **[Attenuation]** node is checked will not make a difference in this case, as the sound file being played is a stereo sound file. Stereo sound files do not spatialize (pan) in UDK but will attenuate over distance if the **[PlaySound]** is targeting an object within the game.

You can play back a sound to emit from any object/Actor in the game world by adding it to the target of a **[PlaySound]**. In the case of 301a, we used a **[Static Mesh]**. With the object selected in the level, just right-click on the target of the **[PlaySound]** in Kismet and select New Object Var using (***).

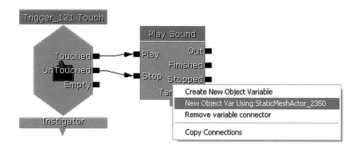

Many designers in UDK like to use the **[Note]** Actor as a useful source to play sounds from, because it is visible within the editor but not in the game. Select **[Note]** in the Actor Classes tab of the Content Browser, right-click in the Perspective viewport, and select Add Note Here. In the properties of the **[Note],** you can also add text (to remind yourself what they are) and a tag (Properties Object/Tag). In the drop-down Show menu in your viewports, you can select the option to Show Actor Tags. This means that the text of your tag will be visible in the editor and is useful for finding things.

301b Mono Attenuation and Spatialization

The next disc (301b) presents the same setup, except this time the **[SoundCue]** is using a mono sound file. Now you can hear that in addition to being *attenuated* the music is also *spatialized*. If you were playing music through an object in the game such as a radio or television, it would be appropriate to spatialize it so that it pans around the speakers according to the player's rotation as you would expect. If you were playing a more film-type score over the top of the action, then non-spatialized stereo files would be more suitable. The nonspatialization of stereo files also extends to any used in **[AmbientSoundSimple]** category Actors or any **[SoundCue]** without an attenuation object.

301c Stereo Ambience

Disc 301c is an example of a streaming stereo ambience. If you have the capacity to stream long ambient sound files, then this can sometimes be a good solution. However, these sound odd if the panning is too obvious. It's often better to combine a nonspatialized stereo ambience with more local spatialized spot effects.

3D Point Sources and Attenuation Curves

Unlike some types of music and stereo ambiences, most sounds within the kind of 3D game environment we've been dealing with emanate from specific points within the 3D world. We provide mono assets and the game system uses the position of these assets to decide how to pan the sound depending on your playback system. If you have a 5.1 or 7.1 speaker setup, then you will hear the sound come from all directions as you rotate around in the game world. If you have a stereo setup, then this information needs to be folded down into a meaningful stereo panning arrangement. Some engines and soundcards also implement HRTF systems for headphone listening. HRTF stands for head-related transfer function and attempts to describe the spatialization cues we get from the way that sounds reaching our ears arrive at slightly different times and are filtered by our head. By applying the same changes to the left and right versions of a sound reaching our ears through headphones, a convincing re-creation of a sense of location for the sound can sometimes be achieved. (Because our heads are all different sizes, the effect is based on an average; therefore, it is not as successful as it could be.) Spatialization gives vital information about the direction of the sound source, so it is particularly important for sounds like enemy weapon fire, footsteps, and dialogue.

301d Point Sources

We looked briefly at how sound attenuates over distance in Chapter 1 (when we discussed the Radius Min and Radius Max settings). Many engines simply have min and max radii with a fixed attenuation curve calculated between them. You may have noticed that UDK offers further options for controlling the way that the sound attenuates over distance under the Distance Model drop-down menu. (This is referred to as the "roll-off factor" in many other engines.)

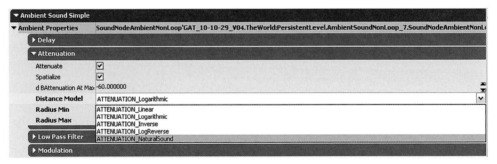

These differences may be easy to overlook and may appear at first glance to be slightly academic, but choosing carefully which model is most appropriate for which sound is critical, both for creating a clean mix within your environment and for giving the player vital audio cues about the location of events and Actors within the game world.

You may be asking yourself at this point why we don't simply replicate the curve of the way sound attenuates in air. We know that in normal outside conditions, the sound pressure level is inversely proportional to the square of the distance from the sound source. "Normal" conditions are actually very rare, and the way sound attenuates is also affected by air pressure, temperature and humidity. In audio terms, a basic rule of thumb is that sounds halve in volume (approx −6 db) every time the distance from the sound source is doubled.

There are a number of reasons why this won't work for games:

- As we observed in Chapter 2, the recording, storage, and playback of sound cannot replicate the dynamic range of the physical world. Typically we record and store sound in 16 bits. The range of numbers this allows does not come anywhere near representing the huge dynamic range of the physical world. (The oft-quoted comparison is the difference between a pin drop and a jet engine.)

● As discussed earlier, game distances are not the same as real-world distances—partly because operating a game character is a lot more clumsy than you think (so they need additional space to avoid getting stuck in furniture all the time) and partly because this would make many games an endlessly boring trudge.

● If we were to imitate the natural attenuation curve of sound, then we would have a lot of very quiet, very distant sounds playing almost all the time, as the Radius Max value would be very large. This would have negative implications for the mix (the addition of all these quiet sounds would take up "headroom," a significant chunk of our available 65,565 numbers) and for the number of voices (simultaneous sounds) we were using (which, as you will discover later, is quite limited).

There is no substitute, when deciding which attenuation curve to use for which sound, to actually previewing it in the game engine itself. Depending on the nature of the sound source itself and the specifics of what's going on at the time, you will find it more appropriate to use your ears than to use these starting points. (The following graphs are reproductions of items in the UDK documentation.)

301d Linear

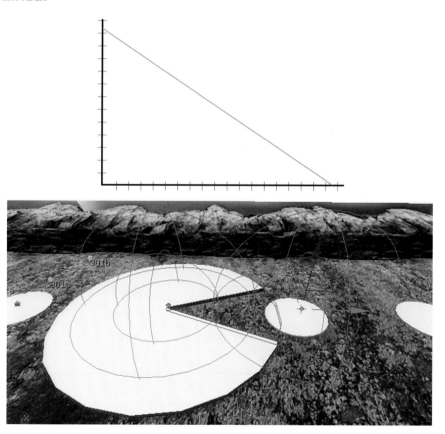

This is a simple linear drop-off over distance. It can be good for looping room tone–type ambiences where you want the fall-off to behave in a predictable way. Sound does not attenuate like this in the real world and this will sound unrealistic for most sounds, but it can be useful for more predictable overlapping/crossfading between ambient loops.

The combination of these two overlapping sounds dropping off to the Radius Max setting should produce a result that does not significantly drop in volume as you pass across the two, as the addition of the two always produces an equal value.

301e Logarithmic

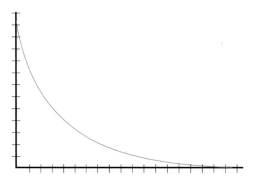

This is a good choice for sounds that you only want to hear within a relatively short distance from their source. Depending on the exact circumstances, this may be a good option for enemy weapon sounds where you have multiple enemies within a relatively small area. The curve will give you a precise idea of the position of the sound source without allowing the sounds to be heard too far from the source, which might muddy the mix.

301f Inverse

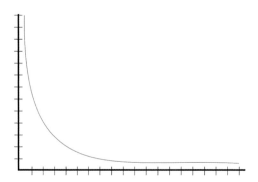

As you can see, this sound can be heard from a significant distance away, but the amplitude only really ramps up when very close. This is good for very loud and distant objects. They will feel really loud up close, and will be heard from a distance as you would expect, but won't completely dominate the mix as they might otherwise do.

301g LogReverse

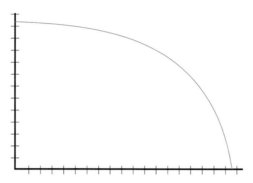

These sounds will be loud right up to their Radius Max value and then suddenly drop off. They are useful for stopping sounds up against walls where other solutions (see occlusion, discussed below) are not practical.

301h NaturalSound

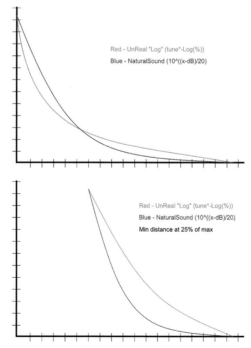

This is an attempt at a more realistic attenuation curve that may be appropriate for certain sounds.

The Game Audio Tutorial

Non-point Sources
301i Non-point Sources

In some cases, a sound source will not come from a specific point but from a larger area such as a large piece of machinery or a waterfall.

In this case, it may work to have a quite large Radius Min value. Having a linear or log reverse curve and a larger Radius Min value will make the sound less directional so that it doesn't pan as much. Remember that we can also remove spatialization, even for mono files, within the Attenuation function of both **[AmbientSound]**s and **[SoundCue]**s. This means that the sound will attenuate over distance but will not pan. This is much more convincing for larger objects where the sound shouldn't appear to be originating from a specific point.

You can turn off spatialization in either the **[AmbientSoundSimple]**

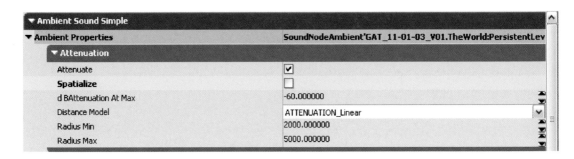

or in the Attenuation object of the **[SoundCue]**

▼ Attenuation	
Attenuate	☑
Spatialize	☐
d BAttenuation At Max	-60.000000
Distance Algorithm	ATTENUATION_Linear
Distance Type	SOUNDDISTANCE_Normal
Radius Min	400.000000
Radius Max	4000.000000

Exercise 301i_00: Sound Sources

Put the sources from Exercise 301i_00 folder into the supplied game level. Choose the appropriate 2D or 3D playback method for each, and adjust the attenuation curves appropriately to create a convincing game environment.

Tips

The sounds consist of a large machine sound, some radio dialogue, and some stereo music. Read back through the previous pages to choose the most appropriate method of attenuation for each.

Multichannel Surround Sources
301j Multichannel Sources

UDK also offers the opportunity to import multichannel files. Like stereo files, these are locked to particular speakers on playback and don't pan. One use of these files might be for big explosions or for events that you want to really envelop the player. You could also use these for distant ambiences, but if you have good multichannel recordings you may do better by attaching the individual files to invisible objects in the game so that as the player rotates the sounds move accordingly. The most common usage would be for surround music files.

The **[Trigger]** in the middle of this bridge starts a **[PlaySound]** that contains a **[SoundCue]** referencing our multichannel file. You'll notice that this SoundNodeWave contains all the channels as they are encapsulated into one file on import.

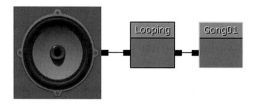

When importing your files, you need to follow a specific naming convention so that the tracks will be panned to the correct speaker. In this case there is a 5.1 piece with each instrument attached to a specific speaker for illustration.

	Filename Extension	4	5.1	6.1	7.1	Example 301c
FrontLeft	_fl	☺	☺	☺	☺	Gong01_fl
FrontRight	_fr	☺	☺	☺	☺	Gong01_fr
FrontCenter	_fc		☺	☺	☺	Gong01_fc
LowFrequency	_lf		☺	☺	☺	Gong01_lf
SideLeft	_sl		☺	☺	☺	Gong01_sl
SideRight	_sr		☺	☺	☺	Gong01_sr
BackLeft	_bl			☺	☺	
BackRight	_br				☺	

These relate to the typical setups for surround-sound speakers.

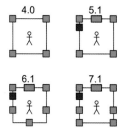

The good thing about surround sound in games is that it's optimized for one person, unlike in the cinema where anyone sitting outside the "sweet spot" is getting a different experience. The problem is that although multichannel music has been used effectively in games, the kind of specific spatialization as heard in this example would be very distracting. The surround channels in games play a vital role in terms of immersion and to provide the player with vital gameplay information (such as the location of NPCs), so any distinct spatialized sound is usually considered to be part of the game world. In situations where you want the music to unnerve the player, it can work well to play on this ambiguity; in general, however, the more subtle approach of putting some of the music's reverb in the surrounds often works better.

Exercise 301j_00: Multichannel Ambience

Try out a multichannel ambience in this factory room.

Tips

1. In the Sound Library there is a quad ambience of a factory. Import these files into a UDK package:
   AMBIENCE_factory_fl.wav
   AMBIENCE_factory_fr.wav
   AMBIENCE_factory_sl.wav
   AMBIENCE_factory_sr.wav
2. You should find that because they have the correct file extensions, they will be automatically combined into a single soundnodewave called AMBIENCE_factory. Create a looping **[SoundCue]** using this file and place it in the level. Walk around the level to see how this sounds.
3. Now take it out. Remove the file extensions (_fl, _fr, etc) from the AMBIENCE_factory files and import each to a separate sound file.
4. Add some **[Note]**s to your level (from the Content Browser/Actor Classes tab), and place them in a quad (4.0) configuration (see the preceding diagram). Use a **[SoundCue]** (including an **[Attenuation Node]**) and a **[PlaySound]** object for each sound, and target the appropriate **[Note]** in the level to re-create the surround-sound ambience.

Directionality

> Sounds often have a particular direction in which they are loudest/unfiltered. Few actually emit equally in all directions. Think of your voice, for example, or a megaphone. Using these controls can greatly help the "reality" of your soundscape.

Many game engines offer the opportunity to specify a directional *cone* for each sound source. This more accurately represents the directional quality of sound from many types of source. Many sound sources have a clear "front" where the sound is clear and "back" where the sound may be attenuated in or filtered. These cones usually take the following form:

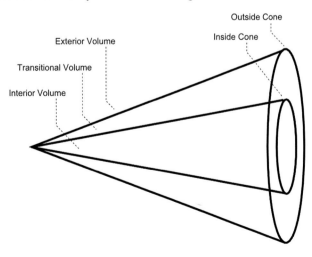

Within the inside cone the sound is at its maximum volume; in the outer cone it drops to a given volume. Outside of the outer cone it is set at this given volume and has a low-pass filter applied. This will give an effect that is similar to walking around behind someone who's speaking. (Try it to see what it sounds like; you'll definitely freak them out). Unfortunately, UDK does not have this functionality as of yet, so we cannot give you a practical example. If this feature becomes available in the future, we'll provide an update on the website, as this is of key importance for being able to localize sound sources.

Filtering Over Distance

301k Attenuate with Low Pass Filter

In addition to the volume of sound attenuating over distance, air also acts a little like a low-pass filter, removing the higher frequencies over distance, as well. Some game engines automatically apply a filter to sound over distance. In others you will have hands-on control of this effect to simulate the absorption of sound into air.

You've already used a low-pass filter in the Aircon room (Room 202) and exercise, but this time we're not just using it to add variation to a sound; this time we're trying to approximate the real-world physics.

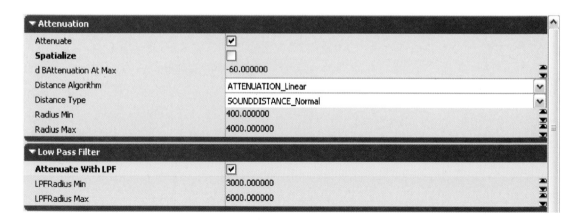

If you use the **[Trigger]** shown in the previous illustration, a randomized explosion will begin in the distance above where the arrow is located. Leave the explosions going and walk toward them. You will hear that not only does the volume get louder, but the filter is gradually removed, going from a "duller" sound to a "brighter" sound.

This has been achieved by using the LowPassFilter option within the **[Attenuation]** node of the explosions **[SoundCue]** (GATA_Sound.Explosion.Explosionfilt).

You can also see other examples where this filter-over-distance technique has been used, such as for the existing Shock rifle weapon. If you look at this **[SoundCue]** (UDKGame/Content/Sounds/Weapon/A_Weapon_Shockrifle), you can see that the high frequencies begin to roll off starting at 2,400 units away from the source.

Applying a low-pass filter over distance in this way is very effective in creating a sense of distance, making sounds appear far away or close by. If you were going to get slightly obsessive about it, you could even have different versions of **[SoundCue]**s (using the same Sound Wave but with different Low Pass Filter settings) playing depending on the atmospheric conditions (e.g., hot sunshine or dense fog).

Exercise 301k_00: Filter Over Distance

The bot on the hill over yonder is shouting for some assistance. Remake the **[SoundCue]** so that the voice is correctly spatialized and attenuates over distance with filtering to make the sound more realistic.

Tips

1. Make a copy of the existing **[SoundCue]**, and re-reference the **[PlaySound]** to your new cue.
2. Edit the **[Attenuation]** node settings to enable Spatialization, Attenuation, and Attenuate with LPF.
3. Experiment with different LPF (Low Pass Filter) Radius Max and Min values.

Faking Filter Over Distance

In some game engines, you need to fake the way that air filters sound over distance. You might do this by apply filtering in your digital audio workstation (DAW) and then crossfading between the "dry" normal sound and the filtered "wet" one over distance.

If your game engine does not have a filter-over-distance setting, such as the one in UDK, then you can fake it by *crossfading* between two wave files depending on your distance from the source. Although the Attenuate with LPF features can be very effective, the way that the frequencies of sound are affected over distance is much more complex than applying a simple low-pass filter, and you may want more control. You could use your audio editor to filter your sounds more precisely and then combine two or more versions within your **[SoundCue]**.

301 Propagation Filter

You can see an example of this technique in the outside of area 301a. As you walk up to the waterfall, you are actually crossfading between two prerendered files. The more distant sound is a version that has already been filtered in an audio editor.

To control the way these sounds crossfade over distance, use the appropriately named **[Distance Crossfade]** node in the **[SoundCue]** (GATA_Sound.Liquid.WaterfallFakeOverDistance).

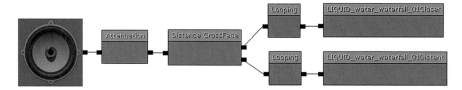

For each input to the **[Distance Crossfade]** node, you apply the following settings:

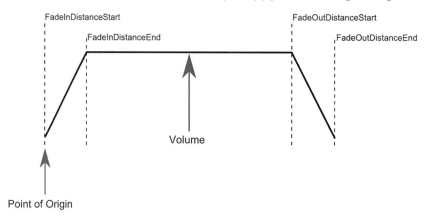

▼ Sound Node Distance Cross Fade	
▼ Cross Fade Input	... (2)
▼ [0]	(FadeInDistanceStart=0.000000,FadeInDistanceEnd=0.000000,FadeOutDistanceStart=
Fade In Distance St	0.000000
Fade In Distance Er	0.000000
Fade Out Distance !	500.000000
Fade Out Distance I	3000.000000
Volume	1.000000
▼ [1]	(FadeInDistanceStart=500.000000,FadeInDistanceEnd=2000.000000,FadeOutDistance!
Fade In Distance St	500.000000
Fade In Distance Er	2000.000000
Fade Out Distance !	3000.000000
Fade Out Distance I	6000.000000
Volume	1.000000

As you can see from the waterfall example, it would be usual for your first sound, the one closest to the point of origin, to have both "Fade in distance start" and "Fade in distance end" values set at zero.

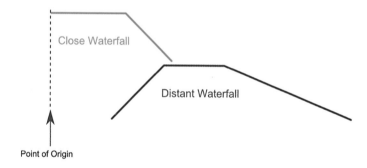

The **[Distance Crossfade]** node has many other applications that we will be exploring later.

Reveal Detail Over Distance

> To simulate some of the effects of sound in air, you may also want to add/remove layers of detail from the sound depending on our distance from it. Typically you would add smaller high-frequency details the closer you got to the sound source. This can also be useful for weapons to keep the mix cleaner when you have multiple enemies.

301m Propagation: Crossfade Detail

Crossing over the bridge by the waterfall, you come to a switch that will power up a large machine at a distance down the river. As you approach the machine, you can hear that the sound not only gets louder, and reveals more high frequency elements, but actually reveals additional details to the sound.

Rather than simply crossfading the machine's sound with a filtered version of itself here, we are adding sounds so you only get the full combined machine sound when you are right up against it. A large and complex sound source would in reality be made of many separate components, each attenuating over distance differently given their volume, position, and frequency content. The **[Distance Crossfade]** node is used again here to reveal this detail as you get closer to the sound source.

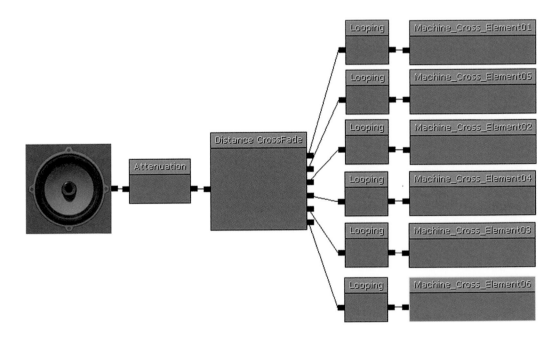

All of these elements are at their maximum volume at the sound source and so the "Fade in distance start" and "Fade in distance end" values are set at zero.

	Fade out distance start	Fade out distance end
Sound 0:	4,000	5,000
Sound 1:	2,500	3,500
Sound 2:	2,000	2,500
Sound 3:	1,000	2,000
Sound 4:	400	1,000
Sound 5:	200	600

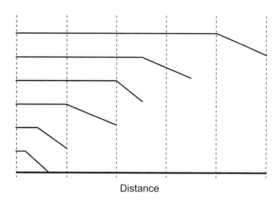

Distance

Exercise 301m_00 Propagation Crossfade

The Temple of Ra is set upon a hill. In the center of the temple, a roaring jet of burning plasma shoots skyward. The low rumble of this furnace can be heard for miles around. As worshipers approach the temple, the hissing of the air fills their senses. Make it so.

Tips

1. Place an **[AmbientSound]** object in the center of the temple, and use this to reference your **[SoundCue]**.
2. Within your **[SoundCue],** use the **[Distance Crossfade]** object to crossfade between a number of sounds depending on the distance from the source.
3. Make sure that your **[Attenuation]** matches up with your farthest sound.
4. Consider also using the LPF over distance if appropriate.

Occlusion, Obstruction, Exclusion

It's a great deal cheaper in computational terms to "fake" the occlusion that takes place when you hear (or don't hear) sound through walls.

We've looked at how sound describes the characteristics of a room as it is reflected around (reverb) and how the effect of sound traveling through air (attenuation and filtering) gives a sense of distance and localization. The other aspects of the acoustics of sound that we have to engage with when designing and implementing sound for games are occlusion, obstruction, and exclusion. As we saw in Chapter 1, "The Walls Problem," by default many engines do not take account of walls/windows to apply the natural changes in volume and filtering that would occur within the real world.

The problem we are dealing with here is occlusion—when a object or surface comes between the listener and the sound source, completely blocking the path so that the sound must pass through the obstacle.

When a sound is occluded, both the dry and reflected sounds are muffled. The extent to which the sound is attenuated in volume and altered in frequency content will depend on the material of the obstacle. Brick has a pretty significant effect as you can imagine, whereas if the sound were occluded by the paper walls of a traditional Japanese house, the effect would be different. In Chapter 1 we looked at the problems that can arise when an **[AmbientSoundSimple]** overlaps a wall, and we looked at two possible solutions:

1. Using multiple smaller sounds, you can better shape these around the geometry and avoid over-lapping walls. This is time consuming to implement, uses up lots of voices, and can in some instances lead to phasing issues.
2. Using a **[TriggerVolume]** to toggle sounds depending on whether the player is "inside" an area or "outside," we can switch on and off the ambiences for each area, creating the impression of a change in the environment.

302 Occlusion: Switching Sounds On/Off

Area 302 replicates the techniques we came across in Chapter 1. This one is a real cheat but can work surprisingly well. To simulate occlusion when you are inside a room or outside, have one group of sounds for the inside, one group for the outside, and simply switch between them.

Area 302 has three **[AmbientSoundSimpleTogglable]**s (shown in the red circle) for the wild-life sounds of outside the building and one (shown in green) for an internal room tone. As the player enters or exits the room, a **[TriggerVolume]** in the doorway is used to toggle off/on the **[AmbientSoundSimpleToggleable]**s.

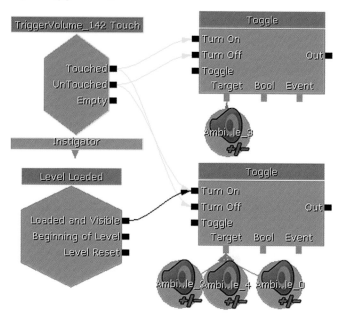

These **[AmbientSoundSimpleToggleable]**s also have a short fade in/out to ease the transition.

▼ Ambient Sound Simple Toggleable	
Fade On Toggle	☑
Fade In Duration	1.000000
Fade In Volume Level	1.000000
Fade Out Duration	1.000000
Fade Out Volume Level	0.000000

Of course, there are a number of drawbacks to this approach:

● Unless you're going to make your own filtered/attenuated versions of the inside and outside sounds, then you will either get only the inside sounds or only the outside sounds, which is not the most realistic occlusion. This can be absolutely fine for some environments where because of the noise levels, or the degree of occlusion, you wouldn't hear these anyway.
● If the players are quickly entering and exiting rooms, then they can become aware of this trickery and this can affect their immersion in the game.
● The nature of a switch is that it is either one or the other; there is no midpoint. So a player hovering in the doorway is going to have a pretty odd experience of constant switching between the two states.

Most modern game audio engines do ray-tracing for detecting occlusion. A simple path is traced between the sound emitters and the listener. If any geometry or objects interrupt this path, then a filtered version of the sound is played (either by filtering in real time or by playing a prerendered filtered version of the sound). Other engines require us to define the geometry for them. Making these calculations in real time to apply changes to the sounds with any degree of real accuracy is beyond the scope of the amount of processing power currently dedicated to audio, so, like we did with many other areas discussed in this chapter, we have to fake it.

Ambient Zones

> The games engine often has no awareness of the positions of walls in regard to occluding sound, so even if you do have a built-in occlusion system, you will have to do some work to define "rooms" for this system to work.

UDK provides a system for occlusion called *Ambient Zones*, which will allow you to avoid many of the issues outlined earlier. This functionality is actually available as a subsection within the **[ReverbVolume]**s that we've already come across.

▼ Reverb Volume	
Priority	1.000000
▶ **Settings**	(bApplyReverb=False,ReverbType=REVERB_Default,Volume=0.500000,FadeTime=2.000000)
▼ **Ambient Zone Settings**	(bIsWorldInfo=False,ExteriorVolume=0.100000,ExteriorTime=0.500000,ExteriorLPF=0.20000(
Exterior Volume	0.100000
Exterior Time	0.500000
Exterior LPF	0.200000
Exterior LPFTime	0.500000
Interior Volume	0.300000
Interior Time	0.500000
Interior LPF	0.400000
Interior LPFTime	0.500000

Using these volumes, you can specify the geometry for the audio system so that it will attenuate and filter sounds depending on whether you are inside or outside of this volume. For example, you could have a rain sound that covered your entire level and add Ambient Zones placed around each building in the level.

Old way: Trying to use multiple rain sound emitters around the building's geometry:

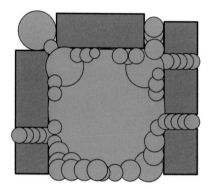

New way: Using Ambient Zones to define the building geometry for occlusion:

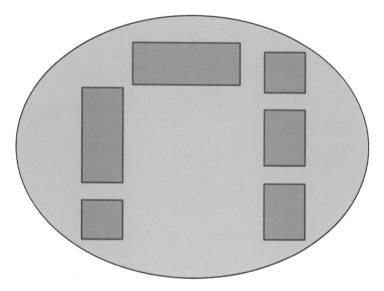

If you had an underground laboratory or a tower block, you could have one ambient sound for the whole of each floor and use the Ambient Zones to separate them out horizontally so that they do not overlap or "bleed through."

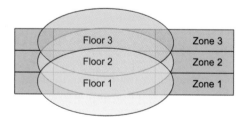

The settings for the Ambient Zone are as follows: Exterior Volume, Exterior LPF, Interior Volume, Interior LPF, and the times it takes to transition between the effect of each one. These settings are explained in the following diagram.

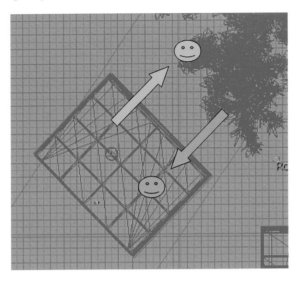

Interior Volume	Exterior Volume
The volume of things inside when heard from the outside.	The volume of things outside when heard from the inside.

Interior LPF	Exterior LPF
The amount of filtering to apply to things inside when heard from the outside.	The amount of filtering to apply to things outside when heard from the inside.

Ambient Zones Only Affect Ambient Sounds

Before we go rushing off in giddy excitement at all the possibilities this feature presents, we should remember an important caveat with the Ambient Zones system in UDK. It will only affect Actors from the **[AmbientSound]** category, or sounds belonging to the Ambient SoundClass.

Any sound waves attached to these Actors will work without any adjustment:

> **[AmbientSoundSimple]**
> **[AmbientSoundNonLoop]**
> **[AmbientSoundSimpleToggleable]**

However, if you are using anything that references a **[SoundCue]**, (**[AmbientSound]**, **[AmbientSoundMoveable]**)), or a **[PlaySound]** from Kismet, then that **[SoundCue]** must be defined as belonging to the Ambient SoundClass.

We'll be looking at SoundClasses in more detail in Chapter 6, but for the moment it's enough to know that if you want your **[SoundCue]** to work with Ambient Zones, you should right-click it within the Content Browser and select Sound Classes: Master/SFX/Ambient. Then save your package. This will define the **[SoundCue]** as belonging to this SoundClass. We do not advise that you change the SoundClass of any of the existing UDK or tutorial-level assets, as this can have unintended consequences later on.

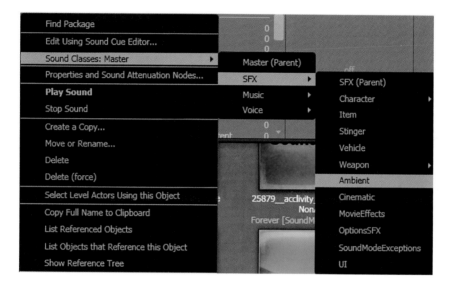

Ambient Zones: Simple

302a Ambient Zones Simple

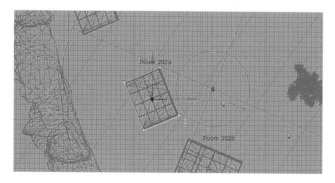

In this area there are some birdsong **[AmbientSoundSimple]**s outside the building and a room tone **[AmbientSoundSimple]** inside the building. Using an Ambient Zone, we have specified that the sounds outside of this zone (defined by a **[ReverbVolume]**) will be quiet when we are inside the volume/building, and when we are outside the volume/building the room tone from inside will be attenuated.

You'll see from these settings that we have also applied a low-pass filter so that things sound slightly muffled. Start the level and walk in and out of this building to hear the effect.

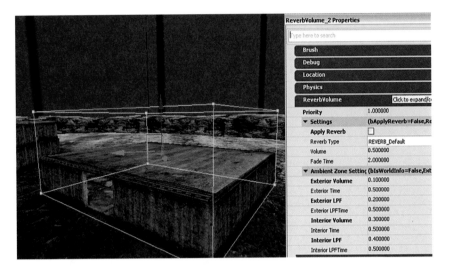

Exercise 302a_00 Ambient Zones Exercises

In this exercise we have an outside area where aircraft are flying past and an inside hangar area. Using Ambient Zones ensure that the sounds are correctly attenuated when inside or outside the hangar.

Tips

1. Add a mechanical room tone to the inside of the hangar as a looping **[AmbientSoundSimple]**.
2. Now you will want to create a **[ReverbVolume]** around the hanger, as this is what also defines the Ambient Zone.
3. Select the hangar in the Top viewport and press Ctrl + P to mould the Builder Brush to its shape.
4. Now select the **[ReverbVolume]**. Because it's exactly the same size as the building itself, you may find it tricky to select. Press W to hide the **[StaticMesh]**s (what the building is made of) to make it easier to select.
5. Alter the Interior/Exterior settings. Remember to also apply some filtering.
6. You will not hear your Ambient Zones take effect until you rebuild the geometry for the level. Do this from the top menu bar: "Build/Build geometry for current level."

Multiple Ambient Zones

302b Ambient Zones Room Within a Room

You will often have multiple rooms within a building and you may want to use Ambient Zones to stop sounds from leaking from one room to another. Unlike **[ReverbVolume]**s, which can over-lap (although you can then use a priority system to decide which will apply), you cannot have overlapping Ambient Zones therefore, you need to carefully sculpt them to the size of each room.

In these rooms there is a separate room tone for the large main room and for the room at the back, together with an outside ambience.

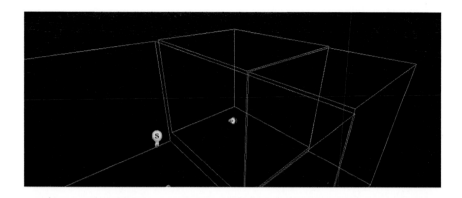

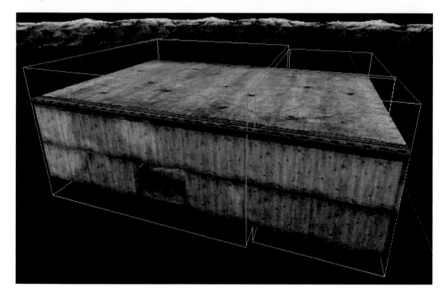

It is possible to edit the shape of the **[ReverbVolume]** into more advanced shapes using the Geometry tool. See the UDK documentation for advice on how to do this.

Additive Effects of Ambient Zones

302c Ambient Zones Area

In Area 302c, the building on the left has a loud alarm sound in it, and the building on the right has a quiet insect. There is also the continuing outside ambience of birds.

Note that the Interior settings (the volume and filtering of things inside the zone when heard from the outside) are not reset by entering a new zone but instead are combined with the exterior settings of that zone. For example, when you leave the alarm building on the left, the alarm sound is attenuated to 0.3 along with a LPF setting of 0.3.

▼ Reverb Volume	
Priority	1.000000
▶ Settings	(bApplyReverb=False,ReverbType=REVERB_Default,Volume=0.500000,FadeTime=2.000000)
▼ Ambient Zone Settings	(bIsWorldInfo=False,ExteriorVolume=0.300000,ExteriorTime=0.500000,ExteriorLPF=0.20000(
Exterior Volume	0.300000
Exterior Time	0.500000
Exterior LPF	0.200000
Exterior LPFTime	0.500000
Interior Volume	0.300000
Interior Time	0.500000
Interior LPF	0.300000
Interior LPFTime	0.500000

This continues to apply when you enter building 2 on the right, but this Ambient Zone has an Exterior setting of 0.2, so this will also now be applied to attenuate the sound further. This is consistent with what would happen in the physical world.

▼ Reverb Volume	
Priority	0.000000
▶ Settings	(bApplyReverb=True,ReverbType=REVERB_Default,Volume=0.500000,FadeTime=2.000000)
▼ Ambient Zone Settings	(bIsWorldInfo=False,ExteriorVolume=0.200000,ExteriorTime=0.500000,ExteriorLPF=0.20000(
Exterior Volume	0.200000
Exterior Time	0.500000
Exterior LPF	0.200000
Exterior LPFTime	0.500000
Interior Volume	0.300000
Interior Time	0.500000
Interior LPF	1.000000
Interior LPFTime	0.500000

Ambient Zones and Filtering
302d Ambient Zones Area

So far we've used the attenuation of volume and the low-pass filter in combination, but there are particular circumstances in which you may wish to apply the filter without significant volume attenuation.

In the building in Area 302d, there is a window. For this case, two Ambient Zones have been set up. The one by the window just filters the sound without attenuating the volume and the one where the character's voice would be occluded by the wall has additional volume attenuation. For cases in which the engine does not support native occlusion, it may be useful and effective to take the time and effort to set up specific details like this for particular circumstances.

Exterior volume is attenuated when hearing the bot through the wall:

▼ Ambient Zone Setting (bIsWorldInfo=False,ExteriorVolume=	
Exterior Volume	0.100000
Exterior Time	0.500000
Exterior LPF	0.200000
Exterior LPFTime	0.500000
Interior Volume	1.000000
Interior Time	0.500000
Interior LPF	0.300000
Interior LPFTime	0.500000

Exterior sound is only filtered, not attenuated when hearing the bot through the window:

▼ Ambient Zone Setting (bIsWorldInfo=False,ExteriorVolume=	
Exterior Volume	1.000000
Exterior Time	0.500000
Exterior LPF	0.200000
Exterior LPFTime	0.500000
Interior Volume	1.000000
Interior Time	0.500000
Interior LPF	0.300000
Interior LPFTime	0.500000

Obstructions and Exclusions

We've looked at how sound is affected when the path between its source and the listener is blocked by an obstacle of some sort. In addition to occlusion we must also consider two other scenarios. The first are Obstructions, which occur when there is an obstacle between the listener and the sound object but the reflected sound, emanating from the object and bouncing off the walls, still reaches the listener.

302e Obstruction

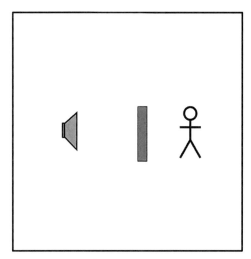

Often there may be an obstacle between the source and listener, but the sound reflected around the room from the source still reaches the listener. This sound obviously differs from the one you hear when all the sounds are on the other side of a wall, for instance. As we've discussed, the calculations for implementing this properly in real time are demanding. However, because the chief effect is a filtering of the sound, it can be worth, under circumstances that demand it, applying the Ambient Zones system.

In this instance, the wall is blocking the direct path of the sound, so an Ambient Zone is created behind the wall with a filter applied to Exterior sounds. This produces a rough approximation of an obstruction effect. Take a look at this in area 302e of the tutorial level.

302f Exclusions

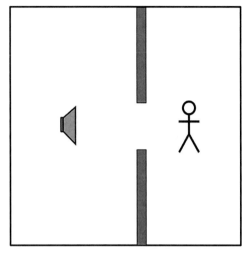

Exclusions are when the sound reaches the listener directly from the sound source, but the reflections hit the obstacle. This would typically occur if a sound and listener were lined up through a doorway, for example.

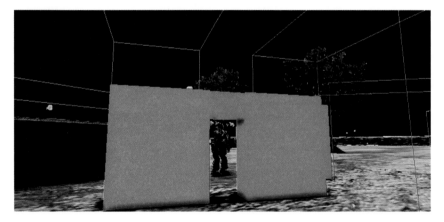

As 302f demonstrates, you can produce a cheap imitation of the effect by having an Ambient Zone for each of the walls while leaving the sound coming through the doorway itself unattenuated. We've made the two zones slightly narrower than the walls to feel more natural, as sound will only gradually be attenuated and filtered as you go around a corner due to refraction.

Summary

- Occlusion: Both the direct and reflected sound are muffled.
- Obstruction: Only the direct sound is muffled.
- Exclusion: Only the reflected sound is muffled.

Although the processing requirement of calculating real-world physics in real time for sound currently means that we have to fake it, we've looked at many examples that demonstrate the importance of understanding sound propagation and occlusion for your game audio design.

Exercise 302f_00 Ambient Zones 02

This environment presents many challenges for the sound designer. Use Ambient Zones where appropriate to better recreate a more real (and better sounding) audio environment.

Tips

1. Use the **[ReverbVolume]**'s Ambient Zone settings to isolate sounds in different areas.
2. Consider where it is appropriate to attenuate the volume, filter the sounds, or do both.
3. Look for areas where you might also attempt to imitate obstruction or exclusion effects.

"Real" Sound for Gameplay

Stealth 101

303 System-Based Occlusion Fudge

One limitation of our use of the Ambient Zones system so far is that it is fixed. If the player could open a window or door (or blow a massive hole in the wall), then the sounds would no longer be occluded and therefore we would no longer apply the Ambient Zones settings. This kind of thing is especially important if the artificial intelligence (AI) of your nonplayer character (NPC) is going to demonstrate any awareness of sound.

In stealth-based games, it is important that players have a sense that their actions can be "heard." A player may then need to adopt a range of strategies in response to this awareness:

1. Choose a "silenced" pistol.
2. Be aware of what surfaces the they are jumping/walking on.
3. Be aware of the different volume of sound produced by running, walking, or "sneaking."
4. Close doors to attenuate sound.
5. Distract enemies by deliberately causing sound (e.g., knocking on the wall, throwing objects, or placing sound-emitting objects to draw the NPC to the sound source).

Room 303 demonstrates a more dynamic use of Ambient Zones for occlusion to illustrate case 4).

You need to sneak into the room behind the guard and steal the plans from the safe (press E to open the safe). If you attempt to do this without first closing the door of the inner room, the guard will "hear" you and come running (and shooting). If you use the button on the wall (by pressing E) to close the door first, then you should be able to open the safe and make your escape without being detected.

As you enter the inner room, you should hear some LPF applied to the room tone of the outside room. This is done using the Ambient Zone settings of the first **[ReverbVolumeToggleable]**. (Note that this volume differs from the standard **[ReverbVolume]** we have been using up until now.)

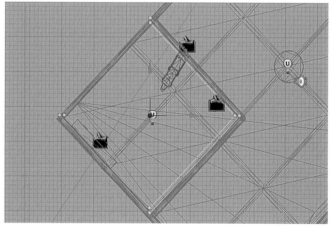

As you close the door to the inner room, you can hear that the outer room tone is occluded more, with volume attenuation and additional low-pass filtering being applied. When you open the door again, this effect is then removed as you might expect. We are able to do this because we are using two overlapping **[ReverbVolumeToggleable]**s in this room. We have made them slightly different sizes so they are easier to see; refer to the yellow cubes in the previous picture.

When the level starts up, the second one is toggled off and the first is toggled on.

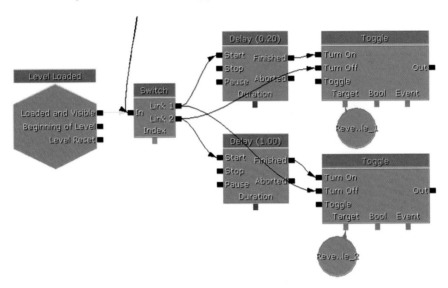

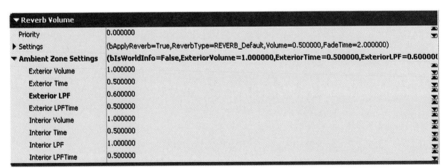

▼ Reverb Volume	
Priority	0.000000
▶ Settings	(bApplyReverb=True,ReverbType=REVERB_Default,Volume=0.500000,FadeTime=2.000000)
▼ Ambient Zone Settings	(bIsWorldInfo=False,ExteriorVolume=1.000000,ExteriorTime=0.500000,ExteriorLPF=0.60000(
Exterior Volume	1.000000
Exterior Time	0.500000
Exterior LPF	0.600000
Exterior LPFTime	0.500000
Interior Volume	1.000000
Interior Time	0.500000
Interior LPF	1.000000
Interior LPFTime	0.500000

When the door is closed, the first one is then toggled off and the second one applied. As you can see, this attenuates the exterior volume and applies a more significant low-pass filter.

▼ Reverb Volume	
Priority	0.000000
▶ Settings	(bApplyReverb=True,ReverbType=REVERB_Default,Volume=0.500000,FadeTime=2.000000)
▼ Ambient Zone Settings	(bIsWorldInfo=False,ExteriorVolume=0.200000,ExteriorTime=0.500000,ExteriorLPF=0.10000(
Exterior Volume	0.200000
Exterior Time	0.500000
Exterior LPF	0.100000
Exterior LPFTime	1.000000
Interior Volume	1.000000
Interior Time	0.500000
Interior LPF	1.000000
Interior LPFTime	0.500000

In some game systems you can trace the actual volume heard at a specific geographic point in the game (i.e., the enemy "hears" the player). Accessing this functionality is not straightforward in UDK, but we can "fudge" it so that this appears to be happening, when actually the system is a great deal more straightforward. You'll often read articles in magazines about how advanced the AI is in the latest game, and sometimes there is some genuinely clever stuff going on, but you'd also be surprised by how a lot of it is faked under the hood with simple scripting. In this case, the **[Trigger]** that you use to open the safe also alerts the guard to start shooting at you. If you close the inner door first, a **[Gate]** (New Action/Misc/Gate) is applied to the message, meaning that it no longer reaches the guard.

You can set a **[Gate]** to be initially open or closed within its properties, and you can set it to close after it has received a given number of messages. We will be seeing more of the **[Gate]** as we go on.

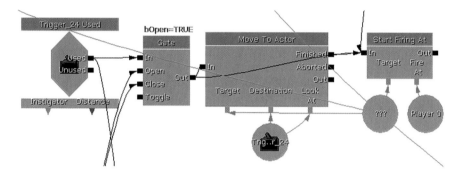

(For advice on setting up and manipulating your own bots, see Appendix C: UDK Tips.)

Exercise 303_00 Dynamic Ambient Zones

In the second room of this exercise, there is an annoying song playing on the radio. Go and close the door!

Tips

1. Add a **[ReverbVolumeToggleable]** to the room with the radio in it.
2. From the **[Trigger]** that closes the door, toggle the **[ReverbVolumeToggleable]** to become active.
3. Set its interior volume (the volume at which things inside are heard when outside) and filter to attenuate the sound when you close the door.
4. Set it to toggle off again when you open the door.
5. Experiment with different times and delay settings until you achieve a natural result.

Stealth and Distraction

303a Stealth and Distraction

Sneak over to the door, taking care of surface types (stepping on a metal surface will alert the guard). When you get near, you can throw a coin to distract the guard from his position so you can get into the building unnoticed.

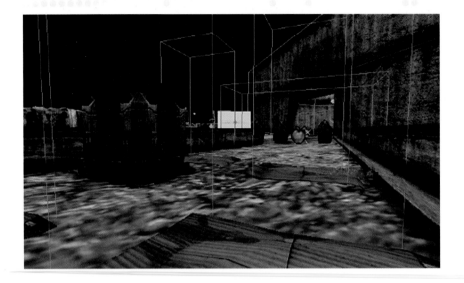

On entering the first **[TriggerVolume],** players are warned about taking care of what surface they walk on so as not to alert the guard. At the same time, a **[Delay]** loop is started, which resets the **[Int Counter]** every second by using a **[Set Variable]** object (New Action/Set Variable/Int). The **[Set Variable]** action allows us to change the value of an existing variable.

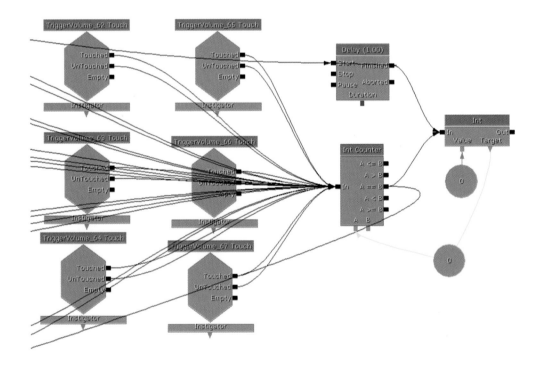

Every time an **[Int Counter]** receives an input, it increments its Value A by the increment amount (in this case set to 1). It then compares its current Value A with Value B, which is set in its properties. In this example, Value B is set at 2. This means that if the **[Int Counter]** receives more than two inputs, then a signal will be output from $A==B$. In the Kismet system, this is then set to "alert" the guard (i.e., move and start firing at the player). However, you'll remember that the Value A of the **[Int Counter]** is being reset to 0 every second. This means that the player who moves slowly can get away with walking on the "noisy" surface, as long as this isn't done twice within one second.

Each "noisy" surface increments the **[Int Counter],** as it has a **[TriggerVolume]** around it.

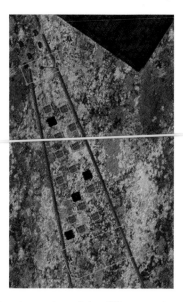

Top-down view of the different surfaces.

If the player reaches the end **[TriggerVolume]** nearest the guard without "alerting" him, then the **[Play Announcement]** "Well done! Throw something ("H") to the left to distract the guard" is triggered, which begins the next system that makes the bot go over and investigate, allowing you to sneak past.

As you can see, all of this is yet again faked. The guard doesn't really "hear" the player or the distraction. Although, as we've explained, there are systems set up in some game engines to enable this type of AI "hearing," the reality is that the combination of the lack of sophistication of the audio physics systems and complexity and unpredictability of the AI systems often mean that it's simply a lot easier to "script" specific scenarios such as this one.

In this example, you'll notice that the metallic floor materials that caused the "noise" problem did in fact have a different footstep sound from the other "grass" materials around them. Let us now look at collisions.

(As we're getting into more complex Kismet systems, now would be a good time to read Appendix C: UDK Tips/Kismet.)

Collisions and Physics

Manual Collisions: Using [TriggerVolume]s

304 Manual Collisions

In the entrance to this large hangar, you will come into contact with various objects and they will produce a suitable "collision" sound. Using **[TriggerVolume]**s to call a **[SoundCue]** for your collisions is probably the simplest (but possibly most laborious) approach to collisions.

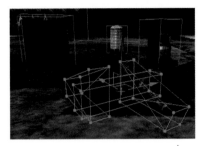

These **[TriggerVolume]**s have been created in the usual way (using the Builder Brush). As the objects you're going to collide with are rarely nice rectangles, we'd had to then edit the shape of some of the **[TriggerVolume]**s to approximate the boundaries of these objects. (To make more detailed changes to the shape of your **[TriggerVolume]**s than is possible with the resize widget, you have to use Geometry mode). Note that the **[PlaySound]** in Kismet targets the static mesh of the objects themselves so that the sound appears to emit from the objects.

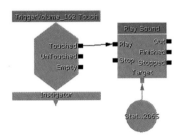

Pressing the key 'C' whilst in the Perspective Viewport shows you that these Static Mesh Actors actually already have Collision boundaries, so you might be wondering why we are going to the effort of adding **[TriggerVolume]**s instead of using a touch event from these. Unfortunately collisions only work if the object is converted to a KActor or Mover (which we'll come onto soon), however the by-product of this is that the player can then pass through the object.

Although you will want your **[TriggerVolume]**s to trigger every time the player collides with them, you may wish to add a retrigger delay to avoid multiple collision sounds being played quickly in succession.

This is easy to implement, but obviously we don't want to have to do this for every possible collision in the game. More importantly, this system will not work for what is probably the most frequently heard collision, player footsteps.

Exercise 304_00 Clumsy

Add **[TriggerVolume]**s to this room so that the player is more aware of colliding with the objects in it.

Tips

1. Create a **[TriggerVolume]** around the area or object where you want the impact to take place.
2. Edit the **[TriggerVolume]**s shape in Geometry mode if necessary.
3. In Kismet, right-click to create a **[TriggerVolume]** Touch event, and link this to a **[PlaySound]** that references your collision **[SoundCue]**s.
4. Use some of the methods discussed in Chapter 2 to ensure sufficient variation in your impact/collision sounds.

Automated Collisions: Footsteps and Surface Types

304a Collision Room Surface Types

Along with providing information about the location of NPCs, footstep sounds are often important in games for giving the player a sense of presence in the world. Without them, the player can feel disconnected and "floaty." However, given the frequency with which you will hear them, footsteps can make sound designers curse. Often the overly repetitive footsteps are not the sound designers' fault. In addition to throwing assets at the problem, a wider variety of surfaces and animations in the game can resolve this dilemma.

In Room 304a (the large warehouse), you can see that there are numbers on certain areas of the floor. When you walk on these numbers, you can hear that the sound of your footstep changes. This is because these materials have different surface types. Whether it's the *Level geometry* (BSP), a *Static Mesh*, or *Terrain*, each of these has a "*Material*" that designates the image displayed.

To make it easy to find the materials, these floor tiles are actually BSP (see Appendix C: UDK Tips) so you can find their material by right-clicking on them and choosing "Find in content browser." This will take you straight to the material they are using.

To find the material that a BSP surface or Static Mesh uses:

- Select the BSP or Static Mesh, right-click and "Find in Content Browser" or "Materials/Find Material in Content Browser."

For Terrain:

● Select the Terrain and press F4 to open its properties. Then, in the Terrain menu, go to Layers/ Setup.

Find this TerrainLayerSetup in the Content Browser and open it. You will see that it references a material that you should again find in Content Browser. Open this *TerrainMaterial* and you will finally find a normal material that references a physical material in the usual way. Phew!

Go back to the material of one of the numbered floor areas (right-click/Find in Content Browser). Double-clicking this material will now open the Material Editor.

In the Material Properties window at the bottom of the screen, you can see that this references a physical material. If you click on the magnifying glass (select "Find object in content browser"), then you will be navigated to the Physical Materials package (UDKGame/Contents/Environment/ PhysicalMaterials).

The physical materials you have available by default in the game are the following: Default, Dirt, Energy, Foliage, Glass, Liquid, Metal, Sand, Stone, Water, Water_Shallow, Wood. Any new material added to the game needs to reference one of these (or a new physical material) if it is to play back an appropriate footstep sound when stepped on (collided with).

Exercise 304a_00 Footloose

Open the package Ex304a_00 Materials, then open the exercise level. The materials in the level have not been set up to reference the correct physical materials so every surface sounds the same. Fix this.

Tips

1. Select a surface on the floor, then right-click and select Find in Content Browser.
2. In the Content Browser, right-click and select Edit using Material Editor.
3. In the materials Properties menu, you can see an entry for Physical Material.
4. Navigate to the Physical Materials package (UDKGame/Content/Environments/) to choose an appropriate material for this surface. When this is selected in the Content Browser use the green arrow to add it to the materials Properties.
5. Exit the Material Editor and save.
6. When you now play the level, the surface should respond with the appropriate footstep sound.

The materials in a level are usually set to reference a particular physical material by the artists or designers. In turn, these physical materials reference the **[SoundCue]**s for footsteps for each different material or surface type. If you look into the properties of the physical materials (Right-Click/ Properties), you can see that they theoretically reference **[SoundCue]**s for impacts (UDKGame/ Content/Environments/).

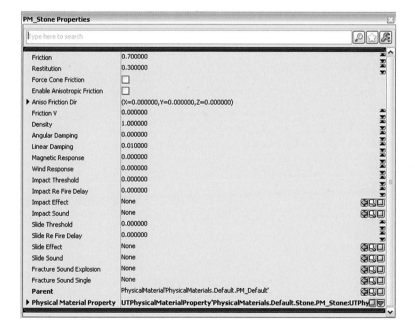

You can also see, however, that these are blank. Adding your own sounds here will not work, as these are actually hard-coded within the player's script file. If you want to add your own footsteps sounds to a game (and of course you do), there are two ways to do it. The first is simple, but potentially problematic.

The **[SoundCue]**s referenced by the *Physical Materials* script are actually here: UDKGame/Content/ Sounds/A_Character_Footsteps. You could open these **[SoundCue]**s, import your own wavs, and then save them.

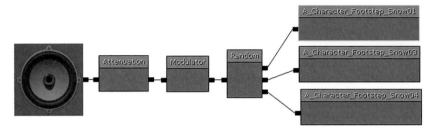

Although this might work very well for you, the unfortunate by-product will be that whoever uses this copy of UDK from now on will have your **[SoundCue]**s playing rather than the default ones.

If you'd rather not upset people, get confused yourself, or if you want to add your own custom physical materials (you may be working on a game level where the floor is made of thick yogurt, for example), then you're going to have to delve into the script files. Don't worry. It's going to be scary and intimidating at first, but we're right behind you.

Scripting 101

Most games engines, although built on a foundation of C++ code, have some kind of higher-level programming language, or scripting, to add or modify features in the game. Although we'd encourage you to investigate it further if programming appeals to you, this mostly falls outside of the remit of this book. So despite the outcries of any programmers out there, we are not going to take you through basic programming concepts. Instead, we're going to dive straight in and tell you what you need to know to achieve what you want. Normally, of course, you would be working with a team of programmers, but even if you are, it's worth getting your hands dirty when working and prototyping by yourself. Like natives of a foreign country, programmers always appreciate it when you try and learn a little bit of their language.

Before you continue, you're going to need to go to Appendix C: UDK Tips/Scripting to confirm that you've got UDK set up correctly for scripting. Read this section before continuing here.

Custom Footsteps Sounds

The default player character in UDK uses the UTPawnSoundGroup.uc script (C:\UDK\UDK(***)\ Development\Src\UTGame\Classes) to determine its sounds, including the footstep sounds we're currently interested in.

Navigate to this folder now and double-click the file. This should open by default in Windows Notepad or Wordpad.

At the top of the page you should see the following:

```
/**
 * Copyright 1998-2010 Epic Games, Inc. All Rights Reserved.
 */
```

```
class UTPawnSoundGroup extends Object
    abstract
    dependson(UTPhysicalMaterialProperty);
```

This simply means that this UTPawnSoundGroup class extends the Object class (i.e., it inherits all the properties of the class named Object but also extends these with additional properties of its own). (If you want to have a look at the Object class, it's here: C:\UDK\UDK(***)\Development\Src\Core\Classes. Good luck!)

Looking down to the bottom of the script we can see where the player character calls the different footstep sounds depending on the physical materials the player is currently walking on:

```
FootstepSounds[0]=(MaterialType=Stone,Sound=SoundCue'A_Character_Footsteps.
FootSteps.A_Character_Footstep_StoneCue')
FootstepSounds[1]=(MaterialType=Dirt,Sound=SoundCue'A_Character_Footsteps.
FootSteps.A_Character_Footstep_DirtCue')
FootstepSounds[2]=(MaterialType=Energy,Sound=SoundCue'A_Character_Footsteps.
FootSteps.A_Character_Footstep_EnergyCue')
FootstepSounds[3]=(MaterialType=Flesh_Human,Sound=SoundCue'A_Character_Footsteps.
FootSteps.A_Character_Footstep_FleshCue')
FootstepSounds[4]=(MaterialType=Foliage,Sound=SoundCue'A_Character_Footsteps.
FootSteps.A_Character_Footstep_FoliageCue')
FootstepSounds[5]=(MaterialType=Glass,Sound=SoundCue'A_Character_Footsteps.
FootSteps.A_Character_Footstep_GlassPlateCue')
FootstepSounds[6]=(MaterialType=Water,Sound=SoundCue'A_Character_Footsteps.
FootSteps.A_Character_Footstep_WaterDeepCue')
FootstepSounds[7]=(MaterialType=ShallowWater,Sound=SoundCue'A_Character_Footsteps.
FootSteps.A_Character_Footstep_WaterShallowCue')
FootstepSounds[8]=(MaterialType=Metal,Sound=SoundCue'A_Character_Footsteps.
FootSteps.A_Character_Footstep_MetalCue')
FootstepSounds[9]=(MaterialType=Snow,Sound=SoundCue'A_Character_Footsteps.
FootSteps.A_Character_Footstep_SnowCue')
FootstepSounds[10]=(MaterialType=Wood,Sound=SoundCue'A_Character_Footsteps.
FootSteps.A_Character_Footstep_WoodCue')
```

When the Player Pawns feet come into contact with a material, a function is called within the UTPawn.uc script (also in the C:\UDK\UDK(***)\Development\Src\UTGame\Classes folder) that identifies the material (and therefore the physical material) and then passes that information to this script, which then defines which **[SoundCue]** to play. (Stay with us, it gets harder.)

You could edit this script to point toward your new **[SoundCue]**s to implement your own footstep sounds, but this would then apply also for any levels you opened.

So that you don't cause untold havoc with the default UDK settings, we've actually set up the Game Audio Tutorial Level to reference a different version of this called GATPawnSoundGroup.uc (C:\UDK\UDK(***)\Development\Src\UTGame\Classes\).

If you open this script, you can see that the process looks a lot simpler. This is because this script extends the UTPawnSoundGroup class. When you extend a class, you only need to provide references to properties of functions that you want to override. (If you're confused, this is normal. Go back and read Appendix C: UDK Tips/Scripting again.)

You can see here that we've extended the range of surface types to include a couple of new ones (11 and 12).

```
FootstepSounds[0]=(MaterialType=Stone,Sound=SoundCue'A_Character_Footsteps.
FootSteps.A_Character_Footstep_StoneCue')
FootstepSounds[1]=(MaterialType=Dirt,Sound=SoundCue'A_Character_Footsteps.
FootSteps.A_Character_Footstep_DirtCue')
FootstepSounds[2]=(MaterialType=Energy,Sound=SoundCue'A_Character_Footsteps.
FootSteps.A_Character_Footstep_EnergyCue')
FootstepSounds[3]=(MaterialType=Flesh_Human,Sound=SoundCue'A_Character_Footsteps.
FootSteps.A_Character_Footstep_FleshCue')
FootstepSounds[4]=(MaterialType=Foliage,Sound=SoundCue'A_Character_Footsteps.
FootSteps.A_Character_Footstep_FoliageCue')
FootstepSounds[5]=(MaterialType=Glass,Sound=SoundCue'A_Character_Footsteps.
FootSteps.A_Character_Footstep_GlassPlateCue')
FootstepSounds[6]=(MaterialType=Water,Sound=SoundCue'A_Character_Footsteps.
FootSteps.A_Character_Footstep_WaterDeepCue')
FootstepSounds[7]=(MaterialType=ShallowWater,Sound=SoundCue'A_Character_Footsteps.
FootSteps.A_Character_Footstep_WaterShallowCue')
FootstepSounds[8]=(MaterialType=Metal,Sound=SoundCue'A_Character_Footsteps.
FootSteps.A_Character_Footstep_MetalCue')
FootstepSounds[9]=(MaterialType=Snow,Sound=SoundCue'A_Character_Footsteps.
FootSteps.A_Character_Footstep_SnowCue')
FootstepSounds[10]=(MaterialType=Wood,Sound=SoundCue'A_Character_Footsteps.
FootSteps.A_Character_Footstep_WoodCue')
FootstepSounds[11]=(MaterialType=BoringFootstep,Sound=SoundCue'GATA_Sound.Foley.
FSWoodNorm')
FootstepSounds[12]=(MaterialType=ConcatFootstep,Sound=SoundCue'GATA_Sound.Foley.
FSWoodConcatenate')
```

(If no physical material has been applied to a material, then a default **[SoundCue]** will be called. This setting actually resides in a different script: *C:\UDK\UDK(***)\Development\Src\UTGame\Classes\GATPawnSoundGroup_GATCharacter.uc.*)

Instead of overwriting the existing types to reference our new **[SoundCue]**s, we are using a couple of new physical materials. This way, all the existing materials in UDK will continue to work as normal, but we can also choose to define some, or all, of the materials in our level as belonging to our new types, and therefore get new footsteps.

Before we go on, it's worth making a copy of the GATPawnSoundGroup.uc and putting it somewhere safe. That way, if things do go pear shaped, you can always just put this back to set things back to normal.

Exercise 304a_01 Custom Materials for Custom Footsteps

Open the Exercise 304a_01 room. This is simply an empty room for you to use to create your own custom physical materials for footsteps. When a pawn (player) steps on the surface, UTPawn.uc identifies the material being stepped on. This material's properties reference a physical material and the *GATPawnSoundGroup.uc* then looks through its array of physical materials to find the matching one and play the appropriate **[SoundCue]**.

Tips

1. First you will want to create a new physical material. Within the Content Browser, select New and choose Physical Material to create a new named Material in one of your packages. (You can also do this by right-clicking in the Thumbnail view of the browser.)

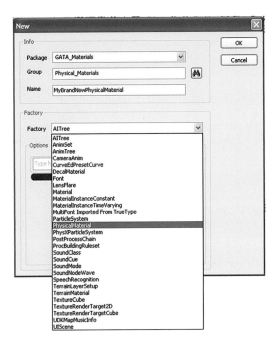

2. Right-click your new physical material to open its properties, then add a UTPhysicalMaterialProperty using the blue arrow. Enter a name that you will use for your material type (we've chosen "Test1").
3. For the parent, browse to and choose UDKGame/Content/Environments/PhysicalMaterials/PM_Default. This means that if there are any problems, it will return to the default sound.
4. If you add your new physical material to an existing material within the game, then all other instances of that material will be affected, so for now we'd recommend that you choose one of the GATSpareMaterials (within the GATG_Graphic_Assets package) and drag and drop this onto the floor. Now double-click this material to open the Material Editor. With your new physical material selected in the browser, use the green arrow to assign it to this material.

5. Open the script: C:\UDK\UDK(***)\Development\Src\Core\Classes\GATPawnSoundGroup.uc. To create a new entry for your new material type, you will need to add a line at the end of the existing footsteps list. For example, here we've increased the array value [13], as the previous existing one (ConcatFootstep) was [12], referenced our new Physical Material Property ("Test1:) and the **[SoundCue]** we want to play:

```
FootstepSounds[0]=(MaterialType=Stone,Sound=SoundCue'A_Character_Footsteps.
FootSteps.A_Character_Footstep_StoneCue')
```

```
FootstepSounds[1]=(MaterialType=Dirt,Sound=SoundCue'A_Character_Footsteps.
FootSteps.A_Character_Footstep_DirtCue')
FootstepSounds[2]=(MaterialType=Energy,Sound=SoundCue'A_Character_Footsteps.
FootSteps.A_Character_Footstep_EnergyCue')
FootstepSounds[3]=(MaterialType=Flesh_Human,Sound=SoundCue'A_Character_Footsteps.
FootSteps.A_Character_Footstep_FleshCue')
FootstepSounds[4]=(MaterialType=Foliage,Sound=SoundCue'A_Character_Footsteps.
FootSteps.A_Character_Footstep_FoliageCue')
FootstepSounds[5]=(MaterialType=Glass,Sound=SoundCue'A_Character_Footsteps.
FootSteps.A_Character_Footstep_GlassPlateCue')
FootstepSounds[6]=(MaterialType=Water,Sound=SoundCue'A_Character_Footsteps.
FootSteps.A_Character_Footstep_WaterDeepCue')
FootstepSounds[7]=(MaterialType=ShallowWater,Sound=SoundCue'A_Character_Footsteps.
FootSteps.A_Character_Footstep_WaterShallowCue')
FootstepSounds[8]=(MaterialType=Metal,Sound=SoundCue'A_Character_Footsteps.
FootSteps.A_Character_Footstep_MetalCue')
FootstepSounds[9]=(MaterialType=Snow,Sound=SoundCue'A_Character_Footsteps.
FootSteps.A_Character_Footstep_SnowCue')
FootstepSounds[10]=(MaterialType=Wood,Sound=SoundCue'A_Character_Footsteps.
FootSteps.A_Character_Footstep_WoodCue')
FootstepSounds[11]=(MaterialType=BoringFootstep,Sound=SoundCue'GATA_Sound.Foley.
FSWoodNorm')
FootstepSounds[12]=(MaterialType=ConcatFootstep,Sound=SoundCue'GATA_Sound.Foley.
FSWoodConcatenate')
FootstepSounds[13]=(MaterialType=Test1,Sound=SoundCue'MyPackage.Footsteps.YoghurtFloor')
```

Replace this with your physical material name and the **[SoundCue]** you want to reference. The reference to the **[SoundCue]** needs to be the full path, so right-click on your required **[SoundCue]** in the Content Browser and choose "Copy Full Name to Clipboard." Then use Ctrl + V to paste this into your script.

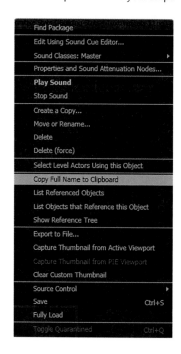

6. When you've made any adjustments to a script file, you will need to recompile the game in order for them to take effect. Save the script file. Close the UDK editor.

Now navigate to C:\UDK\UDK(***)\Binaries and open the program UnrealFrontEnd.exe.

Clicking on the Script/Compile Scripts button will now compile your new script. When you reopen the editor and play the room with your new material, you should hear your chosen **[SoundCue]** being played for the footstep sounds.

Well done! You've just done you first bit of scripting. We hope you've enjoyed the feeling of smug satisfaction when it works. If you didn't enjoy this process, then the bad news is that there's plenty more coming in Chapter 7. The good news is that it is really no more difficult than what you've just done.

(To add footstep sounds to newly imported characters, you would need to be supplied with a script along the lines of the UTPawnSoundGroup that can receive a call from an AnimNotifyFootstep attached to the animation itself. See the section titled "Adding Sounds to Animations" in Chapter 7.)

Custom Movement Sounds

Repetitive footstep sounds do seem to irritate people more than most aspects of game audio. The first thing to do is to stop thinking of them as footstep sounds. Unless you have a particularly unusual anatomy, you do not take steps in isolation from the rest of your body. Therefore, we should consider them "movement" sounds, not footstep sounds. Here are our top tips for avoiding FRM (Footstep Repetition Madness).

1. Obviously we start with several wavs, randomly chosen with a little pitch and volume variation (don't overdo the pitch). If you've got the option, then try other DSP effects like varying the ADSR (Attack, Decay, Sustain, Release) envelope or the filter on each repetition.
2. Try concatenating heel/toe samples (see Chapter 2, the section titled "Concatenation: Footsteps").
3. We don't want each wav to sound identical, nor do we want them to sound too different. A particularly characteristic footstep will jump out noticeably and make the system feel more repetitious than it is. Either don't use it or set its weight in the **[Random]** node to be low.

4. You may want to set up a left/right foot rhythm using slightly different samples for each one (people do lean more heavily on one side). A **[Random]** node with two inputs and "Randomize without replacement" checked will in fact alternate between its two inputs.

5. As stated earlier, movement is about more than feet. You should layer in randomized Foley cloth sounds together with weapon/items jangling together with your footsteps. Alongside a friendly programmer you could layer in different sounds depending on the equipment that the player is actually carrying, such as the type of armor. This would not only vary the footstep/movement sounds but would also provide useful feedback to the player.

6. People don't just walk. Sometimes they have been known to run, jump, slide, trip, and to do all these things with a variety of velocities. All of these will result in different sounds. Running tends to have only one impact, rather than the heel-toe rhythm of walking, for instance. The more developed the animation system you're working with, the better you can make your movement sounds. If you do have walk-run animations, then also try a "start to run" and a "slowing down" sound or crossfade sounds depending on the player's velocity. Look at the real world. People do not suddenly run at full speed.

7. Think about when sounds should and when they shouldn't be there. Be flexible in your mixing (see Chapter 6). If there's a firefight, you won't hear the movement sounds and they are just taking up valuable headroom and channels (voices). Perhaps play the sound louder when surface type changes to provide the feedback needed, but then drop the volume. When it comes to sound it often works well to "Make a point, then go away". (© r.c.stevens 2011:)

8. It's not actually about the footsteps, it's about the variety of surface types and how often they change. Distances are not the same in games as the real world. I can walk around my living room in five paces (and that's not just because of my salary). For various reasons (not least the relative clumsiness of the control mechanisms), the spaces between objects in games need to be much larger than in reality, hence more footsteps. This already puts us at a disadvantage when it comes to repetition, but we rarely have continuous surface types in the real world. If you recorded yourself walking at the same speed on a continuous surface (if you can find one), then you would probably find the sounds very repetitive. Work with your artists to create and define a larger number of surface types and change them more frequently.

9. Think about how your walking or running changes depending on how you are feeling. Perhaps there's opportunity for some more subtle feedback to the player than a health bar here. Your footsteps could transition to a heavier set, depending on player health.

10. Any repetition in footstep sounds will be particularly acute if you have multiple NPCs all referencing the same **[SoundCue]** within a confined area. Here are a few approaches to discuss with your programmer.
    - Have a priority system for NPC footsteps. Limit the number of footsteps that can play at any given time (see Chapter 6, the section titled "Voice Instance Limiting") or keep the one nearest to the player (or the one the player is actually looking at) at normal volume but slightly attenuate the others.
    - Along the same lines, perhaps you could have adaptive distance attenuation curves. When X number of bots are within a certain radius of the player, swap their attenuation curves so that their footstep sounds are a lot tighter to the center of origin. (Definitely consider different attenuation curves for single player versus multiplayer games.)

● In terms of our perception, we usually class things as one, two, or many (i.e., if there are more than two things we consider them to be a group rather than individual units). Again, you (and your programmer) could develop a system whereby if there are more than X number of NPCs within a given area, you will not actually play their individual footstep (movement) sounds anymore but will instead play the **[SoundCue]** "ManyNPC'sMovement." This will not work under all circumstances (as the player will often need to locate individuals), but it could save on the number of voices used and make them more convincing than the tat, tat, tat of repetition that you sometimes get.

Exercise 304a_02 Footloose 2: Bigger, Cornier, and More Callous

This room has four different surface types: custard, gravel, springs, and a hydroquantumpseudoscientifc electric field (sounds a bit like electrified glass). Create a new physical material and sound cue for each material.

Tip

1. See Exercise 304a_01 for a guide to creating and adding your own physical materials.

Physics

304b Physics

Scaling and setting thresholds for variables are extremely important tasks when dealing with physics variables.

Using your mouse wheel, switch to your physics gun. Walk over to this object in the hangar 304b, and use the left mouse button to push it or the right mouse button to pick it up and throw it around.

What the game system is attempting to do here is to somehow replicate the interactions of different materials that produce sound. A great deal of research is available on the physical processes that create sounds, and there is an increasingly important branch of game audio research that looks at how these sounds can be implemented in games without the vast processing overheads of truly accurate simulations. The detail of this subject, termed procedural audio, is for another book (see the bibliography for a good one). The reality is that within the processing power currently available for games audio, we are only at the earliest stages of this brave new world; so once again for us, there is the need to fake it.

The object you have just been throwing around is a **[KActor]**. A **[KActor]** is essentially a **[Static Mesh]** that has additional properties so that it is movable and it uses the physics engine to enable collision with the world's geometry (and other **[Kactor]**s). Any **[Static Mesh]** can be converted to a **[KActor]**. This Actor can then send out events when it collides with another rigid body. The event [Rigid Body Collision] within Kismet will output the collision event together with the Impact Velocity.

When dealing with variables arising from games physics, it is important to be able to scale these variables into a useful and meaningful range of numbers for your audio. To *scale* means simply to take an incoming range of numbers and convert it into another range of numbers. In addition to scaling the variables from physics events, it's also often useful to set thresholds (a "cap" for the numbers) so that the sometimes extreme numbers that might appear unpredictably do not result in an extreme audio event.

In this example, you can see that the impact velocity of the collision of the object passes through a **[Divide Float]** object where it is divided by 100 to scale the numbers into a useful range for the **[PlaySound]**'s Volume Multiplier. This means that we not only get a sound when the **[KActor]** collides with something, but we are also adjusting the volume of this sound depending on how fast it was going when it collided (and consequently how loud the impact sound will be).

Exercise 304b_00 Bang! Physics Impacts for Dummies

This room currently contains three **[Static Mesh]**es. Alter them so that the player can interact with them using the physics gun. Give each one an appropriate impact sound.

Tips

1. Right-click the **[Static Mesh]** and select Convert/Convert Static Mesh Actor to KActor.
2. Open your new **[KActor]**'s properties (F4), and within the DynamicSMActor/Static Mesh Component/Physics menu enable Notify Rigid Body Collision.

▼ Physics	
Never Become Dynamic	☐
RBDominance Group	15
Disable All Rigid Body	☐
Skip RBGeom Creation	☐
Notify Rigid Body Collision	☑

---

3. With your **[KActor]** still selected in the viewport, right-click in Kismet and select New Event Using KActor (***)/Rigid Body Collision.
4. Right-click on this event's Impact Velocity output and select Create New Float Variable.
5. Create a **[Divide Float]** (New Action/Math/Divide Float) and a **[PlaySound]** (hold the S key and click).

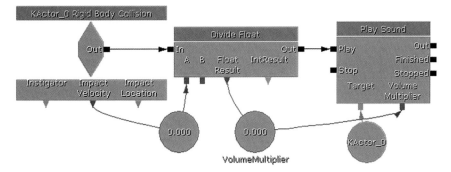

6. Set the **[Divide Float]** object's **Value B** initially to 100 in its Properties window (Seq Act_Divide Float). (You may want to experiment with this later.)
7. Expose the **[PlaySound]**'s Volume Multiplier (right-click the **[PlaySound]** object).
8. Create a New Variable/Float/Float and connect it up to the Result of the **[Divide Float]** and the **[PlaySound]** Volume Multiplier.
9. Do the same for the Impact Velocity output of the **[Rigid Body Collision]** and the Value A of the **[Divide Float]**.
10. Select your **[KActor]** in the viewport, and right-click the **[PlaySound]**'s target to create a New Object Variable using this so the sound is played back from the origin of the **[KActor]** itself.
11. Construct an appropriate **[SoundCue]** and reference it from your **[PlaySound]**.
12. Test and adjust the **[Divide Float]** values and the properties of the **[Rigid Body Collision]** events to get a satisfactory result.

Of course, the velocity of an impact changes considerably more than simply the volume of the sound produced, and you could extend this system to play different **[SoundCue]**s for different ranges of *Impact Velocity*.

By law you are not allowed to call your game a "game" unless it has a barrel in it.

The second object in this location, the barrel, goes through the same scaling process to change the range of values of the impact velocity (approximately 0 to 2,000) into an appropriate range for volume, but then it decides which impact sound to play: hard, medium, or soft, depending on this range.

(As our systems are getting complicated now, we've started to use subsequences to avoid a spider's web of connections. When you create an External Variable within a subsequence (New Variable/External Variable), an input to that sequence appears so you can attach your variable to pass it through. See Appendix C, the section titled "Kismet Tips," for more.)

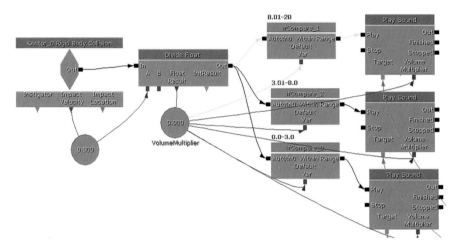

The subsequences contain a compare system that looks to see if the velocity/volume falls within a given range. Two **[Compare Int]** objects look at an inner and outer range. If both conditions are satisfied, then both the A and B input of a third **[Compare Input]** will be 1, and therefore the A==B output is triggered. The **[Finish Sequence]** (*New Action/Misc/Finish Sequence*) object outputs back up to the upper sequence to then trigger the appropriate **[PlaySound]**.

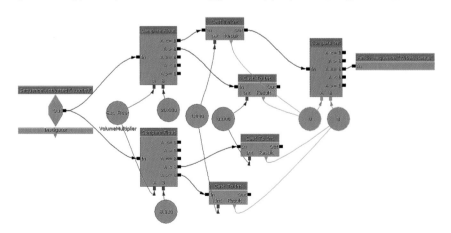

Other physical interactions such as Sliding/Scraping or Rolling are accessible within many game engines. Theoretically they are available in UDK via the Physical Materials, but this feature is currently not supported.

Although dependent on many variables (and the robustness of your game engine's physics), both sliding and rolling are usually implemented with a relationship between velocity and both volume and pitch.

Although the values from the impact velocity are being scaled, they still have a linear relationship with the volume of the impact. For a more sophisticated audio response to physics events, we would need to start looking at the use of curves so that the changes in velocity are not directly related but instead read through a curve that we can control. You can use some simple maths to transform the velocity-to-pitch relationship within Kismet. Better still, talk to your programmer about accessing a range of *distribution curves*.

Linear relationships

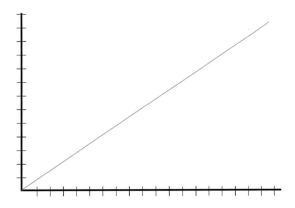

Square root relationship

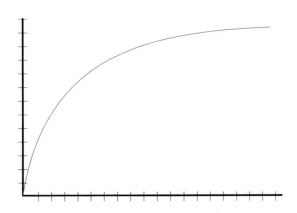

Power of 2 (Squared) relationship

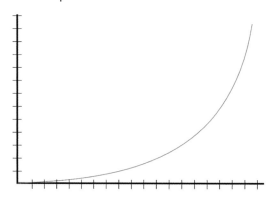

We'll be dealing with another important type of collision in games (that of bullets with soft flesh) later in the Weapons section.

Cascading Physics

304c Cascading Physics

> You'd imagine that if you take the sound of one rock falling and applied it to 20 rocks, when they fell you would have the sound of 20 rocks falling. You'd be wrong.

In this area you have four buttons from left to right:

Button 01 = One random rock falls.
Button 02 = Three to five rocks fall.
Button 03 = They all fall and the normal **[Rigid Body Collision]** triggers the **[SoundCue]**.
Button 04 = They all fall but this time when the number of impacts get beyond a given threshold, a "Rocks falling" sound is played instead of the individual collisions.

When responding to physics, it's easy for your sound system to become overwhelmed with the number of events. Simply reusing the same rigid body collision for each individual collision does not work beyond a certain density of events because (1) it can lead to too many voices being used, (2) it can lead to phasing, and (3) it just doesn't sound right. You could limit the number of occurrences of this sound to stop it from taking up too many channels (using the **[SoundCue]**'s Voice Instance Limiting feature discussed in Chapter 6), but this would not improve the sound beyond perhaps eliminating some of the phasing. The complex interference of soundwaves when many collisions are occurring simultaneously means that any attempts to re-create 20 rocks falling, or 20 shards of glass, by playing back 20 individual impact sounds is doomed to failure.

What we need to do is to implement a system where we can monitor the number of collisions within a given time frame. If that number reaches our permitted threshold, we will then override the individual collisions system and instead play a prerecorded sound of these many collisions. (This is reminiscent of the one, two, many concept described in the discussion of footsteps presented earlier.)

Like the Stealth and Distraction system (303a), this system counts the number of individual collisions that occur within a given time period by using a **[Delay]** to reset the count of an **[Int Counter]**. In this case, if more than four individual rock collisions occur within a 0.3 second period then a RocksMultiple **[SoundCue]** is called instead of the individual ones.

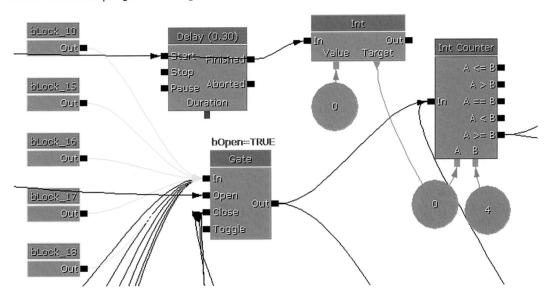

Movers and [Matinee]

> Whether the source is visible or not, making sounds move creates a more realistic and believable audio environment.

Sounds that Move

305 Moving Sound: Fly-by

As you climb the stairs (305) out of Room 304, you'll notice that there are a number of pesky mosquitoes buzzing around your head. (This is another version of the flies **[SoundCue]** we came across in

209 that uses an oscillator to vary the pitch and volume). If you have a 5.1 or 7.1 sound system, you'll really hear them moving around you; in stereo you'll hear them pan left and right. These sounds are produced by the **[AmbientSoundMoveable]** Actor. Note that **[AmbientSoundMoveable]**s will loop their **[SoundCue]**s, irrespective of whether that **[SoundCue]** has a loop in it. This Actor allows you to define a movement path for your sound so that its movement can then be triggered or looped.

Adding an **[AmbientSoundMoveable]** is straightforward. Select the **[SoundCue]** you want in the Content Browser, then right-click in the Perspective viewport and select Add AmbientSoundMoveable: (***). To make it move, we need to look at UDK's tool for any kind of movement, **[Matinee]**.

Matinee

If we look at the Kismet sequence for Room 305, we can see that both of the **[AmbientSound Moveable]**s in this area are attached to a **[Matinee]** object. By double-clicking the **[Matinee]**, we can see how this operates. In the **[Matinee]** there is a movement track that contains several *Keys* (shown by the small triangles). With the Matinee window open, click on the different Keys (triangles). You can see the **[AmbientSoundMoveable]** in the Perspective viewport move to these different locations:

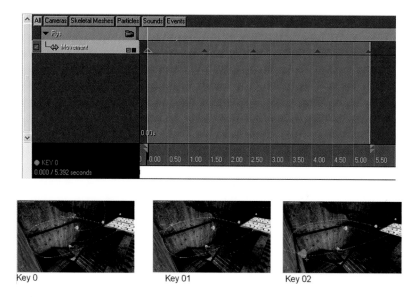

Key 0   Key 01   Key 02

If you click on the Play looped Section button at the top of the window, you can see the whole movement sequence play out in the viewports.

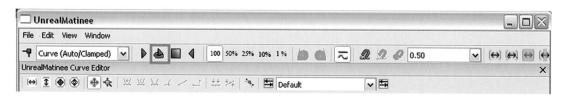

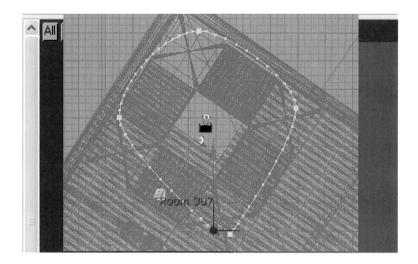

The **[Matinee]** sequences here are triggered by a **[Trigger]** that covers the whole stair area, and when it is untouched they stop.

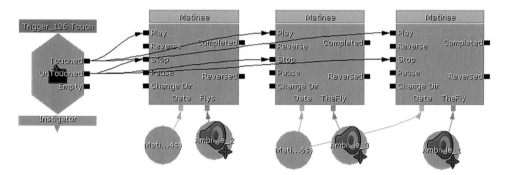

The best way to understand the **[Matinee]** system is use it, so have a go at the following exercise.

EX305_00 Moving Sounds Wooded Area

Using the bird sounds provided in the Sound Library, make this woodland area come alive with movement.

Tips

1. Add your sound at the position you want the movement to start from. Select the **[Soundcue]** in the Content Browser and right-click in your level. Choose Add AmbientSoundMoveable: (***) here.
2. With this **[AmbientSoundMoveable]** selected, open Kismet and right-click to select New Matinee.
3. You'll want this **[Matinee]** to start up when the level starts, so right-click and create a new Event/Level startup and connect the Out of this to the Play of the **[Matinee]**.

4. Now double-click on the **[Matinee]** to begin adding your movement.
5. In the bottom left of the **[Matinee]** screen, right-click and select Add New Empty Group and name it something appropriate. Right-click next to this name when you have entered it and select Add New Movement Track from the drop-down menu. You'll see that this already has the first triangle or Key, which is your starting position.

6. With the Movement Track option selected on the left, click on the timeline at the bottom of the screen and press Enter. This will add a new Key. Now go back to your viewport and move your **[AmbientSoundMoveable]** to the position you'd like it to be at for this key (use the arrows of the movement widget). You can delete or move Keys (hold down Ctrl to move them) later but don't attempt to move the first Key. Create some more keys, and move the sound to a new position for each Key. Press Play from the top toolbar at any time to check your movement sequence.
7. You'll also see some green markers and some red markers on the timeline. The red markers indicate the start and end of your sequence, and the green markers indicate the part of the sequence that will be looped if you enable looping. For the moment, move both the green and red markers to encompass your whole sequence.
8. Once you're happy, close the **[Matinee]** window, select the **[Matinee]** object, and in its properties (Seq Act_Interp) check the box marked Looping.
9. Now you should be able to play your level and hear the movement of the sounds.

Movers that Sound

Doors, elevators, and many other objects in the game make sounds when they move. These movable objects are called **[InterpActor]**s. Any **[Static Mesh]** in the level can be converted into an **[InterpActor]** and made to move. We can add these sounds in two ways, either directly into the properties of the **[InterpActor]** or via a Sound Track feature in a **[Matinee]**.

Doors

305a Door

The button on the right controls the doors leading out to the roof area. The **[Matinee]** for these doors has been set up so that, instead of moving position, they rotate. This is done in exactly the same way as any other movement is established, by adding a Key to the Matinee Movement track and then moving the object to the position, or in this case, the rotation, that you want. To make both doors finish opening at exactly the same time, the Key in **[Matinee]** allows you to right-click and choose Set Time to enter a precise time for the key event.

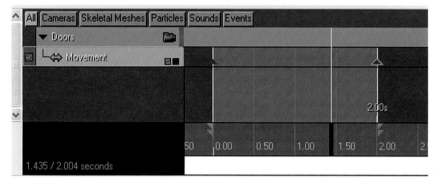

The sounds for these movements are defined within the door **[InterpActor]**s.

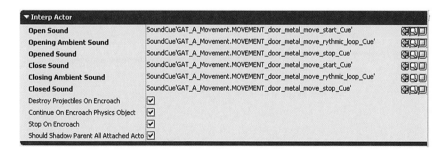

- *Close sound*: This is when it starts to close (when the **[Matinee]** is in reverse).
- *Closed sound*: This sound plays when it has finished closing.
- *Closing*: This sound is a loop that will play while the **[InterpActor]** is moving between Close and Closed.
- *Open*: This sound will play when you start to open—in other words, when the **[Matinee]** movement begins.

- *Opened:* This will play when the **[InterpActor]** has finished its movement, when you have gotten to the end of the **[Matinee]**.
- *Opening*: This is a sound that will loop while the **[InterpActor]** is moving between Open and Opened.

All of these sounds are actually triggered from the timings of the **[Matinee]**. This is why it's very important that the markers in your **[Matinee]** are in the correct position. If the red end marker, for example, is after the final Key where the **[InterpActor]** ends its movement, then you will not hear the Opened sound until it reaches this time—that is, it will not play simultaneously with the end of the movement.

Exercise 305a_00 Matinee Doors

In this room there are two types of door, a metal door and a stone door. Using the sounds from the Sound Library or your own, add sounds to these door movements.

Tips

1. The first door system (the metal doors) is set up for you. You just need to select the **[InterpActor]** and go to its properties (F4) to add the appropriate **[SoundCue]**s.

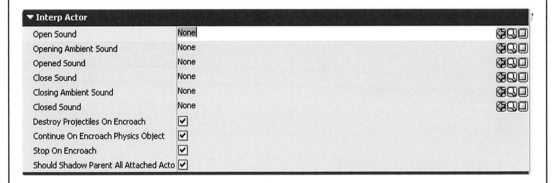

2. In the second system, the doors are not working yet, so you'll have to use **[Matinee]** to make them rotate correctly.
3. Once the **[Matinee]** is working, you can add sounds via the **[InterpActor]**'s properties as you did earlier.

Elevators or Lifts

305b Elevator

The elevator that takes you back down to the ground is also an **[InterpActor]** whose movements are controlled by the **[Matinee]** and whose sounds are attached within its properties.

You'll notice that the lift does not necessarily have to be triggered by the switch but will also work when the player simply steps onto it. You can sense these events by using a Mover Event feature. With the **[InterpActor]** selected in the viewport, right-click in Kismet and select New Event using (***)/ Mover. This will bring up the Mover Event option, which will output when a pawn (player or NPC) is attached to (on) the **[InterpActor]**. This will automatically create a **[Matinee]** already set up with groups and a Mover Track control for this specific object, so you just need to double-click the **[Matinee]** to edit it.

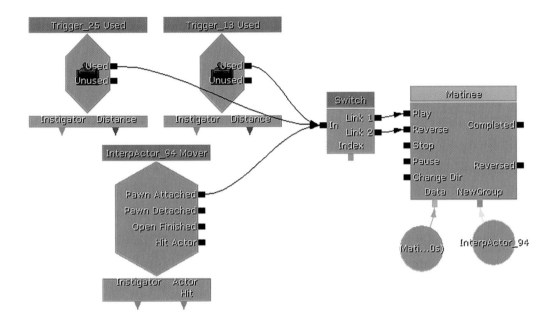

Exercise 305b_00 Pawn Attached Mover

In this exercise, there is a moving platform that will take you across the gaping chasm of death. Set up a system so that this starts automatically when the player stands on it.

Tips

1. Create a **[Matinee]** that moves the platform across the chasm.
2. Select your **[InterpActor]** platform, then right-click in Kismet to create a "New Event using (***)/Mover."
3. Now open the **[Matinee]** (double click), click on the Timeline at the start and press Return to create the first Key. Create another Key later in time then drag the **[InterpActor]** to it's new position for this Key. Continue to add Keys and positions until you are happy with the movement across the chasm. (Make sure that the red and green markers on the Matinee timeline encompass all your Keys.)
4. Now see if you can extend this system so that your player can get back.

Variable Speed Matinees

305c Speed Machine

By the river at the bottom of the elevator there is a machine that consists of several movers. By changing the *play rate* of the **[Matinee],** we can speed the machine up or down. The first switch starts and stops the **[Matinee]**, and the other two increase (button A) or decrease (button B) its speed.

This time the sounds have been embedded within the **[Matinee]** itself by creating a *Sound Track* (right-click in a Matinee group/Add New Sound Track). When you have selected a **[SoundCue]** in the Content Browser press Enter while on the matinee timeline to add a Key, the **[SoundCue]** will be added at this point. You can also edit this Key to set the sound's volume or pitch.

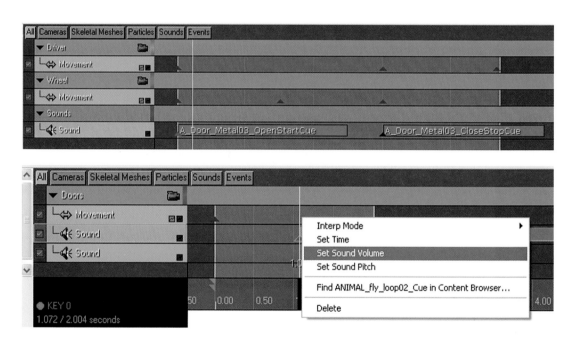

Because the sound is generated by individual samples triggered from the **[Matinee]**, rather than a single longer sample, the sounds will match the speed of the machine as the **[Matinee]** is played back at different speeds.

The initial **[Trigger]** starts the **[Matinee]** and sets the variable play rate (1.0 is normal speed) via a **[Set Float]** object (New Action/Set Variable/Float).

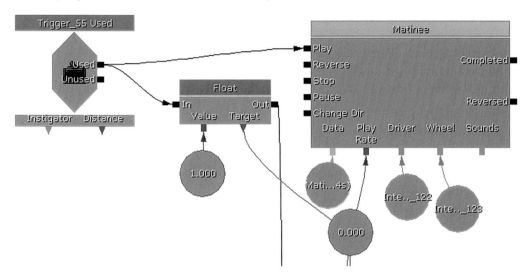

Input *A* to the **[Add Float]** object is the current Play Rate variable. The two other **[Trigger]**s set the *B* value and trigger the **[Add Float]** object so that it performs the calculation A + B. It then sends the *Float Result* back to the play rate of the **[Matinee]**. As a result, either 0.2 is added to the current speed or −0.2 is added (i.e., 0.2 is taken away).

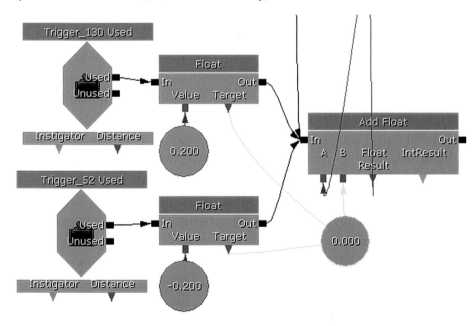

Using separate sound elements to make up the complete sound of a moving object in your game means that you have variable control over the speed without needing to pre-make a separate sound file for each speed.

Interruptible Matinees

305d Crane

If you stand inside the area around this crane, you can use the H on your keyboard to switch it on. While the key is held down, the **[Matinee]** will play; when the key is released, it will stop.

(The magnet on the end of the cable is the only thing that actually moves. The cable is scaled within the **[Matinee]** to get shorter and longer.)

This system uses a combination of sound-producing systems. The Key Press event is used to trigger the **[PlaySound]** start and stop events, whereas the looping sound (while moving) is controlled by the **[InterpActor]** (or strictly speaking by the **[Matinee]** telling the **[InterpActor]** what state it is in and therefore what sound to play).

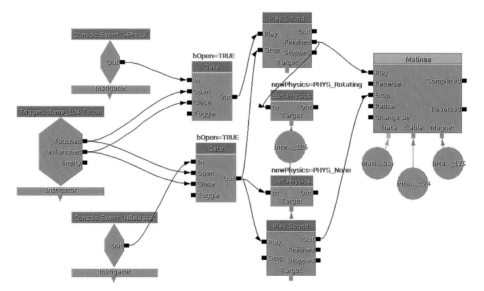

The reason it is necessary to use both of these systems is that we want to be able to stop and start the crane while it is midway through its **[Matinee]** sequence. As explained previously, the **[InterpActor]**'s Close/Closed and Open/Opened **[SoundCue]**s are only called when the red Keys (*Sequence start/Sequence end*) of **[Matinee]** are passed. As these are at the start and end of the sequence, this would not give us the starting/stopping sounds we wanted in this situation.

The **[TriggerVolume]** is there to control a **[Gate]** so that the Key Press messages do not get through to this system unless you are within the immediate area of the crane. We want to use the Key Press H elsewhere in the level too, so if we didn't have this blocking the input, then a key press of H from anywhere in the level would have started this crane. (For more on adding and using your own custom keyboard keys, see Appendix C: UDK Tips.)

Funky Bridge

305e Bridge

Press the button and a bridge will construct itself in front of you to enable your passage across the river.

Each of these **[InterpActor]**s has the same movement sounds embedded within it. Rather than doing this multiple times, the original **[InterpActor]** was simply copied and pasted. For systems like this (where something is constructed for a change rather than destructed), it's often easier to start with the complete object and work backward, then play the **[Matinee]** in reverse. When doing this, remember that the Open/Close sequence of the **[InterpActor]**s sound will also be reversed.

Cut-Scenes, Cameras, and Sound

Cut-Scenes with No Audio Control

> Cameras and sound don't follow each other naturally—what works visually often does not make sense for sound. You need separate control over these elements.

306 Cameras and Sound

The two buttons in this area will present two different versions of this cut-scene conversation between these two bots. One is heard from the default sound setting, which is from the *point of view* (location and view) of the camera. The other overrides this option to play the sound track via the matinee.

Cut-scenes and cinematic sequences in games use either prerendered video files or are created in real time within the game engine itself using scripted animation and movements. The ability to sound-design a linear sequence such as a prerendered cut-scene remains an important skill for the game sound designer. These skills are the same as those used for film or animation sound design, so we're not going to dwell on them here. In-game engine cut-scenes do require some implementation knowledge on your part, so we'll focus on them. As well as being the controller for character animations or object movements, Kismet also takes care of the camera during these sequences.

When the **[Trigger]** on the left is used, Cinematic mode is enabled, which switches the camera from the usual player's perspective to that of whatever camera you designate.

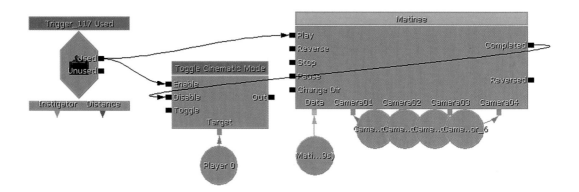

The cameras have movement tracks within the **[Matinee]** object like the other movements we have dealt with, but they also have a Director track, which controls how the cut-scene might switch, or "cut," between cameras.

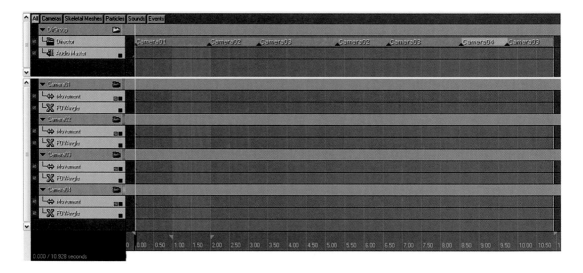

If you watch the cut-scene after clicking on the left-hand switch, you will notice an issue regarding the sound track. In this simple scene there are five sound sources: two characters, a machine, the electric field blocking the door, and the birds in the trees.

As the Director track cuts between each camera, the orientation of the sounds relative to each camera is different. This gives the effect of sounds suddenly panning from one side of the screen to the other. Although this may be strictly accurate, it is distracting to the player. The problem is, of course, well known in cinema, and to avoid it the sound track is often not panned according to the camera movements but instead maintains a separate continuity. For us to avoid this distracting panning during cutscenes, we need to essentially switch off the normal game sounds, which are heard from the point of view of the camera, and play a more cinematic sound track that we have more control over instead.

Cut-Scenes with Audio Control

Pressing the right hand switch will show you an example of the same scene where the in game sounds have been muted, and the audio has been re-created using a *Sound Track* in a **[Matinee]** instead. A new group and an *Event Track* has been added. This outputs an event from the Kismet object that you can link up to any other object in Kismet. In this case it has been linked to a **[Set Sound Mode]** object. We'll be looking at *Sound Modes* in more detail in Chapter 6, but essentially this is going to silence all sounds in the game that have not been designated as belonging to the "*Cinematic*" *SoundClass*, and in this case this means that all of the ambient sounds in the area will be muted.

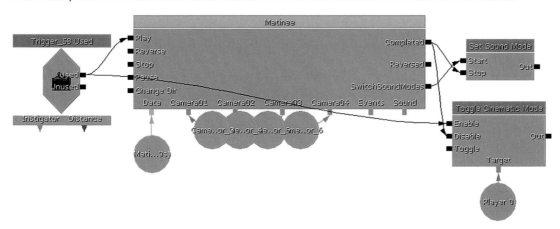

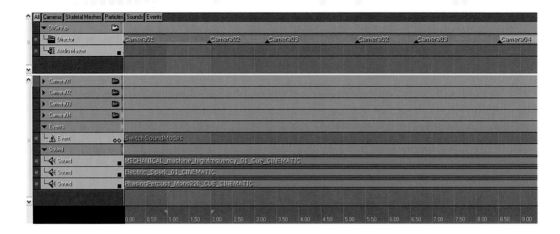

Another group contains the *sound tracks* where **[SoundCue]**s have been added to re-create the sound of the scene.

In the Director group you can also right-click and select Add New Audio Master Track. This will allow you to control the overall level of all your sounds in the sequence and also apply fades using the Curve editor. The Curve editor is enabled using the check box indicated in the following figure.

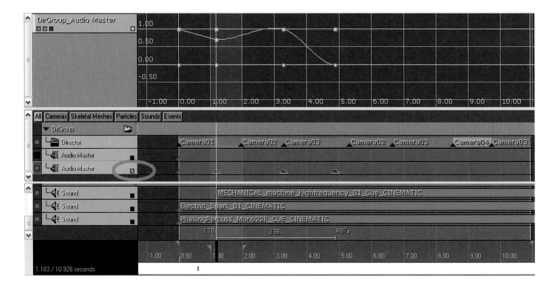

It is highly unlikely that you would be directly involved in directing the in-game cut-scenes. However, it's important that you make the point that they need to be controlled and mixed just as carefully as a linear cut-scene would. Simply leaving it up to the automated 3D sound engine to provide a mix from the point of view of the camera is not going to produce polished results.

Exercise 306_00 Lights, Camera, Action

In this cut-scene, the sound is quite distracting as it pans according to the camera movement rather than being a more appropriately "Cinematic" sound. Re-create the sound for the cut-scene using the Sound Track feature of **[Matinee]**.

Tips

1. Any **[SoundCue]**s that you want to hear during cut-scenes should be identified as belonging to the "Cinematic" SoundClass. Right-click them in the Content Browser and select SoundClasses/Master/SFX/Cinematic. You'll have to duplicate the **[SoundCue]**s currently used to re-create the scene.

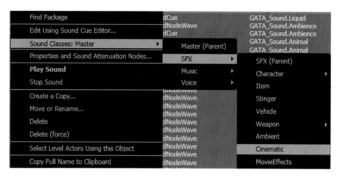

2. The **[Matinee]** and **[Set SoundMode]** are already set up for you, so you can focus your attentions on re-creating the scene. (The **[Set SoundMode]** is currently unattached so you can hear the scene first. Once you start work you should link it up so that it mutes the current sounds.)
3. Open the **[Matinee]**, and in the left-hand panel right-click and choose New Empty Group. Then in this group right-click again and select Add New Sound Track.
4. With your **[SoundCue]** selected in the Content Browser, you can now click on Matinee Timeline and press enter to add the currently selected **[SoundCue]** at this position. You can move these around later by Ctrl + left-clicking on their Key points.
5. Try adjusting their Volume properties by right-clicking on their Keys; consider adding an audio master track in the Director group to control the Master Volume feature.

Level Fly-Throughs

306a Fly-Through

Of course, there may be situations when you want to hear the world from the camera's point of view, in which case there is no need for this more "cinematic" approach. On a level fly-through, for instance, you'll probably want to hear the sounds emitted by the Actors as you fly past them. Once you're past the bots, try pressing the button in the corridor for a quick level fly-through example.

Where's My Head At?

One issue that will require the careful consideration of your team is where the sound a player hears will come from. For a first-person game this is obvious—you will hear the world from the location of the player's head (i.e., the camera's location). For 2D, third-person, or fixed isometric view games, it is less clear. In some instances the sound remains attached to the player, but more often it is heard from a location in space somewhere offset from the players themselves (i.e., the camera's position). Some games also allow you to swap from between different types of view.

First Person View

Third Person View

When using a third-person camera, we get a wider perspective than we get in first-person view. We may see things that are out of sight of the player's character. Sound from the camera's point of view can lead you to hearing things that you can't actually see, or to hearing the indoor ambience when the player character is still outdoors and vice versa. There is no single solution to this problem, and it often comes down to a matter of taste. It is, however, something you should be looking out for to avoid circumstances in which the sound track will be at odds with what the player sees.

If you want to see a simple example of where camera panning and sound can produce some unwelcome effects, then jump ahead to the racetrack in area 700 of the tutorial level. Pick the standard Scorpion vehicle on the right-hand side (shown in red in the image that follows) and use your mouse to move the camera (and the turret) around while driving. You'll notice that as the engine sounds are spatialized, they pan around the stereo (or surround) field. In terms of the logic of the player's position in the vehicle and in terms of the lack of elegance in the panning, this is less than ideal.

Conclusion

Although not yet fully implemented in UDK the power of the latest generation of consoles gives us the opportunity to replicate real-world physics as never before with ray tracing for occlusion, real-time delayed reflections, filtering, and convolution reverbs. As this technology continues to improve and become accessible, it will allow us to create a convincing and consistent impression of the "real" to validate and support what is, after all, just a 2D image of pixels changing color. Next we need to consider when and how to move beyond the "real," to use the emotional impact of sound and music on the player to support the gameplay or narrative. We'll return to this topic in Chapter 6: Making It Sound Good after a trip to the other end of the reality spectrum to consider the unfathomable power of music.

Music Systems

Introduction

Music is one our most powerful tools to affect how players feel in games. The systems described in this chapter will give you an understanding of some of the key techniques involved in implementing music in games. You will be able to try out your music in these systems and to prototype new ones. It is unlikely that many of these systems would operate in exactly the same way in an actual game engine because you would have a dedicated programmer to implement them at a lower level. However, an understanding of how the systems and prototypes operate will enable you to describe to the programmer precisely the effect you are after. By looking at the systems you have built in Kismet, your programmer will be able to replicate them a lot more efficiently. We'll focus here on techniques to get your music working and sounding good in a game. Although music is typically streamed from disk, it is not immune to the concerns over memory that we discussed in Chapter 2. See the section titled "Streaming" in Appendix B for some specific advice on memory management for music.

As you're reading this section, you're obviously interested in writing or implementing music in games, so we're going to assume some musical knowledge. If you don't know how to write music then we'd suggest you put this book down, and go and learn about pitch, rhythm, harmony, timbre, texture, instrumentation, and how to structure all these things into a successful musical whole.

You're back. Well done! Now let's move on.

If you want to write music for games, you need to learn to write music ... for ... games. It's not a shortcut to that film music job you always wanted. You need to play, understand, and love games and, yes, if you skipped straight to this chapter in the hope of a shortcut, you will have to go back and read the earlier chapters properly to understand the implementation ideas ahead. Your music works alongside, and hopefully with, the sound in games, so you need to understand both.

If you take a flick through the following pages and are thinking "but I'm a composer, not a programmer," then we can understand that initial reaction. However, in games audio you cannot separate the creation from the implementation. If you want your music to sound the best, and be the most effective that it can be, then you need to engage with the systems that govern it. As you will no doubt recognize from the discussions that follow, the production and recording methods involved in producing music for games share a great deal with those used for film, but there are some important differences. As these are beyond the remit of this book, we'll provide some links to further reading on this topic in the bibliography.

Don't worry. Writing good music is possibly one of the most complicated things you can do. If you've mastered that task, then this part is easy.

Styles and Game Genres

Certain genres of games have become closely associated with particular styles of music. That's not to say that these traditions can't be challenged, but you should acknowledge that players may come to your game with preexisting expectations about the style of music they will experience. This is equally true of the producers and designers who may be commissioning the music. The following list of game categories is intended to be a broad overview.

Social/Casual/Puzzle

The music for this type of game is often repetitive. Perhaps there is something in the mesmeric quality of these games that suits the timelessness or suspension of time implied by a repeatedly looping music track. The more pragmatic answer is that by nature many of these games are often fairly undemanding in terms of processing so that they can be accessible to older platforms or work on the web. They will also often be played without the audio actually switched on (in the office), so music is not thought to be a great consideration and typically receives little investment. This leads to simple repetitive loops, which are the easiest to process (and the cheapest music to make).

Platformer/Arcade

In the public's imagination, it is this genre that people still associate most closely with the idea of "game music." The synthesized and often repetitive music of early games has a retro appeal that makes music in this genre really a case of its own. What might be considered repetitive level music within other genres is still alive and well here, the iconic feedback sounds of pickups and powerups often blur the line between "music" sounds and "gameplay" sounds, and it is not unusual to find an extremely reactive score that speeds up or suddenly switches depending on game events.

Driving/Simulation/Sports

Driving is closely associated with playing back your own music or listening to the radio, so it is not surprising that the racing genre remains dominated by the use of the licensed popular music sound track. In the few cases where an interactive score has been attempted, it has usually been in games that have extended gameplay features such as pursuit. In a straightforward driving game where race position is the only real goal, perhaps the repetitive nature of the action and limited emotional range of the gameplay would make any attempts at an interactive score too repetitive. Simulations typically do not have music (apart from in the menu), and sports-based games aim to closely represent the real-life experience of a sporting event, which of course does not tend to have interactive music, apart from perhaps some responsive jingles. On the rare occasions where music is used, it tends again to be the licensed "radio" model consisting of a carefully chosen selection of tracks that are representative of the culture or community of the sport.

The music in this genre is often important in defining both the location and the culture of the player's immediate surroundings (see "Roles and functions of music in games," presented later) although it often also responds to gameplay action. Attempting to provide music for an experience that can last an indefinite amount of time, together with the complexities of simultaneously representing multiple characters through music (see the discussions of the "Leitmotif," below) means that this genre is potentially one of the most challenging for the interactive composer.

Adventure/Action/Shooter

Probably the most cinematic of game genres, these games aim to use music to support the emotions of the game's narrative. Again this presents a great challenge to the composer, who is expected to match the expectations of a Hollywood-type score within a nonlinear medium where the situation can change at any time given the choices of the player.

Roles and Functions of Music in Games

There are usually two approaches to including music in a game. The first is to have music that appears to come from inside the reality of the game world. In other words, it is played by, or through, objects or characters in the game. This could be via a radio, a television, a tannoy, or through characters playing actual instruments or singing in the game. This type of music is commonly referred to as "diegetic" music. Non-diegetic music, on the other hand, is the kind with which you'll be very familiar from the film world. This would be when the sound of a huge symphony orchestra rises up to accompany the heartfelt conversation between two people in an elevator. The orchestra is not in the elevator with them; the music is not heard by the characters in the world but instead sits outside of that "diegesis" or narrative space. (The situation of the game player does confuse these definitions somewhat as the player is simultaneously both the character in the world and sitting outside of it, but we'll leave that particular debate for another time, perhaps another book.)

Whether you choose to use diegetic or non-diegetic music for your game, and the particular approach to using music you choose, will of course be subject to the specific needs of your game. Here we will discuss a range of roles and functions that music can perform in order to inform your choices.

You're So Special: Music as a Signifier

Apart from anything else, and irrespective of its musical content, simply having music present is usually an indication that what you are currently experiencing is somehow special or different from other sections of the game that do not have music. If you watch a typical movie, you'll notice that music is only there during specific, emotionally important sections; it's not usually wallpapered all over this film (with a few notable exceptions). The fact that these occasions have music marks them as being different, indicating a special emotional significance. In games, music often delineates special events by signifying the starting, doing, and completion of tasks or sections of the game. By using music sparsely throughout your game, you can improve its impact and effectiveness in highlighting certain situations. If music is present all the time, then it will have less impact than if it only appears for certain occasions.

This Town, is Coming Like a Ghost Town: Cultural Connotations of Instrumentation and Style

Before you write the first note, it's worth considering the impact of the palette of instruments you are going to choose. Although the recent trend has been for games to ape the Hollywood propensity for using large orchestral forces, it's worth considering what alternative palettes can bring. The orchestral score has the advantage that it is, to some extent, meeting expectations within certain genres. It's a sound most people are familiar with, so it will probably produce less extreme responses (i.e., not many people are going to hate it). Of course, the melodies, harmonies and rhythms you use are also essential elements of style, but instrumentation remains the most immediately evocative. By choosing to use a different set of instruments, you can effectively conjure up a certain time period or geographical area (e.g., a Harpsichord for the 17th century, Bagpipes for Scotland). If you think of some of the most iconic film music of the previous century (leaving John Williams to one side for a moment), there is often a distinct set of instruments and timbres that has come to influence other composers and define certain genres (think of Ennio Morricone's "spaghetti westerns" or of Vangelis' synthesized score for *Blade Runner*).

In addition to conjuring up a specific time and place, these instruments—and, of course, the musical language—also bring significant cultural baggage and hence symbolic meaning. Different styles of music are often closely associated with different cultural groups, and by using this music or instrumentation you can evoke the emotions or culture ascribed to these groups. This is particularly effective when using diegetic music (e.g., from a radio), as you are effectively showing the kind of music that these people listen to and therefore defining the kind of people they are.

You Don't Have to Tell Me: Music as an Informational Device

Sometimes it is appropriate to make explicit the link between the music and the game variables so that the music acts as an informational device. Music often provides information that nothing else does; therefore, you need it there in order to play the game effectively. The music could act as a warning to the player to indicate when an enemy approaches or when the player has been spotted. The details and consequences of linking music to the artificial intelligence (AI) in such a way must be carefully considered. Depending on your intentions you may not want the music to react simply when an enemy is within a given distance, as this may not take orientation into account. Do you want the music to start even when you can't see the enemy? Do you want it to start even when the enemy can't see you? Again, your answer will depend on your particular intentions and what is effective within the context of your game.

He's a Killer: Music to Reveal Character

One of the most powerful devices within film music is the "Leitmotif." Originally a technique associated with opera, it assigns specific musical motifs to specific characters. For example, the princess may have a fluttery flute melody, and the evil prince's motif may be a slow dissonant phrase played low on the double bass. The occurrence of the motif can, of course, inform the player of a particular character's presence, but additionally the manipulation of the musical material of the motif can reveal much about both the nature of the character and what the character is feeling at any given time. You may hear the princess's theme in a lush romantic string arrangement to tell you she's in love, in a fast staccato string arrangement to tell you that she's in a hurry, or with Mexican-type harmonies and instrumentation to tell you that she's desperately craving a Burrito.

You might choose to have explicit themes for particular characters, for broad types (goodies/baddies), or for particular races or social groups. What you do musically with these themes can effectively provide an emotional or psychological subtext without the need for all those clumsy things called "words."

In Shock: Music for Surprise Effect

A sudden and unexpected musical stab is the staple of many horror movies. One of the most effective ways of playing with people's expectations is to set up a system that's a combination of the informational and character-based ideas described earlier. In this scenario, the music predictably provides a warning of the approach of a particular dangerous entity by playing that character's motif. By setting up and continually re-establishing this connection between music and character, you set up a powerful expectation. You can then play with these expectations to induce tension or uncertainty in the listener. Perhaps on one occasion you play the music, but the character does not actually appear, on another you again override this system in order to provoke shock or surprise by having the danger suddenly appear, but this time without the warning that the player has been conditioned to expect.

Hey Mickey, You're So Fine: Playing the Mood, Playing the Action

With a few notable exceptions, music in games tends toward a very literal moment-by-moment playing of the action and mood of the game, rarely using the kind of juxtaposition or counterpoint to the visuals you see in films. When music is used to closely highlight or reinforce the physical action on the screen, it is sometimes referred to disparagingly as "Mickey Mousing." This derives, of course, from the style of music in many cartoons which imitates the actions very precisely in a way that acts almost as a sound effect, with little in the way of a larger form of musical development. You can do this in a linear cartoon as the action occurs over a fixed and known time period; this way, you can plan your music carefully so that it is in the correct tempo to catch many of the visual hits. Although game music is rarely so closely tied to the physical movement or action taking place (partly because of the difficulty in doing so), it often responds to communicate the game situation in terms of shifting to different levels of intensity or mood depending on gameplay variables such as the presence of enemies, the number of enemies within a given distance of the player, player health, enemy health, weapon condition, amount of ammo, distance from save point or target location, or pickups/powerups. Along with these reactive changes in intensity there might also be "stingers," short musical motifs that play over the top of the general musical flow and specifically pick out and highlight game events.

Punish Me with Kisses: Music as Commentary, Punishment, or Reward

Related to playing the action of a game, music can also fulfill an additional function of acting as a punishment or reward to the player. You might use music to comment on actions that the player has just undertaken in a positive or negative way, to encourage the player to do something, or to punish the player for doing the wrong thing.

It's a Fine Line between Love and Hate

The way in which music and narrative interact could be seen as a continuum between Mickey Mousing at one end and actively playing against the apparent emotion of the scene at the other:

Hitting the action (Mickey Mousing)
Synchronising musical gestures with the physical action on the screen

Playing the emotion (Empathetic Music)
The music works in empathy with the emotions of the character or characters on the screen

Playing the meta-emotion (Narrative Music)
Here music might not directly reflect the moment to moment emotional state of the characters but instead might play a more over-arching emotion for the entire scene or indicate some larger scale narrative point

Counterpoint (Anempathetic Music)
This music will actually play against or be indifferent to the emotions that appear visually. The juxtaposition of happy upbeat music with a tragic scene for example.

Choosing the degree to which music is going to respond to the game action or narrative emotion is a difficult decision. If the music is too reactive, players can feel that they are "playing" the music rather than the game, and this can break their immersion in the game world. If there is too little reaction, then we can miss opportunities to heighten the player's emotion through music.

Together with the game designer, you need to make emotional sense of the combination of the games variables. Music is effective in implying levels of tension and relaxation, conflict and resolution. Choosing whether to score the blow-by-blow action or the larger emotional sweep of a scene will depend on your aims. You can avoid the relationship between the game system and the music becoming too obvious by sometimes choosing not to respond, as this will reduce the predictability. However, sometimes you may want a consistent response because the music may be serving a more informational role.

Here are some questions to think about when deciding on how to score the action or mood:

- Are you scoring what is happening in terms of highlighting specific actions?
- Are you scoring what is happening in terms of the underlying mood or emotion you want to convey?
- Are you scoring what is happening now, what has happened, or what is about to happen?

Making the Right Choice

Bearing in mind some of the possible functions of music just described, you and your team need to decide upon what you aim to achieve with the music and then implement an appropriate mechanism to deliver this aim. Let's be clear, it is perfectly possible to implement music into games effectively using simple playback mechanisms. It depends on what is appropriate for your particular situation. Many people are totally happy with simple linear music that switches clumsily from one piece to another. Look at the time and resources you have available together with what the game actually needs. Some circumstances will be most effective with linear music, and others may need a more interactive approach. Your experience with the prototypes outlined here should help you to make the right choice.

Music Concepting/Spotting/Prototyping/Testing

> Most game producers, like most film directors, have little or no understanding of music and how to use it. The difference is that in film it doesn't matter as much because the producer hands over the final edit to the composer and they can make it work. The problem for the composer for games is that the game producer, who doesn't really understand music, will not have built a proper system to use it effectively. Either on your own or together with a game designer you should demonstrate your ideas and get involved with the process as early as possible.

It is not always meaningful to separate out these process into these stages because the implementation can (and should) often affect the stylistic considerations, but we will attempt to do so for the purposes of illustration.

Concepting

It's quite likely that you will have been chosen for a composition role because of music you have written in the past or a particular piece in your show reel. Although this may seem like an established starting point, before you spend lots of time actually writing music consider putting a set of reference tracks together to establish the kind of aesthetic or tone your producer is after. This may differ from what you thought. Words are not accurate ways of describing music, especially to most people who lack the appropriate vocabulary, so some actual musical examples can often save a lot of confusion.

Editing together a bunch of music to some graphics or illustrations of the game can be an effective shortcut to establishing the style that the producers are after. You should also discuss other games (including previous games in the series) and movies as reference points. Certain genres of Hollywood film composition have become so established that they are a kind of shorthand for particular emotions (think of John Williams' mysterious Ark music from *Raiders of the Lost Ark,* for example). There are many other approaches that could work; so rather than just pastiche these musical archetypes, why don't you try to bring something new to the table that the producers might not have thought of? (If they hate it, that's fine, as you will have also prepared another version in the more predictable style.)

Spotting

Spotting is a term taken from the film industry that describes what happens when a director and composer sit down and watch the film together to establish where the music is going to be. During this discussion they not only decide on start points and end points but also discuss the nature of the music in detail, the emotional arc of the scene, and its purpose. Unfortunately, when writing music for games you are often working on an imaginary situation with possibly only a text-based game design document to go on. Along with the producer or designers, you should discuss the roles you want music to play, the desired emotion or goal of the scenario, and how it might reflect the conflict and resolutions within the gameplay or the tempo of the action. You should establish particular events that require music, start points, end points, and how the music will integrate with different gameplay variables such as player health, enemy health, and so on. It's important to have access to the right data so that you are able to discuss how to translate that data into emotional, and therefore musical, meaning.

During this process you should try to get involved as early as possible to act as a convincing advocate for music. *Importantly, this also involves, where appropriate, being an advocate for no music!*

Prototyping

As part of the concepting process, it's important that you try not to be simply reactive, just supplying the assets as requested. To develop game music, you should be an advocate for its use. This means putting your time and effort where your mouth is and demonstrating your ideas.

It's a continuing irony that decisions on interactive music are often made without it actually being experienced in an interactive context. Often music will be sent to the designers or producers and they will listen to it as "music" and make decisions on whether or not they like it. However, music for games is not, and should not be, intended to be listened to as a piece of concert music. Its primary goal should be to make a better game. Therefore, it should be heard in the interactive context within which it will be used. (This is not to say that there are not many pieces that are highly successful as concert music, just that the primary purpose of game music should be to be *game music*.) This problem is exacerbated by the fact that people's musical tastes are largely formed by their exposure to linear music in films (and mostly of the "Hollywood" model).

Some people continue to argue that it is not necessary for composers to write music with the specifics of gameplay in mind, that they should simply write music in the way they always have, and then the game company's little army of hacks will come along to cut and splice the music for interactive use. In some cases this process can be perfectly adequate, but there should be opportunities for the more intelligent composer to face the challenge more directly.

Although it is possible to prototype and demonstrate your music systems in some of the excellent middleware audio solutions (such as FMOD by Firelight Technologies and Wwise by AudioKinetic), an in-game example is always going to be more meaningful than having to say, "Imagine this fader is the player's health, this one is the enemy's proximity, oh, and this button is for when the player picks up an RBFG."

Either by developing example systems on your own, based on the examples that follow, or by working directly with a game designer, the earlier you can demonstrate how music can contribute to the game, the more integral it will be considered. Remember, the aim is to not only make the use of music better but by extension, and more importantly, to make the game better.

Testing

The importance of testing and iteration can never be underestimated in any game design process and music is no exception. As you address these issues, keep in mind that the degree of reactiveness or interactivity the music should have can only be established through thorough testing and feedback. Obviously you will spend a significant amount of time familiarizing yourself with the game to test different approaches yourself, but it is also valuable to get a number of different people's views. You'd be amazed how many QA departments (the quality assurance department, whose job it is to test the games) do not supply their testers with decent quality headphones. Of those actually wearing headphones, you'd also be surprised at the number who are actually listening to their friend's latest breakbeat-two-step-gabba-trance-grime-crossover track, rather than the actual game.

In addition to determining whether people find that Bouzouki intro you love a bit irritating when they have to restart that checkpoint for 300th time, you may also discover that users play games in very different ways. Here are a few typical player approaches to "Imaginary Game": Level 12c:

1. *The Creeper.* This player uses stealth and shadows to cunningly achieve the level's objectives without being detected at any point (apart from just before a rather satisfying neck snap).
2. *The Blazer.* This player kicks open the door, a pistol on each hip, and doesn't stop running or shooting for the next three minutes, which is how long it will take this player to finish the level compared to the creeper's 15 minutes.
3. *The Completist.* This player is not satisfied until the dimmest crevice of every corner of the level has been fully explored. This player will creep when necessary or dive in shooting for some variation but will also break every crate, covet every pickup, read every self-referential poster and magazine cover, and suck up every drop of satisfaction from level 12c before moving on.

You should also note the positions of any save points, where and how many times people restart a level. Do you want your music to repeat exactly the same each time? By watching these different players with their different approaches, you may find that a one-size-fits-all solution to interactive music does not work and perhaps you need to consider monitoring the playing style over time and adapting your system to suit it.

The Key Challenges of Game Music

Once you've decided on the main role, or roles, you want the music to play in your game, two fundamental questions remain for implementing music in games, which will be the concerns of the rest of this chapter:

1. **The transitions question:** *If the music is going to react to gameplay, then how are you going to transition between different pieces of music, when game events might not happen to coincide with an appropriate point in the music?* This does not necessarily mean transitioning from one piece of music to another, but from one musical state to another. The majority of issues arising from using music effectively in games arise out of the conflict between a game's interactive nature, where events can happen at any given moment, and the time-based nature of music, which relies on predetermined lengths in order to remain musically coherent.
2. **The variation question:** *How can we possibly write and store enough music?* In a game you typically hear music for a much longer period than in a film. Games may last anything from ten hours up to hundreds of hours. Given huge resources it may be possible to write that amount of music, but how would you store this amount of music within the disk space available?

The only way to decide what works is to try the music out in the context to which it belongs—in an actual game.

Source Music/Diegetic Music

Sometimes the music in games comes from a source that is actually in the game world. This is referred to as "diegetic" music in that it belongs to the diegesis, the story world. This is more representative of reality than the music that appears to come from nowhere; the "non-diegetic" score you more usually associate with film. The style of diegetic music you choose can carry a strong cultural message about the time, the place, and the people listening to it.

400 Radio Days

Outside of, and on the approach to, Room 400 you can hear two sources of diegetic music—that is, music that originates from "real" objects in the game world, in this case a Tannoy and a Radio. This kind of music can be used to define the time period, location, or culture in which we hear it. For example, if you heard gangsta rap on the radio it would give you the distinct impression that you weren't walking into a kindergarten classroom!

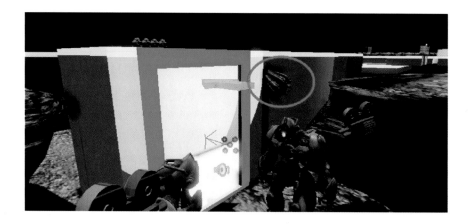

As well as defining the place where you hear it, you can use sources of music in your games to draw the player toward, or away from, certain areas. The sound of a radio or other source playing would usually indicate that there are some people nearby. Depending on your intentions, this could serve as a warning, or players may also be drawn toward the source of the music out of curiosity.

You can interact with this radio to change channels by pressing E. This plays a short burst of static before settling on the next station. If you so wish, you can also shoot it. You did already, didn't you?

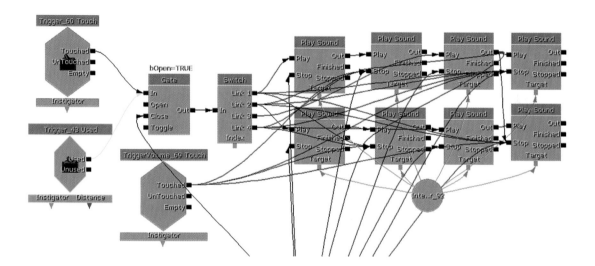

When you enter the outer corridor, a **[Trigger]** goes through the **[Switch]** to start the first **[PlaySound]**, which holds our first music **[SoundCue]**. Notice that the target for the **[PlaySound]** object is the **[StaticMesh]** of the radio itself so that the sound appears to come from the radio rather than directly into the player's ears. This spatialization will only work with mono sound files. As explained in Chapter 3, stereo sound files do not spatialize. (If you really want the impression of a diegetic stereo source that appears spatialized in game, then you'll have to split your channels and play them back simultaneously through "left" and "right" point sources in the game.)

When the **[Trigger]** surrounding the radio is used, it then switches a new track on (with a **[PlaySound]** in between for the static crackles) and switches all the others off. In the **[Switch]**'s properties it is set to loop, and so after switch output 4 has been used it will return to switch output 1. Finally there is a **[TriggerVolume]** when leaving the room that switches them all off so that this music doesn't carry over into the next room as well.

The **[Gate]** is there so that if or when the player decides to shoot the radio the Touch messages no longer get through. The **[Take Damage]** event destroys the radio **[InterpActor]**, fires off an explosion **[Emitter]** and sound, and turns off all the **[PlaySound]**s. (For more on **[Take Damage]** events, see Appendix C: UDK Tips).

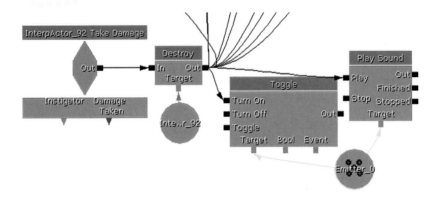

Exercise 400_00 Diegetic Music

In this room there are several possible sources for music. Add music to the sources. Perhaps include a "use" action to switch them on/off or to change the music that is playing.

Tips

1. In Kismet create a new **[PlaySound]** object (Right-Click/New Action/Sound/PlaySound, or hold down the S key and click in an empty space in the Kismet window).
2. Add your **[SoundCue]** to the **[PlaySound]** as usual by selecting it in the Content Browser and then clicking the green arrow in the **[PlaySound]**'s properties.

3. To choose where the sound plays from, select a **[StaticMesh]** in your Perspective view and then right-click on the Target output of the **[PlaySound]**. Choose "New Object Var Using Static Mesh (***)."
4. Remember from Chapter 3 that any stereo files will be automatically played back to the player's ears, so if you want your music to sound localized to this object, you should use mono files and adjust the **[Attenuation]** object's settings within your **[SoundCue]**.
5. To start your **[PlaySound]**, either use a **[Level Start]** event (Right-Click New event/Level Startup), a **[Switch]** (New Action/Switch/Switch), or a **[Trigger]**.

Linear Music and Looping Music

The music for trailers, cut-scenes, and credits is produced in exactly the same way as you might create music for a film, animation, or advert. Working to picture in your MIDI sequencer or audio editor, you write music to last a specific length of time and hit specific spots of action within the linear visuals.

Composing and implementing music for trailers or cutscenes is not unique to games audio. Because they last a specific length of time, you can use the same approach you would use to write music for a film or animation. We're interested here in the specific challenges that music for games throws up, so we're not going to dwell on linear music. Instead we're going to work on the presumption that you want your music to react (and perhaps interact) with gameplay in a smooth, musical way.

Perhaps an exception in which linear audio starts to become slightly interactive would be in so-called looping "lobby" music that might accompany menu screens. It's "interactive", as we can stop it to enter or exit the actual game at any time. This is a source of many heinous crimes in games audio. Producers that will lavish time and effort on and polishing every other aspect of a game will think nothing of brutally cutting off any music that's playing during these menu scenes (and Pause menus). We understand that if players want to start (or exit) the game, then they want an immediate response. It would be possible to come up with more musical solutions to this but the least your music deserves is a short fade out.

Using the Fade Out functionality of the **[PlaySound]** object in Kismet would at least improve some of the clumsy attempts to deal with this issue.

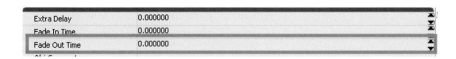

If you don't respect the music in your game, it shows that you don't respect your game. After all, the music is part of your game, isn't it? Don't cut off music for menus or do clumsy fades—it's just not classy!

Avoid the Problem: Timed Event Music

Often the most effective, and least complex, way of using music in games is to use it only for particular scenarios or events that last a set amount of time. This way you can use a linear piece of music that builds naturally and musically to a climax. Although it appears that the player is in control, the scenario is set to last for an exact amount of time, whether the player achieves the objective or not.

Linear music can be very effective if the game sequence is suitably linear as well. An event that lasts a specific amount of time before it is either completed or the game ends allows you to build a linear piece to fit perfectly.

401 Timed Event

On entering this room you are told that the "Flux Capacitor" barring entry to the next room is dangerously unstable. You've got to pick up six energy crystals and get them into the Flux Capacitor before she blows. If you manage it, you'll be able to get to the next room. If you don't...

Around the room are a number of **[InterpActor]**s. Each one has a **[Trigger]** around it so it will sense when it is being "picked up." As you enter the room, a **[Trigger]** Touch object starts the music track and a series of **[Delay]**s. The total value of all the **[Delay]**s is two minutes precisely. After the first delay time, one of the **[InterpActor]**s is toggled to Unhide by a **[Toggle Hidden]** object. At the same time, a **[Gate]** object is opened to allow the **[Trigger]** that surrounds this **[InterpActor]** to be utilized. This can then play the pickup sound and destroy the **[InterpActor]**. When the player then runs over to deposit this into the flux capacitor, a **[Trigger]** around this object is allowed through an additional **[Gate]** to play the **[Announcement],** telling the player how many are remaining.

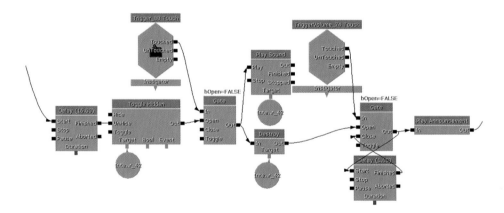

Each time the pickup is "deposited," the **[Play Announcement]** outputs to an **[Int Counter]**. As we saw earlier, this object increments its value A by a set amount (in this case 1) every time it receives an input. It then compares value A to value B (in this case set to 5). If value A does not equal value B, then the **[Gate]** that leads to the explosion event is left open. As soon as value A does equal value B (in other words when all five of the energy crystals have been picked up and deposited into the flux capacitor), the A==B output is triggered. This closes the explosion **[Gate]** and opens the triumph **[Gate]** so that when the music has finished, its output goes to the appropriate place. This also destroys the **[DynamicBlockingVolume]** that so far has been blocking our exit.

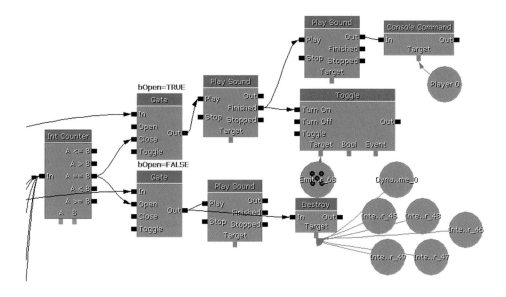

If you can still read this through your tears of bewilderment, the good news is that in terms of the actual music part of this system, it is probably the simplest you can imagine. When the events are started by the initial **[Trigger]** touch, this goes to a **[PlaySound]** object, which plays the music **[SoundCue]**.

The **[SoundCue]** targets the **[Player]** so it is played back to the player's ears and does not pan around. This is the most appropriate approach from music that is non-diegetic (i.e., music that does not originate from a source object within the game world).

Avoid the Problem: Non-Time-Based Approaches Using Ambiguous Music

The problems with musical transitions in response to gameplay events discussed earlier (and continued in the following examples) can in certain circumstances be avoided by using music that is ambiguous in tonality and rhythm. People will notice if a rhythm is interrupted, they will notice if a chord sequence never gets to resolve, and they will notice if a melody is left hanging in space. If none of these issues were there in the first place, then you won't have set up these expectations. So avoid rhythm, tonality, and melody? You might ask if there's any music left? Well, if you're working in the horror genre, it's your lucky day as this typically makes use of the kind of advanced instrumental and atonal techniques developed by composers in the 20th century that can deliver the kind of flexible ambiguity we're after.

402 Fatal Void

In this room there are three "bad things." Each of these bad things carries a "scare" rating of 1. So if two overlap where you're standing, then you have a scare rating of 2. If you are in the area where all three overlap, then things are looking bad with a scare rating of 3.

These scare ratings are associated with music of a low, medium, and high intensity. The music itself is fairly static within its own intensity. As you listen, notice that no real rhythmic pulse has been established, nor is any particular chord or tonality used. This makes it less jarring when the music crossfades between the three levels. (This is our homage to the music of a well-known game. If you haven't guessed already, see the bibliography.)

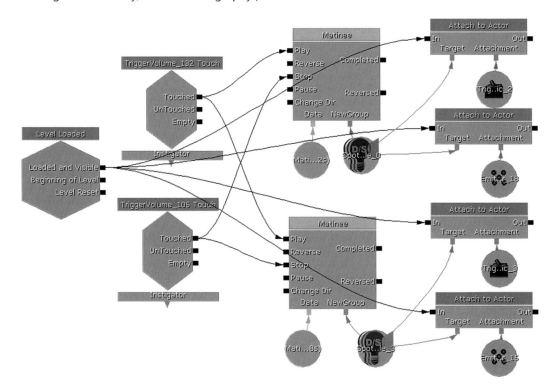

On the level start a **[Trigger_Dynamic]** (Actor Classes/Trigger/Trigger_Dynamic) and a **[Particle Emitter]** are attached to the two moving lights using an **[Attach to Actor]** object. A **[TriggerVolume]** on entry to the room starts the movement of the two colored lights, which is controlled in the usual way by a **[Matinee]** object. The **[Trigger_Dynamic]**s are movable triggers, which will now follow the movement of the lights. As the lights are higher up and we want the triggers to be on the floor, we have offset the triggers from the lights by 400 units in the vertical plane.

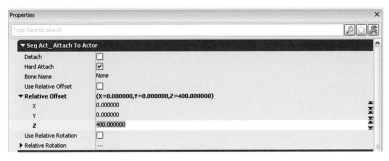

Attach to Actor properties.

When any of these triggers (including the central light area, which does not move) are *touched*, it adds to a central variable; when it is *untouched*, it subtracts from it. This central variable therefore represents our "scare" factor. Three **[Compare]** objects compare this variable to the values 3, 2, or 1 and then play the corresponding sound file. If the "scare" variable is the same as their compare value, they *play* their sound; if it differs, then they *stop* their **[Playsound]**. Each **[PlaySound]** object has a Fade in time of two seconds and a Fade out time of five seconds to smooth the transitions between the different levels of intensity.

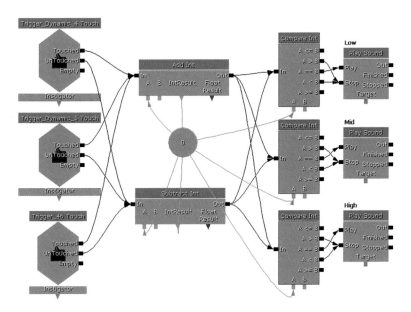

The use of music that is ambiguous in its tonality and rhythmic structure can make the transitions necessary in interactive games appear less clumsy.

Exercise 402_00 Ambiguous

In this room there are four switches. The more that are switched on, the greater the danger. See if you can adapt the system and add your own ambiguous music so that the music changes with any combination of switches.

Tips:

1. Add a **[Trigger]** for each of the switches. Right-click in the Perspective viewport and choose Add Actor/Add Trigger. With the **[Trigger]** selected, right-click in Kismet and choose New Event using (Trigger***) Used.
2. In the **[Trigger]** Used event properties in Kismet, uncheck Aim to Interact and change Max Trigger count to zero.
3. In Kismet, duplicate the system from Room 402 so that your triggers add or subtract from a central variable.
4. By changing value B within the properties of the **[Compare Int]**, you can choose which one triggers which level of music.
5. Experiment with different fade in/fade out lengths for your **[PlaySound]**s until you achieve a satisfying crossfade.

Avoid the Problem: Stingers

Sometimes you don't want the whole musical score to shift direction, but you do want to acknowledge an action. Perhaps the action is over too quickly to warrant a whole-scale change in musical intensity. "Stingers" are useful in this regard, as they should be designed to fit musically over the top of the music that is already playing.

403 Music Stingers

A stinger is a short musical cue that is played over the top of the existing music. This might be useful to highlight a particular game event without instigating a large-scale change in the music. Two bots are patrolling this area. If you manage to shoot either one, then you are rewarded with a musical "stinger."

When you enter the room, the **[TriggerVolume]** begins the background music via a **[PlaySound]** and also triggers the bots to start patrolling.

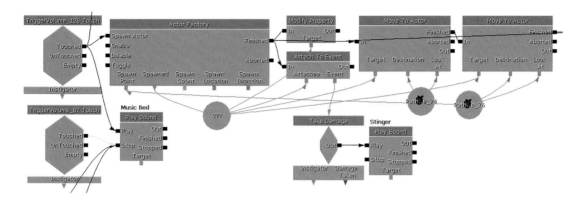

The bots that are spawned can send out a signal in Kismet when they **[Take Damage],** and this is used to trigger the musical stinger over the top via another **[PlaySound]**. (See the Spawning and Controlling Bots section of Appendix C: UDK Tips).

The stinger **[SoundCue]** is made up of five brass stabs that are selected at random.

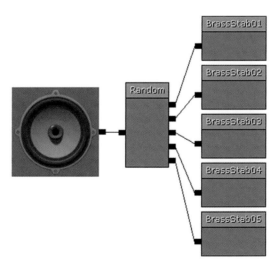

This example works pretty well because the background music is purely rhythmic. This means that whatever melody or harmony the stinger plays over the top will not clash with the music already playing. If you want to put stingers over music that fits more rhythmically or harmonically, then we need to extend the system's complexity to take into account of where we are in the music when the stinger is played.

Exercise 403_00 Stingers

The player needs to jump across the lily pads to get to the other side of the river. Set up a music background that loops. Now add a stinger so that every time the player successfully jumps on a moving pad there is a rewarding musical confirmation.

Tips

1. Set up your background using a looping **[SoundCue]** in a **[PlaySound]** triggered by either Level Start (New Event/ Level Startup) or a **[Trigger]** touch.
2. The **[InterpActor]**s are already attached to a matinee sequence (created by right-Clicking in Kismet and choosing New Event using InterpActor (***) Mover). This has a **[Pawn Attached]** event, which you can use to trigger another **[PlaySound]** for your stinger(s).

403a Rhythmically Aware Stingers

With certain types of musical material, it could be that the stingers would work even better if they waited until an appropriately musical point to play (i.e., until the next available beat). To do this you would need to set up a delay system that is aligned to the speed of the beats and then only allow the stinger message to go through at the musical point.

At **[Level Loaded]** we make a simple calculation to work out the length of one beat in seconds. A minute (60 seconds) is divided by the tempo (the number of beats in a minute) to give us the length of a beat. As this is unlikely to be a whole number (and as a **[Delay]** object only accepts floats anyway) we then need to convert this integer to a float before passing it as a **[Named Variable]** to a **[Delay]** object.

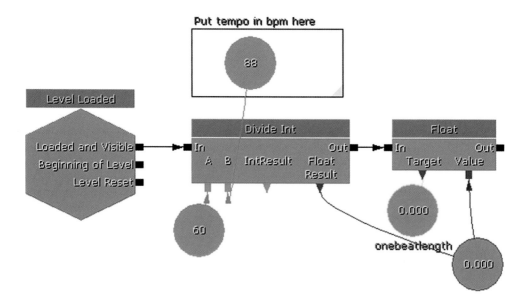

The **[Delay]** will now send out a pulse for every beat. This goes into the gate to go through and trigger the stinger (via the **[PlaySound]**) on the beat. It is only allowed to go through and do this, however, when the bot's **[Take Damage]** event opens the **[Gate]**. Having taken damage, the **[Gate]** opens, the stinger plays on the beat (triggered by the **[Delay]**), and the **[Gate]** then closes itself.

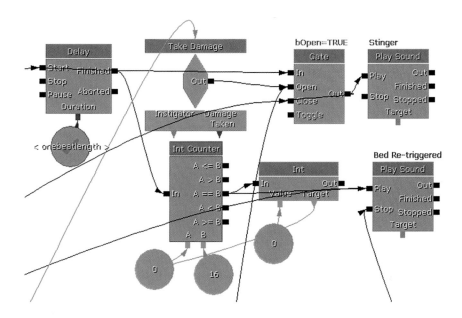

There is also an additional system at work just to make sure that the looping background musical bed remains in time with the beat pulse. Instead of using a looping **[SoundCue]** for the musical bed, we are retriggering it. An **[Int Counter]** is set to increment by 1 every time it receives a beat from the **[Delay]** object. When this reaches 16 (the length in beats of this particular **[SoundCue]**), the music is retriggered. This helps avoid any slight discrepancies in the timing that may arise from using a looping sound.

Exercise 403a_00 Aligned Stingers

Now adapt your system so that the stingers only play on the next available beat. You'll notice that this version also has some flowers that act as pickups; give them a different musical stinger.

Tips

1. You will have to calculate the tempo of your track, then add a bit. The timing system within UDK is not accurate, so some trial and error will be necessary. These timing of these systems will also run unreliably within the "Play in editor" window, so you should also preview your systems by running the full Start this level on PC option.

2. The system in Room 403a uses a **[Delay]** of one beat length to get the stingers in time. Copy and adapt this system for your exercise so that you're using your **[Pawn Attached]** event instead of the **[Take Damage]**. Adjust the delay length and number of beats to match the length of your background piece of music. (You'll need to use another version of your piece from 403_00, as the original **[SoundCue]** would have had a loop in it and now you are looping manually.)

403b Harmonically and Rhythmically Aware Stingers

Percussive-based stingers are easiest to use because they will fit with the music irrespective of the musical harmony at the time. Using more melodic or pitch-based stingers can be problematic, as they may not always be appropriate to the musical harmony that's currently playing. For example, a stinger based around the notes C and E would sound fine if it happened to occur over the first two bars of this musical sequence, but it would sound dissonant against the last two bars.

Chord of C Major	Chord of A Minor	Chord of F Major	Chord of G 7

To make this work, we would need to write a specific stinger for each specific harmony that was in the piece. Then if we can track where we are in the music, we can tell the system to play the appropriate stinger for the chord that's currently playing.

As the system is getting more complex, **[Activate Remote Event]** actions are used to transmit both the beat pulse and the measure event that retriggers the bed to make it loop. Passing events like this can help to stop your Kismet patches from becoming too cluttered. (See Appendix C: UDK Tips.)

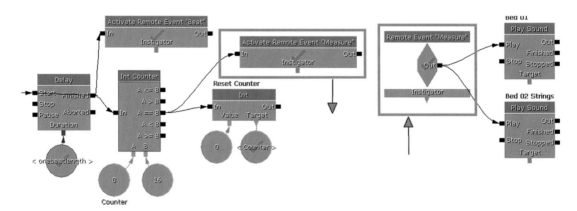

Although our rhythmic bed remains 16 beats long, now we have an additional harmonic element provided by some strings. This is in two halves of 8 beats each. To monitor which half is playing, to therefore choose the appropriate stinger, another **[Int Counter]** is used. This counts to 8 and is then reset. Each time it reaches 8, it equals the B variable and therefore outputs to the looping **[Switch]** to send either a value 1 or 2 to a named variable "Bar no."

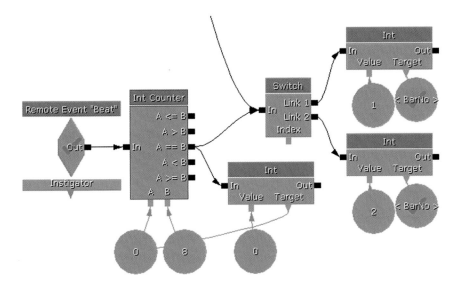

A **[Compare Int]** object is used to look at these numbers and then play either stinger 1 (if bar 1 is currently playing) or stinger 2 (if bar 1 is currently not playing).

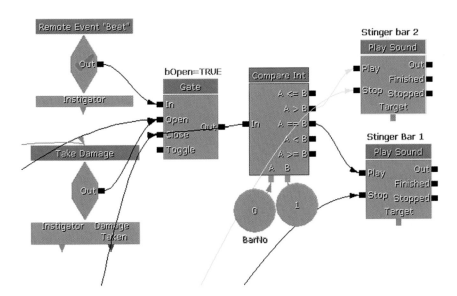

You can see how this system could be extended and developed significantly so that we could have both harmonically variable music and stingers that fit with what's currently playing. It would be even better if the system could transpose the stingers to play at a pitch appropriate to the current harmony. This would be trivial to do if we were using MIDI, and in theory this would be possible in

UDK if one were to calculate the relationship between the pitch multiplier and "real pitch" (see the earlier Mario example if you really want to know.). Of course, the problem would be that the playback speed would also be altered.

Stingers have a role to play in highlighting game actions through musical motifs. However, when a significant change in musical state is required, we still need to tackle the issue of how we move from the piece of music that is playing now to the piece of music we want. This is referred to as the Transition Problem.

Transitional Forms/Horizontal Switching

Clunky Switching

Location-Based Switching

> If you have different music for the different locations in your game, the issue is how you transition between them. The problem for the music is that the player may move between these locations at any given time and not necessarily at a nice "musical" moment like the end of a bar or even on a beat. This can upset the musical flow when you have to suddenly switch from one track to another. We call this "clunky" switching.

404 Music Switch

The idea of having different pieces of music playing in different game locations is common in genres such as MMOs (Massively Multiplayer Online game). The system in Room 404 represents the simplest (and most musically clumsy) way to implement this feature.

The floor tiles mark out two different locations in your game, and each has a **[Trigger]** to start the music for its particular location. (Obviously this would be happening over a much larger area in a game, but the principle still applies.) When each one is touched it simply plays the music cue through the **[PlaySound]** object and switches the other piece of music off.

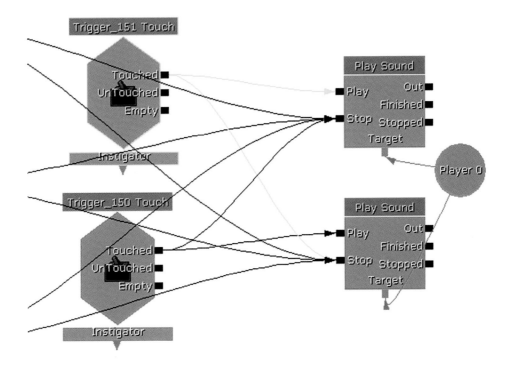

This fails to take account of where we might be in musical terms within piece A or whether it's an appropriate place to transition to the beginning of piece B (they may even be in completely different keys). Any of the three scenarios (and more) at the bottom of the image below are possible.

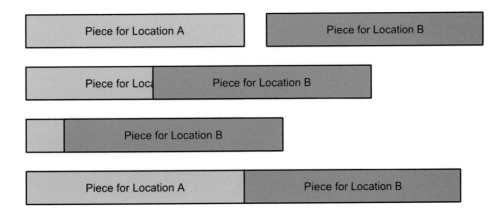

These fairly brutal music transitions to the start of piece B are pretty clunky.

Gameplay-Based Switching

Like a change in location, gameplay events can also occur at any given time (not always musically appropriate ones). You want the music to change instantly to reflect the action, but the transition between the piece already playing and the new piece can be clunky.

404a Spotted

As you cross this room you are inevitably spotted by a bot. Fortunately, you can run behind the wall and hide from his attack. By an even happier coincidence, you notice that you are standing next to an electricity switch, and this happens to lead (via a smoldering wire) to the metal plate that the bot is standing on (what are the chances, eh?). Flick the switch (use the E key) to smoke him.

On entrance to the room a **[TriggerVolume]** is touched and triggers the initial ambient musical piece via a **[PlaySound]** object. (In case you show mercy and leave the room without killing the bot, there are also a couple of **[TriggerVolume]**s to switch off the music.)

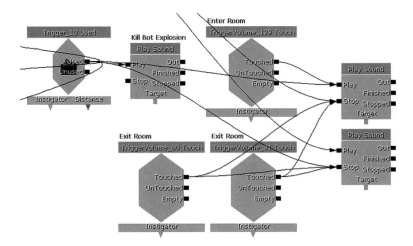

A bot is spawned in the room, and when the player falls within the bot's line of sight, a **[See Enemy]** event stops the music and starts the other **[PlaySound]** object which contains a more aggressive intense "combat" piece.

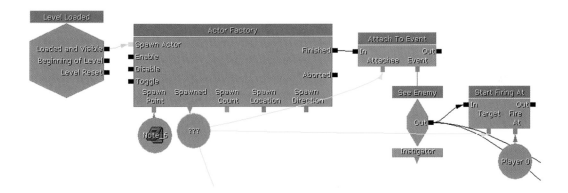

Although the inputs may be different (a game event rather than a change in location), you can see that this is effectively exactly the same system as the location based switching above and shares the same problem in that the musical transition is less than satisfying. In some circumstances this sudden "unmusical" transition can work well, as it contains an element of shock value. In others (most), we need to develop more sophistication.

Smoke and Mirrors

Simple swapping between two pieces of music dependent on either the location of the game or the current situation can sound clumsy. Masking the transition between the two musical states with a sound effect, so you don't hear the "join," can be surprisingly effective.

404b Smoke and Mirrors

Using a piece of dialogue, an alarm sound (or, as in this case, an explosion) to "mask" the transition between two pieces of music can mean that you can get away with simple switching without drawing attention to the clunky nature of the transition.

When you enter this room you'll notice that the door locks behind you. You get a message that states, "They're coming through the door; get ready." The tension music starts. The other door glows and gets brighter until Bang! The action music kicks in as bots come streaming through the hole.

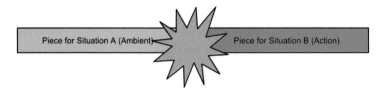

After the door closes, a **[Delay]** is set while the particle emitters build in intensity. When the **[Delay]** ends and the **[Matinee]** blows the door open, a loud explosion sound is heard, and the second music track is triggered. "Ducking" the currently playing music (lowering its volume temporarily) below a piece of important dialogue can also be useful in masking the transitions between your musical cues. We'll discuss ducking in more detail in Chapter 6.

Better Switching: Crossfades

> Rather than simply switching one track off and another track on, a short crossfade to transition between them can work. This method works best when the music is written in a fairly flexible musical language without strong directional melodies or phrases.

405 Music Crossfade

In this room there are four musical states. Enter the room and wander around before succumbing to temptation and picking up the 'jewel' (press E). This launches a trap. Now try and make it to the end of the room without getting killed.

Now restart the level, and this time allow yourself to be killed to hear how the music system reacts in a different way. (We're using the "Feign death" console command here to "kill" the player because a real death would require the level to be restarted. When you "die," simply press "fire" [left mouse button] to come back to life.)

The tracks are as follows:

> *Ambient.* For when the player is just exploring.
> *Action.* In this case, triggered when you "pick up" (use) the jewel.
> *Triumph.* If you then make it to the end through the spears.
> *Death.* If you allow the spears to kill you.

This works better than the location based or instant switching examples partly because we are now using a short crossfade between the cues and partly because the musical language here is more flexible. Writing in a musical style that is heavily rhythm based or music that has a strong sense of direction or arc can be problematic in games, as the player has the ability to undermine this at any time.

As you enter the room, the first **[TriggerVolume]** plays the "Ambient" **[SoundCue]**. When you *use* the jewel on the plinth to pick it up (okay, we know it's a HealthPack, but use your imagination), this first **[SoundCue]** is stopped and the "Action" **[SoundCue]** is started. In the **[PlaySound]** object, the fade out time of the "Ambient" **[SoundCue]** is set to 1.5 seconds, and the fade in time of the "Action" **[SoundCue]** is set to the same, allowing these to crossfade for the transition between these two cues.

If the player is hit by any of the spears flying across the room (the **[InterpActor]**s Hit Actor event), then an impact sound is played, the "Action" is stopped (the fade out time is one second) and the "Death" **[PlaySound]** comes in (the fade in time is one second). Likewise if the player reaches the end then the **[TriggerVolume]** in this area will stop the "Action" (the fade out time is one second) and play the "Triumph" **[SoundCue]** (the fade in time is one second).

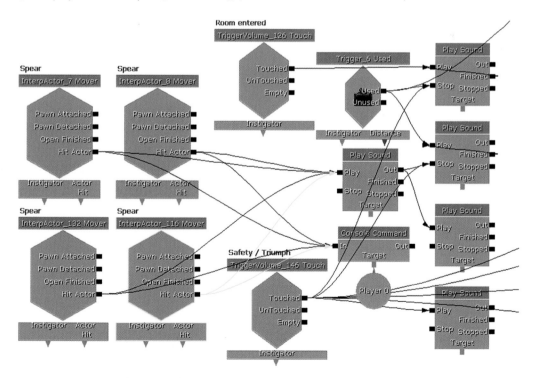

189

If you play the room through several times, you'll see that the player could spend much longer exploring the room before picking up the jewel (in which case the transition to "Action" would be from a different part of the "Ambient" music) or remain on "Action" for some time while carefully navigating the spears. Or else the player could run just through the whole thing. For example, the music could be required to transition at any following points.

Or a different player with a different approach might result in this:

The more impulsive player might even get this:

When combined with the right musical language and the occasional masked transition, the use of simple crossfades can be quite effective.

Exercise 405_00 Music Crossfade on [Trigger]

In the center of this room is a valuable diamond (seem familiar?). Start the level with "Ambient" music, which then switches to "Action" if the player goes near the diamond. If the player defeats the bot that appears, play a "Triumph" track, if the player is killed, play a "Death" track.

Tips

1. In the Kismet setup there are four **[PlaySound]** objects. Add appropriate **[SoundCue]**s for "Ambient," " Action," "Triumph," and "PlayerDeath" tracks.
2. For each **[Playsound]** object, set an appropriate Fade in/Fade out length.
3. Use the game events as commented in the given Kismet system to play the appropriate **[PlaySound]** object and to stop the others.
4. After "Triumph" has finished, you may want to go back to the "Ambient" track. Take a message from its finished output to play the "Ambient" **[PlaySound]**.

UDK's (Legacy) Music System

You may be wondering by now why we have been using the **[PlaySound]** object within Kismet rather than what appears to be more appropriate, the **[Play Music Track]**. The reason is that this offers little in terms of functionality and much that is broken or illogical as part of Unreal's legacy music system.

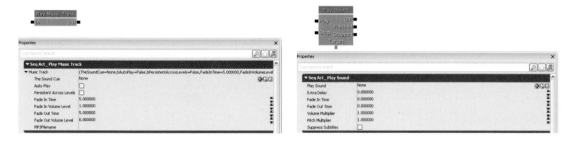

The **[Play Music Track]** will allow you to fade your music in up to a given volume level, but this could be set in your **[SoundCue]** anyway. It then appears to offer the ability to fade back down to a given level, which could be useful for dropping the music down to a background bed, for example. However, the problem is that unlike the Fade Out features of the **[PlaySound]**, which is triggered when the **[PlaySound]** is stopped, there is no apparent way of triggering a **[Play Music Track]** to apply this Fade Out feature, nor indeed is there any way of stopping a **[Play Music Track]** once it has been started. If you want one piece of music to play throughout your level irrespective of where in the level the character is or what situation the character is facing, then this could be a useful object for you. If that is your approach to music for games, then go back to the bookstore right now and try and get your money back for this book. (Once you've done that, you can go and crawl back under your rock.)

If you've been playing some of the Unreal Tournament 3 maps that come with UDK (C:\UDK\ UDK(***)\UDKGame\Content\Maps), then you will have noticed that there appears to be an interactive music system at work. In the UDKGame/Content/Sounds/Music folder you can see these music tracks grouped into Segments and Stingers. You can also see a package called Music Arrangements. Open up the properties of one of these by double-clicking on it.

These arrangements govern how music used to work in UT3. If you open the map VCTF-Necropolis from the UDK maps folder and select World Properties from the top View menu, you can see that it was possible to assign one of these arrangements to your map.

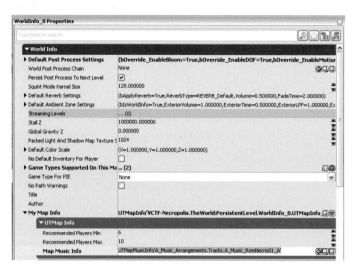

You'll also note that although you can create a new **[UDKMapMusicInfo]** item within UDK that appears to be the equivalent of these **[Arrangement]** objects, you cannot actually add these to a new UDK map because this functionality has been removed.

The music in these items is triggered by game events and allows some musical transitions by allowing you to specify the tempo and the number of measures/bars over which the music will transition between states. Although this might be potentially effective for certain styles of music, it is not working and so we won't dwell on it anymore here.

(If you want to try it out, you can replace the map music info in one of the UDK example maps with your own by copying one of the existing **[Arrangements]** files. Using a new **[UDKMapMusicInfo]** will not work.)

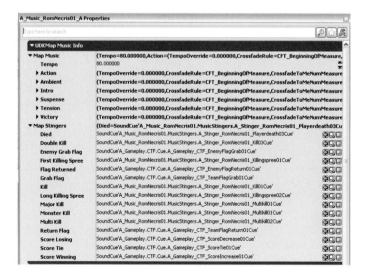

Maintaining Musical Structures: Horizontal Transitions

Write in Chunks

> Although musical crossfades can be effective, they are never going to be totally satisfactory from a musical point of view, and if it doesn't work musically, it's less effective emotionally. If we write our music in relatively short blocks and only allow the transitions to be triggered at the end of these blocks, then we can react relatively quickly to game events while maintaining a musical continuity.

406 Searchlight Chunks

If the cameras in this room spot you, then you must hide behind the wall. The guards will quickly forget about you and the music will return to its more ambient state.

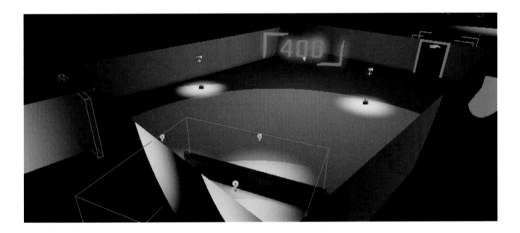

As in Room 402, a **[Trigger_Dynamic]** is attached to the search light (at a Z offset so that it is on the ground), and when this is touched it changes the music to the "Action" track. When you go behind the wall, the **[TriggerVolume]** starts a five-second delay before switching back the "Ambient" track. (The guards have a very short attention span; we blame Facebook).

Using a simple system, this effect could be achieved with the following steps. As the player enters the room, there is no music. When the **[Trigger_Dynamic]** (attached to the spotlights) hits the player, the first track is played and its gate is closed so it does not retrigger. At the same time, this action also opens the second gate so that when the player hides behind the wall and comes into contact with the **[TriggerVolume]**, this is allowed to go through and adjust the switch to play the second track.

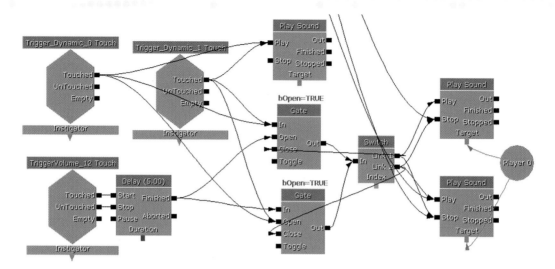

However, now we want to improve the system by only allowing changes at musical points. Out of these tracks only the "Ambient" track is able to be interrupted unmusically. We allow this because we want the music to react instantly when the player is spotted by the searchlight.

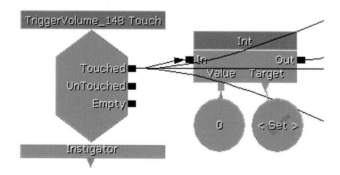

On entrance to the room, a **[TriggerVolume]** triggers a **[Set Variable]** Action to set the variable named 'Set' to zero.

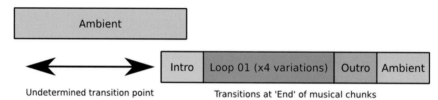

This action triggers a **[Compare Int]** object, which compares the number 1 with the variable 'Set'. In this case, input A is greater than B, so the result comes out of A > B and triggers the **[PlaySound]** for the "Ambient" track.

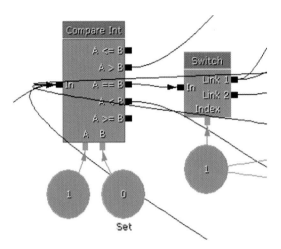

The room entry **[TriggerVolume]** also opens the **[Gate]** so that when the **[Trigger_Dynamic]** (searchlight triggers) are touched they can go through and change the variable 'set' to 1. The **[Gate]** then closes itself to avoid retriggering.

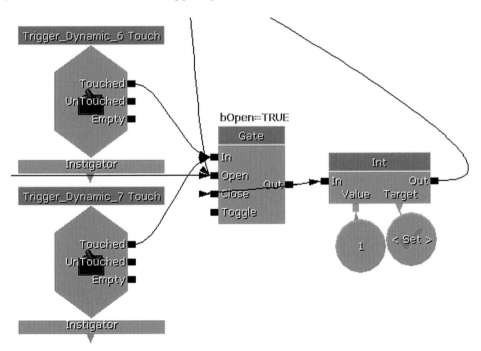

When the **[Trigger_Dynamic]**s (searchlight) have been touched, the variable 'Set' is the same as input A of the **[Compare Int]**, so a trigger comes from the == output into the **[Switch]**. This initially goes through output 1, plays the "Intro," then plays the "Action" track. When the "Action"

track is finished, it sets the switch to go to output 2. That means that when the signal comes through the **[Compare Int]** again (assuming nothing has changed and we're still in the "Action" state), the trigger will go straight to play the "Action" cue again instead of playing the "Intro." Although the **[SoundCue]** does not have a **[Looping]** object in it, this system effectively "loops" the "Action" cue until the circumstances change.

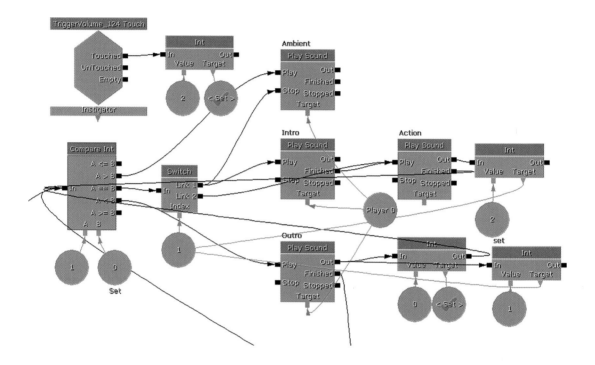

When players hide behind the wall, they come into contact with another **[TriggerVolume]**, which now changes the variable 'Set' to 2, causing an output from A < B. This plays the "Outro," resets the 'Set' variable to zero, and resets the **[Switch]** to 1 (so on the next switch to "Action" it will play the "Intro" first). "Outro" then opens the **[Gate]** for the **[Trigger_Dynamic]**s. (This will make more sense by examining the system in the tutorial level. Honest.)

The key to this system is that triggers are only entering the **[Compare Int]** object when each track has come to its end using the **[PlaySound]**'s Finished output (with the exception of the move from "Ambient" to "Action" already discussed). This means that the changes will happen at musical points. You could put any music into this system with chunks of any length and it would work because it's using the length of the pieces themselves as triggers. A typical use of this sort of system would be to check whether the player was still in combat. The "Action" cue keeps going back through the **[Compare Int]** object to check that the variable has not changed (i.e., we're still in combat). If you anticipated being in this state for a significant length of time, you could build in variation to the "Action" **[Soundcue]** so that it sometimes plays alternate versions.

Exercise 406_00 Chunk

Adapt the system you used for 404, but this time instead of crossfading, choose music that would suit switching at the end of the bar. Again there is to be an "Ambient" track on level start, an "Action" track when the diamond is approached, and "Death" or "Triumph" tracks.

Tips

1. The system is illustrated with triggers below, but you should connect up the appropriate game events as described in the comments of the exercise.
2. As the "Ambient" finishes it goes back around through the **[Gate]** and starts again (as long as the gate remains open). It also goes to all the other **[Gate]**s so that if the situation has changed and one of them has opened then the new **[SoundCue]** will be triggered at this time (i.e., at the end of the ambient cue).

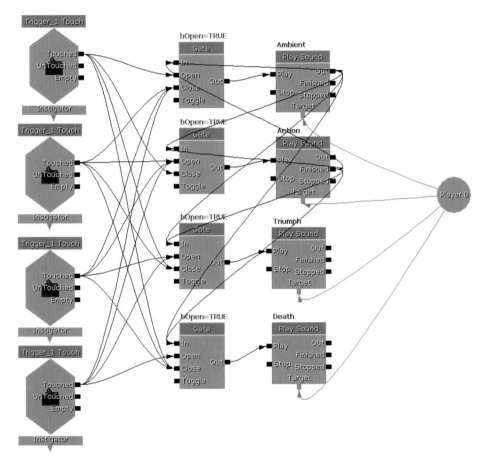

3. The "Action" does a similar thing so that it is relooped while "Action" is taking place. The "Death" and "Triumph" **[PlaySound]**s simply play and then stop, as they are a natural end to the music. When the "Action" is triggered it should open the **[Gate]** to the "Action" cue and close all the others.
4. Each **[PlaySound]** is triggered by the Finished output of another. In this way, the end and the start of each are correctly synchronized (presuming your tracks are properly edited).

Transitions and Transition Matrices

If you consider the range of musical states you might want for a typical game scenario, you can quickly see the challenges that face the composer in this medium. Let's take a relatively straightforward example based in one general location at a particular time of day (you may wish to have different sets of pieces dependent on these variables, but we'll leave this additional complexity to one side for now).

"Stealth 01", "Stealth 02":

Two stealth cues of slightly different intensities.

"Action 01", "Action 02":

Two action cues, one for the normal guard combat, one for the boss combat.

"Action 02a":

One additional action intensity for the boss combat (when the boss's health gets low).

"Death":

The player dies.

"End":

The player defeats the guards.

"Triumph":

The player defeats the boss.

"Bored":

If the player loiters on stealth for too long switch the music off.

"Stingers":

The player lands a blow on the boss.

If we discount the "Stingers," "Death" and "Bored" (because they don't transition to any other cue), then we have seven musical cues. If we allow for a game state where it might be necessary to transition between any of these to any other, then there are 127 different possible transitions. Of course, not all of these would make sense (e.g. "Stealth 01" should not be able to transition straight to "End" as there would have been some combat "Action" in between), but nevertheless writing music that allows for this kind of flexibility requires a different mindset from composing traditional linear scores. Before beginning, the composer needs to consider which pieces will need to be able to link to which other pieces, and the ways in which you want to handle each of these transitions. This is sometimes referred to as a *branching* approach to interactive music because it can be reminiscent of a tree-like structure. At the planning stage, a flow diagram such as the one that follows can be useful.

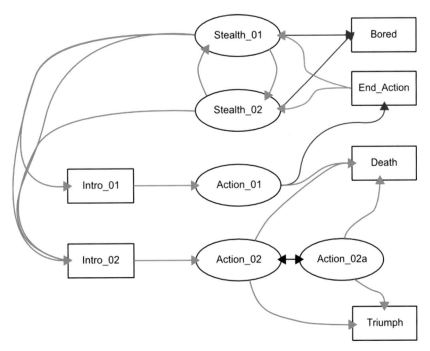

Next you need to decide on the best way for each of these cues to transition between one another.

Transition Times/Switch Points

There are, of course, a variety of ways to move from one piece of music to another, some more musical than others. You need to make a choice that is preferably reactive enough to the gameplay to fulfill its function while at the same time maintaining some kind of musical continuity. Here are some illustrations of the types of transition you may want to consider.

The arrow indicates the time at which the transition is called by the game.

Immediate
This immediately stops the current cue and plays the new cue from its beginning.

Crossfade
This transition fades out the current cue and fades in the new cue.

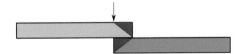

At End

This transition waits until the end of the currently playing cue to switch to the new cue.

At Measure

This transition starts the new cue (and silences the old one) at the next measure (bar) boundary.

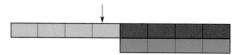

At Beat

This transition plays the new cue at the next musical beat of the currently playing cue.

At Beat Aligned

This transitions at the next beat, but to the same position in the new cue, rather than the start of the new cue—that is, we exit cue A at beat 2, and we enter cue B also at its beat 2. More about this later.

Transition Cues

Often it is not satisfactory to simply move from one cue to another. You may need a "transition cue" to smooth the path between the two main cues. This is a specific cue whose role is to help the music move from one cue to another; of course, these cues can begin at any of the transition times described earlier.

A transition cue might take the form of an "End" to the current cue before starting the new one, on an "Intro" to the new cue (or a combination of both of these options (e.g., Cue 1/EndCue1/IntroCue2/Cue2).

Here is the transition cue leading from "Main Cue 01" to "Main Cue 02":

Here are the transition cues leading from "Main Cue 01" to "End" to "Intro" to "Main Cue 02":

A transition cue will normally ease the shift in intensities by leading down, building up, or managing a change in the tempo between the old and the new. It might also act as a "stinger" (! - see image) to highlight an action before then leading into the new cue.

A Transition Matrix

A table like the one shown here is useful for considering these kinds of systems. There is a blank template version for your own music available to download from the website. This defines which cues can move to which other cues and the transition time at which they can move. In this example, you can see that the "Intro_01"/"Intro_02" and "End_01"/"End_02" cues serve as transition cues between the main pieces.

	Stealth_01	Stealth_02	Intro_01	Intro_02	Action_01	Action_02	Action_02a	End_01	Death	Triumph	Bored	Stingers
Stealth_01		Bar/Measure	Beat	Beat	Beat via Intro_01						Bar/Measure	Immediate
Stealth_02	Beat		Beat	Beat	Beat via Intro_01	Beat via Intro_02					Bar/Measure	Immediate
Intro_01					At End							Immediate
Intro_02						At End						Immediate
Action_01	Bar via End_Action	Bar via End_Action						Bar/Measure	Beat	Beat		Immediate
Action_02							Bar/Measure	Bar/Measure	Beat	Beat		Immediate
Action_02a						Bar/Measure			Beat	Beat		Immediate
End_01	At End	At End										Immediate
Death												Immediate
Triumph												Immediate
Bored												Immediate
Stingers												

Reading from left to right:

> When moving from "Stealth_01" to "Stealth_02" the system should do it at the next measure.
> When moving from "Stealth_01" to "Action_01" you should do it at the next available beat via the transition cue "Intro_01."
> When moving from "Action_01" back to "Stealth_01" or "Stealth_02" do it at the next available bar/measure using the "Action_End" cue to transition.

Although this might seem like a slightly academic exercise when you sit down to compose, the time you spend now to work these things out will save you a lot of pain later.

407 Transitions

This series of rooms contains a "stealth" type scenario to illustrate a system of music transitions.

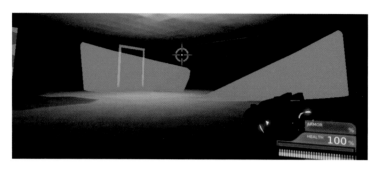

Because the system is reasonably complex, we'll present it in both narrative and diagrammatic forms.

First, here's the story of 407. Upon entering the first room, the "Stealth 01" cue begins. The player must avoid the security cameras to get to the next room undetected. If the player is detected, then "Intro 01" leads to "Action 01" as a bot appears and they do battle. When the enemy is defeated, the cue "End 01" leads back into "Stealth 01."

In Room 02 the situation gets slightly more tense, so we switch to "Stealth 02" (a slight variation of "Stealth 01"). Here the player needs to get the timing right to pass through the lasers. If these are triggered, then again "Intro 01" leads to "Action 01" for a bot battle. This time a different end cue is used, "End 02", as we're not going back to "Stealth 01" but returning to "Stealth 02."

The player needs the documents contained in the safe, so there's nothing to do but to open the safe and be prepared for the boss battle that follows. The music in the room, initially remaining on "Stealth 02," switches on the boss's appearance to "Intro 02" to lead to "Action 02." During the battle when the enemy's health gets low, the music goes up in intensity to "Action 02a" and there's also the occasional "Stinger." Defeating this boss leads to the final "Triumph" cue.

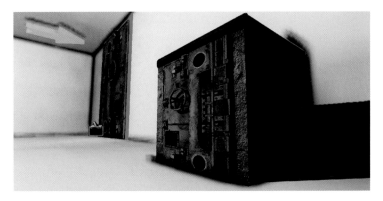

In all the rooms, another two cues are available: "Death" if the player is defeated by the enemy at any time, and "Bored."

The "Bored" Switch

"Bored" is a version of "Stealth 01" that has a fade to silence. Part of music's power is to indicate that what is happening now is somehow of special significance or importance. If we have music playing all the time, it can lose its impact (and make your system look stupid). It's useful to always have a "bored" switch (™ Marty O'Donnell;), so if the player remains in one musical state for an unnaturally long period, the music will fade out.

The diagram shown here also represents this music system.

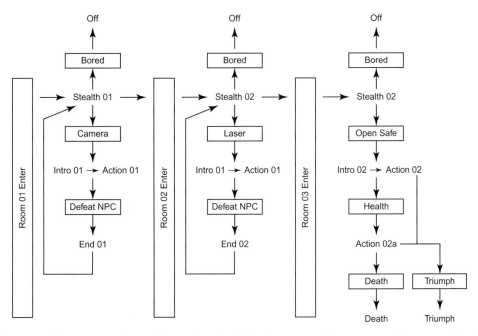

(For the gameplay systems themselves, take a look in the room subsequences. These are simple systems based on triggers, dynamic (moving) triggers, bot spawning, bot take damage, and bot death.)

Here is a screen shot for the implementation. Sadly this is our idea of fun.

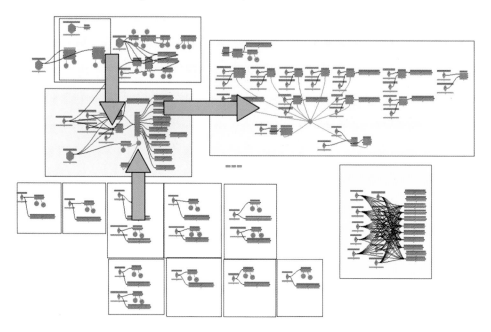

First a pulse is established that matches the tempo of the music. From this we get two outputs via **[Activate Remote Event]**s: the beat (407 Beat) and another signal on the first beat of a four-beat bar/measure (407 Measure). These will allow us to control transitions so that they occur on either the musical beat or Bar/Measure line.

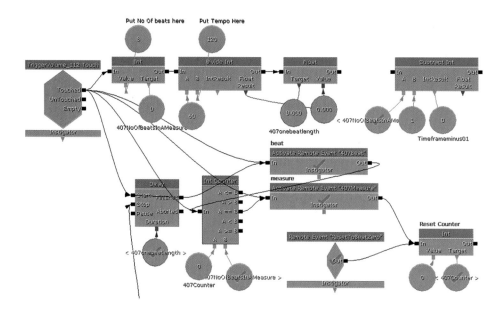

Both these are received via **[Remote Events]** at our main switching system. (You can double-click on a **[Remote Event]** to see the **[Activate Remote Event]** that it relates to.)

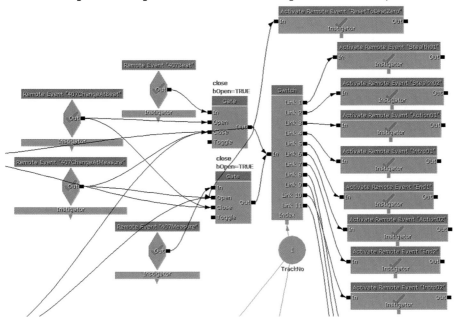

This switching system receives a message from a game event, which comprises two parts:

Which track should I play?
> (**Named Variable** "Track No")

When should I switch to it?
> (**[Remote Event]**s "407ChangeAtBeat"/"407ChangeAtMeasure")

On receipt of this message the *track number* goes straight to the **[Switch]** and changes its index so that the next message received by the **[Switch]** will go out of the appropriate *link number* of the **[Switch]**. You can see that these then go to further **[Remote Event]** objects, which then go to actually play the music when received by the **[PlaySound]** objects.

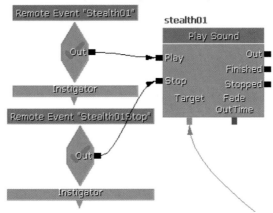

This message will only be sent out of the **[Switch]**'s link when the **[Switch]** receives an input, and this is governed by the second message that determines whether this will be at the next beat or the next bar/measure. Both impulses are connected to the **[Switch]** via a **[Gate],** and the choice of transition type (407ChangeAtBeat or 407ChangeAtMeasure) determines which pulse goes through by opening/closing their respective **[Gate]**s. (When a ChangeAtBeat message goes through to the switch, the **[Int Counter]** that counts the length of a measure is also reset so that the next measure is counted starting again at beat 1.)

How these transitions occur is under the composer's control; all the game designer needs to do is to call one of the remote events named T0 to T9 (Trigger 0 to 9). You can then set these up to call a particular music cue, at a designated time.

Which track should I play?
    (**Named Variable** "Track No")
When should I switch to it?
    (**[Remote Event]**s "407ChangeAtBeat"/"407ChangeAtMeasure")

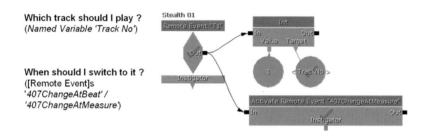

At the moment they are set to do the following:

T0: Play "Intro 02" at next beat // Then play "Action 02"
T1: Play "Stealth 01" at next bar/measure
T2: Play "Intro 01" at next beat // Then play "Action 01"
T3: Play "End 01" at next bar/measure // Then play "Stealth 01"
T4: Play "Stealth 02" at next measure
T5: Play "End 02" at next bar/measure // Then play "Stealth 02"
T6: Play "Stinger" (this plays over the top and therefore operates outside of the usual switching system)
T7: Play "Triumph" at next bar/measure (this then stops the system)
T8: Play "Death" at next beat (this then stops the system)
T9: Play "Action 02a" at next bar/measure.

You will notice that many of these actually trigger two changes. In these cases, the second part of the system receives a **[Remote Event]** when the first music cue has finished playing.

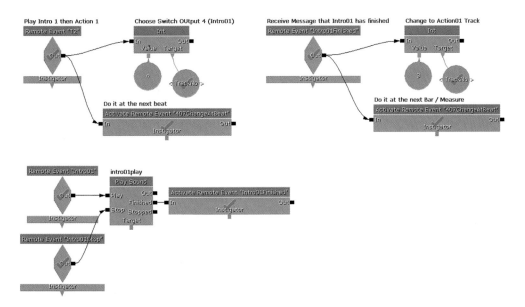

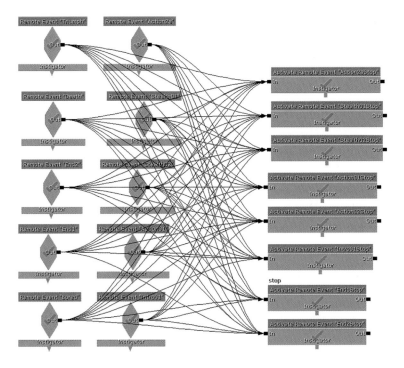

Finally (you'll be relieved to hear) we have what's known in Yorkshire as a "Belt and Braces" system to stop all the cues apart from the one that is currently supposed to be playing—just in case. (We also did this because it makes a pretty pattern.)

As you can see, setting up a system for musical transitions is not trivial, but once you've got your head around the system here you can adapt it for your needs.

Postscript: The Bored Switch

When a "Stealth" track is triggered, a **[Delay]** starts (how long to give it before you get bored and fade out the music). If this time passes then we change at measure to a new track (track 7). This triggers the **[Remote Event]** "Bored," which comes back and starts a **[PlaySound]**. This **[PlaySound]** is actually playing the "Stealth 01" cue again, but this time it has had a fade out applied. It also closes the **[Gate]** so that it only plays once before ending. The music will not start again until there is a change in state that flicks the playback switch to a different track.

Exercise 407_00 Transitory

This exercise contains a copy of the game level and music transitions system from Area 407 of the tutorial level. Use some of your own music to experiment with the transition systems.

Tips

1. Try to understand what the hell is going on.
2. Add you own music cues to the existing **[PlaySound]** objects.
3. Within the pulse creation section, make sure you adjust the tempo and number of beats in a measure variables to match your music.
4. Try creating your own triggers that call a designated track at either the next beat or the measure/bar.

Switch Points: Marking Up Existing Tracks

A few games have attempted to use commercial tracks interactively in games, with some success. One approach has been to apply DSP effects to the track. For example, in a racing game when the player performs a jump, apply a low-pass filter to the music while the player-character is in the air. When the player gets a speed boost, play the track back faster by pitching it up, or apply a filter to temporarily boost the bass frequencies.

Another approach would be to identify parts of the track/song that have different intensities and note the possible in and out points. Moving to different parts of the track in response to game events can work if the track's possible transition points (or switch points) are carefully (and musically) identified.

'Banging Track no. 87'

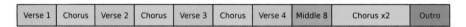

| Verse 1 | Chorus | Verse 2 | Chorus | Verse 3 | Chorus | Verse 4 | Middle 8 | Chorus x2 | Outro |

Having identified which sections are of what intensity, the programmer can then call these particular sections at relevant times using transition points on bar/measure boundaries.

If the track is at a consistent tempo, then you should be able to calculate these points easily and either supply the timings to your programmer or slice up the track in your digital audio workstation (DAW). (See the downloadable spreadsheet file "Markup" on the website.)

For example, Tempo = 120, 4 beats per bar.

	Time per Beat (Seconds)	Time per 4 beat bar / Measure	First Beat of Bar No	Time first beat of Bar / Measure No
	0.5	2	1	0.00
		2	2	2.00
		2	3	4.00
		2	4	6.00
		2	5	8.00
		2	6	10.00
		2	7	12.00
		2	8	14.00
		2	9	16.00
		2	10	18.00
		2	11	20.00
		2	12	22.00
		2	13	24.00
		2	14	26.00
		2	15	28.00
		2	16	30.00

Your DAW will have a Bars and Beats option for its timeline where you can see these timings, and some will also have the functionality to set markers at the beat or bar lines automatically.

Many audio editors have the ability to store extra information in the wav file, which contains a header with non-audio information known as metadata. Using metadata to hold your markers is better than chopping up the wav itself, as your programmer can call these but will also have the original sound file in order to enable a short volume envelope to fade the music out. This can avoid the kind of clicks you will otherwise get from editing music at arbitrary points in the Wav file (see Appendix D). Methods for marking up users' music tracks with data automatically are already available, and this is likely to be an area of growth in game audio research. Many games already enable or encourage players to use their own music within the game, but the potential to make this music interactive using embedded metadata about the track itself has yet to be fully exploited.

You'll be aware that musical sounds are no respecters of bar lines, and the "Decay" of a note will often fall across where you are likely to edit. This is known as the "decay problem."

The Problem of Decay

Although a few styles of music can work well when split into "chunks," for interactive use most have instances where the tails of notes, or the decay of the reverb, falls across the bar line and into the next bar. If we chop our music up at bar line points, then we won't hear these decays and the music will sound unnatural.

408 Decay

We've seen how a matrix of transitions between pieces can be musically challenging, but there's an additional technical challenge that we also need to consider. The following four-bar/measure loop might be our music for a "Stealth" sequence. We want to export it from our sequencer and use it in the game initially as a loop. In our sequencer it sounds fine, but when exporting it as a wav file it suddenly sounds unnatural. In Room 408, use button 01 to hear this version.

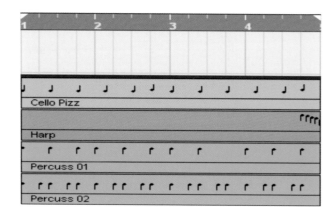

As you can see, the harp has a short descending motif just before the loop point. In our sequencer this sounds okay because the sample-based instrument allows these notes to decay naturally even though the sequence has returned to the start of the loop. However, when exporting, the decay of these notes is not preserved as they fall outside of the fourth bar.

By selecting a section to export that's longer than the actual MIDI files, you can see that there is a significant decay to the sound. Within your sequencer you will continue to hear this as the pattern loops around to the start; by exporting the audio for just the loop, however, this is lost. In the selected area (white) you can see the natural decay of these notes. In the unselected area (black) is the actual exported wav file we get.

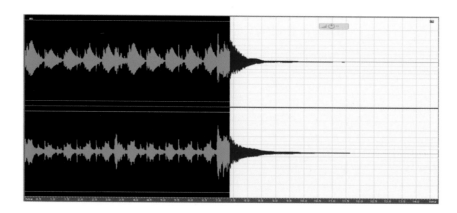

There are two approaches for preserving the decay for a looping sound, both of which have the same effect of mixing the decay of the end of the sample back into the start of the sample.

Copy and paste your sequence so that it is repeated and then export this to a new file.

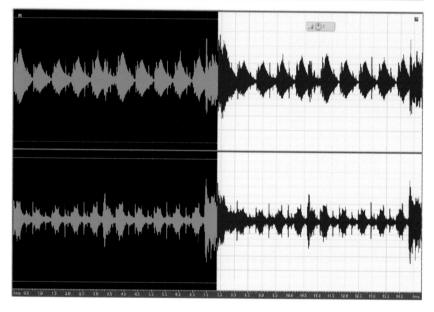

Selecting the second half of this wav file (divide the total length by 2 and start your selection at this point, then "Trim" to keep only your selection) will give you a version of your loop that includes the decay of the Harp notes. This means that when this is looped around it will now sound more natural because these are not cut off. Use the second button in the level to hear this version looping. The other method to achieve the same effect would be to export the original sequence, but with a few following empty bars included. Then you can select the decay portion and mix-paste (blend) it back into the start of the loop.

This is fine while it's looping, but you will have noticed that the first playing has decaying portions at the start (shown below in blue) of notes that have not actually been played yet.

The result, of course, is that you need both, either as separate files as shown here or the ability to select loop points within one file.

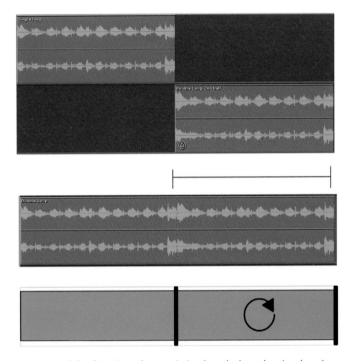

One version is used the first time the music is played; the other is a looping version.

These issues also apply to transitions, of course. Where one block of music switches to another the decay of the instruments from the first is lost. You can have a short crossfade so that some of the decay is there, but, of course, so are all the other notes. You might consider recording a separate decay sample for each of your blocks so that on transition this could be played to overlap with the new music.

This method is entirely possible although laborious. (Some sequencers have the ability to export with a "Capture effects tail" option that makes it slightly less tiresome). You'd also need to rework the previous transition systems to add this new decay sample of the previous piece to the first playing (and first playing only) of the new cue.

Here's a question we'll leave you to ponder until we return to the subject at the conclusion of this chapter: Have you ever tried getting a symphony orchestra to play in one bar's chunks so that you can get a natural decay for each musical block? Would you want to?

Parallel Forms/Vertical Layering

> By dividing the music into separate tracks or stems, we can keep the music aligned while at the same time mixing layers up and down to change the intensity.

We've looked at some of the issues and solutions to interactive music using a horizontal approach—that is, the transitioning between a series of tracks depending on the game state. Another approach is to consider that it might be possible to generate music for many of the circumstances you want by using the same piece of music. By exposing the different layers or tracks, we can bring them in and out of the mix to change the arrangement:

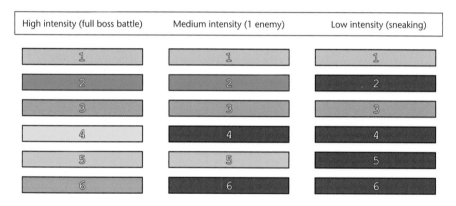

When tracks 1 through 6 are all playing, this could be your "very intense, many enemies, health low" musical state, whereas muting all the tracks except for track 1 might give you your "ambient sneaking" version.

The term "stems" is commonly used to describe these individual layers as these might consist of individual "tracks" in the sequencing/recording sense, or might be a group of tracks. The idea of stems is most commonly associated with film postproduction where a sound track might be grouped into the dialogue stem, the music stem, and the effects stem, although it's also used in music production to represent the output of a particular subgroup or bus.

Simple Mute/Unmute

409 Vertical Mix Tension Layers

Press the button to start the game. Objects appear in random places/at random times. You need to collect these to score points and get bonus time (the countdown started when you pressed the button). Some health packs have been damaged—picking these up will give you a time penalty.

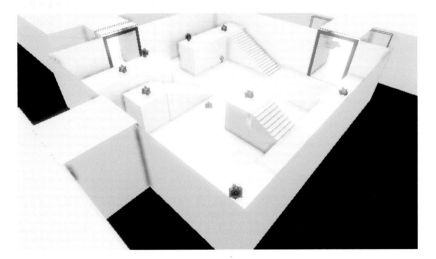

When the game is started by using the central **[Trigger]** all six **[PlaySound]** objects containing the six stems/layers are triggered. When the **[PlaySound]** object number 1 finishes, it retriggers itself and all the rest again. This ensures that they keep in time.

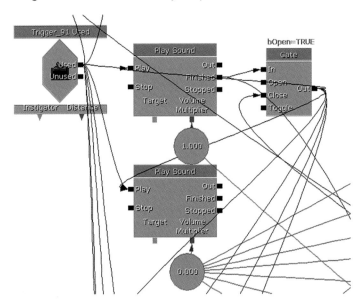

For the game aspect, a random **[Delay]** is triggered (sometime between zero and six seconds); when this is complete the first pickup is unhidden, and a **[Gate]** is opened allowing the invisible **[Trigger]** around the pickup to pass through. This now plays the pickup **[SoundCue]**, destroys the pickup **[InterpActor]**, and triggers an **[Announcement]** informing the player of the points just won. This then goes on to trigger the next randomized **[Delay]** to unhide the next pickup, open its **[Gate]**, and so on.

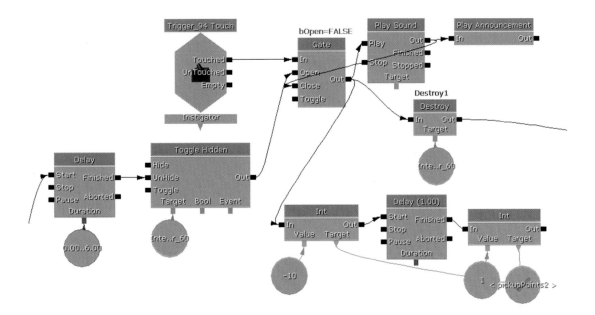

The timing system starts with an initial value of 60, from which the value 1 ('PickupPoints2' named variable) is subtracted every second by a **[Delay]**. (For more on named variables, see Appendix C: UDK Tips.)

While the announcement is made, a value is sent to the countdown clock depending on whether this was a "good" pickup or a "bad" pickup, adding a bonus of 10 seconds or subtracting a penalty of 10 seconds. To add/take away these values from the time remaining, a **[Set Variable]** is sent to alter the 'PickupPoints2' variable to +10 or −10, which is added to the current remaining time. This is then set back to 1 to continue incrementing the countdown in seconds.

As explained earlier, all the separate tracks that make up the full intensity arrangement are playing throughout. The Time Remain value is then used to mute or unmute certain stems in order to produce different versions of the full arrangement for our lower intensity levels. The relationship between the Time Remain variable and the music arrangement is outlined in the following diagram.

Time Remain = Less than or equal to 60 and more than or equal to 51

1
2
3
4
5
6

Time Remain ≤50 and ≥41

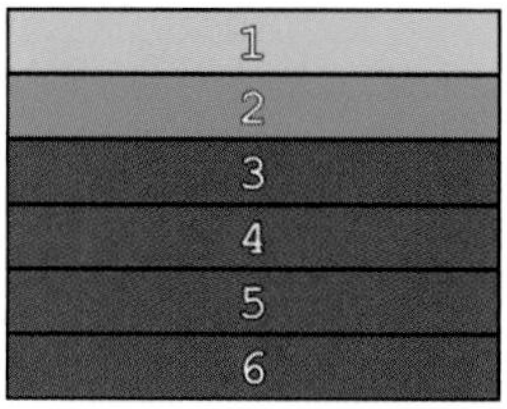

Time Remain ≤40 and ≥31

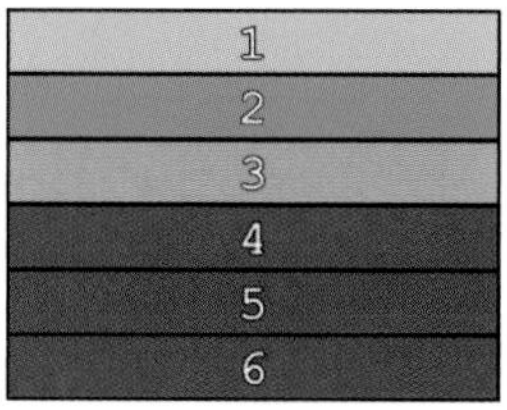

Time Remain ≤30 and ≥21

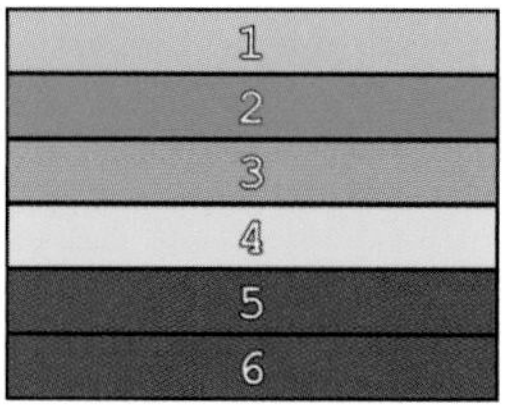

Time Remain ≤20 and ≥11

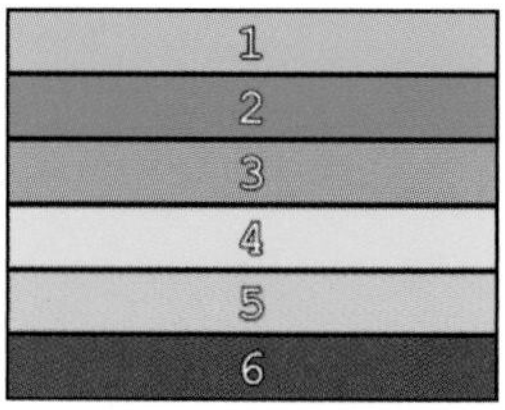

And when Time Remain ≤ seconds, all the tracks play for the arrangement of fullest intensity.

A series of subsequences compare the Time Remain variable with their settings; if it is within their range, then they unmute the appropriate track. For example, this sequence checks to see if the Time Remain variable is less than or equal to 60 (≤60) and more than or equal to 51 (≥51).

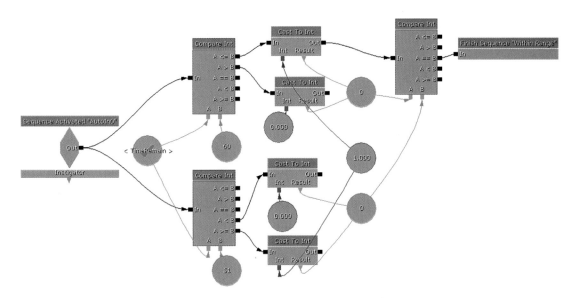

This result is checked by the **[Delay]** pulse (every second). In theory it shouldn't be a problem with the parts being unmuted at any given time as they are all aligned in time. If part 3 happens to be unmuted while we are three seconds into the music, it will be okay because you will hear part 3 at three seconds (which, of course, is written to fit with all the other parts at three seconds), not the start of part 3 as in previous systems. We could have several versions of each part for variety and a system that mutes and unmutes in the following ways and it would (theoretically) still function musically.

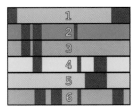

You may notice that in the UDK system although the numbers change and possibly unmute at second intervals the musical parts do not appear to actually change until they are retriggered. This is not a huge problem in this instance because the musical parts are short and therefore the system appears relatively responsive. However, if our parts were a minute long, we wouldn't actually hear the change in the arrangement until these were retriggered after 60 seconds.

Here's the problem. Although you have access to the Volume Multiplier variable of the **[PlaySound]** object, this is the volume set when it begins to play that sound. You cannot change the volume of a currently playing sound.

Exercise 409_00 Vertical Simple

The music should reflect the player's health as they navigate this maze. The maze includes electric shocks, falls, and debris landing on the player. (Unlike the end of a typical night out in Leeds that this is reminiscent of so far, the level also fortunately contains some health pickups).

Tips

1. Use three or more music layers that will come in/out depending on the players health. Set up three **[PlaySound]**s and use the first as the master timer that re-triggers them all so they are all constantly looping. There are several ways you could get the health variable to change the volume of the different **[PlaySound]**s in order to layer in parts for different intensities.
2. Try feeding the health variable into a number of **[Compare Int]** objects as value A, set value B to be the health value at which you want the new **[Playsound]** to start being heard (e.g. health = 90 for one **[PlaySound]** layer, health = 70 for another). When A is less than B in the Compare objects (triggered from the out of the **[Get Property]**) then send a **[Set float]** to alter the volume multiplier of the appropriate **[PlaySound]**.

Mixing Layers

409a Music Layers 01

You have to sneak up on the guards in this area and silently dispose of them (press E when close behind them).

In this example the music indicates proximity from the enemy. This might be useful in a stealth-based game. There are four music stems (in this case single tracks): "Sticks," "Shakers," "Bell"

and "Bass." The "Bass" and "Bell" tracks are mixed up or down in volume depending on the player's distance from the enemy, the idea being that the closer the player is to the enemy the more tense the music should be, and therefore we bring up the "Bass" and "Bell" elements to indicate this tension. In addition to the mixing of layers there's also a stinger element that plays when we get within a certain proximity of the bot, and another when you attack him.

Instead of simply switching tracks bluntly on or off at the end of each loop as we did earlier, we'd like to be able to have smooth transitions in volume to change the mix of the full arrangement in real time in response to gameplay variables. If you like, it's an analogue scale, using a range of numbers rather than a binary on/off switch system.

Binary

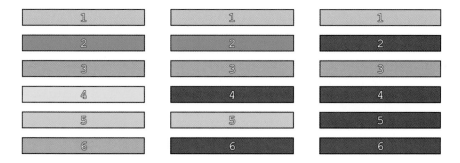

High intensity (full boss battle), Medium intensity (1 enemy), and Low intensity (sneaking)

Analogue

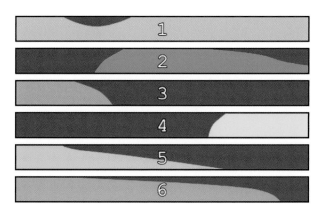

The **[TriggerVolume]** on entry to the room plays all the **[SoundCue]** layers, and they continue to loop (they have **[Loop]** nodes within their **[SoundCue]**s). When the bots are spawned, we get the distance between the player and the bot and do some maths on this number so that it falls into a more appropriate range of values to control the volume of our "Bass" and "Bell" stems.

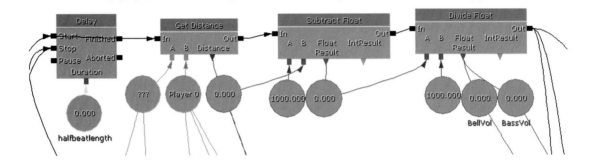

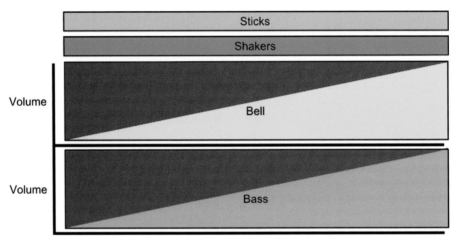

Distance from Enemy

This example is musically simple to illustrate the point, but we could have several stereo stems streamed from the disk simultaneously, and if they were all built over the same harmonic structure, we could dynamically mix them to produce different intensities through changes in the orchestration, texture, and instrumentation. You could say this was similar to the "Fatal Void" system (Room 402), but this time our music can be rhythmic and harmonic as long as the tracks are kept aligned in time.

The ability to control the volume of several separate music tracks that maintain their alignment in time is a fundamental requirement of interactive music. Because UDK's **[PlaySound]** object disappointingly does not allow us to change the volume of a sound while it's currently playing, we've had to make our own.

*Introducing the **[GATPlaySound]** object!*

This is a custom Kismet object and is found in (right-click) New Action/GATKismetActions/ GATPlaySound.

The **[GATPlaySound]** object allows you to select a **[SoundCue]** and control its volume. The volume level can be set by the fade level variable. Whenever a signal is received at the Trigger Fade input, the volume will go to this fade level over a time period designated by the Fade Time variable.

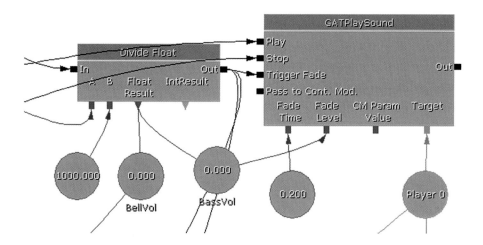

Here the output of the **[Get Distance]** object is then scaled and sent to the Fade Level (BassVol). Each time this value changes, the **[Divide Float]** object is also sending a signal to the Trigger Fade input to enact a volume change, which then occurs over 0.2 seconds.

In this case, the variable is the distance from the enemy, but it could be anything, such as the number of enemies in the area, the amount of ammo you have left, player health, player hunger, proximity to pizza....

409b Music Layers 02

This room switches to an imitation 2D platformer style level. You have to avoid the lasers and the falling crates to reach the end. The music uses a vertical layering system based on two variables; the player's distance from the objective **[Get Distance]**, and the player's health **[Get Property]**.

All the music **[SoundCue]**s are started by the **[Trigger]** on entry to the room. A **[Delay]** is polling the player's health every 0.1 seconds, and this is scaled by some maths to give an appropriate range for the volume of the "Health" cue. As we want this cue to increase in volume as the player's health declines, it is divided by 100, and the result is subtracted from 1.0. This has the effect of inverting the value (i.e., health high = volume low, health low = volume high.) The **[GATPlaySound]** object is used again here as it allows us to fade to these changing levels while the music is playing.

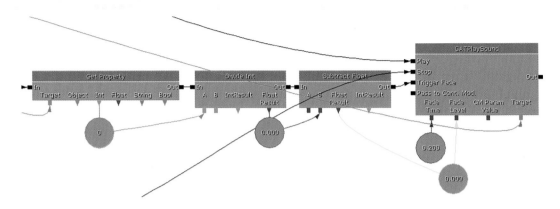

The second variable (the player's distance from the "end" objective) is also scaled and controls the volume of the three other music tracks. For these tracks we did not want a simple linear (or inverted linear) relationship between the variables' values and the volume of our cues, so we have extended the system to allow us to define different volume curves. A switch is set up and the scaled variable reads through the index of the switch and outputs the value attached to that link. In programming terms, this is the equivalent of reading through an array of numbers. Your programmer can get you access to UDK's distribution curves, which can perform a similar function, but for now we've chosen to make this system explicit so you can see what's going on and have easy access to the values yourself.

If we plot the array horizontally, it's clearer what this allows us to do. The Volume values are held in the **[Set Variable]** actions attached to each switch output link.

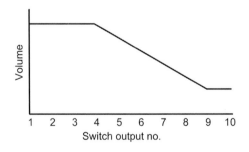

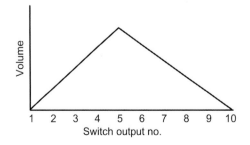

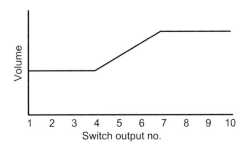

Having control over the relationship between the game variables and the volume of your stems is where the real power of a vertical layering approach lies.

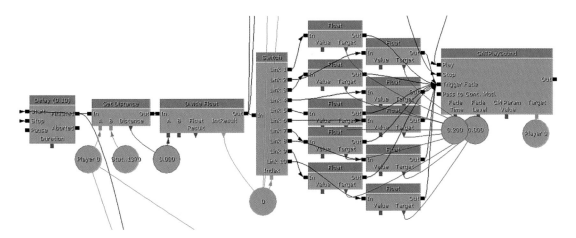

This idea is often more elegantly implemented and referred to as "Real Time Parameter Controllers" (RTPC's). Audio Middleware like FMOD and Wwise are very good at allowing you to tie in different volume curves for your music layers in response to the game variables in a much more composer-friendly way. Unfortunately, at the time of writing you need to already be working for a game developer to get hands-on with this middleware in conjunction with the Unreal engine. Until this is opened up to the audio community, you can have fun testing out these approaches with your music using the models we have provided here.

Exercise 409b Real-Time Volume Changes

This exercise has a simple boss battle. It's made slightly more interesting by the fact that the boss's health recharges over time, and there's the random appearance of health pickups for the player. Both the player health and boss health variables are already linked up to the indexes of some switches. Add your own music layers to this scenario and change the values with the **[Set Variable]** floats to try out ways in which your layers could vary in volume in response to these variables.

Tip

1. It may help to think of your switch variables array like this:

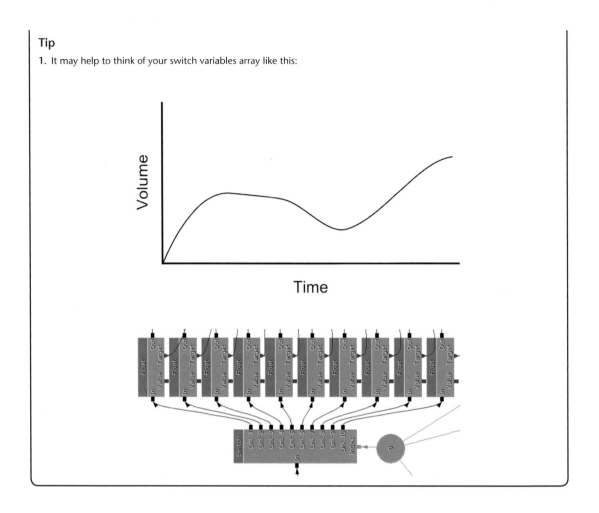

Leitmotifs and the Combinatorial Explosion

410 Leitmotifs

> One of the most powerful techniques from the world of film music is the idea of Leitmotifs. Originally inspired by techniques found in opera, a Leitmotif is a musical element (most typically a melody) that becomes associated with a particular character.

By associating a melody or motif with a character, we can be made aware of the character's presence (real or implied) and gain insight into how that character feels by the different ways in which the character's leitmotif is presented. A solo flute version of the motif might mean that the character is feeling lonely, whereas a version with blazing brass and drums might tell us that he or she is ready for a fight. (You can have leitmotifs for many other functions besides being attached to a character, but this is its most typical usage.)

In the context of film music where everything is predetermined in terms of time, this works well and is a powerful tool for the composer. For the game composer who wishes to utilize this technique, the problem of combinations arises. We've seen how the exponential growth of possible combinations can be a real help to us as audio designers for games as it can generate many new combinations from relatively few sources, but to understand why this is a problem when it comes to leitmotifs, consider the following game design brief for an MMO.

- Each location should have a particular musical style to define it. There are five locations.
- Each tribe in the game has its own associated melody (leitmotif) that you hear whenever that tribe is in your vicinity. There are five tribes.

With 10 variables this would, in theory, give us a potential of 1,023 possible combinations. However by using a similar idea to the vertical layering, we could write all of the leitmotifs so they fitted over the same harmonic structure. It might be difficult to avoid clashes in the melodies, but the goal is achievable (after all, Mozart seemed to manage it). The five locations could be defined through the instrumentation of the accompanying parts.

In Room 410 there is a gathering of creatures around a campfire. As each creature comes closer to the player, you can hear the creature's leitmotif join the music. Theoretically you could have the music for all the beasts start at the same time (on level startup) and be of the same length. You could then use the attenuation curves on the **[SoundCue]** so that the music is only heard when they get within a given radius of the player. The trouble is that if a player is outside of the max radius, the cue isn't actually played. This is, of course, completely logical. Why play something you can't hear? But it means that the cue will actually be started when the player enters the max radius, not in alignment with the other musical parts.

If we keep the parts aligned, our music should fit.

If we allow the leitmotifs to start at any time (i.e., they are not temporally aligned), then you will get the musical mess that follows. You do not need to be an advanced musician to know that this is not going to sound good.

You can see that this is the same problem we have faced earlier when composing layered music, so it follows that a potential solution would be the use of the **[GATPlaySound]** to synchronize all the musical parts but fade their volume up or down depending on the distance from the player.

On entry to the room, the "Harp" background music starts and loops. The bots that spawn in the area wander around at random time intervals, moving toward and away from the central fire.

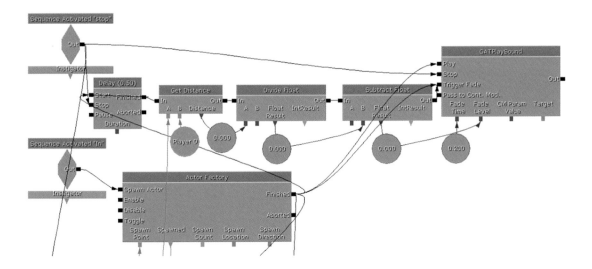

Within each bot subsequence the distance from the player is scaled and used to vary the volume of each bot's leitmotif. The effect is that as each bot enters the area around the player, its leitmotif joins in the musical texture. Because all the music stems are started at the same time (immediately after all the bots spawn on level start), they are all aligned in time, and remain so even when their volume is changed.

As you can see, the ability to keep separate music tracks or "stems" aligned in time and the ability to vary their volume in response to game events can be a partial solution to the Leitmotif problem.

Exercise 410_00 Music Liet

This room is a recreation of Room 410 in the tutorial. Try to compose a tune for each creature. Like those in Room 410, these leitmotifs will be heard when the characters are within a given distance from the player. Potentially they may all be heard at the same time, so they have to all fit together musically.

Tips

1. Just place your **[SoundCues]** into the appropriate **[Playsound]**, the challenge here is a musical one.

The "Variation" Question: Generative or Procedural Forms

An MMO can easily exceed 1,000 hours of gameplay (sometimes a lot more). If we are going to have a lot of music in games, we need it to have variation so that it does not become repetitive. This raises the question of how long it might take us to write this amount of music, and how we store this amount of music within the confines of a console's memory or disk space. Adopting a new approach to musical composition can provide some solutions.

(See the "Streaming" section in Appendix B for some specific advice on memory management for music.)

When composers sit down to write a piece of music, they usually feel that they have complete control and autonomy over what they are writing. In fact, most of the time, if using traditional Western harmony, they are actually doing so within the confines of a well-understood and codified system of rules. It's just that these rules have been so internalized that the composers forget they are there.

Although most music does not need to be as immediately responsive as sound effects and can therefore be streamed from disk, it is not immune to the restrictions of memory and file space. Games can have anything from 10 to many hundreds of hours of gameplay. It is not realistic to write and to store this amount of original music. By moving away from a linear music model to using generative or procedural techniques to create, or at least vary, music on the fly it is possible to avoid a repetitive score while still keeping the storage space required within reasonable limits. Generative music or procedural music—that is, music that is generated by a system or procedure—can have totally predictable output, but to produce the variation we are after for games we need to look at a subset of generative methods usually referred to as aleatoric (from the Latin *alea,* meaning dice). These systems involve leaving some aspects of the output to chance or random events. For many composers, the idea of leaving some aspects of their music to chance is an alien concept. However, once they appreciate that they are just creating the opportunity for different possibilities (the range of which they still have complete control over), many find this an exciting and intriguing approach to writing music.

Vertical Recombinations

411 Vertical Recombinations

This room illustrates how four different music tracks can be randomly combined. Each combination is different and therefore creates variation. This is much like the combination of explosions and debris covered earlier in the book (Room 205). You could relate this to the simple muting and unmuting of layers in Room 409, but this time we are not trying to go up and down in levels of tension but are instead swapping layers in and out to create variation within one tension level.

The switch in this room cycles between two versions of the same music. The first version attempts to get as much variation out of the four music tracks as possible. The **[SoundCue]** randomly picks between these different possibilities by having 1 by itself, then 1 + 2, 1 + 2 + 3, 1 + 2 + 3 + 4, 1 + 3, 1 + 4, and so on.

Track 01															
Track 02															
Track 03															
Track 04															

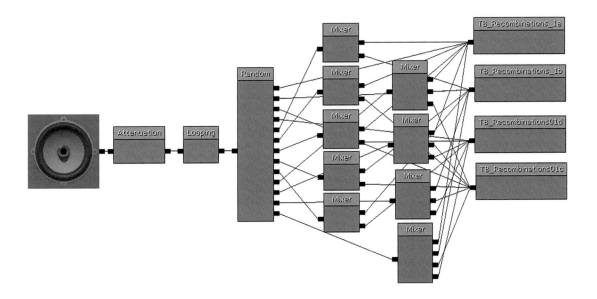

The second version has been tweaked. Using the weightings within the **[Random]** node and by limiting the combinations available, the amount of variation has been limited but the overall effect is more musical.

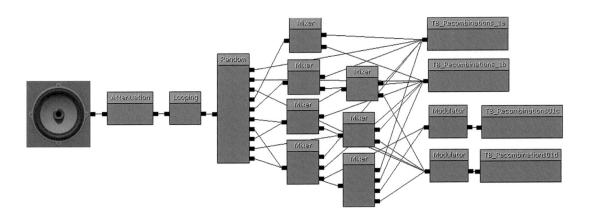

If you have a piece of music that could last an indeterminate amount of time in a game, there are two solutions. The first is to have a timer mechanism so that after a given amount of time the music fades out so that it does not become repetitive and lose its impact. The second is to develop more complex **[SoundCue]**s that have a significant amount of variation built in through the use of controlled random processes.

Here is the old approach:

Here is the new approach:

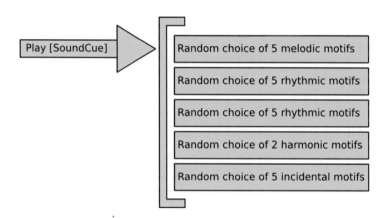

Writing in this style takes some getting used to for the composers because they need to release some level of control, but this can be liberating! The approach that works the best for this type of generative system is to write your music over a static harmony. Writing your motifs over one chord will make their vertical combinations easier, because you don't have to worry about them fitting with each other and with any changing harmonies. Ironically, writing over a single chord will also appear to make the music less repetitive. If we have multiple motifs or ostinati (repeating patterns) based around a single "drone" note or chord, you will avoid the repetitive feeling that a cyclical chord sequence might create. The chord sequence will become quickly predictable, and therefore feel repetitive, whereas without it people will start focusing on different aspects of the music.

Exercise 411_00 Vertical Recombinations

You're working on the new MMORKG (Massively Multiplayer Online Rat Killing Game) called Evercraft. Your player may spend many hours in certain areas of the game. Your producer has requested that there be a constant background of music. Try to adopt a simple "chance" approach to writing your musical parts and place them in the **[SoundCue]** so that the music does not drive the player completely mad with its repetition.

1. In your music sequencer, compose a number of different parts that will all fit vertically with each other.
2. Experiment with muting/unmuting the parts to anticipate how these might sound if placed in a randomized cue.
3. Create a **[SoundCue]** along the lines of the preceding one using a combination of **[Mixer]** objects and **[Random]** objects to create a range of possibilities for the combination of your parts.
4. Consider weighting the **[Random]**'s inputs so that some combinations are more/less likely than others.
5. Consider adding a **[Modulator]** object to vary the volume of each part.

Set Phasing to Stun

411a Music Phasing

Another interesting way of generating musical variation from limited resources involves the idea of "phasing loops." This works best with rhythmic elements, because with harmonic ones the combinations are often too complex to predictably avoid clashes.

If we had one rhythmic loop that lasted 3 bars and another that actually lasted 4 bars, then we would only hear the same music repeated after 12 bars. In other words, what you would hear at arrow marker 1 will not occur again until arrow marker 5. Although the start of part 1 will always sound the same, the overall music will sound different because you are hearing this in combination with a different section of part 2 each time. Only after 4 bars of part 1 (and 3 bars of part 2) will you hear both the start of part 1 and the start of part 2 at the same time like you did in the beginning.

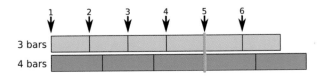

A 3 bar piece looping and a 4 bar piece looping.

A 6 bar and 8 bar combination would only repeat every 24 bars, a 7 and 9 bar combination every 63 bars.

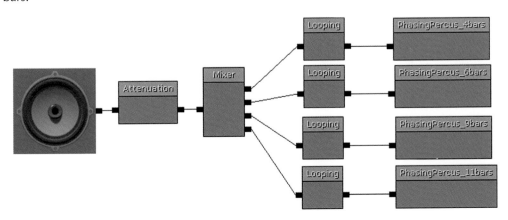

The first example as you enter the room uses files that are stereo 44.1 kHz. It consists of a 4-bar loop (858 kB), a 6-bar loop (1286 kB), a 9-bar loop = (1,715 kB), and an 11-bar loop (2,143 kb). The total for these files is approximately 6 MB.

By looking at the lowest common multiple between them ($2 \times 2 \times 2 \times 3 \times 3 \times 3 \times 11 = 2,376$), we can work out that in order for them to come back in sync and for us to hear exactly what we heard when they all began to play, we would have to play the 4-bar cue $\times$ 594 times, the 6-bar cue $\times$ 396 times, the 9-bar cue $\times$ 264 times, and the 11-bar cue $\times$ 216 times to come back in sync.

The 4-bar loop lasts 4.571 seconds, so that means we get more than 35.5 hours of music before it repeats. (Listen to it for 35 hours and check if you don't believe us.)

If we convert these to mono at a 22-kHz sample rate like the second version in this room then we get the following:

4 - bar loop (197 kb), 6 - bar loop (296 kb), 9 - bar loop (394 kb), 11 - bar loop (474 kb) = 1,361 Kb

Now 35.5 hours of music for just over 1.3 MB of memory footprint is not bad (if this were one file at CD quality, it would have only given us only 8.5 seconds of music).

Obviously, although every detail will not repeat until the cycle is complete, this does not mean that it's necessarily interesting to listen to—it is up to you to make that judgment. This is, however, a useful tool for producing nonrepetitive textures.

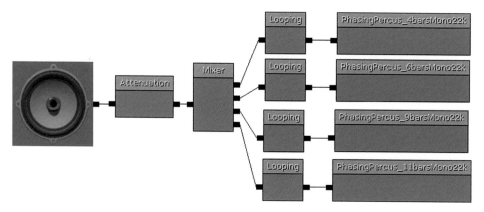

You can get 35.5 hours of interesting music from this? Probably not but...

Exercise 411a_00 Phasing Loops

You're now working on a different land within the world of Evercraft, the Land of the Disproportionate Women. The women in this land are keen on drumming. To encapsulate this culture, the producer wants there to be constant drumming present throughout the 200 hours that the players will typically have to spend in this part of the game while they kill more rats.

Tips

1. In your music sequencer (or with live musicians), create several loops that share the same tempo but are of different lengths (an odd number of bars will give you greater variation than an even number).
2. Use the looping tools of your sequencer to see how they work in combination over a period of many loops. (You'll note that you have to edit them very accurately so that the pulse does not slip out of time over many repetitions.)
3. Recreate this in a **[SoundCue]** by attaching each piece to a **[Looping]** node before mixing them together.

Low-Level Generative Processes

Some game sound tracks have adopted much lower level generative systems where each note chosen to play is the result of a procedural system. Tools such as "Max" (Cycling 74) or "PD" (Miller Puckette) are ideal for this process, but if you find them a little intimidating at the moment, then you can still get a taste of this approach to writing music within UDK.

412 Music Generative 01

Taking these ideas of generative music to their logical extreme, you can build systems that will procedurally create music from very small samples of individual notes or sounds. The rhythmic drumming in Room 412 is actually being entirely generated in real time.

The **[SoundCue]** is a randomized choice of seven samples of a large tin can being hit.

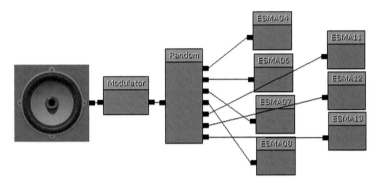

A **[Delay]** of 0.2 seconds is serving as a pulse that enters a looping switch. As this is sending out half beat pulses, it imitates a tempo of 150 bpm (60/0.4 = 150). This serves as a basic sequencer, outputting from each link in turn with the pulse provided by the delay.

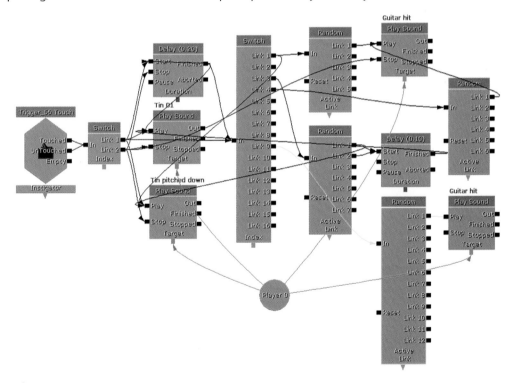

The **[PlaySound]** "Tin 01" receives every pulse directly from the **[Delay]**. This provides the basic quaver (half note) with some **[Modulation]** in the volume of the hits within the **[SoundCue]**. On pulses 1 and 3, a second **[PlaySound]**, "Tin 02," is triggered. This **[SoundCue]** reuses one of the samples of the first, but its **[PlaySound]** object pitches it down (pitch multiplier 0.5) and lowers the volume (volume multiplier 0.5).

Note that it does not always play (that would be predictable) but instead goes through a **[Random]** switch, of which three of the four outputs are empty. This means that there is a one in four chance that this element will play. This system is spiced up a little with the occasional "Guitar being hit by a drumstick" chord that adds another element of unpredictability. This has a one in four chance of being played on pulse 1, a one in six chance of being played on pulse four, and a one in twelve chance of being played on pulse 9.

This is a simple example designed to illustrate a point, but you can see the potential. The total size for the percussive samples used here is 5.1 MB, or 1.5 MB without the longer guitar hits. By programming systems to generate musical output, it is possible to create long non-repetitive sequences with a minimal memory cost.

Exercise 412_00 Micro Generative

The folder Exercise 412_00 contains some individual musical hits. Using a **[Delay]** and **[Switch]** sequencer, build a generative composition.

Tips

1. Get your **[Trigger]** in game to start a looping delay. This should be the length of the shortest "pulse" you want to use.
2. Create a **[Switch]** object (New Action/Switch/Switch).
3. In its properties, add the number of links (pulses) you want in your loop and check the Looping box. (You'd typically be using a "musical" number of pulses such as 8, 16, 32.)
4. Attach your **[SoundCue]**s to the pulses where you want them to be triggered.
5. Consider adding **[Random]** objects with empty outputs so that your **[SoundCue]**s are not necessarily triggered every time they receive a pulse.

The Problem with Generative Music

Aleatoric techniques are very effective for producing "ambient" music that does not feel too repetitive. However, the nature of randomness is that it can be quite predictable—predictably random if you like. This can lead to textures that sound "samey" or "noodly" and lacking in dynamic change. Adding "meta controls" to your procedural system can help alleviate this tendency and bring some drama back into the music.

412a Meta Generative

This room uses a similar "sequenced" approach to producing music with some randomized elements to Room 412. However, this time there is an additional switch that allows for some more global changes to the musical texture.

To add a sense of drama, musical textures should do this:

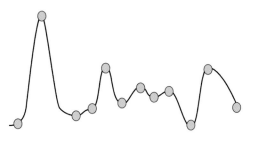

Not this:

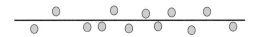

Some calculations are made to determine the length of a half beat at the given tempo; this is sent to the **[Delay]** object, which provides the basic pulse for the switch sequencer. This switch is linked up in various ways to the musical **[PlaySound]** elements, which are organized in terms of intensity layers.

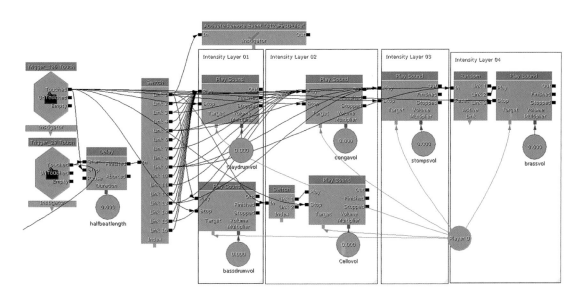

For example, at a low intensity the "Claydrum" plays on every pulse and the "Bass drum" on the first of every group of 16 pulses. At another intensity level the "Stomps" are playing on pulses 1, 5, 9, and 13.

You'll note that the **[Playsound]**s have their volume multiplier exposed, so this means that we can send a variable to these to alter their playback volume, to mute or unmute them. As we know from bitter experience, this will only take effect when the **[PlaySound]** is triggered, not while it's playing back. In this case, as the sounds are made from such short sampled elements the changes should appear to be near instantaneous.

Every 16 pulses, the section of the sequence that controls the volume of each musical element receives a **[Remote event]**.

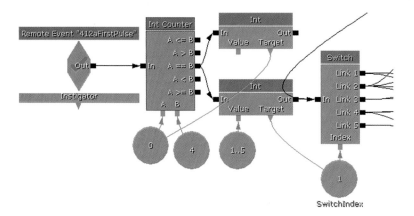

A **[Random]** variable is chosen, and this is used to control the *index* of a **[Switch]** (i.e., which output the switch will switch to). These outputs control various sets of variables, which will set the volume of the various **[PlaySound]** elements and hence govern the musical intensity.

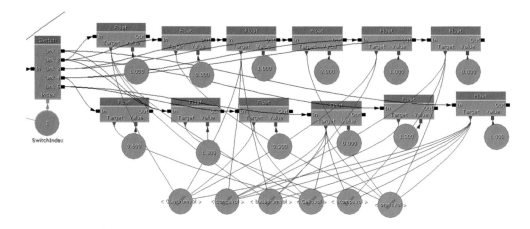

We've noted how textures produced by random systems can perversely become fairly predictable. You can produce more dynamic or dramatic shapes within your music through building procedural systems that react to gameplay via "meta" overarching controls. Ideally we would be able to have a curved or variable parameter that could collate variables from the game state and then control the overall intensity level of your generative music. Have a go - and send us a copy when you're done!

"Interactive" Music: Music as an Input

> The real way for game music to improve (and consequently for games to improve) is to make musical considerations part of the game's decision making processes. As well as the music responding to the game data, the game should have an awareness of the music data. This is *interactive* music, rather than what we mostly have at the moment, which is *reactive* music.

Although we've tried not to dwell too much on abstract theory in this book, there are several terms typically used to describe types of game music (and game sound) and a variety of definitions within the existing literature on the subject. We'd like to take this opportunity to confuse things even further by offering up our own.

Reactive Music System=Adaptive or Dynamic Music

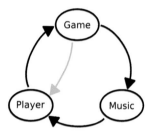

This music responds to the player's actions, as mediated by the game state, or varies according to the game state itself. Players get feedback from the game on their interactions, and they receive feedback from the music. But the music is simply a recipient of commands from the game engine.

The music could be a purely linear piece or could respond to the game state in complex ways using horizontal transitions or vertical layering as described earlier. This is described variously as interactive music, adaptive music, or dynamic music. Although common in many games, we would argue that this music is not interactive (which implies a cycle of feedback between the elements of the system), simply reactive.

Interactive Music System

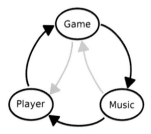

For truly interactive music, there needs to be a feedback cycle between the game engine and the music state. Rather than simply receiving input from the game and responding accordingly, the game state should receive feedback from the music as to its current position and the time to the next musical transition point. This way the game state can decide whether to call the music immediately or whether a more satisfying overall result can be achieved by taking into account the music state within its decision making processes.

Performative Systems

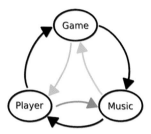

This is an additional category that encompasses situations where the player has some direct control over the music state itself such as in music-based games like the rhythm-action genre.

Let's look at a simple example to explore these principles further.

413 Music as an Input

This room contains three different musical scenarios. It is intended to be a simple demonstration of the concept that when appropriate (nearly always) the game state should consider the music state, as well as the music reacting to the game state.

Each button in this room represents one of three choices. When you press it a bot will appear and you must battle this bot to the death. As you do so, an "Action" cue will loop around playing one of three variations. When the bot dies an "End" cue will be played. The difference between the three scenarios is in the way we transition from the "Action" to the "End" cue.

(A) Instant Death and Instant Music

In this example the bot is set to die when its **[Take Damage]** reaches 14. When this number is reached, it dies instantly and the music instantly switches to the "Triumph" cue.

(B) Instant Death but Music Delayed

In this example the bot is also set to die when its **[Take Damage]** reaches 14. When this number is reached it dies instantly, but this time the music waits until the next "musical" opportunity to transition (i.e., the next bar line).

(C) Interactive Death

The bot is still programmed to die when **[Take Damage]** reaches 14, however this time the actual **[Destroy Actor]** and **[Toggle]** explosion that represents its death are blocked until the music is ready to transition to "Triumph" (at the bar line/measure).

(If you keep getting killed there is also an additional switch (D) to stop the bot shooting at you!)

Play the Room a few times. Which do you prefer, A, B, or C?

(A) Sudden Switch on Enemy Defeat

When the enemy is spawned, the **[PlaySound]** for the "Action" cue is triggered.

An **[IntCounter]** is incrementing every time you land a shot on the enemy via the **[Take Damage]**. When this reaches 14 (outputting from A==B), the **[Destroy]** object kills the bot, the "Triumph" cue is played, and simultaneously the "Action" cue is stopped.

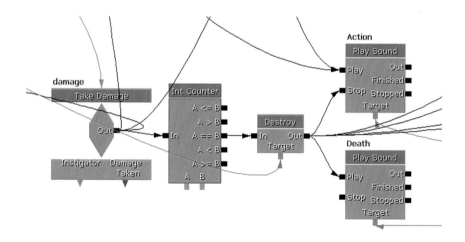

(B) Death Immediate but Music Waits

This time the bot dies as normal; at the instant that the **[Take Damage]**=14, however, the music only switches to the "Triumph" cue at the measure/bar.

When the enemy is spawned, the "Action" cue is triggered. At the same time, a **[Delay]** object one bar/measure long is started, which serves as the retriggering mechanism for the music, initially producing a looping retrigger of the "Action" music. Every time the enemy takes damage, an **[Int Counter]** is incremented. While this value is below 14, the A < B outputs a signal, and the **[Gate]** to the "Action" cue remains open and the **[Gate]** to the "End" cue is closed. When the damage reaches 14, however, the **[Int Counter]** outputs via its == and destroys the bot.

This time, instead of triggering the musical change directly, it now opens the "Triumph" **[Gate]** and closes the "Action" **[Gate]**. The "Triumph" cue will, however, only be triggered when the next **[Delay]** comes through, so in effect it only actually plays on the next measure/bar.

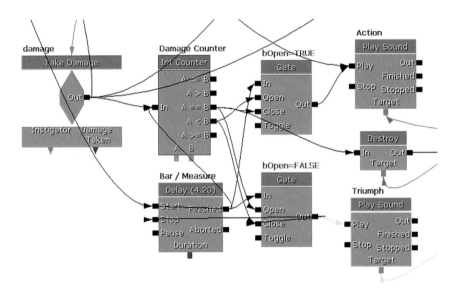

Although this is musically satisfying, it could feel "wrong" or "broken" that the music does not always coincide with the bot's death.

(C) "Interactive" Music: Death Waits for the Musical Measure

In this final example, the whole system becomes properly interactive. In other words the feedback goes both ways, not simply that the music reacts to the game state, but the game state also takes input from the music. This may sound complex, but in fact it involves only the movement of one connector. See if you can spot the difference.

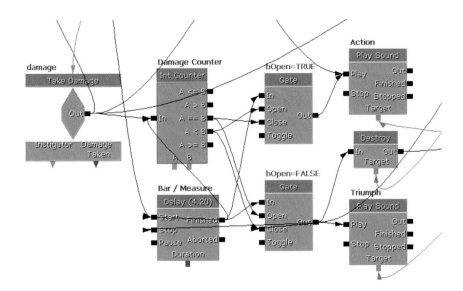

When the Damage **[Int Counter]** reaches 14, it outputs from the == output as usual; however, rather than instantly triggering the bot **[Destroy]**, this object is now connected to the **[Gate]** of the "Triumph" music cue, meaning that the bot will be destroyed on the next musical bar/measure when the music's **[Delay]** signal goes through. (Compare the input to the **[Destroy]** object discussed earlier with the previous image.)

This tiny change means that the game system is now involving the music system and music state in its processes. Rather than simply being *reactive*, this system is now *interactive*.

Challenges and Responses to Interactive Music

A game designer may argue that if the bot takes 14 shots to kill, then it should die when it receives the 14th shot, not later when you may have actually shot it 15 or 16 times. This is a fair argument. However, in the heat of battle who counts the number of shots that have successfully landed on the enemy?

Another scenario could be that you've shot it 14 times, then you stop shooting, only to see it actually die a few seconds later. This actually happens frequently in games and is actually more realistic than the enemy dying in sync with a shot. Sometimes the last shot has killed the enemy, but it takes a few seconds for the enemy to die (we don't know this from personal experience, but we have watched a lot of movies).

Does the satisfaction produced by the synchronization of the death with the musical hit outweigh the need for strict accuracy? We would argue that in many cases it does.

Some games will work fantastically with totally linear music and some with reactive music. However, some demand that we improve the current model of interactivity. Whatever clever methods, present or future, we come up with, they are never going to work musically (and therefore will never be as effective for the game experience as they could be) unless we start to consider music as part of the system, not just as an output. The current state of the music and the available musical transition points should be inputs to the game's decision-making system. It should not simply have to react.

Go and spread the word.

A Short History Lesson: Gains and Losses

Imagine for a moment that you have hired an orchestra to play a piece for your game. They sound fantastic, but there is a problem. Very strict new union rules have been introduced, which means that orchestras are only allowed to play one piece of music, and they also have to play this piece in exactly the same way each time. If you want to change one note within a four-minute piece, you will have to hire a different orchestra to play it. If you decide you want to have a rallentando (slowing down) toward the end of your piece, again a new orchestra will be required. Composers are puzzled. "Why can't I just alter the score (which amounts to a very cheap box of paper) and they can play all the versions I want?"

Isn't this dumb?

Isn't this the equivalent of using wav files for interactive music?

There is an inherent irony at the heart of writing interactive music in that the format we use to deliver it (typically stereo or 5.1 wavs) is not as appropriate for its use as the format we probably used to write it in; MIDI. The majority of composers work using a MIDI sequencer combined with some kind of high-quality sampling or synthesis engine. With the separation of "Orchestra" (the sample banks) and "Score" (the MIDI tracks) you can play any piece you like, solve the decay problem (see the earlier discussion), produce as many variations as you like, plus add tempo changes, controller changes, and the like with roughly zero impact on the overall size of the project (MIDI files are tiny).

It's clear that the greater the level of interactivity, the more flexible music must be and therefore the more granular (note) level control over the music we must have. But by rendering our work out to a wav file, we are essentially creating the "one-track-orchestra." This is big, expensive (in terms of memory), and inflexible (every possible variation, even changing one note, means you have to render the piece out as a separate file). Even with the inclusion of musical states into the game's decision-making processes, argued for above, can we really say that we have interactive music when we actually have control over so few parameters (whether it plays or not + its volume)?

So why can't we have our sample banks in memory (tweaking them so the "Orchestra" isn't too big) and then control our interactive score with MIDI? The answer is that we did have this ability once, but then we lost it.

Early games could use MIDI to control their music, knowing that as all soundcard manufacturers were meeting the "General MIDI Specifications" they could safely assign a track to Program No. 110 and it would be played by a bagpipe. The problem was—what kind of bagpipe? Although there was agreement in terms of the instruments that should be there (i.e., instrument 110 should always be a bagpipe), there was a wide variation in the sounds themselves as these were reliant on the local synthesis or sample-based General MIDI (GM) sound set. So depending on the system or soundcard, you might have bad bagpipes or good bagpipes (at this point you need to take a leap of faith to imagine that such a thing as a "good" bagpipe sound actually exists).

Once again, the MIDI Manufacturers Association (the ones that coordinated the GM specifications in the first place) stepped in with a solution. Initially developed by the Interactive Audio Special Interest Group (IASIG), the DownLoadable Sound (DLS) format specification allowed composers to develop their own "Orchestras"/Sample banks that would be distributed alongside the "Score"/MIDI files to ensure that the music was heard exactly as intended. A very effective development tool appeared from Microsoft called DirectMusic Producer that allowed composers to create and proto-type their music and so all was good in the garden of interactive audio. Until—what's this? A shiny silver disc blocking out the sun?

The ability to stream relatively large music files from CD, then DVD, and now Blu-ray disc has had a huge impact on the development of interactive music. In trying to solve all the problems of interactive music in one swoop, DirectMusic Producer was to an extent a victim of its own complexity and few managed to master its depths. Streaming was, and is, popular for good reason as it gives you absolute consistency, arguably a better sound quality (you can't "master" a MIDI + DLS track in the same way as you can master a stereo or 5.1 track in a good studio with expensive racks), and most importantly, musicians.

The qualities that musicians bring to a performance have been rightly treasured over centuries of human existence and the complex interactions of an ensemble of players are never going to be replicated within a MIDI file, no matter how careful the programming and articulations. Although it's possible to produce fantastic and realistic-sounding instrumental scores with MIDI and good-quality sample sets, there's a reason why people still pay thousands of pounds or dollars an hour to record a professional ensemble in a top-quality studio (and no, it's not just for the marketing department). We're not going to argue that it's anything but entirely appropriate that some music is written and used in this way, that sometimes the gains in musicianship and ensemble playing are worth the losses in terms of flexibility.

But where's the alternative?

Where you still have significant memory or bandwidth restrictions (such as on the Wii, NDS, or mobile phone) or the nature of the music-based game demands note-level granularity, the techniques of MIDI + DLS are still alive, but within the mainstream of game development this technology has been rendered obsolete and its advantages (flexibility = interactivity) dismissed. You can do a lot with streaming wavs (as we've demonstrated in some of the examples), and the makers of current middleware tools such as FMOD and Wwise are continually developing better systems for their use, but there should also be an alternative available for composers to develop more granular interactive scores. Why do we struggle today to get the same degree of interactivity that the team at LucasArts had in the early 1990s? The iMuse system had/has most of the answers when it comes to interactivity and music, but 20 years later there is still no universal platform for writing and testing interactive music without having to first render it out as inflexible wavs.

Where we go from here obviously remains to be seen, but it has already been noted that the processing power of even the current generation of consoles should theoretically allow us to effectively run a DAW/sequencing environment in real time. Others have suggested that the answer lies in leapfrogging over any technical constraints within the console itself to produce the music in the "cloud". Data from the game would be transmitted via the Internet to dedicated servers that could handle the processing of the music and then stream back a complete 5.1 mix. The IASIG continues to develop the iXMF format (Interactive eXtensible Music Format), which aims to be an open standard cross-platform solution to interactive audio that encapsulates both the implementation instructions and the audio data itself (using audio files or MIDI + DLS). Although the design principles of this format are now well defined and we can learn a great deal from the lessons of iMuse, DirectMusic Producer, FMOD, and Wwise, a composer-friendly composition and authoring tool remains the missing link. The question is where this will come from?

The game industry is significant enough now that the big boys and girls of the DAW world must be starting to pay attention, and perhaps even by the time this book reaches the shelves the solution may be out there. In the meantime, we hope you can hone your skills through experimentation with some of the systems we've included here.

One area where authoring tools of a type are beginning to emerge is in the genre where *the music is the game.*

(To get a taste of some old-skool approaches, check out the MIDI + DLS tutorial on thegameaudio-tutorial.com website).

Music-Based Games

> There are whole genres of games that use music itself as a gameplay mechanism, from beat matching and pitch matching to more abstract approaches

The nature of many music-based games is that the player has to attempt to perform the music. The player's success is usually based on the timing of the input or, in the case of microphone-based games, both the timing and the degree of pitch accuracy. The input does not just affect the player's score but also frequently affects what elements of the music are heard, with a correct "note" leading to the music being played as intended or an incorrect one playing back a bum note or error sound.

Given the note-level interaction with the music, most of these games use some kind of MIDI and sample-based playback or advanced stem muting/unmuting system. Some of these games are simply about rhythmic matching for fun and some are driven by the aim of making music creation more accessible to people who are not trained musicians. You can get a good feel for how the rhythm action processes work by creating your own interactive music track for "Rock Band" using the plug-in for the DAW Reaper (see the bibliography for a link).

There is another range of game applications that take a more experimental or abstract approach to both music and interaction. The most interesting ones lie somewhere in the middle.

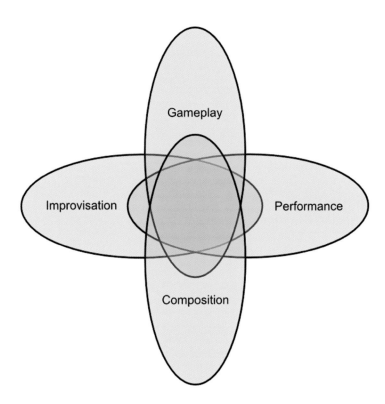

Given their highly specific nature, we are not going to cover these in depth here but would recommend taking a look at some of the examples that follow together with those referenced in the online Bibliography for this chapter in order to get an idea of the range of possibilities in this area.

(The "Peter" and "Piano Master" systems discussed in this section were developed by two of our students on the MSc. Sound and Music for Interactive Games course at Leeds Metropolitan University. Thanks to Andrew Quinn and Phil Briddon for allowing us to use them here.)

Simon

414 Music Game 01: Peter

This room contains a system inspired by the well-known Simon game of 1978. In this game, the player needs to accurately recall and replay an increasingly long sequence of tones attached to the colored areas.

Each colored area of the game has a **[DynamicTriggerVolume]** placed around it that generates a **[Take Damage]** event in Kismet. This toggles a light around the area and plays back a musical tone. Within the Kismet patch there are 32 subsequences that record the randomly generated sequence to play it back each time and to check whether the player has correctly matched the order of sound and lights.

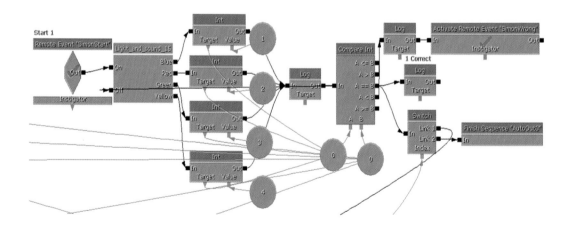

The randomized element of this game is what makes it particularly unique. There are still many games within the rhythm action genre that rely on memory (or a combination of memory and reactions) but mostly within a musical context and with fixed and repeating patterns.

Piano Hero

414a Music Game 02: Piano Master

In this rhythm action type game system, you have to shoot the keyboard to match the timing of the descending notes. Good timing will reveal a well-known tune.

A series of **[Delay]**s generates the sequence of notes for the tune. As each note is triggered, it starts a series of lights that indicate to the player when the note is coming.

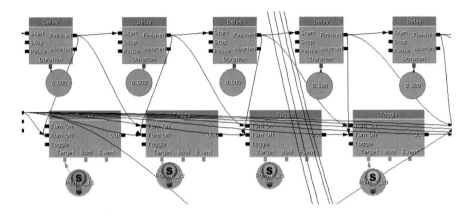

The player input (shooting) is detected by a **[DynamicTriggerVolume]** around each note. In FreePlay mode, the note is allowed to pass through the bottom **[Gate]** directly to a **[PlaySound]** for that note.

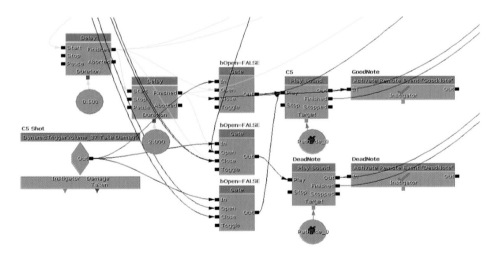

In the game mode, the final light opens the top **[Gate]** to detect the correct note at the correct time (*GoodNote*), and the *Dead Note* **[Gate]** is temporarily closed. Both the *Goodnote* and the *Deadnote* are passed to a scoring system to subtract or add **[Int]**s to the total score.

Abstract Music "Game"

414b Music Game 03: Abstract

This room is an illustration of some of the more abstract things you can do within a game environment that don't necessarily fit with the definition of a game (there are no specific goals or rules) or music (there is no organization or predetermined system of musical events) but instead fall somewhere in-between.

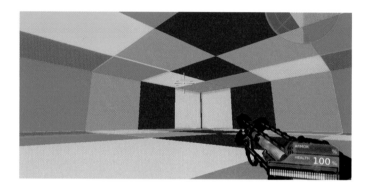

On entry, the player picks up a new weapon that has been adapted to shoot out projectiles that will bounce around the room. As they do so, they will hit the different colored panels on the walls, floor, and ceiling. These are attached to musical notes so the player can construct a piece of music through layering multiple bouncing sequences.

Each panel is encapsulated by a **[TriggerVolume]**, the properties of which have been set to detect the weapon's projectile via a touch event (Block Complex Collisions, Block Zero Extent), which then plays a **[SoundCue]** via a **[PlaySound].** The musical tones have been selected so that they can play in any combination without being dissonant.

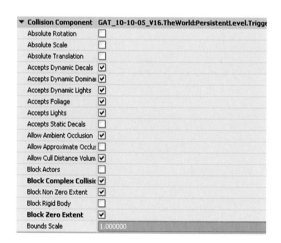

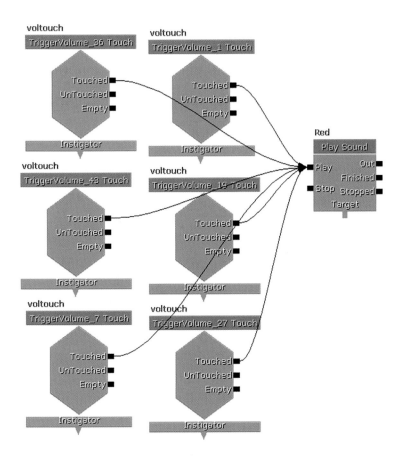

In the UTWeap_Musical, UTProj_MusicProjectile, and UTAttachment_Musical script files, the weapon fire has been altered and the velocity, damping, and lifespan variables to make the projectile bounce and last for longer than its default settings.

Exercise 414b_00 Rhythm! Action!

The exercise provides a simple template for a rhythm action style game. Do something cool with it.

Tips

1. Add your music cue to the first [Matinee]'s sound track.
2. With the Event track selected, play the matinee and press return to create events at musical points in the track.

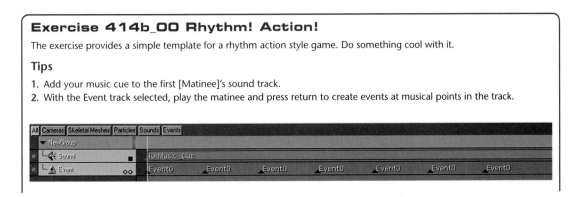

---

3. Enter the tempo and number of beats per bar into the Kismet system provided. This will use these inputs to scale the speed of the animation **[Matinee]**s so that the targets appear in the central aiming area exactly one bar after they are triggered by the Event track. Once you've set these up, you can move your music one bar to the right in the Matinee timeline and then you have yourself a (very rough) rhythm action game.

4. The targets have a Take Damage event to cue a "Success" **[SoundCue]**, and the wall at the back triggers a "Fail" **[SoundCue]** if you miss. You could use the input from these to create a scoring system.

There's lots of interesting stuff going on in the borderlands between games, music, art, and interactivity. Game engines such as UDK could have many applications in this field but are currently limited in their ability to communicate with the kinds of interfaces you might want to use. If you're interested in taking this further after having followed up some of the examples in the bibliography, then we'd highly recommend getting into Max (Cycling 74) or Pure Data (Miller Puckette).

Conclusions

For most games there should not be a music system, there should be music systems. These should work in tune with the particular requirement of the circumstances of the game within different scenarios. One answer to the challenge of interactive music is certainly a deeper integration with the game design itself. This will require producers and designers to understand what music can bring, and how it operates. It should inform the design of the game, not simply be an add-on to it. Sharing this understanding and making this happen is your job.

Although this might seem like a contradiction given the contents of this chapter, we would urge you not to get obsessed about interactive music in games. This is one of our options, and it's an option that we can't yet satisfactorily fulfill, but remember that it is on one end of the continuum of what music can do (see section presented earlier, "It's a fine line between love and hate"). Representing the larger scale narrative or playing against the action on screen could also be options and should have their place. Taking the contradictions one step further still, you will also remember that it is part of your duty to your craft, and to the game, to sometimes argue for no music. As powerful an effect as music can have by being there, it can have an equally powerful effect by not being there. We'll leave you to ponder that thought.

(If we could have embedded the sound of a Tibetan gong into the book at this point, then we would have.)

Dialogue

Game dialogue is an area of game audio that has seen significant improvements in recent years. For some strange reason, in the past many game producers and designers appeared to be under the impression that they were born with an innate ability to write good dialogue, rather than appreciating that, like any other skill, it takes years of practice and application to master.

Trying to avoid clumsy game dialogue is particularly difficult, as there is often a huge burden put on dialogue as the sole driver of a game's narrative. Perhaps not yet as developed in terms of visual storytelling as film, where a couple of shots may convey several key story elements, games often rely on dialogue to not only move the narrative forward but also to provide a great deal of instructional information to the player. Games also tend to operate within well-established genres (action/space opera/Tolkienesque fantasy) where it is hard to avoid cliché. Even if you are an experienced writer this is challenging.

Concepts and Planning

The first thing to appreciate about implementing dialogue for games is that it is, to a large degree, an asset-management problem. You need to approach the whole exercise with excellent organization and management skills if you are going to avoid some painful mistakes.

Obviously your dialogue production process cannot start until the story, characters, and mission details have been completed and signed off by all parties. At this stage, the type of dialogue required may fall into one of these broad categories.

Types of speech

Informational Dialogue

This dialogue provides players with the information they need to play the game. This might be instructions on how to use a piece of equipment or designating a rendezvous point. The key points with the dialogue are that it needs to be (1) clear and (2) heard. It is usually clear and articulate and in complete sentences, very different from natural dialogue. This dialogue might be panned to the center speaker or "radioized" over distance (so that when the attenuation over distance means that it falls below a given volume level, it becomes heard as if over a radio headset) as it is vital that it is heard.

Character Dialogue

This dialogue conveys the thoughts and emotions of the speaker. It is more naturalistic than the informational style because its emphasis is on conveying the emotions of the words. This is more likely to be spatialized in the game world but may still also be "bled" into the center speaker for clarity (see SoundClasses in Chapter 6).

Ambient/Incidental Chatter

This dialogue helps to set the scene for the location or situation you are in. Although crucial for establishing the ambience, the information conveyed by the words is not necessarily vitally important. This would be spatialized to originate from the characters in the game.

Nonspeech Vocal Elements

These are the expressions of pain, dying, and screaming that can make a day in the editing room such a pleasure. Again, these would be spatialized in the game.

The ideal aim is for the informational category to be subsumed into character so that any instructions necessary emerge naturally out of the character's speech. Given the relative lack of dialogue in games and the nature of what are often very specific goal-based narratives, this is often difficult to achieve.

Repetition and Variation

Earlier in the book we discussed how repetition destroys immersion in games. This is a particularly acute problem for dialogue. Since you were a baby, the human voice has been the most important sound in the world to you. It is the thing you pay most attention to and you have spent your life understanding the subtle nuances of frequency, volume, and timbre that can change a compliment into a sarcastic swipe. Our hearing is most acute for the range within which human speech falls. In other words, we are very sensitive to speech. Even if a character says the same line, in the same way (i.e., playing back the same wav) several hours apart from the first time the character said it, the chances are that we will notice and this will momentarily destroy our immersion in the game world.

The nature of games is that we are often in similar situations again and again, and are consequently receiving similar dialogue ("enemy spotted"/"I've been hit"). This indicates that for the most heavily used dialogue for each character, we need to record lots of different versions of the same line.

X 3500000

In addition to needing multiple versions of the same line, you may also need the same line said by different characters. If you have three characters in your group, then you may need three versions of each line, as each character might be in a position where he or she needs to say the line. For example, in our generic military shooter, an enemy might be spotted in a particular position by any of the characters, depending on who got to the location first.

At the start of a game you may be able to choose your character, or at least choose between a male and female character. This will mean at least two versions of every line of your dialogue for the entire game.

The game may have a branching dialogue system where the character's next line will vary according to which response the player chooses. You only have to go a short way along such a dialogue tree to see the number of lines implied. In this example, four sentences are exchanged; however, the number of sound files necessary for all the permutations is 25.

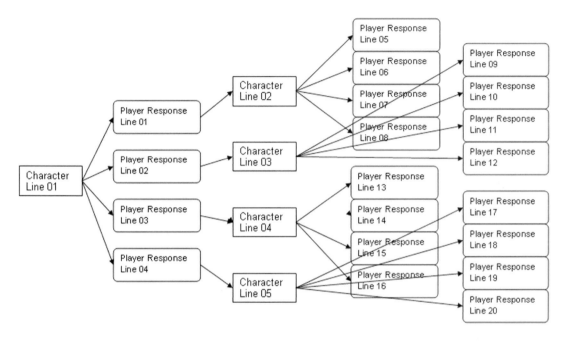

Localization

Once you've got your script with all 30,000 lines worked out, it might dawn on you that most of the world does not actually speak English. The nine foreign-language versions need their dialogue "localized" (if you're lucky it will just be French, Italian, German, and Spanish). Localization can be a huge job requiring specific skills, which is why many outsourcing companies have sprung up to provide this service. These recording, editing, and organizational skills generally fall outside of the implementation remit of this book. However, they are the principles with which you should become familiar:

1. For the in game cut scenes or full motion videos (FMVs), the foreign language dialogue will need to sync to the existing English-language animations. It would cost too much to reanimate to match the timing of the new language. Many foreign-language voice Actors are very experienced in dubbing for films and so are expert at matching the rhythm and flow of the new lines to the visuals. As you will appreciate, however, particularly with close-ups on the face, this is difficult to do. You can use the English recordings as a template for time reference so that the local Actors can attempt to approximate the same timing. Given that some languages will require considerably more words or syllables to communicate the same sentence, this is never going to be ideal, particularly if your English performance is fast.

2. The new language files need to match the exact length of the existing English language assets so that the overall file size does not differ.

The good news is that you may not need to replace the non-word-based vocals such as screams and expressions of pain, although we believe in some regions "aiieee!" is more popular than "arrgghhh!".

Localization is achieved in UDK by keeping your **[SoundCue]** in separate packages from the wavs they reference. This way the wavs package can have a three-letter language code suffix and the appropriate one chosen according to the game's language settings—for example, _KOR (Korean), _DEU (German), or_JPN (Japanese). See the UDK support files on the UDK website for more details.

Casting

Your game characters have the potential to be speaking off screen on many occasions, so you will want to cast voices that are distinctive and easily differentiated from each other. You'll note that despite the reality, where an army platoon would often be from a similar geographical location, in games they are rather more international or at least have distinct localized accents so that the player finds it easier to identify them. Their character is also part of individualizing their voices, so if you have a team then also think about whether you might have the "serious" one, the "joker," the "rookie," and the like (or perhaps something more imaginative). The main characters should be particularly distinctive from the others (it has been known in film that if the supporting character's voice is too similar to that of the lead Actor, for their voice to be completely overdubbed with a new voice in order to help the audience differentiate them).

Despite the continuing delusions of certain producers, there is no evidence to support the premise that having a moderately successful Actor playing the voice of Zarg in your latest game will actually lead to any increase in sales, so it's recommended that you choose a cheaper Actor with some understanding of games. Any budget spent on experienced voice Actors (apart from ones who have done one too many TV commercials) will be wisely invested and may help to preserve your sanity through the long hours ahead.

When specifying the voice talent you are seeking, you should obviously outline the sex, the "voice age" you are looking for (which does not necessarily match their actual age), and the accent. In addition to using well-known voices as references, you may also want to describe the qualities you're after such as the pitch (high/low), timbre (throaty/nasal), and intonation (how the pitch varies—usually closely linked to accent). It may also be useful to refer to aspects of character and personality. You may wish to consider the Actor's flexibility, as a good Actor should be able to give you at least four different characters, often many more.

Recording Preparation

This is the key time to get your organizational strategies in place to save time later on. (You might approach this stage differently if you were recording a session for concatenated dialogue; see the 'Concatenation, Sports, and How Not to Drive People Nuts : Part 2' section below.)

Script Format and Planning

Although Actors are used to a very specific format for their scripts, it is often essential to use a spreadsheet for tracking game dialogue. From this document it is relatively easy to increase the font size so that it's easier to read or if time allows (or if it speeds things up with the Actors), you can copy out the script into a movie format (see the online Bibliography for this chapter) from here.

Your script needs to contain the lines together with key information about the line. Obviously a dialogue line can be read in many different ways so it's important that you, and the Actor, know the context of the line and the tone with which it should be read. A classic mistake would be to have the Actor whispering a line and later realize that this line actually takes place just as he's supposed to be leaping onto a helicopter to escape from an erupting volcano. The line might sound good in the studio, but when put into the game you just would not be able to hear it.

Your spreadsheet should contain at least the following information. (See the downloadable template on the website.)

Character	Line/cue	Actor name	Area/location	Context/Situation	Inflection	Effect	Filename	Take or Variation number	Keep?
Bob	It's no good I just can't write any more	Laurence Olivier	Office	Trying to finish the book	Desperate	None	Bob_Sc23_L23_01.wav	1	
Steve	You have to, the people need you	John Gielgud	Office		Encouraging	None		1	✓
Bob	But my hands, my eyes! I'm falling apart.	Laurence Olivier	Office		Still Desperate	None		1	
Steve	OK, Let's just go for a pint	John Gielgud	Office		Phlegmatic	None		1	

Character. Name of the character.

Line/cue. The actual dialogue you want the Actor to say.

Actor name. The Actor who's playing the character.

Area/location. Informational and character dialogue are often linked to a specific game location, so these items would be tagged with the mission, area, and character name. Non-specific ambient and incidental dialogue could be named "generic" in the mission column.

Context/situation. This should include the setting and scene description to give as much detail on the scenarios as possible (i.e., distance from player, other details about the sound environment). You might even consider bringing screenshots or video footage from the game. This is simple to do and could save you time. Your characters may be saying the same line under different circumstances, so the Actors will need to know the context.

Inflection. Conversational, angry, sarcastic, panicked, fearful, whisper, shout. (You should agree on a predetermined preamp setting for lines tagged "whisper" or "shout" and make sure this is consistently applied to all lines.)

Effect. Any postprocessing effects, such as "radioize", that will be applied to the recording later.

Filename. You need to come up with a meaningful system for naming your files (see Appendix A).

Line I.D. You will need some kind of number for each line for identification.

Take or variation number. You'll usually try to get at least two different versions of the line, even if the first is fine, to give you flexibility later on. In the case of incidental dialogue that may be needed repeatedly, you would try to get many versions.

Keep? It may be immediately obvious that the line is a "keeper" (i.e., good) so it's worth noting this at the time to save trawling through alternative takes later.

There are three other elements you should try to have with you in the studio if at all possible:

1. *The writer.* This person knows the context and the intention of the dialogue better than anyone.
2. *A character biography sheet.* This should include some background about the character together with any well-known voices you want to reference (e.g., "like a cross between Donald Duck and David Duchovny").
3. *A pronunciation sheet.* If dialogue is going to be part of your life, it's worth spending some time researching phonemes (the individual sounds from which words are formed—discussed further later in the chapter). This will allow you to read phonetically so that you can remember and consistently re-create the correct pronunciation for each word. If your game is based around the city of Fraqu (pronounced with a silent q, "fraoo"), then make sure someone knows the correct way to say it and get your Actors to say it consistently.

Session Planning

Before booking the Actors and recording sessions you are going to need to make a decision regarding your approach to recording. Are your sessions going to be planned around using individual Actors or groups (ensembles) of Actors? There are advantages and disadvantages to both approaches.

The advantage with ensemble recordings is that the dialogue will flow much more naturally as the characters talk to each other, rather than one person simply making statements to thin air. In addition to allowing you to record all sides of a conversation at the same time, you can also get the kind of chemistry between the Actors that can make dialogue really come to life. The downsides are that this chemistry can also work in reverse. More egos in the room means more pressure on the Actors, more potential for problems or misunderstandings, and, of course, more people to make mistakes and therefore more retakes.

Getting the script to the Actors in advance and putting some time aside for rehearsal can alleviate some of these problems. You are in a different (cheaper) space, so the pressure of the red recording light is off and the Actors can get to know each other, the script, and you. If you go down the ensemble route, you can probably expect to plan for 50 to 80 lines per hour for typical (average 10-word) dialogue lines. For an Actor working alone you could sensibly plan for around 100 lines per hour (with an average of 2 takes per line) although this could be up to 200 with an experienced Actor, or as low as 50 for complex emotional scenes.

In your spreadsheet it's as easy as sorting by the character's name column to see all the lines for that individual, then the order in which to record them could be decided. If you're working on a narrative-based game, it would be beneficial for the Actor if you could group them into some kind of linear order so that the Actors can track what their characters are going through in terms of the story. It's more difficult (and hence more time consuming) to skip around in mood from one line to the next. If there are lines where the character is shouting or exerting him or herself, these can easily strain an Actor's voice, so you should plan to have these lines toward the end of your session.

In addition to the documentation, you should prepare and bring the following items to your session to help make your voice Actors more comfortable and therefore more productive:

- Pencils
- Warm and cold water (avoid milk, tea, and coffee as these can build up phlegm in the throat)
- Chewing gum (gets saliva going for dry mouths)
- Green apples (helps to alleviate "clicky" mouths)
- Tissues (for all the spittle)

Good studios are expensive places, so an investment of time and effort into this planning stage will save a lot of money and effort in the long run.

Recording

Wild Lines

The most common recording to be done for a game is a "wild line," which is a line that is not synced to any kind of picture or pre-existing audio. The dialogue will be recorded first and the animation and lip-sync will then be constructed to match the previously recorded dialogue.

Studio Prep and Setup

You may have to record dialogue in multiple studios, sometimes with the same Actor many months apart, yet you need to ensure that the final lines still have the same characteristics so that one does not pop out as sounding obviously different from another. To ensure consistency between multiple takes and different locations, accurately note your setup so that you can reproduce it again. Avoid using any compression or EQ at the recording stage, as this allows you greater flexibility later on. As noted in the discussion of the spreadsheet, consider establishing particular preamp settings for getting the best signal-to-noise ratio for normal, whispered, and shouted lines.

Make a note of all the equipment you are using (mic, preamp, outboard FX) and take pictures and make measurements of the positions of this equipment within the room and relative to the Actor. Note these in your DAW session.

You will need a music stand or equivalent to hold the script just below head height so that the Actors can read and project their voices directly forward. If the script is positioned too low, they will bow their heads and the dialogue will come out muffled. It's common to put the mic above the Actor's heads and angled slightly toward their mouths. In addition to being out of the way of the script, this also helps, in combination with a pop shield, to alleviate the "popping" of the microphone that can occur with certain plosive consonants that result in a sudden rush of air toward the microphone's diaphragm (such as "p" and "t").

You might also consider placing a second mic at a greater distance from the Actor, which can come in useful for lines that require the voices to sound more distant (see the discussion of outdoor dialogue in the "Voices at a Distance" section).

Performance

The most important thing about any studio session is not the equipment, it's the performance of the Actor. Post-Production editing can cover a multitude of sins, but it cannot make a flat performance come to life.

The ideal is to have a professional Director. These people know how to communicate with Actors and will get you the very best results. If it's down to you, then it is about knowing what you want (which your script planning should have provided for you), communicating it effectively to the Actors, and making them comfortable and relaxed. Few things are going to upset an Actor more than being directed by someone who can't decide what they want. It's fine to try different approaches, but it's important to exude the confidence that you know what you're doing (even if you don't).

- Talk about the character and context with the Actor.
- Have a good idea of what you want, but be prepared to be surprised by any original angle the Actor may bring—be flexible enough to run with it if it works.
- Be clear and specific in your comments.
- Try to avoid reading the line and getting the Actor to imitate it. Most Actors don't like "feeding," and this should be used only as a last resort.
- Get and track multiple takes.

Near and Far (Proximity Effect and Off-Axis)

With the script and microphone in place, it's unlikely that your Actors will be doing so much moving around that they affect the quality of the sound. However, it's worth considering the nature of the microphone's pickup pattern for a moment, as the distance and direction from which the sound source comes to the microphone can have a dramatic effect on the sound. A "normal" distance could be anything from 8 to 18 inches depending on the mic's characteristics, but you may want to go outside of this range for specific effects.

Proximity Effect

You will no doubt be familiar with the rumbling boom of the dramatic movie trailer voice, or the resonant soothing lows of the late night radio DJ. Both are aided by the proximity effect of directional microphones. When you are very close to a microphone, the bass frequencies in your voice are artificially increased. Although this may be great for your dramatic "voice of God" sequence, you should avoid it for normal dialogue.

Although the distances where this effect becomes apparent can vary from mic to mic, the chances are that any voices within three inches will start to be affected. In addition to helping with "pops," your correctly positioned pop shield is also a useful tool for keeping an overenthusiastic Actor at a safe distance from the mic.

Voices at a Distance

It is notoriously difficult to get voices that have been recorded in a studio environment to sound like they are outside. Because this is a frequent requirement for game audio, we need to examine the possible solutions.

The first and most important thing is to get actors to project their voices as if they are outside. This takes some practice and skill to overcome the immediately obvious environment they're in. You can help them by turning down the volume of their own voice in their ears, or even playing back some noisy wind ambience that they feel they need to shout over the top of. You certainly need to avoid the proximity effect, but you should also experiment with placing the microphone at different distances from the Actor and at different angles (your room needs to be properly acoustically treated and "dead" for this). The "off-axis" frequency response of a microphone is significantly different from that when facing it straight on and can be effective, together with the performance, in creating the impression of outside space.

(Other techniques you can try, after the session, to make things sound like they are outside are discussed in the online Appendix E.)

ADR Lines and Motion Capture Recordings

In the film world, "automated" or "automatic" dialogue replacement (ADR) (sometimes referred to as "looping"), is used when the dialogue recorded on the set is of unusable quality. The Actors will come into the studio, watch their original performances on the screen, and attempt to synchronize their new recording with the original dialogue.

On occasion you will also need to use this process for game audio cut scenes. Cut scene animations are either animated in the engine by hand or are based on animation information gathered during motion capture sessions (usually a combination of both). The most natural results in terms of the dialogue are of course derived from a group of Actors working together on the motion capture stage.

Through the use of wireless headset mics or booming (using a boom microphone) the Actors it is possible to get good results, but not all motion capture stages are friendly places for sound, so this situation may require ADR.

Even if you know that the dialogue recorded on the stage is not going to be of sufficient quality, you should record it anyway. Listening back to the original "scratch track" can help the Actors remember their original performances and synchronize more easily to the video.

Editing and Processing

A good dialogue editor should be able to nearly match the production rate in terms of productivity (50 to 100 lines per hour). To get the dialogue ready to go into the game, there are a number of processes you may need to apply to the recorded tracks.

Editing

Get rid of any silence at the start and end of the line (top "n" tail). Remember, silence takes up the same amount of memory as sound.

High-Pass Filter

If you recorded in an appropriate environment you likely won't have any problems like hiss or high-end noise, but you may want to get rid of any low elements like mic stand or feet movements by using your EQ to filter off the low end. You can normally filter off anything below around 100 to 150 Hz for male voices and 150 to 200 Hz for female voices without significantly affecting the natural timbre of the voice.

Clicks and Pops

Despite your care with the pop shield, the odd pop may occasionally get through. You can zoom right in and edit the waveform manually or use a click/pop eliminator tool (normally found in the noise reduction/restoration menu of your DAW).

Breaths

What you do with the breaths will depend on the circumstances within which the dialogue will be used. Leaving breaths in will give a more intimate feel, whereas taking them out will leave the dialogue sounding more formal or official. Sometimes they are part of the performance, so you should leave well alone but experiment with the settings on your expander processor that will drop the volume of any audio below its given threshold by a set amount. (Extreme settings of an expander serve as a noise gate.)

De-Essing

There are a number of strategies for reducing the volume of sibilant consonants like "s" and "z," which can be unnaturally emphasized through the recording process, but your DAW's de-esser will usually do the trick by using a compressor that responds only to these sibilant frequencies.

Levels

Dialogue can vary hugely in dynamic range from a whisper to a shout, so you will often need to use some processing to keep these levels under some kind of control. No one is going to be able to do this better than an experienced engineer riding a fader level, but this is rarely possible given the amount of time it would take to sit through all 350,000 lines. Automatic volume adjustments based on average values of the wav file are rarely successful, as perceived volume change depends on more than simply a change in the sound pressure level (db). (See Appendix E for a recommended software solution.)

Rapid Prototyping for Dialogue Systems

Often you will want to get dialogue into the game quickly for testing and prototyping reasons. In addition to simply recording it yourself, you could also try using your computer's built-in speech synthesizer or one of the many downloadable text-to-speech (TTS) programs. Many of these programs will allow you to batch-convert multiple lines to separate audio files which will allow you to get on with prototyping and testing, and will give you a general indication of the potential size of the final assets. Fortunately for us, UDK has its own built-in text-to-speech functionality that we'll be using in the next example.

Implementation

Branching Dialogue

500 Branching Dialogue

A guard is blocking the door to Room 500. You have to persuade him to let you through to the next area.

This is a simple example of branching dialogue. The game is paused while an additional interface is overlaid that allows you to choose your responses. Different lines are synthesized using the text-to-speech (TTS) function available within a **[SoundCue]** to react appropriately to the different responses you might give.

The system uses UDK's Scaleform GFx functionality which allows you to build user interfaces in Flash. These provide the buttons for the player to click on in order to interact and navigate the conversation. (See the UDK documentation for more on GFx.) Depending on how polite you are, the conversation will end with the bot either graciously standing to one side to allow you through or attempting to annihilate you with it's mighty weapons of death.

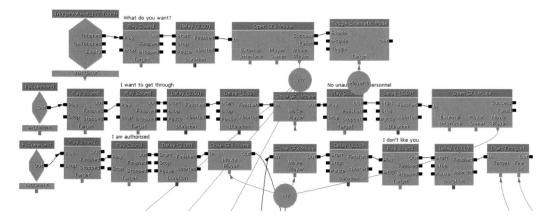

The branching dialogue tree is shown below. The boxes in bold indicate that the outcome is that the bot will attack; the lines boxed with a hashed line indicate where the bot has decided to let you through.

Although this dialogue tree relies on the simple playback of dialogue lines you can appreciate how it can create a narrative problem (given the complexities that can arise), an asset problem (given the number of sound files it may require), and an organizational problem (to keep track of this number of lines). The real solution is to work with your programmer to call your **[SoundCue]**s from a database, as trying to build a visual system (such as the Kismet one here) quickly becomes nightmarish.

The speech itself is created using TTS functionality within the **[SoundCue]**. After importing a fake (very short) SoundNodeWave into the **[SoundCue]**, the Use TTS checkbox is ticked and the dialogue entered in the Spoken Text field. You'll note that the duration of the SoundNodeWave updates to reflect the length of this dialogue, and the actual SoundNodeWave you imported is not played at all. Using a combination of the duration and sample rate, you can record these figures to give you a good indication of the likely size of your files when the final dialogue goes in.

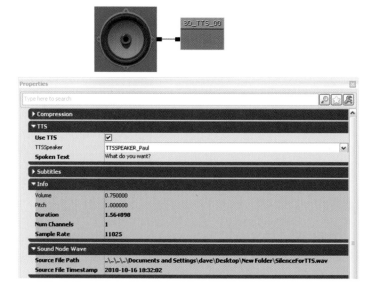

You have to be aware that although the duration appears to have changed, the **[PlaySound]** object will still be flagged as finished after the duration of the original imported SoundNodeWave, so you should add a **[Delay]** of the approximate length of your line as we have in the Kismet system for this example.

AI, Variation, and How Not to Drive People Nuts: Part 1

Dialogue is very effective in making your game AI look stupid. A non-player character (NPC) saying "It's all quiet" during a pitched battle or saying nothing when you crash an aircraft immediately behind him will instantly break the believability of the game. Dialogue is often an indicator for a change in AI state ("I think I heard something"), and you feel more greatly involved in the game when the dialogue comments on your actions. You are reliant to a great extent on the effectiveness of these AI systems to ensure that your dialogue is appropriate to the current situation. The more game conditions there are, then the more specific you can be with the dialogue. Obviously situational "barks" that occur frequently will need the greatest number of variants. You also need to work with your programmers to determine the frequency with which certain cues are called (or if they're not listening, put some empty slots into those cues).

501 Abuse

In this room there is a poor bot just waiting to be repeatedly shot. As the bot is shot, he responds with a vocal rebuke. Because this incident (shooting a bot) may occur many times in your game, you want to ensure that the dialogue does not repeat the same line twice in quick succession.

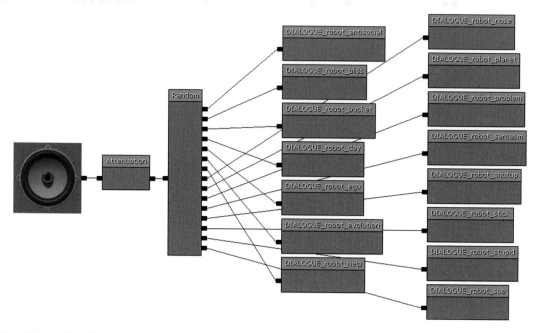

The **[SoundCue]** for the bot's responses uses the **[Random]** node where the 15 dialogue lines are equally weighted (and therefore equally likely to be chosen). Within the **[Random]** node you'll see that the additional option "Randomize Without Replacement" has been chosen. This tracks which input has been triggered and then randomly chooses from the remaining options. This selection results in a random order of choices but at the same time ensures that the same line will be chosen at the longest possible time interval from when it last played.

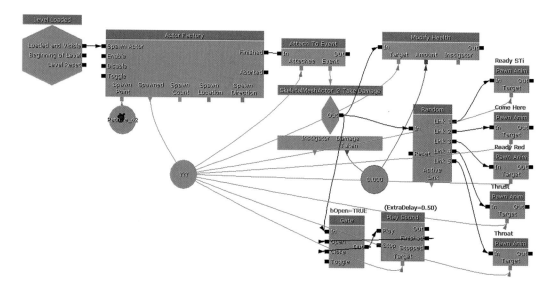

The system in Kismet also uses a **[Gate]** (see image above) so that a dialogue line, once begun, is not interrupted by another. When each line is finished, the **[PlaySound]** object opens the **[Gate]** to allow the next line through.

Exercise 501_00 I think I heard a shot!

To get into the safe, you need to shoot the door 10 times. Each time you do, the guard in the next room thinks he hears something. If you pause for a few seconds, he will then return to normal duty. If you don't wait, he will be alerted and you will have failed the mission.

Tips

1. Put a **[DynamicTriggerVolume]** around the safe. (These are easier to set up for link gun weapon damage than a normal **[TriggerVolume]**).
2. In the Collision menu of the properties of this Actor (F4) make sure the blockrigidbody flag is checked and make sure the Collision type drop down menu refers to COLLIDE_BlockWeapons. Then within the Collision Component menu check the first flag named Block Complex Collision Trace.
3. With the **[DynamicTriggerVolume]** selected in the level right-click in Kismet to create a New Event Using **[DynamicTriggerVolume]** (***) Take Damage. In the properties of this event (Seq Event_Take Damage) set the damage threshold to 1.0.
4. Send the out of this event to a **[SoundCue]** that has "Randomize Without Replacement" on at least 10 lines that convey the message "I think I heard something". Also pass it through a **[Gate]** (ctrl + G) to a **[Delay]** (Ctrl +G) object. This will set the delay before the guard thinks the threat has passed.
5. After this **[Delay]** go to another **[SoundCue]** that indicates the bot has given up and is back to normal ("Oh well, must have been the wind.")
6. Link the out of the **[Take Damage]** event to an **[Int Counter]** to count the number of shots. Set the value B to 2. If the player shoots twice in quick succession then A=B. Link this to a **[SoundCue]** to play an alert sound. (Also link it to the guard spawn command that we've provided in the exercise.)
7. Use a looping **[Delay]** of around 3 seconds to send an Action/**[Set Variable]** of zero to value A of the **[Int Counter]** so that the player who waits can then fire again without being detected.
8. Use another **[Int Counter]** that you don't reset to also count the shots fired. When this =10 send this output to the explosion **[Toggle]** and **[Matinee]** provided that opens the safe.

(If you just want to focus on the dialogue then open EX501_00_Done where we've provided the whole system for you !).

Concatenation, Sports, and How Not to Drive People Nuts: Part 2

In terms of dialogue and sound, sports games present huge challenges. Dialogue is there for authenticity, reinforcement, information, and advice. At the same time as fulfilling all these functions the speech and the crowd, camera, and graphic overlays all need to match and make sense.

Some elements can be highly repeatable. We've seen how informational sounds that carry meaning are less offensive when repeated because we're interested in the message they convey rather than the sound itself. Likewise, in sports games we can get away with unmemorable expressions of words like "Strike!" that simply acknowledge an oft-repeated action. Other dialogue cues such as remarks about specific situations or jokes will be much more readily remembered. Your system also needs to show an awareness of time and memory by suppressing certain elements if they repeat within certain time frames. In natural speech we would not continually refer to the player by name but would, after the first expression, replace the name with a pronoun, "he" or "she." However, if we came back to that player on another occasion later on, we would reintroduce the use of his or her name. As you might begin to appreciate this is a complex task.

Sports dialogue can be broadly separated into two categories, "play by play" and "color" commentary.

The play-by-play commentary will reflect the specific action of the game as it takes place. The color commentator will provide background, analysis, or opinion, often during pauses or lulls in the play-by-play action and often reflecting on what has just happened. Obviously some events demand immediate comment from the play-by-play commentator, so this will override the color commentary. After an interruption, a human would most likely come back to the original topic but this time phrasing it in a slightly different way ("As I was saying"). To replicate this tendency in games we'd have to track exactly where any interruption occurred and have an alternative take for the topic (a "recovery" version). However, where the interruption occurred in the sentence would affect how much meaning has already been conveyed (or not). We'd need to examine how people interrupt themselves or change topic midsentence and decide whether to incorporate natural mistakes and fumbles into our system.

In sports games, everything tends to be much more accelerated than it would be in reality. This makes life in terms of repetition more difficult, but more importantly events happen faster than your speech system can keep up. A list of things to talk about will build up, but once they get a chance to play they may no longer be relevant (e.g., play has continued and somebody else now has the ball). You need a system of priorities and expiry times; if a second event has overtaken the first or if some things haven't been said within a certain period, then they are no longer worth saying.

All these challenges would be significant in themselves but are heightened by (1) our innate sensitivity to speech and language and (2) the huge amount of time that many players spend playing these games. The commentator dialogue will be a constant presence over the many months or even years that these games are played. Rarely are games audio systems exposed to such scrutiny as this.

Let's examine a typical scenario for a sports game to look at a particular challenge regarding the speech. In the English Premier football league there are 20 teams. In a season each team will play each other team twice, once at home and once away, giving each team 38 games. At the start of the match we'd like the commentator to say: "Welcome to today's match with Team A playing at home/away against Team B. This promises to be an exciting match."

To ensure that this sentence states each of the possible matches in the football season, we'd need to record this statement 760 times to have a version for each of the possible combinations of teams. Now imagine that we have 11 players on each team (not including subs) and each player might intercept a ball that has been passed by another player (or pass to, or tackle, or foul).

Similarly in a baseball league there might be hundreds of named players, so our combinatorial explosion has returned once again!

You can perhaps appreciate from the football/soccer sentence above that it's only actually certain words within the sentence that need replacing. We could keep the sentence structure the same each time but just swap in/out the appropriate team names or the word "home" or "away." This method is called concatenation or "stitching." We've already come across the **[Concatenator]** node in the **[Soundcue]** that will string together its inputs end to end, and this is what we want to happen to our sentence elements.

Sentences usually comprise one or more phrases. By using a phrase-based approach, you can create a compound sentence by stitching together an opening, middle, and end phrase. This can work well with speech of a relatively relaxed, low intensity. The challenge here is to get the flow of pitch and spacing over the words feeling right across all versions. It is often the spacing of words that stops the phrases from sounding natural and human. (If you want to hear some examples of bad speech concatenation, try phoning up your local utility service or bank.) You can also appreciate how a recording session for a concatenated system would differ from a normal session in that you'd want to construct a script so that you get the maximum number of the words you want in the least amount of time.

502 Football/Soccer

In Room 501 you can see a prototype of a football kick around (five-a-side) for illustration purposes. When you press the button you can see that there is a pass made between random players (represented by the colored spheres).

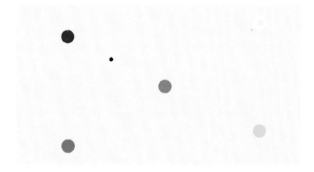

This system works very simply by tracking which player has passed to which player via two variables, StartingBot and EndingBot. When the player passes the ball (press the E key), the opening phrase "Nice pass from" is played. Then the first variable StartingBot is compared against the variables for each player (1 to 5) and the appropriate player name **[PlaySound]** is chosen. The linking word "to" is played by the central **[PlaySound]**, and then the EndingBot variable is compared to see which player name should be used to complete the sentence.

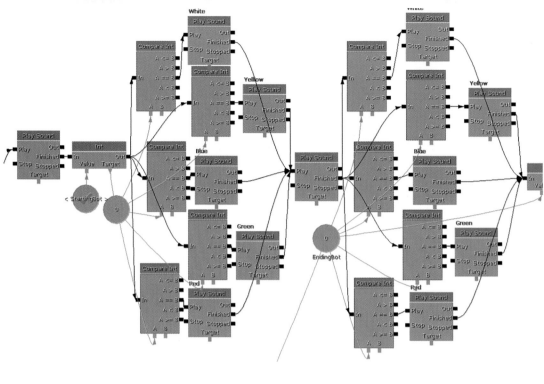

"Nice pass from"   *" "*   *" to"*   *" "*

Although functional, you can hear that this does not really sound in any sense natural. In a real match these comments would also vary in inflection depending on the circumstance; for example, a pass of the ball a little way down the field would be different from a pass that's occurring just in front of the goal of the opposing team with only 30 seconds left in the match. It might be that you record two or three variations to be chosen depending on the current game intensity level. The problem with more excited speech is that we tend to speak more quickly. Even in normal speech our words are often not actually separate but flow into each other. If you say the first part of the phrase above "Nice pass from player 01" you'll notice that in "nice pass" the "s" sound from "nice" leads into the "p" sound of "pass." In this case it is not too much of a problem because it is unvoiced (i.e., does not have a tone to it). The "m" of "from," however, is voiced; even when your mouth is closed the "m" is a tone that then leads into the tone of "p" from "player." An unusual jump in this tone, produced for example by the words "from" and "player" resulting from two different recording sessions or a different take of the same session, will again feel unnatural.

More "seamless" stitching can be achieved, but it requires a deep understanding of aspects of speech such as phonemes and prosody that are beyond the remit of this introductory book. See the bibliography of this chapter for further reading suggestions.

Crowds

A reasonable approximation of a crowd can be created simply by layering in specific crowd reactions against a constant randomized bed of general crowd noise. This is the nature of sports crowds themselves and so can work well, particularly if linked with some variable fade in/fade outs within the **[PlaySound]** objects.

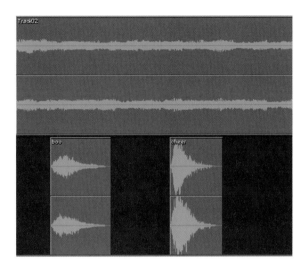

For more complex blending of sourced crowd recordings, we need to have control over the volume of these sounds while they are playing in order to be able to fade them up or down depending on game variables. This is similar to the approach we used for interactive music layers. By using variables to read through arrays containing volume information, you can control the curves of how the different **[SoundCues]** respond to the variables. The good news is that as this isn't music, you won't need to worry about aligning them in time.

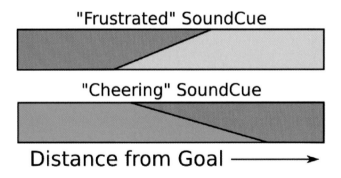

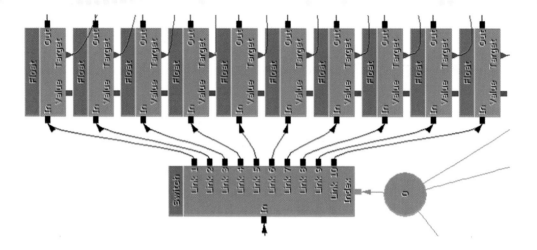

Exercise 502_00 Concatenation

In this exercise you have a fairground game where you have to shoot the colored ducks.

The game allows the player to shoot three targets (each of which are worth a different number of points) in a row, and then it will recap what the player hit and the total points scored. You have to add the dialogue.

This is the playback system.

"You shot (***), (***) and (***)"

"You scored (***)"

Tips

1. Consider the elements of dialogue you need.
    a. "You shot" and "You scored"
    b. Ducks. The colors of the Ducks hit ("Red" – worth 15 points, "Green" – worth 10 points, and "Blue" – worth 5 points)
    c. Scores (work out the possible scores you can get from all the combinations of these three numbers: 5, 10, and 20)
2. The system has been set up for you so you just need to add your **[SoundCue]**s. The challenge lies in (1) recording and editing the dialogue for the smoothest possible delivery of each line and (2) seeing if you can improve upon the current system.

In-Engine Cut Scenes: A Dialogue Dilemma

Your approach to dialogue in cut scenes will depend on whether they are FMV (Full Motion Video) or in-game. If they are FMV, then you will add the dialogue as you would in a normal piece of linear video such as an animation or a film. This would conventionally be panned to the center speaker, but some panning could work depending on the setup of the particular scene. If the cut scene takes place in game, then you have the same problem that we first came across when discussing cut scenes in Chapter 3. The sound is heard from the point of view of the camera, which can result in some extreme and disconcerting panning of sounds as the camera switches positions. The solution proposed in Area 305 was to mute the game sounds (via SoundModes) and to re-create these via the use of SoundTracks in Matinee. The additional consideration for dialogue here is that since the dialogue will no longer be emitted from an object in the game, then it will not be affected by any attenuation or reverberation effects. If you are going to use this method, you will have to apply these to the sound files themselves in your DAW so that the dialogue sounds like it is taking place within the environment rather than playing the acoustically dry studio recording.

Conclusions

It's pretty clear from the inordinate amount of effort involved in recording dialogue, and the complexities involved in developing effective concatenation systems, that this is an area of game audio desperate for further technological solutions. We can only hope that it's only a matter of time before more effective synthesis and processing techniques help to ease some of this often laborious and repetitive work. That way we can get on and concentrate on *making it sound good.*

Making it Sound Good

Now we've got all the elements (sound, music, dialogue), we can start to bring them together. Before you begin you should always ask, "What am I trying to achieve?" Ideally you're asking this question alongside the game producer and game designers in weekly design meetings. Even if you are working without this kind of support, you need to have a good understanding of the intended purpose of the gameplay from moment to moment, and the type of emotion you want your player to experience so that your soundscape can effectively support it.

For a long time sound has developed with the aim of matching the increasingly photo-realistic look of games, hence "making it sound real." It's true that to some extent the role of sound is to support the visuals by creating a sense of "reality," adding weight and substance to what are, after all, simply a bunch of pixels. However, the exclusive pursuit of realistic sound displays a lack of understanding about how the human brain deals with sound. Here's the key point, and it's a biggie. With regard to the human sensory system, there's no such thing as "reality" when it comes to sound. Take a moment, breathe deeply, and we will explain.

If you had 40,000 speakers, then it might be worth trying to accurately represent a real sound field; then we could use our perceptual mechanisms in a way that is akin to how we use them in the real physical world. As this isn't realistically possible (yet), we need to realize that the usual ways of listening do not apply. The phenomenon described as the "cocktail party effect" explains how the brain uses the difference in the time between the sound arriving at each ear and the difference in the sound itself (that results from the head filtering one ear's version depending on the direction of sound) to enable us to tune in or focus our aural attention on things of interest. For example, at a cocktail party where there are many sound sources, you can still tune in to the fascinating conversation of the couple by the door who are discussing what an idiot you are.

Without a fully functional sound field, the listener is no longer able to do this. Therefore, it is our job, whether as a film sound designer or game sound designer, to decide from moment to moment what the most important sounds are for the listener/player. If we try and play all of the sounds all the time, then we're going to end up with sonic mud that the user cannot decipher. If were to you put a microphone in the middle of the cocktail party, make a recording, and listen to it, the result would be chaotic (unless it was a very boring cocktail party). With your own *subjective* listening, you can choose to tune into different voices; with the microphone's *objective* hearing, however, when you listen back to the recording, you won't be able to make anything out. In other words, microphones *hear,* people *listen.*

The realization that it's our job to control and manipulate the sound track actually opens up a range of creative opportunities for giving the player a better emotional experience. The emotional use of sound in games is currently limited when compared to the creative use of sound in movies. This is in part because of a lack of sophistication in the tools available but also because of the inherent conflict that arises from the dual function of sound and music in games, where we have to balance the role of providing information to the player with the aesthetic role of communicating emotion.

Audio Concepting

> People, including sound designers, are generally not very good at talking about sound. Instead of writing design docs and talking about it, do it. If you've got a great idea about a gameplay mechanic based on sound or an audio feedback mechanism that you think would work really well, don't tell your producer about it, make a mockup and show her.

You need to understand your tools well enough to break them, use and abuse them in ways not intended in order to illustrate your point. Whatever the engine you will eventually be using, if you can mock the idea up in UDK or Cycling 74's Max, then if the idea gets accepted the programmers can implement it properly for you later.

As well as understanding the game's mechanics, you should also get your hands on any early concept visuals as soon as possible. In Windows Movie Maker or iMovie, take a still image of this concept art, drag it across the timeline, and add an audio track to it. Try creating a one-minute environment ambience for this location or do the same with an animation. With just the still image on the screen (or a series of images), create an imagined scenario where a character or creature will interact with things. Get the movement sounds and vocalizations in. To try out visual concepts quickly, sometimes artists will grab a bunch of imagery or video clips from a variety of sources and roughly put them together (sometimes referred to as "ripomatics"). If you're pushed for time you could take a similar approach, taking bits of the sound track from your favorite films or games and blending them together to see quickly if this is the direction that people are after.

Putting in the extra effort early on to provide audio concept tracks will achieve a number of objectives:

1. It will tell you quickly what people don't want. People are generally not good at articulating what they do want (particularly in terms of audio where most people lack the vocabulary) but are very good at telling you what they don't like when presented with an example. Don't get too precious or attached to your sound ideas, because they will no doubt change a number of times. (Always keep them, though, for when the producer comes around in six months' time looking for some "new" sounds for one of the creatures. That's when you play your original sounds, which the producers had rejected earlier. This time around, they'll probably think the sounds are perfect. Either that or they'll sack you.)

2. The great thing about making mockups and concept tests is that they can feed into other areas. If you make a concept sound for the creature that you've got some art for and then show it to the animator the chances are that consciously or not, some of your elements will influence the final animation.

3. Providing early concept sounds will also form an early association with particular characters or objects. People will get used to hearing them with your sounds, so that the game will begin to sound "not quite right" without them.

4. Using sound to illustrate aspects of gameplay will get other people interested in the sound of the game, to realize its potential impact, to get into discussions, and to offer input and ideas. This increase in communication is what you want if you are to have a positive impact on the game design.

Of course, the element that will drive your concepts more than anything is an understanding of the nature of the game itself and of the roles and functions you want the sound and music to achieve.

Spotting, Roles, and Functions of Sound in Games

When talking to designers about the goal of the player in a particular scenario or the arc of emotion they want the player to experience, you should have a good understanding of how sound can contribute to gameplay and emotion so that you can help achieve their goals and, where appropriate, make the case for using sound more creatively. This chapter deals with the crucial issues of how sound can support gameplay and narrative not only by adding characterization to objects and characters but by also being responsive to game events via the use of interactive mixing.

Sound obviously shares many roles and functions with music. Unlike music, which frequently falls outside of the reality of the game world (as non-diegetic audio), sound tends to derive mainly from objects and characters within the game world. (Although there can be considerable crossover between music, musical sounds, and sounds that play the role of music.)

Reality, Mood, Information

A primary function of sound that differs from that of music is to make the sometimes-unconvincing two-dimensional image feel real. It also provides information to the players, both in terms of aiding navigation and describing what is around them in the off-screen space, and in terms of providing feedback about their actions and their status. Sound not only reinforces the image to make it more convincing but also describes the image, giving it a substance and character. Sounds can have strong links to memory and therefore to the feelings evoked by those memories. In addition to giving the player a sense of presence in the world, it also immerses the player, setting the mood and guiding the player's emotions, most powerfully experienced through the subjective point of view of the character. From the pleasing reward of the coin successfully collected to the shocking boom of your BFG, sound makes things cool. (Put this book down and play your favorite game—only with the sound switched off. See what the experience is like without the audio there to provide immersion and feedback.)

Too often the process of adding sound to a game level turns into the simple routine of supplying a list of assets that are checked off a spreadsheet. As with music, it's important to spend time with the designers or the producer "spotting" the level for sounds you will need. But as you do so, you should have uppermost in your mind the purpose or function of the sounds you are intending to implement. What does this sound bring to the game experience?

Make sure you have thoroughly familiarized yourself with any design documents available so that you have a proper awareness of what's actually going to be taking place within the level. (You'll often be starting to implement sound before many of the game mechanisms or scripting are in place.) This way you can talk about how they want the player to feel at a given place/moment and what's happening with the gameplay or narrative. Consequently you can try and avoid the spreadsheet mentality of "See a ventilation shaft, hear a ventilation shaft." As discussed later in "Interactive Mixing and the Power of Subjectivity," you should look for opportunities for the player to experience subjective or interpretive audio, sound that is heard via your character's emotional state or focus, as opposed to the strict "realism" of simply representing what's there. Don't be afraid to let go of the "real."

We'll deal with each of these topics in more detail through the examples that follow.

Reality and Characterization

> When we see and hear something at the same time the brain automatically fuses the object itself and the sound the object makes into one event. Sound gives us information about the material and nature of objects and this fusion (sometimes referred to as synchresis) between the audio and visual aspects allows us to get away with layering different sounds together for a specific object to give it a different feel or character, while still convincing us that it originates from that object. When game reviewers talk about the relative weight and power of weapons, they are getting most of this information from the sound.

600 Characterization Corridor

The first thing to remember when designing the sounds for your game is that sound has the power to change what we see. By choosing the sound to put together with a certain image (or object/ animation), you can make this object feel very different. It's interesting to note that when films are rated for age appropriateness, it is often the sound effects that are revised to make the action feel less violent. (Appendix E on the website offers some tips on sound asset creation/design.)

Along these corridors you will pick up three weapons in turn. Although graphically they all look exactly the same, they are characterized as different by the sounds that are attached to them. By choosing how to characterize a weapon, we can affect how the player feels. The choice as to whether you give the player a big, powerful sounding weapon, or a weaker sounding one will affect not only the players emotion but will also probably affect their gameplay style.

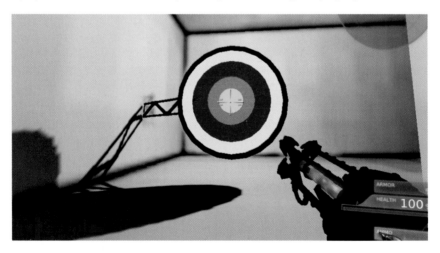

(To make sure that the player only has the weapon we want him or her to have, we are providing an inventory that is empty just before the player arrives at each weapon's locker. We do this by using the **[Give Inventory]** Action (New Action/Pawn/Give Inventory).)

The locker for each of the three weapons contains a shock rifle. We have swapped out the usual sounds and replaced them with our own. (For more on weapon sounds, see Chapter 7.)

At the end of the weapons corridor, the light flickers and goes out; we attach a light to the player to act as a torch using the **[Attach to Actor]** object (New Action/Actor/Attach to Actor). In the next room the floor drops away and the player enters the spooky tunnels under the level. The falling floor is actually a **[KActor]** that you'd usually control with the **[Matinee]** feature. In this case, it's simply in its original position as a floor; when the player enters the **[TriggerVolume]**, its physics is changed to PHYS_Falling (New Action/Physics/Set Physics), which means it will fall until it hits the surface below.

Define the Environment: Immersion and Emotion

Immersion in a game is when the player loses sense of the outside world and is, for a moment, "lost in the flow."

601 Spooky Sounds

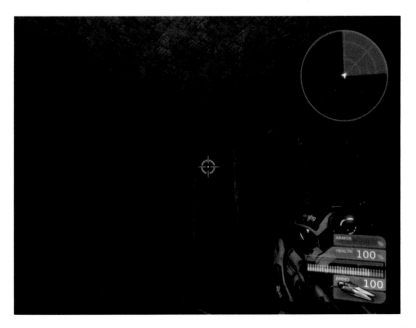

As well as characterizing particular objects, sound also characterizes an environment both through acoustic properties such as reverb and through the sounds and their location in the off-screen space. We've looked already at how even a simple room tone can have a significant aesthetic and emotional effect. Ambiences and sound environments do not have to be real to be immersive, but sounds that might have a source in reality (however strange) are often the most convincing.

Many games aim at the visceral thrills of fear and excitement. As you walk through the maze of corridors that make up Area 601, you'll hear a variety of sounds that are aimed at immersing the player in this environment.

Symbolic Sounds

The first approach to creating a spooky atmosphere is to use sounds that have become synonymous with danger. The sounds used in this area are either triggered via the usual **[Trigger]** or **[Trigger Volume]** Actors or are produced by **[AmbientSoundNonLoop]**s. The ambience contains some of these elements:

Dogs barking = Danger
Glass breaking = People doing things they shouldn't
Whispers = Ye olde reverse reverb effect (see Appendix E), a horror staple
People in pain = Danger
Low-frequency bangs, groans, or rumbles = Danger. (These types of sound often mean that something significant or structural is breaking; either that or something large is coming our way to have us for breakfast.)
Baby crying = This sound produces a natural tension. (Not many babies were harmed in the making of this book!)

Expect the Unexpected

Tension is created by playing with expectations. It is the unknown or unexpected that often generates a fear response. As illustrated in the level, sudden sounds can produce a shock effect but what is also effective, and used much less often, is to actually stop a sound. As you enter one of the areas, a room tone that has been present since the start suddenly stops for no apparent reason. This change leads the player to expect something to happen, and there's a tension in this anticipation.

Space, the Final (Technique) for Tears

For sound to be immersive, of course, it's important for it to be all around you, with no gaps or holes, to literally "immerse" you, but its direction and source can also have a powerful emotional effect. Evolution has conditioned us to be aware of danger, and we rely on our hearing to inform us of things that are either out of our field of view, hidden, or at a great distance. Sounds that are placed behind the player increase the perception of threat, and any sound source whose location is hard to identify also boosts tension. If a sound source is large enough for there to be ambiguity as to its point of origin, this can be as effective as sounds from the rear. (You'll obviously only notice this effect in the level if you're listening via a 5.1 or above surround sound setup.)

One way to achieve this effect would be to mix a surround ambience in your DAW and then import it as a multichannel sound source as described in Chapter 3. In this instance, however, we're illustrating a different approach.

To put a sound behind the player in order to spook them out we use the **[Attach to Actor]** object again. This time a **[TriggerDynamic]** is attached at an offset to the player (behind and above), and the sound is played back through this trigger.

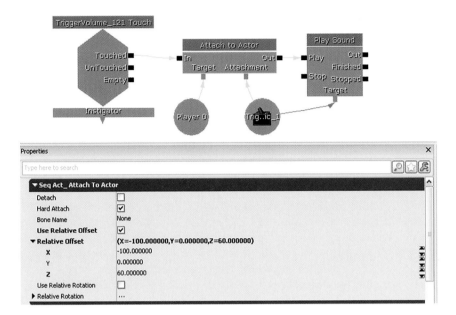

Characterization through sound design is, of course, absolutely key to the sound designer's job. We've only touched on a few ideas here (and there's more discussion in Appendix E), as other books already cover this aspect comprehensively. See the bibliography for further reading.

Exercise 601_00 Characterization

Make two versions of this exercise room to characterize it in two different ways. Firstly as a normal office, then as the setting for a new comedy horror game, 'The Office, a Transylvanian workplace'.

Tips

1. The easiest mood to evoke in sound is a disturbing one. Think of sounds that evoke this particular feeling.
2. Consider the strategies used in the tutorial level.
3. To generate shocking sounds, use sudden changes in volume and experiment with expectations. For example the first time you open the door it opens simply, the second time when the player presses open there is a dramatic scream !
4. Position sounds in space to have an unnerving effect and create some movement with **[AmbientSoundMovable]** Actors.
5. Add some low-frequency sounds for their "threatening" connotations.

Information and Feedback

One of the crucial differences between sound in film and in games is the reliance on sound in games to give the player critical gameplay information.

All of the points below relating to sound's role in providing information to the player apply equally to all games, but some are more equal than others. Multiplayer gaming is a special case in that information, both in terms of what the sound or music represent and in terms of its spacial location, is critical. A good multiplayer-level designer will use sound as a design tool, using footsteps to indicate not only location but character type, and placing items and weapons in areas that the designer knows will give off audio cues (such as in water) to alert the other players as to the first player's location. For now, consider how the following points apply particularly to multiplayer games. As soon as we can play for longer than 15 seconds without receiving a headshot and a derogatory remark from an 11-year-old American boy, we'll write a book specifically about multiplayer sound too (probably never).

Instruction

In its simplest form, sound often directs you to objects of interest through speech. Through Room 601, you were guided by various direct (specific instructions via an imaginary "headset") and indirect (via overheard comments, items on the radio) speech. These examples have been "futzed" to make them sound like they are being played back through these various playback media. (For more on how to create these futzed effects yourself, see Appendix E.)

Games often put a heavy burden on dialogue to instruct the player, either directly or indirectly and this can impact negatively on the "realism" or naturalness of the dialogue. (See Chapter 5 for more discussion on dialogue.) There are many ways to convey information without instructional dialogue, but it remains a fundamental part of many games. The most obvious (but sometimes overlooked) concept to bear in mind is that your instructional dialogue must be audible. In some circumstances you will have control over all the sound sources in a room, in which case you can balance them so the dialogue is easily heard. However, there may be other situations (in the heat of battle, for example) where the audibility of dialogue is more problematic.

One approach is to designate your dialogue **[SoundCue]** as belonging to the DialogLoud SoundClass. This technique boosts the volume of the dialogue in the center speaker, which can help it cut through a busy mix.

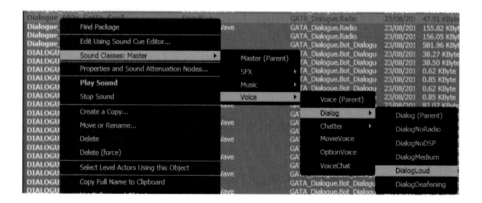

It may also be necessary to turn down the volume of other sounds that are playing to ensure that the player is able to hear the dialogue. The final room before exiting Room 600 provides an example of this approach, where the sounds in the area are "ducked" so that the player can hear the lines. We'll look at both SoundClasses and ducking in greater detail later in the chapter.

Feedback

> In addition to the very direct form of instructional dialogue, a great deal of other information is fed back to the player through sound.

Confirmation of Action Feedback

In the physical world sound is often used to provide a user with a confirmation of their action. Think of your mobile/cell phone or the ATM machine. Sound gives you the message that the button you've just pressed has in fact been acknowledged. This kind of confirmation sound is even more important in games, where the amount of feedback you get through their physical interface is often limited. Some interfaces may have "rumble" functionality where you can get some (haptic) feedback to confirm your actions, but many have none. Therefore, it's important to have the player's interactions confirmed with sound as a proxy for the tactile feedback of the physical world.

602 Weapons Locker Room

There are two doors leading into the weapons locker room. To open the door, you need the key-code that you overheard in the previous area. (If you've forgotten already it's 1, 2, er 3, ... 4.)

The panel on the left is silent. The panel on the right has sounds attached so that when you "press" the buttons your choice is confirmed with a beep. Which one is more satisfying to use?

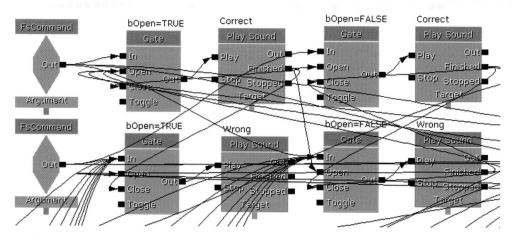

The interface for the Keypad is created using Adobe Flash and accessed via the **[Open GFx Movie]** Action. When you click on each number pad on the screen they output an **[FsCommand]** event. These go through a series of **[Gate]**s. As you get each stage of the combination right, the next **[Gate]** is opened until finally a **[Matinee]** object is triggered, which opens the door.

HUD/UI Feedback

This kind of audio feedback on your actions is equally important as part of any menu navigation user interface (UI) or heads-up display (HUD) that you interact with.

602a (in Room 602) HUD

In the room next to this one there are turrets that are protecting the weapons locker room. If you attempt to enter this room, you will undoubtedly get killed. The good news is that the weapons locker in this room carries a modified shock rifle with a grenade launcher attachment—handy, eh? When you've picked it up, press F10 to activate your inventory. Navigate this menu to select the new weapon.

When designing sounds to be used for menu navigation, you need to use sounds that somehow convey the notions of:

"Forward"/"Backward"
"Accept"/"Decline"

It is difficult to generalize about which sounds might have these kind of positive (forward/accept) or negative (backward/decline) connotations. A rule of thumb from speech patterns might be that positive meanings are often conveyed by a rise in pitch, whereas negative meanings are suggested by a fall in pitch. By using slight variations on a few sound sources, it is easier to produce a "positive" or "negative" version that conveys this meaning than it would be to use completely different sounds. This method also gives these sounds an identity as a family of related sounds rather than simply a collection of unrelated ones.

Your sounds will have more coherence and unity if you link them with the theme of the game world itself or with an aspect of the object that you're interacting with. If your game is set within a dungeons-and-dragons type of world, then the sounds on the UI menu might be made of armour and sword sounds; if your game is set in a sci-fi world, the sounds might be more electronic in nature. If you're going to have menu music playing while the game is in this mode, then you might consider how the UI sounds will fit with this. You can pitch-shift your UI sounds so that they are in the same key as the music so that they do not sound too abrasive against it, or you can use musical tones that fit with the style and notes of the background music. This option may not be appropriate in all cases, but it can add a nice sense of polish to your menus.

Look in the Sound Library "Feedback" folder to see if these items fit any pattern in regard to their positive or negative feedback.

As noted in Chapter 5, UDK's system for UI menus is based around Scaleform's GFx plug-in that allows developers to port across interfaces constructed in Adobe's Flash motion graphics software. This technique is a little too involved to deal with here, but all you need from your designer is the names of the events that the buttons on the interface will call. With a GFx movie opened (New Action/GFx UI/Open GFx Movie), you can get named events from the interface to trigger your sounds using the **[FSCommand]** (New event/GFx UI/FS Command).

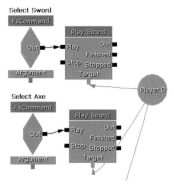

You can also do this via UDK's SoundThemes. Using a SoundTheme, you can then attach these to specific **[SoundCue]**s. You can see the SoundTheme for the UDK front-end menu system by using the Search toolbar in the Content Browser (search "Soundtheme").

To create your own, you need to go to the Actor Classes tab of the Content Browser. Uncheck the two boxes at the top (use "Actor" As Parent and Placeable Classes Only?), navigate down to the UTUISoundTheme Actor, right-click, and select Create Archetype.

See the UDK documentation for more on SoundThemes.

Exercise 602_00 Simple HUD

This exercise presents you with two game menus. The first menu is for a weapon selection menu in a MMOTDG (Massively Multiplayer Online Time Decimating Game) set in the ancient world of Turgeron. The second is the menu for selecting the super nano enhancements in the game "Star Paws", which revolves around the exploits of a genetically modified dachshund set in the year 2215. Create and add appropriate sounds for both these UI's.

Tips

1. The systems are already set up for you in this exercise. Simply replace the sounds in the appropriate **[SoundCue]**s.
2. Try to choose sounds that might somehow relate to the theme of the games.
3. Try using variations of one or two elements instead of a completely different sound for each action.
4. Test your sounds with your friends to see if you can get people to agree on what sounds right for forward/back/positive/negative feedback sounds.

NPC Status Feedback

One of the most essential pieces of information that sound often provides us with is that of the current status of enemies or other non-player characters (NPCs) in the game world.

602b Turret Guards

If you confront the turrets in the next room head on, they will kill you immediately; so you need to select the grenades weapon (via the inventory menu F10 or keyboard key 1) and fire at them from around the corner.

In many circumstances it's important for the player to get feedback on the enemy's status, and sound can be the most effective way of providing this information. Obviously the speech (or dying gasps) of your enemy give you an indication of the enemy's health, but other more symbolic sounds are also often used. In this example, when a turret is fully destroyed it emits a high-pitched whine like a heart monitor "flatline" sound. This is relatively straightforward to do and gives useful information to the player. However, there are two turrets in this room, and you need to know whether you have successfully disabled both.

If we kept the system as it is and the two turrets were destroyed simultaneously or immediately after one another, the two tones would overlap and blend in to appear like one constant tone. For the feedback to be clear, we must monitor if the first turret's tone is still playing. If it is, we should alter the second tone so that it is differentiated from the first and we can clearly tell that a second turret has also been destroyed.

When an enemy is killed, an integer of 1 is added to a variable. When this sound has finished playing, an integer of 1 is taken away from the variable. This variable will therefore only become 2 when two enemies have been killed and the first enemy's flatline sound effect is still playing. Because a single pitched tone combined with another tone at the same pitch will blend into one another (and just sound like a slightly longer single tone), we play the second tone at a slightly higher pitch if they are sounding simultaneously.

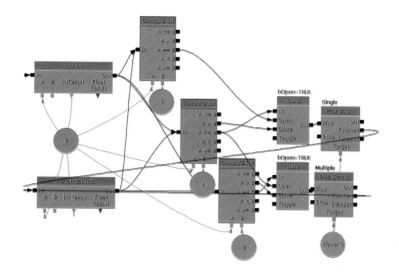

When the variable is greater than 1—that is, two enemies have been killed within this time period (and so their flatline sound would be overlapping)—the **[Gate]** to the "Single" is closed and the **[Gate]** to the "Multiple" **[SoundCue]** is opened. This is a second version of the original sound; the only difference is that its pitch has been raised within its **[SoundCue]** properties.

The default bot NPCs have some sound feedback already built in with their pain reactions. You can see these in the following folder within the Content Browser: UDK Game/Sounds/INT/A_Character_ CorruptEnigma_Cue. You could change these to your own by altering the references in the script:

C:\UDK\UDK(***)\Development\Src\UTGame\Classes\UTPawnSoundGroupLiandri.uc
```
HitSounds[0]=SoundCue'A_Character_CorruptEnigma_Cue.
Mean_Efforts.A_Effort_EnigmaMean_PainSmall_Cue'
HitSounds[1]=SoundCue'A_Character_CorruptEnigma_Cue.
Mean_Efforts.A_Effort_EnigmaMean_PainMedium_Cue'
HitSounds[2]=SoundCue'A_Character_CorruptEnigma_Cue.
Mean_Efforts.A_Effort_EnigmaMean_PainLarge_Cue'
```

Don't forget that any changes to a script will need recompiling and will affect all players on your version of the game from now on. For a reminder about basic scripting, go back to the "Scripting 101" section in Chapter 3 and see the "Scripting" section in Appendix C.

Player Status Feedback

Sound is often used to inform the player about his or her own character's status and health.

602c Ammo Storage Basement

By going down the ladder, you will find yourself in the ammo storage area. You'll need to pick up the weapon here and some additional ammo for the next section. However, the dastardly enemies have stored all their ammo in a radioactive liquid. You should be all right as long as you don't stay in too long. As soon as you hit the water, the danger beep starts. Pick up as much ammo as you can before the radioactivity irreparably damages your health.

As you enter the radioactive liquid, a **[TriggerVolume]** starts the health damage system. After a delay of five seconds, the looping **[Delay]** starts. Each time this **[Delay]** completes, it increments a variable by 0.02. This is then subtracted from a constant of 1 to give a new delay time (0.98, 0.96, 0.94, etc.). The result is that the warning beep emitted by the **[PlaySound]** object gets faster and faster the longer the player is still touching the **[TriggerVolume]** (i.e., still in the radioactive liquid).

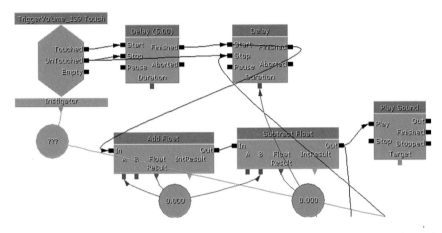

If the player stays in the water too long, a pain **[SoundCue]** is played and the player has a short time to get out before being killed. A **[Compare Float]** object compares the **[Delay]** variable to 0.2; if this is true, then a **[PlaySound]** leads to a **[Modify Health]** to kill the player.

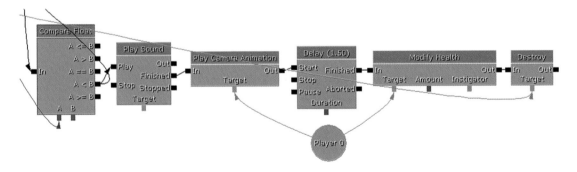

You'll note that if you stay actually *under* the water too long, the built-in damage of the UDK **[UTWaterVolume]** also takes effect. The **[UTWaterVolume]** (added like a **[TriggerVolume]** from the Volumes menu) also has enter and exit sounds.

A second **[TriggerVolume]** just under the surface of the water is used to fade in and out the underwater bubbling sounds.

Weapon Status Feedback

Do you watch the ammo counter on your HUD when you're in the heat of battle? Most people don't, so it's up to the sound to give them feedback on the status of their weapon, such as its condition and how full the clip is.

602d Weapons Target Practice

When you shoot the weapon you pick up in this firing range, you will get audio feedback to let you know the status of the weapon. In this case, the weapon uses a new variation of its firing sound when the ammo count gets below 25.

We'll look at how this is done in the weapon script presented in the "Weapon Systems" section of Chapter 7. This example reflects the way that some real weapons firing sound changes in character depending on the number of bullets left in the clip. You could also adapt this system so that a weapon's sound alters as it gets damaged with over-use, or there could be a sound for the clip ejecting when empty. Whether it represents the reality of the weapon itself or not, getting audio feedback from their weapon is very useful to a player.

Symbol/Punishment/Reward

In certain genres of games (particularly platformers), the repetitive nature of the pickup sounds serves as a kind of conditioned response to punish or reward the player. Whether it's picking up stars, coins, or powerups, the sounds are there to reward the player with a pleasurable confirmation of achievement.

602e Punishment/Reward

You need to regain some health, so go through these corridors and pick up the, er, pickups. Beware! Some have degraded and therefore will actually damage you.

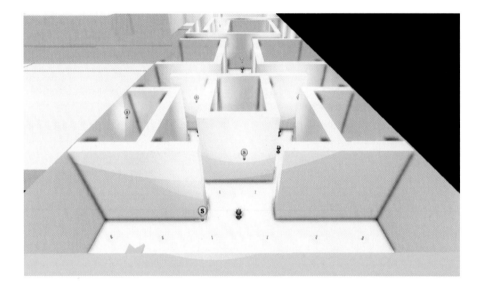

Rather like the UI menu sounds, it is hard to generalize as to what makes a satisfying reward or punishment pickup sound that will withstand being listened to for thousands of repetitions. The repetition makes the sound drive a conditioned reflex to seek/avoid certain sounds. You need each one to have a clearly different sound so that you can recognize what it is; at the same time, the sounds cannot be so varied that they feel part of a different game.

Although we have droned on a great deal about the need for variation in your sounds, these type of feedback sounds are an exception to the rule. These sounds are the equivalent of "earcons" in computer software that tell you you've got mail, in that they are sounds that carry specific meaning. Although a typical "coin" or "star" pickup sound may go up in pitch if you collect more within a given period of time, for symbolic sounds like these we are interested in the information they convey rather than the sound itself, so the repetition of the same audio sample is less of a problem than it has been in other circumstances. The player is concerned with the learned meaning of the sound rather than any information conveyed by the nature of the sound itself. We don't want the distraction of variation where the player might be forced to think about the sound more. If there were variations in the sound, the player would be forced to consider "Why is this sound different? What is it trying to tell me?" rather than simply being able to acknowledge the information that the presence of the sound has provided.

The existing health pickup script is here:

C:\UDK\UDK(***)\Development\Src\UTGameContent\Classes\UTPickupFactory_HealthPack.uc

Try the following exercise to create your own health pickups, and add different sounds to give each one a different meaning or character.

Exercise 602e_00 A Quick Pick-Me-Up

Your player has been trapped in an electromagnetic pulsar field. Help is on its way, but the only way for the player to survive the next three minutes is to continually replenish his or her health. Luckily, the health pickups are being continually regenerated around the room.

Tips

1. Add lots of health pickups to the level. In the Content Browser/Actor Classes tab navigate to Pickups/Health/ UTPickupFactory_Healthpack.
2. Attach these to the **[Toggle]** objects in the Kismet system provided so that they will randomly appear.
3. Extend this by now adding your own pickup sounds through creating some new Health pickups. Close the editor.
4. Navigate to the C:\UDK\UDK(***)\Development\Src\UTGameContent\Classes folder and open the UTHealthPickupFactory.uc script with the Windows notepad. Edit the references to **[SoundCue]**s and replace them with your own. Now save the file with a new name in your My Mod/Classes folder: (C:\UDK\UDK(***)\ Development\Src\MyMod\Classes). For example we would name ours GATHealthPickup.
5. Make sure your new name for this pickup is reflected within its own script file—that is, for our new pickup 'GATHealthPack' the third line down of the script would read
   class UTPickupFactory_GATHealthPack extends UTHealthPickupFactory.
6. Using the Unreal Front End, recompile your scripts using the Script/Compile Scripts command.
7. Now re-open the editor and you should see your new pickups in the menu of the Content Browser/Actor Classes/ Pickups/Health/.

Navigation

Attract

Part of the challenge of designing games based in three-dimensional (3D) worlds is helping your player to navigate the world without becoming lost or frustrated. Subtle visual clues can be effective in attracting players toward certain areas without being as clumsy as a big pointing arrow. Sound and music can also play a specific role in helping players navigate the space or in drawing their attention to certain objects. This technique is all the more effective if the players are unaware that they are being manipulated.

603 Navigation

As you enter this area, you will hear a distant beeping. Without needing to give any specific instructions to the player, all but the most perverse will probably be attracted to seek out the source of this sound.

When you touch the **[TriggerVolume]** leading outside, an **[AmbientSoundSimpleToggleable]** is switched on. This starts the beeping sound, which is located in the same place as the pickup the player is being encouraged toward. Upon reaching the destination ammo pickup, this is toggled off and the **[KActor]** is hidden.

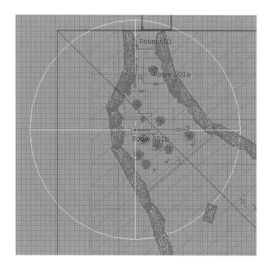

This is an example of how sounds can be used in simple but effective ways in the level design to help navigate players toward areas or objects of interest.

Repel

603a Radioactive

As you navigate your way to the mysterious beeping object, the player's path will also be to some extent dictated by the audio from the "radiation" zones.

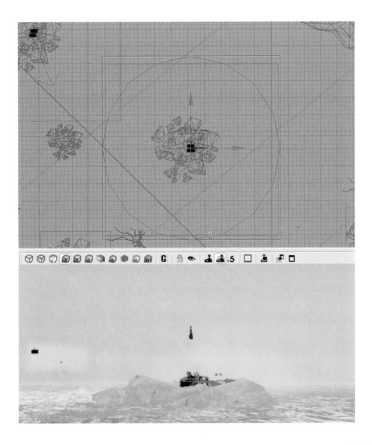

In addition to attracting players, sound can also guide them away from potentially hazardous areas. As a player passes the initial **[TriggerVolume]**, a low Geiger counter (radiation monitor) crackle is started along with a camera animation and motion blur effect to indicate that the presence of this sound is not a good thing.

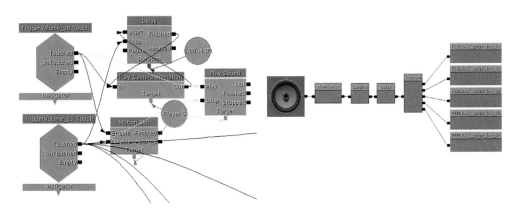

Around each radiation area are two **[Trigger]**s. The outer **[Trigger]** plays back a Geiger_High **[SoundCue]** to warn the player of the danger. If the player chooses to ignore this warning and continues, then the inner **[Trigger]** applies a **[Modify Health]** object to damage the player.

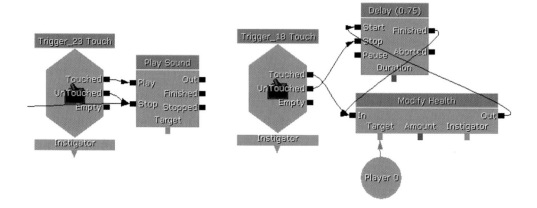

When a player leaves the immediate proximity of a radiation area, the **[Trigger]** is "UnTouched" and turns the Gieger_High **[SoundCue]** off. When the player finally leaves this area, another **[TriggerVolume]** turns the low Geiger counter and camera animations off to let them know that they are now in the clear.

Exercise 603a_00 Manipulate

This series of rooms represents a maze. Guide your player through the maze using sound as the only navigation device.

Tips

1. Try using **[AmbientSoundSimpleToggleable]**s to lead your player in certain directions.
2. Set up **[TriggerVolume]**s to toggle these like the example in Area 603.
3. You could also use **[Trigger]**s to warn of danger or to act as rewards.

Tracking Devices

Some games make use of an audio tracking device to enable the player to locate objects or NPCs. These kinds of audio tracking devices are often at their most effective (and scary) when the visuals are deliberately obscured either through fog or darkness. This forces the player to rely more on the audio and taps into the tension of knowing that there's something there, but not knowing quite where it is.

603b Enemy Tracker

At the ammo drop you pick up an enemy tracking device. This emits a beep that changes in rate, pitch, and volume the closer you get to the enemy. Find the enemy.

The enemy is spawned at the location of **[Note_8]** and the distance from the player to this point is used to control the duration of a **[Delay]** object. The **[Get Distance]** object is rechecked and updated every 0.1 seconds by a looping **[Delay]**. To use the distance variable directly would lead to the **[Delay]** duration being 1,000+ seconds, so it is scaled by the **[Divide Float]** object (/1000) to get it into a more useful range of values.

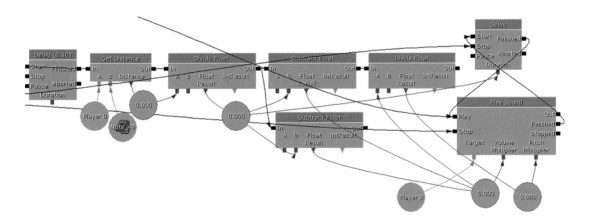

This number is then also subtracted from 1.4 to give the **[PlaySound]**'s volume multiplier, and it is subtracted from 1.6 and then divided by 2 to give the **[PlaySound]**'s pitch multiplier. This means that the volume gets louder, and the pitch higher, the closer you get to the enemy. Either of these feedback mechanisms can also work well in isolation.

You could extend this system so that the **[SoundCue]** changes depending on the player's distance from the enemy using a series of Compare subsequences like the system in the Physics area (Room 304b). This would play a different **[SoundCue]** when the player's distance from the enemy fell between different ranges.

Exercise 603b_00 Tracker

The player has to find the red keycard to get out of this area. It must be on the body of one of the guard bots, which have been deactivated. Fortunately, players have a tracking device to help them find it. Use the player's distance from the guard holding the keycard to control the speed of the tracking device beeps.

Tips

1. The guard's location is marked with a **[Note]** object.
2. Use a **[Get Distance]** action with inputs A being the player (New Variable/Player/Player) and B the **[Note]** (select the note in your viewport, then right-click the B input of **[Get Distance]** to create a New Object Var using Note (***)).
3. Set up a **[Delay]** that retriggers the **[Get Distance]** action to update the distance from the player to this **[Note]** every 0.5 seconds.
4. Create another **[Delay]** object that retriggers a beeping **[SoundCue]**.
5. Create a New **[Float]** variable for the duration of this **[Delay]** (right-click the duration input and select Create New Float Variable).
6. Use some maths (Right-click/New Action/Math) to scale the values you are getting from the **[Get Distance]** Distance output into ones that are appropriate for the varying length of the beeping **[Delay]**. (Send the float result of this math to the **[Delay]**'s duration variable.)

Orientation

We have already discussed the importance of sound in describing off screen space in reference to ambient sounds, but knowing where your enemies are coming from in games is crucially important.

603c Town Square showdown/Orientation

After you have found and shot the Rebel leader in the town square, you will find enemies charging toward you from various directions. The vocalizations will cue you as to the direction of their approach before you are able to see them. Note how we need to return to the concepts around sound sources and spatialization in order for the directional cues given by these sounds to be clear enough.

The bot dialogue here uses two different **[SoundCue]**s, each with different Distance Algorithm and Radius Min/Radius Max settings (from the **[SoundCue]**'s **[Attenuation]** node). The player's ability to judge the direction from which the enemy is coming will depend on the settings you choose.

Interactive Mixing and the Power of Subjectivity

In order for any of the intended functions of sound or music to be achieved the audio mix needs to be considered. Before you start thinking about the various audio elements and their appropriate volume level you need to be clear on what you want to be heard, and why.

In the opening to this chapter we discussed how the sound field within a game differs from that in the real world and how consequently we need to actively control the mix of the different audio elements in order for the player to be able to make sense of them.

The mix on sounds and music that we hear at any one time is the product of several factors:

- The volume of the sound sources
- The number of these sound sources
- The timbral nature of the sound sources (their frequency content)
- The spatial nature of the sound sources (3D spatialized, stereo, multichannel)
- The attenuation over distance settings of the sources
- The reverberant environment in which they take place
- The impact of occlusion systems like ambient zones
- Global, group, or bus-level volume controls

When considering these factors, the key is to be conscious of what you want the player to hear and why these things are important. It may be appropriate at times to have a very dense mix with lots of activity; at other times it will work better if the mix is sparse.

The first requirement that will force you to consider these questions is the fact that there is a hard limit on the number of sound channels, or *voices,* that you are actually able to play back at any one time.

Voice Instance Limiting and Prioritization

All game engines have a limitation on the number of sound channels or voices they can play simultaneously. Although in exceptional circumstances this can be a problem (see the retriggered weapons examples in Chapter 7), it actually works in our favor most of the time because whether we have 48 or (theoretically) 512, it forces us to think about which sounds should be the highest priority.

Before we consider a hierarchy of types of audio to decide which can be lost, or *culled,* if the voice count gets too high, we should take steps to try to make sure that it doesn't get too high in the first place. Within the properties of each **[SoundCue]**, the setting for Max Concurrent Play Count allows us to determine the number of times this cue can play simultaneously before instances are culled. (Right-click/Properties and Sound Attenuation Modes/Max Concurrent Play Count.)

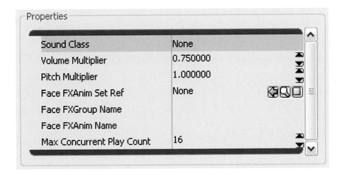

The default is 16, but for some sounds you may wish to consider setting this variable lower. How many instances of the same **[SoundCue]** you hear will be significantly affected by the attenuation over distance curves you apply.

Depending of the nature of the scenario, you may want to be able to hear NPC footsteps from a significant distance, in which case you could potentially get a high number of concurrent instances.

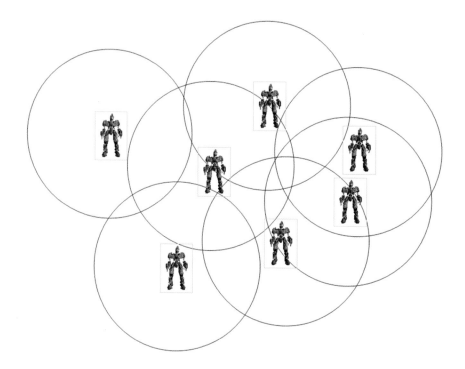

Alternatively there may frequently be many NPCs within a confined area, in which case you may want to reduce their Radius Max or lower the Max Concurrent Play Count for the footsteps **[SoundCue]**. You might consider swapping between two or more **[Soundcue]**s, that actually reference the same sound wave but have differing Max Concurrent Play Counts, depending on the circumstances.

It might be appropriate to consider grouping your **[SoundCue]**s into different categories and devising some general rules as to the number of voices you will allow for each one depending on its importance to the game or the particular scenario. You can select multiple **[SoundCue]**s at once in the Content Browser and adjust their Max Concurrent Play Counts simultaneously.

One, Two, Few

The other thing to remember here is the idea we discussed with regard to cascading physics in Chapter 3. Perceptually we tend to view things as a group when there are more than two of them, so it's worth considering if you need specific instances of a sound to sync precisely beyond a certain number, or whether it would be better to discuss a method with your programmer of switching instead to a different "group" sound file.

Prioritization

Given the interactive and dynamic nature of games, no matter how carefully you plan there will always be instances where the system becomes overloaded. When this happens, you don't want to be listening to the great ambience and footsteps all around you while the player weapon is actually the voice that is being culled.

Along with the voice instance limiting systems, all audio engines have some way of making sure that there is a hierarchy of sounds so that in such circumstances the lower-priority sounds are culled but the high-priority sounds continue to play. Typically you'd consider your sounds in groups such as Mission Dialogue, Player Weapons, NPC Weapons, Explosions, Dialogue Chatter, Ambience, and so on, and then you would tag these groups by their relative importance. In UDK, things are somewhat less sophisticated than this at the moment. What we do have is an option within the SoundClasses to choose "Always Play," which will prioritize any sound assigned to this SoundClass above others in a limited voice count situation. SoundClasses are discussed again later in the chapter.

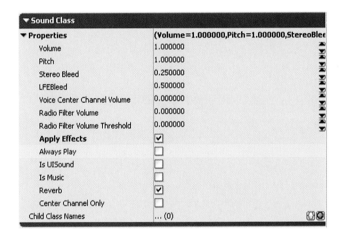

With the advances in the capabilities of current gaming platforms, the use of a simple limiting system on the number of concurrent versions of a particular sound is usually sufficient. However, with the expansion in the number of voices available, we are faced with this dichotomy: now that we can play everything, perhaps not playing everything is the way forward. Read on.

(Also see "Audio Optimization and Tracking the RAM Budget" in Appendix B, for instructions on how to track your voice count.)

Listening Levels

Mixing for cinema has long established a reference level to mix at, which is then replicated exactly in the cinema. Within this controlled environment, you know that the audience is going to be experiencing the film at exactly the same level at which you are mixing. Unfortunately, as of yet, games have no established reference level for mixing but it's important to bear in mind that games are a home entertainment medium and as such should be considered alongside similar media such as TV or DVD. People play games in a variety of environments and circumstances, and through a variety of mediums, from a mono television to a 7.1 THX-certified surround-sound setup. If you are not mixing within a professional environment (and as beginners we'll assume that most of you aren't), then one reference level it is worth paying attention to is the console's startup sound and any dashboard/interface sounds (on the PC, people usually set their default volume levels according to the notify sounds, such as that used for incoming mail; unfortunately, particularly on older versions of Windows, these are blisteringly loud). People are not going to want to have to jump up and down (or even reach for the remote) to adjust the volume for your game, so setting your own playback levels to a point where these sounds are comfortable can give you an indication of the volume at which a significant proportion of people are going to be listening to your game. (For a proper discussion of game mixing levels, see the links in the bibliography for this chapter.)

Planning for a Dynamic Mix

The concept of "mixing" actually starts with the design of the game itself. The events in the game will govern the density and nature of the sound and music at any given moment. In the past, game audio was too often treated as a fixed system, a network of processes put in place and then left to get on with it. Mixing a game needs to be integrated with the game design and should be dynamic and responsive to gameplay. We don't mix to make sure that everything is heard (we've established that in terms of presenting a "reality" that is impossible); we mix to make sure that the sounds we want to be heard are heard. Our choices are based on the gameplay or narrative function of the sound or music at that moment.

The first issue to consider is that not only does our perception of the frequency content of sound change depending on the volume at which it is played back, but our perception of volume is actually very subjective. Humans do not have an built-in reference level for sound, and so perceive loudness as a comparative level, not an absolute. We will compare the volume of a sound to the volume of the other sounds we have heard within a recent time window. If you are sitting quietly in the kitchen in the middle of the night trying to finish writing a book and accidentally knock your cup of coffee off the table, sending it crashing to the floor, this is loud. As you walk over to the aircraft that is warming up on the runway, then you will also consider this to be loud. Intellectually you know that the jet engine is probably a lot louder than the cup breaking, but psychologically, at the time, the cup felt louder.

You will want to use the full dynamic range that you have available in order to highlight the differences between your quiet sounds/music and your loud sounds/music. In order for an event to feel loud, the other events around it must be by comparison relatively quiet. Unfortunately, in some genres there can be an expectation that loud equals good without an understanding that if everything is loud all the time then (1) your players will simply turn the volume down and (2) nothing will actually feel loud because your players have not experienced a quiet sound to compare it to. Increasingly people are using visual maps of the events in the game to help plan these moments of light and shade, these peaks and valleys. Here's what a map of activity in a game might look like.

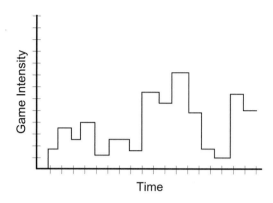

Gradually game designers are realizing that in order to have an impact, the loud/intense sections of a game need to be balanced with quiet/tense sections. (These intense sections are sometime referred to as an "action bubble".) In terms of audio, this is helpful but we need to consider the timescales over which to plan these dynamic contrasts. If we were to parallel a film approach, we might decide to save our loudest, most dramatic, sounds and music for a key climactic point in the game. This might happen, for example, at around eight hours into play. The difference is that the volume levels within cinema are known and controlled so members of the audience will know/feel that this section is really loud/intense compared to what they saw before within a relatively narrow timescale. A game player, however, may be returning to the game after several weeks away and will also likely be playing the game at a different volume level than he or she was using before. So in terms of a dynamics map for the mix of a game, we need to work over smaller contained time windows. These might be delineated by save points, levels, or exploration/conflict sections.

Planning for a Full Mix

So you've set up some voice limiting and prioritization systems, you've set the volume of your menu music and UI sounds so the players will set their volume levels appropriately to give you some dynamic range to play with, and now you're looking at your action bubble in which pretty much everything is going to kick off. Where do you start?

Although we've tried to make the case for variety in terms of having less and more dense periods of activity, and consequently thinner and thicker sound textures, there are some genres that by their nature are typically intense for a significant proportion of the time. There are some parallels to be made between the discipline of mixing sound for films and that of mixing for games, but perhaps a more fruitful one is to look toward music production. Film's language of distant, medium, and close-up shots means that the nature of the sound track is often that of a shifting focus rather than an attempt to represent the soundscape as a whole. If you listen to an action sequence in a film, then you will notice that the mix is radically altered from moment to moment to focus on a particular sound or event; therefore, it is actually quite unlike the mix for games where, as the player is in control and the perspective fixed, we sometimes need to try to represent many events simultaneously. We can use focus for specific effect (see "Subjective Sound States" presented later in the chapter), but in the main, the need to provide information to the player means many elements will be present and that the challenges are more akin to those of music production than film production.

In a music mix, you have a number of simultaneous elements that you want the listener to be able to hear and choose from. You are allowing the listener the possibility of selective listening. To achieve this goal, you might think in terms of the arrangement, the panning, the relative volumes of instruments, compression/limiting, EQ, and reverb. In a typical soundscape for a game, our concerns are similar:

> *Arrangement.* The number of simultaneous sound sources; a product of the game's activity map, voice instance limiting, and occlusion.
> *Panning.* The spatialized nature of the sound sources.
> *Volume.* A product of the actual volume of the source together with the source's attenuation curve.
> *Compression/limiting.* The overall headroom limitations of combining 16-bit sound sources.
> *EQ.* The design and nature of the sound sources themselves in terms of their frequency content.
> *Reverb.* The different game environments and their reverberant nature.

Some of these aspects are *predetermined* (i.e., they are set in place before the game runs), some can be *automated* by processes at run time, and some are best controlled via triggers (*triggered*) from specific events or variables at run time. (The latter are sometimes referred to as *active* mixing types and the two former types as *passive*.)

Predetermined Mix Elements

This would include the *arrangement* (amount of activity) that is predetermined depending on the game design. The panning and reverb are also determined by the game's system for spatializing sound and the design of the level. The sound source's attenuation curves are also typically predetermined before run time. Although EQ can be varied during gameplay, the fundamental nature of the sound and its frequency content is predetermined.

All of these factors will impact upon the mix and need to be considered in light of the circumstances within the game. For instance, it might be more realistic to have a long hall reverb type in a particular game location, but if you know that the game design decisions mean that there's going to be a battle taking place, then this will affect (1) your decision to have the reverb there at all and (2) your decision regarding the wet/dry mix of the reverb. You will also make different decisions about attenuation curves and panning depending on the number of potentially simultaneous events, the distances involved, and the relative importance of being able to identify point sources.

If you know that a set of 40 sounds and a specific piece of music are to be used in one area, then you should consider the frequency content of those sounds and perhaps identify different bands of frequency for different types of sound so they're not all fighting for space. A typical example would be to dedicate certain ranges for the music and other ranges for the main power of the sound effects. In the sound field represented here, the different elements have some overlap in terms of their frequency range but are different enough so that when they are heard at the same time (imagine the image being squashed in from each side), each one still has some (vertical) room.

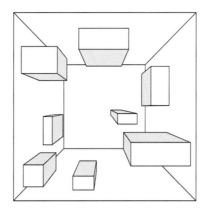

Plan the frequency ranges for elements that you know are likely to be played simultaneously.

At a very basic level, it's worth considering the relative volumes of the different elements of your sound-scape. Some have approached this by setting some general ground rules for different types of sound; for instance, the UDK guidelines suggest the following volume levels: dialogue ~1.4, music ~0.75, weapons ~1.1, and ambience ~0.5. This is, of course, based on the premise that the raw sound files are themselves at equal volume in the first place. We know that there's no such thing as "equal" volume because our perception of loudness is (1) subjective and (2) dependent on the frequency content of the sound, not its amplitude. Having said this, most people find that some kind of normalization strategy applied to groups of sounds in their DAW can save a lot of individual tweaking later. (Normalization is a basic function of any DAW that will scan the audio file to find the peak value then increase the gain of the whole file so that this peak does not exceed a given value.)

Theoretically you should normalize all assets to 100%, as every good sound engineer knows that mixing should be a process of gain reduction, not boosting, but in reality it's quicker and easier to run a batch process on a folder of sounds to set some general ballpark levels within your DAW than it is to edit the properties of each sound wave after it's been imported into UDK. (For tips on batch processing, see the online Appendix F.)

All these things are examples of how you should always be considering the final mix and making mix decisions before you even get near what is typically characterized as the mixing stage.

Automated Mixing Systems

All platforms have some sort of built-in limiting system to stop distortion. These are often clumsy and unpredictable, so it's really best to avoid having to apply these systems in the first place. There are also, however, increasingly intelligent systems of automation that can really help the overall mix of the game. Given the huge dynamic range of sounds in the physical world and the limited dynamic range that can be represented by 16 bits of information, it is not surprising that achieving the feeling of a wide dynamic range in games is a particular challenge. We've discussed how the level design can contribute to this effort, but we also need systems in place that will allow the intelligent management of which sounds are playing, and how many, so that the combinations of these sounds do not cause clipping and bring in the blunt instrument of the limiter. Chirping insects may add an important element of immersion to a game environment when you are creeping around, but in the midst of battle you will not hear them because they will be masked by the louder sounds. An automated system that monitors the current levels of the sounds at the player's location and culls the quieter elements, which you won't hear anyway, will both clean up the mix in terms of frequency content and create some additional headroom for the sounds you do want to hear.

A considerable amount of clever work has been done on interactive mixing for games audio in recent years that falls outside of the introductory parameters of this book. We would encourage you to undertake some further reading in this area, starting with the bibliography for this chapter.

(Various mixing-related changes such as volume ducking may be implemented as an automatic process for a particular subset of sounds, but as this is still a triggered event—albeit an automated one—capable of being overridden during run time, rather than a constant background process, we are going to consider it within the Triggered mixing category.)

Triggered Mixing Systems

Obviously we do not want to have to specify mix settings for every single sound or music element in game, so like a traditional mixing console we can use the idea of a group or bus that will control the volume of a given subset of sound types. By routing several channels to a group (or, in our case, routing the sounds themselves), you have quick and easy control over their volume. Rather than having to move 10 faders while maintaining their relative volumes to each other, you can just move the Group fader. A typical use in music production would be to have a group for drums to control the overall volume of the kit as a whole in relation to the other elements. The default groups (SoundClasses) in UDK are listed in the figure below.

A collection of mixer settings is sometimes referred to as a mixer snapshot or mixer state. These will contain the volume levels for each group or bus together with other mix settings such as EQ or FX. When triggered, mixer values will be set to any of the different states or snapshots you have defined. These might be aligned to specific modes (such as in-game or menu), locations, or events (power up, shellshock, etc). In our initial discussion we will assume that only one mixer state (or SoundMode in UDK) can apply at any one time and that when called it will override the current mixer state. The changes between states, however, may be applied immediately or over a transition period.

An interactive game level speaks a thousand words, so we will look at these principles in more depth via UDK's mixing system of SoundClasses and SoundModes.

SoundClasses and SoundModes

Each **[SoundCue]** in UDK can be assigned to a Soundclass (we looked at this briefly when discussing AmbientZones). To see which class a **[SoundCue]** is currently assigned to, select the cue in the Content Browser, right-click, and select Properties and Sound Attenuation Nodes.

For instance, in the A_Character_Footsteps package (in the UDKGame/Content/Sounds folder), you can see that the A_Character_Footstep_Default **[SoundCue]** is set to belong to the SoundClass called Character.

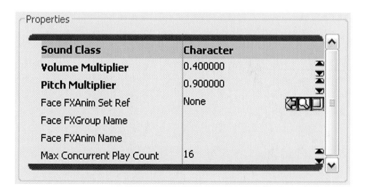

In List view in the Content Browser you can also scroll to the right to see which SoundClass the cues are assigned to by looking at the Custom 1 column. To assign your own **[SoundCue]**s to a SoundClass, use the right-click menu on the **[SoundCue]** which allows you to select from the existing list of SoundClasses.

Note that any sounds that do not belong to a **[SoundCue]** and are played back by the objects below are automatically designated as belonging to the Ambient SoundClass:

> **[AmbientSoundSimple]**
> **[AmbeintSoundNonLoop]**
> **[AmbientSoundSimpleToggleable]**
> **[AmbientSoundMovable]**

SoundClasses are UDK's equivalent of a mix group or bus. If you navigate to the SoundClassesandModes package, you can see how they work (UDKGame/Content/Sounds/SoundClassesandModes).

Double-click on any of the SoundClasses here to open the Sound Class Editor. Here you can see all of the available SoundClasses/Groups/Buses together with a tree structure that defines their hierarchy. It defines the SoundClasses in terms of "Parents" and "Children." (Although there appears to be a separate SoundClass object for each SoundClass, they actually all reference the same hierarchy tree and any changes made in one will be duplicated in all.)

By using this parent/Child grouping system, we can choose to change the parameters of an individual SoundClass, or by going to a higher-level group/parent we can specify a setting for the group as a whole. The default SoundClass hierarchy is shown overleaf.

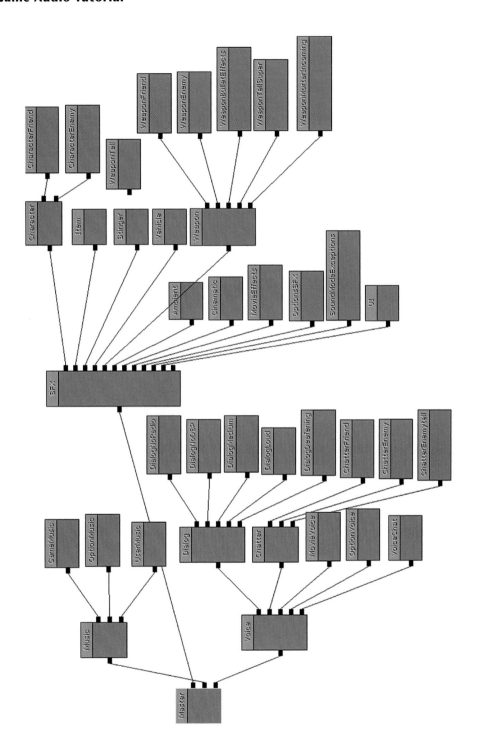

For example, we might choose to change the volume of the enemy weapons (WeaponEnemy), or the volume of all the weapons (Weapon), or the volume of all of the sound effects (SFX).

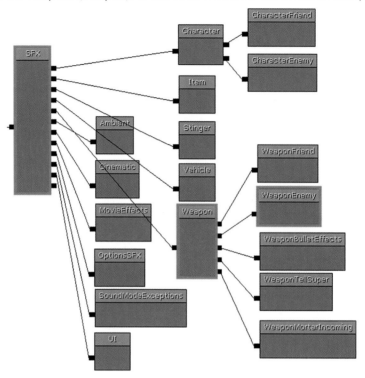

We do this by selecting the option Apply to all Children within a SoundMode, which we'll come to shortly.

The existing parent/child hierarchy is a reasonable place to start; however, if it makes sense for your particular situation, you can edit this tree to set up your own parent/child relationships and create new SoundClasses to position within them. See the SoundClass Bunker example that follows.

Within the Sound Class Editor there are additional properties that will apply to any **[SoundCue]** assigned to these classes:

▼ Sound Class	
▼ Properties	(Volume=1.000000,Pitch=1.000000,StereoBleed=0.250000,LFEBleed=0.500000,VoiceCenterChannelVolume=0.000000,RadioFilterVolume
Volume	1.000000
Pitch	1.000000
Stereo Bleed	0.250000
LFEBleed	0.500000
Voice Center Channel Volume	0.000000
Radio Filter Volume	0.000000
Radio Filter Volume Threshold	0.000000
Apply Effects	☑
Always Play	☐
Is UISound	☐
Is Music	☐
Reverb	☐
Center Channel Only	☐
Child Class Names	... (0)

- The **Volume** and **Pitch** apply a master control to anything attached to this class.
- **Stereo Bleed** refers to the amount of a stereo sound source that should "bleed" into the surround speakers.
- **LFE Bleed** is the amount of sound to bleed to the LFE channel (the Low-Frequency Effects channel that goes to the subwoofer speaker). A portion of the low end frequencies of your sounds is already sent to the subwoofer via the Dolby bass management system so routing additional elements like this can cause a problematic comb filtering effect. If your system allows the sending of unique sounds to the LFE channel then you are better advised to make use of this.
- **Voice Center Channel Volume** is the volume of the source that will go to the center channel or center speaker in a 5.1 and 7.1 speaker setup. This is traditionally reserved for dialogue in the cinema and it can be useful in games if it is more important that the dialogue is heard than spatialized.
- **Radio Filter Volume** is the volume of the radio filter effect. Within the **[SoundCue]**'s Radius Min the sound behaves as normal. Outside of this the signal is treated as if it is now heard over a personal radio by the player i.e. it is heard through the center speaker with 'radioized' effects and does not attenuate over distance. Radio Filter Volume Threshold is the volume at which the radio filter starts.
- **Apply Effects** governs whether sounds belonging to this class have effects such as filtering applied.
- **Always Play** prioritizes the sound above others in a limited voice count situation.
- **IsUISound** determines whether or not the sound will continue to play during the pause menu.
- **IsMusic** designates the class as being music or not.
- **Reverb** controls whether reverb is applied to this class.
- **Center Channel Only** forces the sounds to appear only via the center speaker of a 5.1 or 7.1 system. This can be useful for dialogue.

604 SoundClass Bunker

In Bunker 604, the **[Trigger]** alternates the voice sample among three different **[SoundCue]** versions. The **[SoundCue]**s are exactly the same except that they have been designated as members of the following three SoundClasses, each of which has different properties. In the tutorial level, walk toward and away from the sound source to hear the effect of these properties. Note that these will only be obvious if you are listening on a 5.1 or 7.1 sound system.

GATRadio01

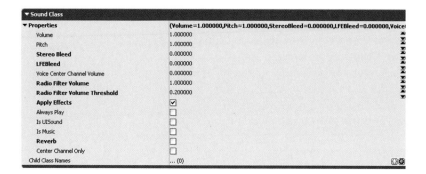

GATVoiceCenterChannel

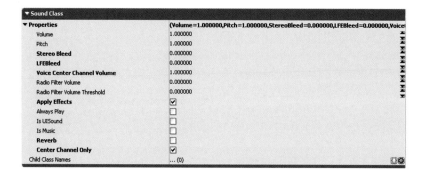

GATVoiceBleed

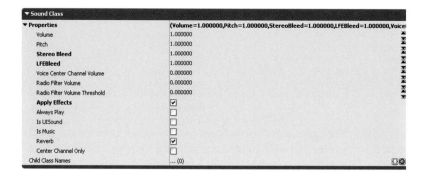

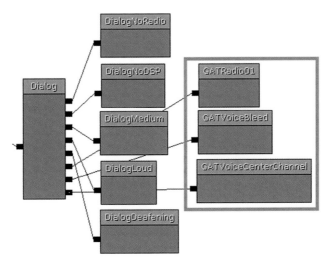

Soundmodes

SoundModes in UDK represent a type of snapshot or state mix described previously. Using these features you can define the volume (as well as the pitch and EQ) to apply to particular SoundClasses or groups of sounds. To explore these items, go over to the fence to (Area 604a) and wait until the cutscene is finished.

There are a number of sounds and music elements here, and you can hear the effect of some different SoundModes while in the Play in Editor mode by opening the console command (press the Tab key or @ key depending on your keyboard language).

In the console dialogue, type "setsoundmode" then type "GATMusicOnly" next.

```
(> setsoundmode GATMusicOnly_
    SetSoundMode <ModeName>
```

The mix should then change so that you are only hearing the music. Now open the console again and try the following in turn:

- SetSoundMode:
  - GATSFXOnly
  - GATDefault
  - LowPass

These 'Only' instances are useful for troubleshooting because they enable you to isolate different parts of the mix, but you can also see that having control over the volumes of different groups of sound can be very useful in terms of responding to gameplay and implementing the type of subjective sound scenarios discussed in this chapter.

In the Content Browser, navigate to the UDKGame/Content/Sounds/SoundClassesandModes package. Double-click on a SoundMode to open its properties menu.

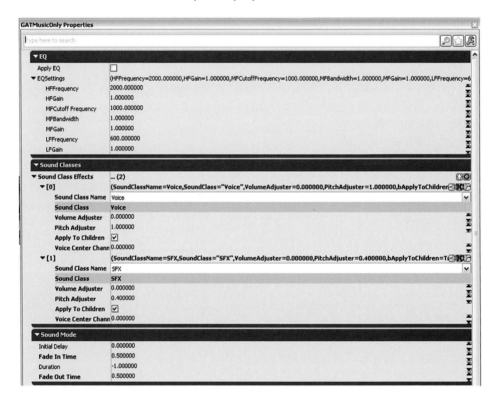

In this example, you can see the GATMusicOnly SoundMode. The three main parents in the SoundClass hierarchy tree are Music, Voice, and SFX. All of the other SoundClasses are children of these parents. By choosing the Voice and SFX classes, giving them a volume adjuster of 0.0, and ticking Apply to all Children, you effectively isolate just the Music SoundClass (and all of its children).

In the bottom SoundMode menu, you can choose whether this takes place immediately (Initial Delay), how long it takes to gradually be applied (Fade In Time), and what time period to undo the changes over (Fade Out Time). You can also set it to last a designated amount of time before switching itself off by entering a time in the duration slot. A duration of −1 means that it will last until a new Set Sound Mode action is triggered.

Also bear in mind that the changes you apply to SoundClasses within a SoundMode are cumulative. In other words, you can apply changes to all children, but you can apply a separate change to one of those children as well. The volume (or pitch) at which the child is heard is the result of combining both these values; see the "super-sense" example presented later.

We will continue to explore interactive mixing, SoundClasses, and SoundModes through the examples that follow.

Ducking

Ducking for Dialogue 01: Volume Ducking

As 5.1 or even 10.2 cannot represent a real sound field, we need to use mixing to focus the player's aural attention on what is important. Typically one of the most important sounds to a player is instructional dialogue. We can ensure this is audible by "ducking" out the other sounds.

604a Electrified Fence

As you approach the electrified fence, a cinematic cut-scene is triggered. In the immediate vicinity of where this dialogue is taking place are several other Sound Actors; crickets, electrical cracking of the fence, and some music. Although not overly loud like some battle sequences might be, we want players to focus their attention on the dialogue, so we use the **[SetSoundMode]** object within Kismet to change the mix.

The **[TriggerVolume]** turns on the Cinematic mode, which stops all input from the player while the cut-scene is taking place. The **[Matinee]** feature handles the camera movement and also includes an Event track that outputs an event we've called TriggerSoundModeChange just before the dialogue starts.

This event leads to a **[SetSoundMode]** Action that sets a mode called GATDuck, then when the dialogue has finished, the completed output of the **[Matinee]** feature calls another SoundMode called Default.

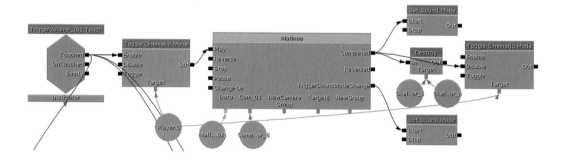

You can see in the figure below that the GATDuck SoundMode applies a volume of 0.2 to the SFX SoundClass (and all its children) and 0.2 to the Music SoundClass (and all of its children). The bot dialogue belongs to the Dialog Medium SoundClass, so it is left unaffected.

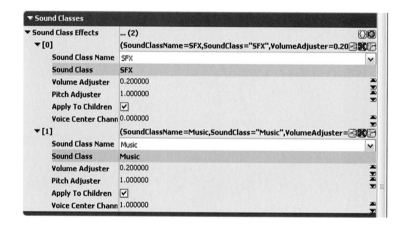

The Default SoundMode does not refer to any specific SoundClasses. In cases where no SoundClass is specified, default settings of 1.0 are applied to all SoundClasses.

EQ	
Apply EQ	☐
▶ EQSettings	(HFFrequency=2000.000000,HFGain=1.000000,MFCutoffFreque
▼ Sound Classes	
Sound Class Effects	... (0)
▼ Sound Mode	
Initial Delay	0.000000
Fade In Time	0.200000
Duration	-1.000000
Fade Out Time	0.200000

This approach is similar to "ducking," which you will be familiar with from radio. With this technique the presenter's voice is used as a controller to duck down the volume of the background music. This enables the voice to always be the loudest sound in the mix. This is particularly important in games where vital gameplay information may be being imparted. (Real ducking works by using the side chain input of a compressor so the speech acts as the control input while the compressor is actually applied to the music signal.)

When the cut-scene has ended you can walk up to the fence and hear that each sound layer has returned to its original volume.

To finish this sequence press H when near to the fence to place and start a small explosive device. This beeps four times and explodes on the fifth, destroying the fence.

An **[Int Counter]** is used to count the beeps; it then turns off the **[Delay]** and triggers the explosion **[PlaySound]**. At the same time, the Fence Panel itself is hidden and its Collision properties changed so the player can walk through the gap where the now invisible fence is.

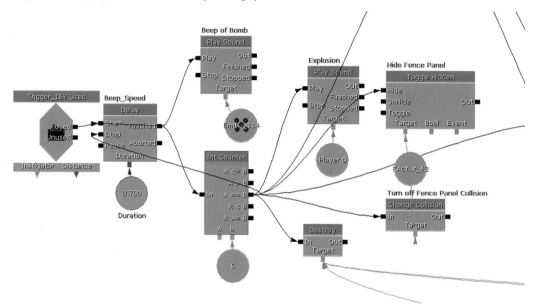

Another method for highlighting critical dialogue is to send it to the center speaker of a multichannel speaker set up. In the SoundMode settings we have the option to apply a multiplier to the SoundClasses default Center Channel Speaker Volume via the Voice Center Channel Volume Adjuster. For example the SoundClass that the **[SoundCue]** belongs to may have a Voice Center Channel Volume of 0.2 . By applying a SoundMode that has a Voice Center Channel Volume Adjuster of 10 the result will be a Voice center channel volume of 2.0.

Exercise 604a_00 Ducking

This room represents a noisy power plant. You need to duck the machinery sounds so that the player can hear the foreman when he gives instructions as to the order of switches needed to turn the machine off. You'd better get it right, or you're history.

Tips

1. The Kismet system will start the dialogue after 4 seconds. Link the output of this **[Delay]** object to a **[SetSoundMode]** (New Action/Sound/Set Sound Mode) Action.
2. Choose one of the existing SoundModes from the SoundClassesandModes package that will duck the volume of the SFX or Ambient class while not affecting the Dialogue class.
3. When the **[PlaySound]** for the dialogue has finished, remember to **[SetSoundMode]** back to default.
4. Some of the SoundModes may only last a limited amount of time (see the duration variable), not long enough for the dialogue to finish. Choose one with a −1 (infinite) duration or edit the existing one. Be aware that any edits made to the SoundClassesandModes package will affect any other part of the game that calls this SoundMode in the future, so it's best to edit it back to the original state when you're done.

Ducking for Dialogue 02: Notching

As well as ducking volume, we can be a bit more subtle by applying EQ to certain groups of sounds to create a "notch" or gap in the frequency range for other important sounds to come through.

604b Notching Out

Once you're through the fence, of course, it all kicks off. So that you're not too busy fighting bots to concentrate on the audio, we've imitated some battle ambience in this area. As you can hear, there's a lot going on so the chances of understanding any important dialogue in this environment are slim.

Over the player's personal radio headset come some important instructions. A ducking technique has been used again here so that you can hear the dialogue. This time instead of simply ducking the volume of all the sounds (a slightly artificial effect), we are using the filter (EQ) within the SoundMode object to notch out the frequencies where our dialogue is centered. This allows the dialogue to poke through the mix in a slightly more elegant way.

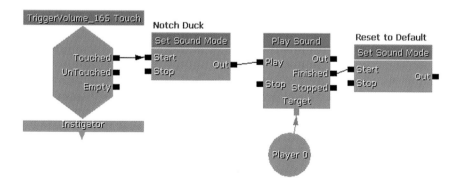

The SoundMode applies to the SFX, ChatterFriend, ChatterEnemy, and Music Soundclasses (all **[SoundCue]**s playing at this time belong to one of these classes). There is no reduction in volume via the volume adjusters but instead we are making use of the EQ available.

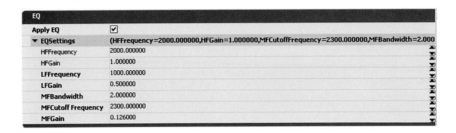

EQ	
Apply EQ	☑
▼ **EQSettings**	(HFFrequency=2000.000000,HFGain=1.000000,MFCutoffFrequency=2300.000000,MFBandwidth=2.000
HFFrequency	2000.000000
HFGain	1.000000
LFFrequency	1000.000000
LFGain	0.500000
MFBandwidth	2.000000
MFCutoff Frequency	2300.000000
MFGain	0.126000

By looking at a frequency spectrum view of the radio dialogue, we can see that its power lies between 500 Hz and 4,000 Hz.

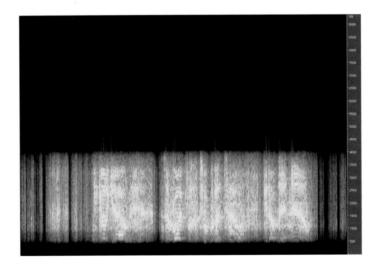

The EQ in the SoundModes properties is a three-band EQ with a high and low shelf, and a parametric mid shelf. The frequency is in Hz, the gain is from 0.0 to 1.0 and the Mid Frequency Bandwidth ranges from 0.1 to 2.0. The precise nature of the filters (and in particular the meaning of the numbers applied to the bandwidth of the mid shelf) remains shrouded in mystery for non-developers, so it will require a bit of experimentation. If you want to get it right, we'd recommend creating a **[SoundCue]** of white noise, applying your SoundMode, and recording the output. You can then see in the frequency spectrum how the SoundMode EQ has affected the sound. In this case, we've created a hole in the frequency spectrum that approximately matches that of the dialogue range. This will allow the dialogue to "punch through" the mix without the need for an obvious duck in overall volume.

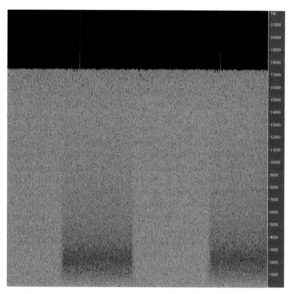

A white noise source with alternating SoundMode off/on.

Although we've used it here for dialogue again, this technique is equally applicable when you want to highlight a big sound effect event while music is playing. Music, particularly a dense orchestral arrangement, often takes up a large range of frequencies so the use of the EQ within the SoundModes function is valuable for notching out a range for a specific sound effect to momentarily shine through without disrupting the musical flow. Record a sequence of your gameplay, and then import this audio track into your DAW. There you can play around with the EQ within a slightly more friendly environment before attempting to imitate these settings within UDK.

(Of course, you won't need to do this as you've meticulously planned your music and sound effects to sit within different frequency ranges so that you have a clean and uncluttered mix—see the "Planning for a Full Mix" section presented earlier.)

Preduck for Dynamic Range

604c Blockage

As we discussed at the opening of this chapter, we notice changes and differences in volume but do not have an awareness of absolute values. If you have a big event happening that you want to have real impact, then the best effect is going to be achieved by preceding it with a quiet section to make the dynamic contrast more dramatic. Of course, this is not always possible, but you can affect a "preduck" strategy that momentarily brings all the sounds down in volume immediately before your loud event.

To get to the tower, you need to trigger another explosive device to get through the wall. Walk up to the device and press the E key. Then move back.

This system is exactly the same as that used for the explosion to get through the electric fence, only this time a SoundMode is triggered immediately before the explosion. The **[PlaySound]** of the explosion has an extra delay built into it so that the SoundMode has time to quickly duck down all other sounds, giving the explosion sound a bigger impact through the contrast in volume levels when it comes in.

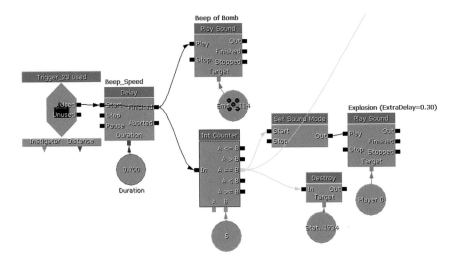

Subjective Sound States

One of the most powerful ways to engage a player's emotions is to present, not a representation of the "reality" of the soundscape as heard from a particular point in 3D space, but one version of reality as experienced through the character's eyes and ears. You might argue that in a first-person perspective game this is true automatically, but hearing is subjective in that we can choose what to focus on, or to listen to. This approach, which is so successful in film, has barely begun to be exploited in games. By changing the mix to focus on or highlight specific elements or to play subjective sounds, we can actually start to really experience the world from the character's point of view (or point of audition) and therefore become further involved and immersed in the game.

Shell Shock (SoundModes +)

In addition to allowing us to focus the player's attention through mixing/ducking, the SoundModes system also allows us to set up some more radical examples of subjective sound such as altered physical or psychological states.

605 Trip Wire

As you pass through this area, you unfortunately set off a tripwire (yes, I know—we tricked you). The explosion deafens your ears, so the sounds around you become muffled and you hear the high-pitched whine of a perforated eardrum. Alongside the whine you hear, the top end comes off the sounds and after a few seconds they return to normal.

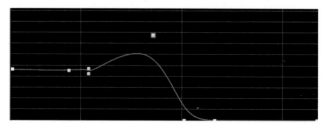

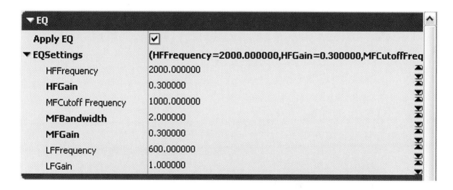

This system combines the ducking and EQ of the SoundModes with additional sounds for a specific circumstance. The **[TriggerVolume]** sets a new SoundMode GATShellShock, plays an explosion, and then plays a high-pitched whine. After three seconds the player regains his or her hearing and the SoundMode is reset to the default. The GATShellShock SoundMode applies both EQ and attenuation to all the SoundClasses (Ambient and Voice) present in the area.

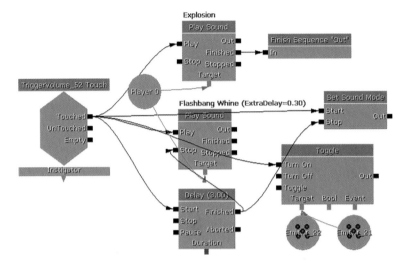

Although we are having to trigger this instance manually, a more typical approach would be to have this kind of effect hard coded so that if an explosion occurred within a given radius of the player, a shell-shock type of filtering and tone would be triggered automatically.

Sniper Focus (Cumulative Effects within SoundModes)

This system simulates how we can block out extraneous sounds when we need to really focus our attention.

605a Sniper

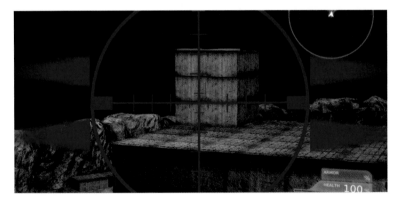

The Game Audio Tutorial

At the top of the tower is a sniper rifle. As every good sniper knows, it takes concentration and attention to your breathing to get the perfect shot. In this instance, you can hold your breath momentarily by pressing the H key to steady your sights. When you do, the player character focuses their attention and the other sounds are filtered out, as they are not important to the character at this moment.

We'll discuss the sniper system itself in further detail in the weapons section of Chapter 7. For the moment we will focus on the use of SoundModes.

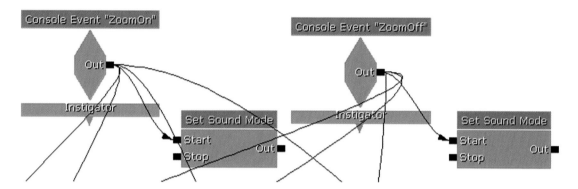

When the H key press is received for the player to hold his or her breathing in Sniper mode, the SoundMode GATSniper is called, and when released, the Default SoundMode is called. The GATSniper Soundmode reduces the SoundClasses Voice, Music, and SFX volumes by half (X 0.5) and does the same to their pitch. So that we don't have to laboriously apply this to every other child of these SoundClass parents, the "Apply to all children" option has been checked.

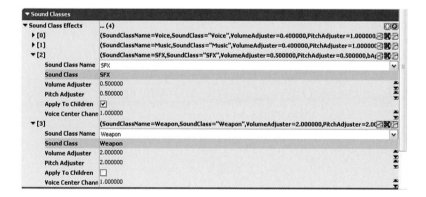

We want the Sniper weapon sound itself to be unaffected, but the problem is that the Weapons SoundClass is a child of SFX and so will be attenuated by 0.5 like all the others. There's a way around this dilemma if we appreciate that within the SoundModes, values act as multipliers, not absolute values. By adding an additional effect to multiply only the Weapon Soundclass by 2.0, we are effectively putting it back to its normal volume as

$$1.0 \ (normal \ volume) \times 0.5 \ (SFX \ parent \ value \ applied) \times$$
$$2.0 \ (additional \ multiplier \ applied \ to \ weapon \ only)$$
$$= 1.0 \ (Back \ to \ normal \ volume)$$

Using the nature of the values applied within SoundModes (acting as multipliers of volume or pitch levels) allows us to combine several commands that affect different SoundClasses in specific ways without having to necessarily refer to each individual SoundClass. (Note: You may have read about ducking snapshots or multiplier snapshots. This is not an example of these. See the discussion at the end of this chapter).

Listen—Don't Hear (Exception SoundClasses)

This is similar to the sniper example presented earlier, but this time we are creating our own SoundClass that we can use as an *exception* SoundClass to stand outside of the normal parent/child hierarchy. Think of this as your slightly odd uncle who pretty much just does his own thing no matter what everyone else is doing.

605b "Listen" Mode

When you enter the building, the doors close and lock behind you. We've received information that a bomb has been planted by the terrorist organization known as the "Leeds People's Front" (not to be confused with the "People's Front of Leeds") at this location. You've got two minutes to find and defuse the bomb.

This room is full of noisy ambient sounds, so identifying the location of the bomb by listening for its ticking sound is not easy. Fortunately, you were pricked by a radioactive cuckoo clock when you were on holiday in Switzerland at the age of 12, so you've developed a "Super-sense" for ticking sounds. To enable this Super-sense mode, press the H key. Unfortunately, this depletes your energy so you can only use it for four seconds at a time, and you will then take four seconds to recover (you knew there had to be a catch).

This time we are focusing our attention on a specific object or source. This is useful if you want to draw attention to a particular object when entering a room or area, or to highlight a particular overheard piece of dialogue. For the ticking bomb, a new SoundClass has been created that stands apart from the parent/child tree.

When the player enters the room, the **[Matinee]** closes the door and the ticking starts. A **[Delay]** counts the 60 seconds, then if it is not stopped it outputs to an explosion event. If the player manages to find the bomb, then he or she can "use it to defuse it." This plays a bomb defused sound and stops the **[Delay]**.

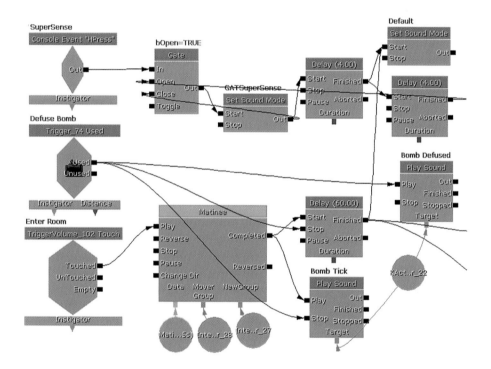

The "Super-sense" **[Console Event]** "H" changes the SoundMode to GATSuperSense, closes the **[Gate]** so this can't be retriggered, and holds this mode for four seconds before setting the SoundMode back to the default. The final delay holds for four more seconds for the player's energy to recharge before allowing another "Super-sense" call through. The Super-sense SoundMode could have been set to simply last for four seconds, but generally it is safer to reset to default manually. (If the **[Delay]** finishes and the bomb goes off, the SoundMode is set to default as well so the bomb blast is not affected by the Super-sense SoundMode.)

The MECHNICAL_Bomb_Tick_01 **[SoundCue]** is designated as belonging to our new SoundClass GATException01. The GATSupersense SoundMode applies to all the main Parents, Voice, Music, and SFX categories with the "Apply to all Children" option selected, but the GATException01

SoundClass is not attached to this tree hierarchy and therefore is not affected. Creating these exception SoundClasses is useful for specific maverick sounds that operate outside the usual laws (on their last day before retirement, etc.).

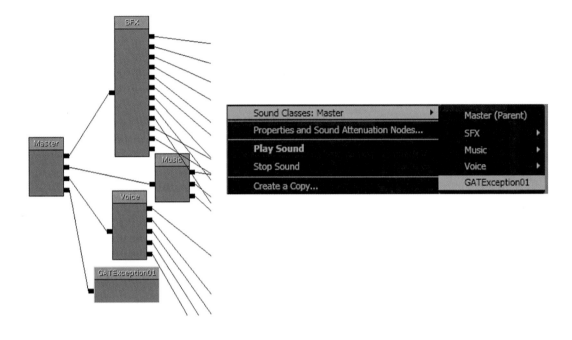

Exercise 604e_00 SoundModes: Children Should Be Seen and Not Heard

Try creating your own SoundMode. When the player approaches the computer in this room, you want to highlight its importance. Create a SoundMode that keeps the computer (which belongs to the Item SoundClass) at its normal volume but slightly ducks all the other sounds in the room.

Tips

1. Your new SoundMode needs to be created in the SoundClassesandModes.upk package. Make sure you make a backup of the original package file before altering it.
2. Select New in the Content Browser and select SoundMode from the Factory menu.
3. After creating or editing SoundModes, you may sometimes find that you need to close down and restart UDK for the changes to take effect.
4. You'll need to find out what SoundClasses the other sounds in this room belong to. (Right-click the **[SoundCue]**s and select Properties and Sound Attenuation Nodes to find out.)
5. Add a SoundClass effect in your SoundMode for each of these types using the green plus symbol to lower their volume.
6. Either set the duration of your SoundMode so that it switches off after a few seconds or use an additional **[Set SoundMode]** Action to return to the default mix settings.

Player Health (Adding to the Mix)

605c Unhealthy Mix

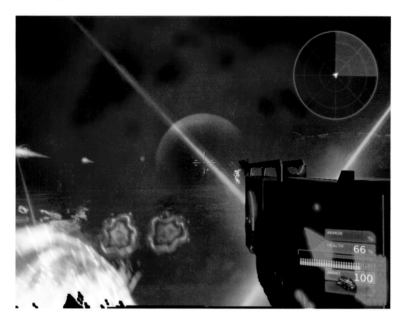

In this area a squadron of bots attacks the player to allow us to demonstrate a couple of reactive mix approaches. The first mode uses the addition of sounds to indicate player health, referred to as "Health", and the second uses the subtraction of sounds (lowering volume and filtering) for a special play mode we're going to refer to as "Fury!!"

In the first part of the system, the player's health is compared to a value of 20 by a **[Compare Int]** object. If this is found to be less than or equal to 20, then a **[PlaySound]** plays a looping heartbeat (we had to get it in somewhere) and also toggles on a **[PostProcessVolume]** and **[Reverb VolumeToggleable]**.

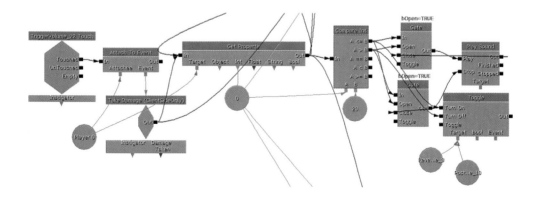

Both of these volumes cover the entire area of play and when they are switched on when the player's health is low, they give feedback to alert the player to this perilous state. They also reinforce the feeling of low health by blurring the image and metaphorically "blurring" the sound through the addition of reverb.

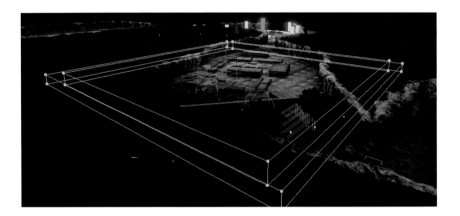

The second part of the system also checks the player's Health property and then scales this to control the volume of a musical choir sound that fades up as the player's health gets lower (inverting the value of the health by taking it away from 1).

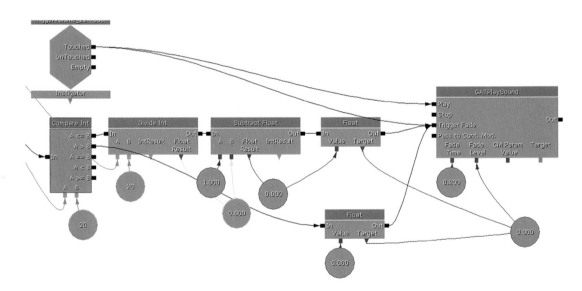

There's also a health recharge system built in here so that if the player is able to evade the bots and remain un-hit for five seconds, the player's Health property is gradually incremented.

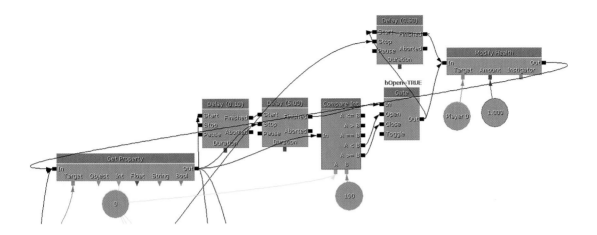

By bringing in or fading up the volume of sounds or music in response to game events or variables, we can change the mix to feel more like the subjective experience of the player character. We can also have an equally powerful effect by taking elements away.

"Fury!!" Mode (Taking Away)

605d Don't Get Mad, Get Mildly Irritated

If the player manages to kill a given number of bots (two) within a certain period of time (10 seconds), then the Fury!! mode is enabled. When the player then presses the H key to instigate the Fury!! mode, the player's weapon becomes super powerful and various effects are applied for this special state.

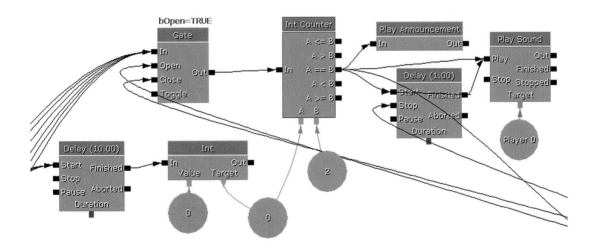

The signals coming into the system from the left are notifications that appear if the player kills any of the bots in the area. An **[Int Counter]** compares the number killed against its variable B (2); if it matches, then an **[Announcement]** is made that prints text to the screen to say, "Fury Ready." The **[Int Counter]**'s variable A is reset every 10 seconds, meaning the player must have killed the two bots within a 10-second time interval to unlock the Fury!! mode.

The announcement also plays an alert sound (you can add SoundNodeWaves to **[Play Announcement]**s) and a looping **[Delay]** is started to retrigger a beeping **[PlaySound]** to also alert the player.

The second part of the system now waits for the player to press H to start the Fury!! mode itself. Once it is pressed, another **[Announcement]** informs the player that he or she is in this mode, Fury!! (this feature also plays a sound to indicate that the player is in Fury!! mode). A new **[SoundMode]** is set to apply a filter to all sounds except the player weapon and music. While in Fury!! mode, a solo voice music piece is played via a **[PlaySound]**. At the same time a **[Modify Property]** action is sent to the player's weapon to increase its power.

After a **[Delay]** of 10 seconds, the Fury!! mode wears off. Another announcement, Fury Off! this time, plays a winding down sound, the **[SoundMode]** is set back to Default, and the modified weapon returns to its normal state. There's also a **[Console Command]** within the system to turn on (slomo 0.5) and off (slomo 1.0), a slow-motion effect during Fury!! mode.

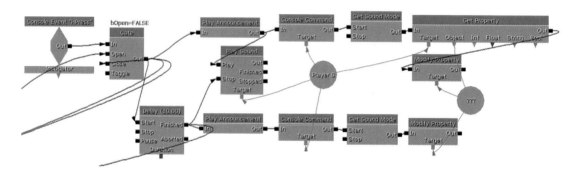

Both the Choir sound from the Health system and the Solo Voice sound from the Fury!! system belong to SoundClasses excluded from the SoundMode change (and they are composed to work together) so they should remain unaffected by either.

Automation

There have been huge strides in the development of processes that can analyze the actual audio output of a game for the purpose of evaluating automatic aspects of the mix. An intelligent system could conduct a frequency analysis of the current mix and from the results decide whether or not you'd actually hear a new sound given the current range of frequencies. It could then decide not to play it or to use a filter or multiband compressor to enable it to come through. These systems are entirely possible on the current generation of consoles and are no doubt being developed as we write. But in the meantime, you don't need to be an audio programmer to implement a bit of intelligent automation.

Like all the best concepts, this next example is very simple but very useful. When the player enters the Health and Fury!! Area, a **[DynamicTrigger]** is attached and moves with the player. It receives Touch events whenever a bot enters its radius (of around 900 units). The system keeps track of the number of bots within this radius and if this number is greater than 2, the ambient sounds in the area are turned off (by stopping one via its **[PlaySound]** and by toggling off the other two **[Ambi entSoundSimpleToggleable]**s).

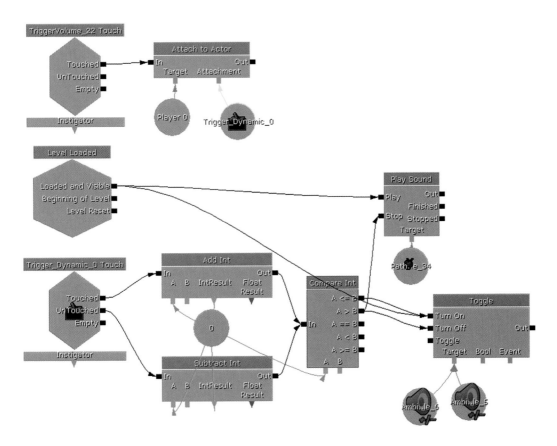

We don't need to conduct real-time signal analysis to appreciate the logic behind this system. If there are more than two bots in close proximity to the player, the number of sound events (weapons firing), and the volume of these events (weapons are loud), means that any quiet ambient sounds will be masked by these louder sounds. As the player will not hear them anyway, we can clean up the mix and provide additional digital headroom by turning them off. Another idea would be to have an ambient sound establish the feel for an area as they player enters but then gradually fade back a little to a lower level, in-keeping with the principle of "make a point, then go away". You could do this with an **[AmbientSoundSimpleToggleable]** or an **[AmbientSoundNonLoopingToggleable]** both of which allow you to fade out to a given volume level. When you're working with intense periods of the game, try to think about simple systems such as this one to keep your mix focused.

Simultaneous SoundModes and the Modifier Mix

Although more flexible than it might first appear, the Soundmodes system is very much that of a Snapshot or Event mix in that only one state can be applied at any given time. (Although you can have multiplier operations within the SoundMode itself, as we saw in the Sniper Focus example, this is more to do with providing a workaround for making the SoundClass tree bus structure more flexible.) The problems with this option are apparent when there are two (or more) simultaneous mix requirements.

While you're battling with the bots in the Health and Fury!! sequence, you'll notice that you also stumble across some carelessly placed landmines. These mines produce an explosion, physics push (via an **[RB_ RadialImpulseActor]**) and a health damage. As you might expect, they also produce a shellshock effect via a low-pass SoundMode and a high-pitched whine. We'll call this the "ShellShock mix."

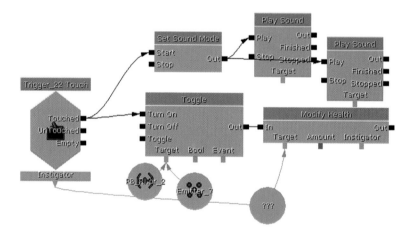

This SoundMode applies an EQ to all classes and takes effect over two seconds (so you have time to hear the initial explosion). It then lasts for three seconds before withdrawing the EQ.

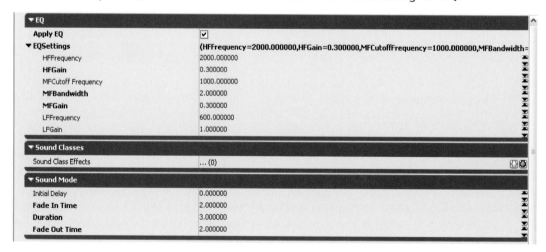

Here's the problem. What if you're in Fury!! mode when this goes off?

With the current SoundModes system operating as a Snapshot mix, the current SoundMode will simply be overridden whenever a new SoundMode is called. Although the **[SetSoundMode]** action within Kismet appears to have a Top Priority option to mitigate against the worst results of this effect (if perhaps a less important SoundMode is triggered while a mission-critical dialogue SoundMode is in place), this appears to be nonfunctional in the current build. What we would need is some kind of system of **[Gate]**s to block the application of a lower-priority SoundMode if a primary SoundMode were still applied.

It would be possible to construct the settings of the Shellshock mode so that it duplicated that of the Fury!! mode with some specific exceptions. This would mean that the change of situation would be noticeable but would still feel like an extension of the Fury!! mode we were already in. The problem is that the system does not keep track of the previous SoundMode state. So when the Shellshock feature turns off, we do not return to the Fury!! mode that should still be continuing but instead go to the Default SoundMode. Again, it would be possible to construct a Kismet system that held a variable relating to our current SoundMode and made sure we returned to that state if interrupted by a different SoundMode event. This is, however, already starting to look like a bit of a headache.

In discussions around a mix type that could operate in combinations, there is sometimes reference to a "Ducking" or "Multiplier" snapshot. The concept is that you can have "Multiplier" mixes occurring simultaneously and the sounds volume/settings are scaled by a factor produced by the combination of the two mix settings. (Please read the bibliography for this section for articles that have a fuller explanation.) We're going to avoid these terms here and propose some new ones because, although the concepts are sound, the terminology can be confusing. To scale the volume of a sound, channel, or group, we are multiplying the numbers that represent the sound's waveform. To make it louder, we multiply by numbers greater than 1.0, and to make it quieter we multiply by numbers less than 1.0. Therefore, the use of the terms "snapshot" and "multiplier" (implying that snapshot is not a multiplier) can be misleading.

In the preceding examples, we have seen situations where we need a hierarchy of mixer states, a tracking system so that we can (easily) return to previous mix states if required, and potentially the ability to have more than one game mode or event (and its related mixer settings) occurring simultaneously.

We'd propose the following solutions.

Primary Snapshot
There can be any number of primary snapshots for a game. However, only one is applied at any one time.

Snapshot Priorities
Each primary snapshot is designated a priority value. If a snapshot with a lower priority is triggered, it will not override the current snapshot; if higher, then it will.

Snapshot Tracking

The currently loaded primary snapshot must be tracked. If a subsequent snapshot is triggered (and is of a higher priority), then this is applied, but if it is then switched off (rather than another snapshot being triggered), we return to the previous primary snapshot.

Modifier Mix

These mix modes can apply to specific groups in response to game events but do not override the primary snapshots. Rather they scale the values of specific groups (SoundClasses) within the primary snapshot. They can occur in combination and the resultant mix will be the outcome of the product of their mix values.

For example, a *Weapons* modifier may duck the player's Foley sounds, and a *Mission dialogue* modifier may apply an additional scaling to duck Weapon sounds.

If we ever recover from writing this book, we'll see what we can knock together along these lines to improve the potential for mixing in UDK. In the meantime if you have a little spare time then let us know when you've cracked it.

Interactive Mixing Conclusion

The UDK method of implementing interactive mixing via SoundClasses and SoundModes is perhaps not the most transparent and certainly has its weaknesses as discussed earlier. Having said that, we do have a tendency to crave more "tech" solutions, when actually there remains a wealth of creative opportunities to engage and excite players within even the most simple systems. Although we will always have to reconcile the sometimes competing demands of providing information and providing emotion, there remains a huge amount to be learned from almost a hundred years of film sound in terms of the power of the subjective mix.

Conclusions

Making it sound good is about using sound and music to chart the emotional landscape of a game (and yes, even Mario has an emotional landscape). Although there are great and compelling game sound tracks out there, we would advise that you also look to other less obvious sources. Play games and learn from games, but try to also bring something new to the creative mix by looking for inspiration in Film, Literature, and Art in all its forms.

Advanced Sound System Design

Many of the examples we've already covered put forward the important concept that in music and sound for games you are not dealing with "an event = a sound", instead, you are constructing a model or system to deliver dynamic content from the static assets of sound waves. Nowhere is this idea more important than when dealing with kinetic systems such as weapons and vehicles. (As you've made it this far we're going to assume that you are going to want to try everything out for yourself so we'll dispense with the separate exercises.)

Weapon Systems

700 Weapons Locker 01

At the start of Area 700 there's a target range and a weapons locker that contains several weapon examples. As you work through the following sections, you can select the appropriate weapon by pressing the number keys on your keyboard. We've removed the bullet impact sounds for these initial weapons so you can more clearly hear the firing sounds. We'll come back to them in the Impact, Whizz-by and Handling sounds section.

All the weapon systems in UDK are scripted, so if you didn't do the scripting examples in Chapter 4 for the player footsteps, now is the time to go back and make sure that you have UDK set up correctly to use our, and your, custom scripts. See "Scripting 101" in Chapter 3 and the scripting discussion in Appendix C.

Our custom scripts are all in C:\UDK\UDK(***)\Development\Src\MyMod\Classes. The scripts for the original UDK weapons these are based on can be found in C:\UDK\UDK(***)\Development\Src\UTGame or UTGameContent.

(Out of interest you can see where any **[SoundCue]**s are referenced by scripts by right-clicking on the SoundCue and choosing "List Objects that reference this object.")

One Shot

Weapon: One_Shot_Pistol

Go to the weapons locker at the start of the target range. Then select the weapon UTWeap_GAT_One_Shot_Pistol (press number 1 on your keyboard).

This weapon fires only once when the trigger or left mouse button (LMB) is clicked.

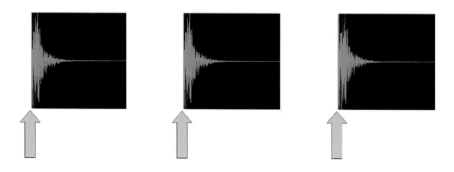

Although it might appear to be unrelated, this weapon actually extends the UDK ShockRifle script.

Open the script for this weapon:

C:\UDK\UDK(***)\Development\Src\MyMod\Classes\UTWeap_GAT_One_Shot_Pistol.uc

In the bottom half of the script you can see the reference to the **[SoundCue]** for the fire sound:

```
defaultproperties
{
  AttachmentClass=class'MyMod.UTAttachment_One_Shot_Pistol'//
  AmmoCount=100       // amount of initial ammo
  MaxAmmoCount=100    // max amount of ammo allowed
  FireInterval(0) = 0.5     // rate of fire --- smaller = faster
  InventoryGroup=1
  GroupWeight=0.5
  // Weapon SkeletalMesh
  Begin Object Name=FirstPersonMesh
    SkeletalMesh=SkeletalMesh'WP_Pistol.Mesh.SK_WP_Pistol_1P'
    AnimSets(0)=AnimSet'WP_Pistol.Anim.K_WP_Pistol'
    Animations=MeshSequenceA
    Rotation=(Yaw=-16384)
    FOV=60.0
  End Object
  Begin Object Name=PickupMesh
    SkeletalMesh=SkeletalMesh'WP_Pistol.Mesh.SK_WP_Pistol_3P'
  End Object
  WeaponFireSnd[0]=SoundCue'GATA_Sound.Weapon.Pistol_One_Shot_Cue'
```

In this instance the **[SoundCue]** uses only one sound file repeatedly, but you could extend it so that it varies slightly in pitch or swaps between several samples using the **[Random]** object. As most weapons are based on the repetition of a mechanical process you will find that they do not vary a great deal from shot to shot. Some very subtle pitch change can work to create some variation and also to alleviate the phasing that can occur with multiple instances of the same weapon.

The other thing to note is that the weapon is stopped from simply looping round and refiring by the ForceEndFire command. This effectively makes the FireInterval (which controls the rate of fire) redundant:

```
class UTWeap_One_Shot_Pistol extends UTWeap_ShockRifle;
simulated function PlayFiringSound() // plays back firing sounds
{
  if ( WeaponFireSnd[CurrentFireMode] != None ) // checks to see if we're in a
particular firing mode - primary or alt
  {
  WeaponPlaySound( WeaponFireSnd[CurrentFireMode] ); // sound to play if enough
ammo ---- CurrentFireMode = left/right mouse button
  }
  ForceEndFire();
}
```

With the next few exercises you're going to be editing the scripts to replace the existing sounds. Before you do, it is a good idea to copy the scripts you are going to alter to a safe place so you can later put back the original versions.

Exercise 700_00 One Shot Weapon

Replace the sound of the pistol with your own sound.

Tips

1. Copy the script UTWeap_GAT_One_Shot_Pistol.uc from C:\UDK\UDK(***)\Development\Src\MyMod\Classes\ and put it in a warm safe place, away from direct sunlight.
2. Right click on the version that remains in the MyMod / Classes folder and via the properties menu make sure that the ReadOnly flag is unchecked (you might want to do this for the whole folder while you're at it). Now open the script in Notepad or any other text editor and change the SoundCue entry to refer to one of your own.
3. Remember, we need the full file path for the **[SoundCue]**. Get this by right-clicking on your **[SoundCue]** within the Content Browser and selecting Copy Full Name to Clipboard. You can then paste this over the top of the existing reference:

   ```
   WeaponFireSnd[0]=SoundCue'GATA_Sound.Weapon.Pistol_One_Shot_Cue'
   ```

4. Save your script and close the UDK editor.
5. As you have now altered a script, you will need to compile these again.
6. Open up the UnrealFrontEnd.exe from C:\UDK\UDK(***)\Binaries and choose Compile Scripts from the Script Menu.

7. Check for any errors. Nine times out of ten errors are the result of spelling mistakes.
8. Now open the Exercise Room 700_00. You see that this replicates the target range from the level.
9. From the weapons locker when you now select the UTWeap_GAT_One_Shot_Pistol weapon you should hear your own firing sound.

To set up your own Weapons Lockers select the Weapons Locker from the Actor classes tab (Actor Classes/Pickups/Weapon/UTWeaponLocker_Content) and right click in your level to add. In the Weapons Locker properties (F4) click the green plus sign to add a Weapon and choose your Weapon from the Weapon Class drop down menu.

Retriggered Firing

Weapon: ReTriggered_Pulse_Weapon

The second weapon UTWeap_GAT_ReTriggered_Pulse_Weapon (press number 2 on your keyboard) will refire for as long as you hold down the LMB until you run out of ammo.

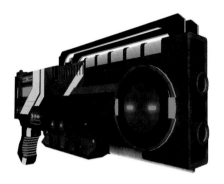

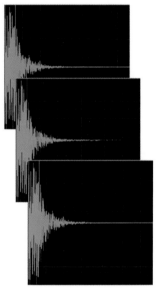

In this example, it's set to a FireInterval of 0.3 seconds, which is a slow 200 rounds per minute (RPM). This is fine for the kind of sci-fi energy bolt it's firing at the moment:

```
defaultproperties
{
  WeaponColor=(R=255,G=0,B=0,A=255)
  FireInterval(0)=0.3
  FireInterval(1)=0.3
  AttachmentClass=class'MyMod.UTAttachment_ReTriggered_Pulse_Weapon' // modded
UTAttachment file to over-ride default impact sound with a silent cue
```

```
// Weapon SkeletalMesh
Begin Object Name=FirstPersonMesh

SkeletalMesh=SkeletalMesh'WP_Shotgun_Green.Mesh.SK_WP_Multi_Shotgun_1P'
  AnimSets(0)=AnimSet'WP_Shotgun_Green.Anim.K_WP_Shotgun'
  Animations=MeshSequenceA
  Rotation=(Yaw=-16384)
  FOV=60.0
End Object
Begin Object Name=PickupMesh

SkeletalMesh=SkeletalMesh'WP_Shotgun_Green.Mesh.SK_WP_Multi_Shotgun_3P'
End Object
WeaponFireSnd[0]=SoundCue'GATA_Sound.Weapon.WEAPON_ReTriggered_Pulse_Cue'
}
```

(You'll notice that it has two FireIntervals; this is because the weapon also has an alternate right mouse button firing mode.)

Depending on your intended use, you could set the FireInterval to be smaller, which would give you a greater number of rounds per minute:

$$Fire\ Interval = \frac{1}{(Rounds\ per\ minute/60)}$$

If you wanted to use this method for a machine gun, which can fire at anything between 600 RPM and 1,200 RPM, then you may find that you run into a couple of problems. We'll deal with these next.

Exercise 700a_00 Making Your Own Retriggered Weapon

Replace the sound of this sci-fi pulse-type weapon with your own.

Tips

1. Copy the script UTWeap_GAT_ReTriggered_Pulse_Weapon.uc from C:\UDK\UDK(***)\Development\Src\MyMod\ Classes\ and put it in a safe place.
2. Open the version that is still in the MyMod\Classes folder and edit the SoundCue entry to refer to one of your own.
3. Again remember, we need the full file path for the SoundCue. Get this by right-clicking on the **[SoundCue]** within the Content Browser and selecting Copy Full Name to Clipboard. You can then paste this over the top of the existing reference:

    ```
    WeaponFireSnd[0]=SoundCue'GATA_Sound.Weapon.WEAPON_ReTriggered_Pulse_Cue'
    ```

4. Change the FireInterval to one appropriate for your sound:

    ```
    (FireInterval(0)=0.3)
    ```

5. Save your script, close the UDK editor, and recompile the scripts using the UnrealFrontEnd.exe.
6. Open exercise room 700_00 again and the UTWeap_GAT_Retriggered_Pulse_Weapon from the Weapons Locker should now use your sound.

Retriggered Firing with Tail
Weapon: ReTriggered_MechwithTail

Retriggered weapon sounds usually work well for mechanical weaponry; however, there are two issues. The first is that as the sounds are overlapping they can use up your voice count (see Chapter 6 Voice Instance Limiting and Prioritization, and "Audio Optimization" in Appendix B) very quickly in environments with multiple weapons. The second is that if your sample is relatively long and your retriggering frequent, you may introduce phasing caused by the interference between the waveforms. You can alleviate phasing to some extent by using a **[Modulate]** node within your **[SoundCue]** to make subtle pitch variations.

Another partial solution to both phasing and voice issues is to use a short fire sound that retriggers but then add the longer tail element when the input trigger is released. You can hear this in effect with the UTWeap_GAT_Retriggered_MechwithTail weapon (select number 3 on your keyboard):

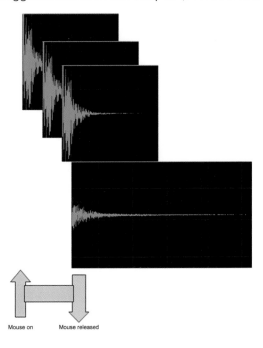

Mouse on   Mouse released

Opening the UTWeap_GAT_ReTriggered_MechwithTail.uc script, we can see the two cues and where they are referenced. As you can see, this script is significantly more complex as it is now based on the rocket launcher, which has alternate firing and weapon load sounds:

```
WeaponLoadedSnd=SoundCue'A_Weapon_RocketLauncher.Cue.A_Weapon_RL_Load_Cue'
WeaponFireSnd[0]=SoundCue'GATA_Sound.Weapon.WEAPON_ReTriggeredTail_Fire_Cue'
WeaponFireSnd[1]=SoundCue'A_Weapon_RocketLauncher.Cue.A_Weapon_RL_Fire_Cue'
WeaponEquipSnd=SoundCue'A_Weapon_RocketLauncher.Cue.A_Weapon_RL_Raise_Cue'
AltFireModeChangeSound=SoundCue'A_Weapon_RocketLauncher.Cue.
     A_Weapon_RL_AltModeChange_Cue'
RocketLoadedSound=SoundCue'A_Weapon_RocketLauncher.Cue.
     A_Weapon_RL_RocketLoaded_Cue'
GrenadeFireSound=SoundCue'A_Weapon_RocketLauncher.Cue.
     A_Weapon_RL_GrenadeFire_Cue'
EndFireSound=SoundCue'GATA_Sound.Weapon.WEAPON_ReTriggeredTail_Tail_Cue
```

This has a FireInterval of 0.1 seconds, which is the same as 600 rounds per minute. By using relatively short fire samples and leaving the tail until the release of the button/trigger, we can avoid some of the worst effects of phasing and limit the voice count. But sometimes we want to go even faster – see the Looping examples below.

Exercise 700b_00 Making Your Own Retriggered with Tail Weapon

Tips

1. Copy the script UTWeap_GAT_ReTriggered_MechwithTail.uc from C:\UDK\UDK(***)\Development\Src\MyMod\ Classes\ and put it in a safe place.
2. Replace the SoundCue references with your own:

```
WeaponLoadedSnd=SoundCue'A_Weapon_RocketLauncher.Cue.A_Weapon_RL_Load_Cue'
WeaponLoadedSnd=SoundCue'A_Weapon_RocketLauncher.Cue.A_Weapon_RL_Load_Cue'
WeaponFireSnd[0]=SoundCue'GATA_Sound.Weapon.WEAPON_ReTriggeredTail_Fire_Cue'
WeaponFireSnd[1]=SoundCue'A_Weapon_RocketLauncher.Cue.A_Weapon_RL_Fire_Cue'
WeaponEquipSnd=SoundCue'A_Weapon_RocketLauncher.Cue.A_Weapon_RL_Raise_Cue'
AltFireModeChangeSound=SoundCue'A_Weapon_RocketLauncher.Cue.A_Weapon_RL_AltModeChange_Cue'
RocketLoadedSound=SoundCue'A_Weapon_RocketLauncher.Cue.A_Weapon_RL_RocketLoaded_Cue'
GrenadeFireSound=SoundCue'A_Weapon_RocketLauncher.Cue.A_Weapon_RL_GrenadeFire_Cue'
EndFireSound= SoundCue'GATA_Sound.Weapon.WEAPON_ReTriggeredTail_Tail_Cue
```

3. Save your script, close the UDK editor, and recompile the scripts using the UnrealFrontEnd.exe.
4. Use the exercise room 700_00 again to test it.
5. Try swapping out some of the sounds for the Alt fire (right mouse button) as well.

Weapon Status Feedback System

Weapon: Feedback_Mech

In Chapter 6 we discussed how useful sound can be in giving feedback to the player and the example was given of a weapon that gives feedback to the player about the status of its ammo through sound.

Swap to the UTWeap_GAT_Feedback_Mech weapon (press number 4 on your keyboard).

This weapon retriggers while the fire button is held down, but when the ammo level gets below 25 it swaps to a new **[SoundCue]** as a warning to the player that the ammo is about to run out.

Ammo full:

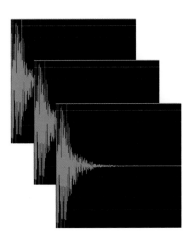

Ammo low (<25):

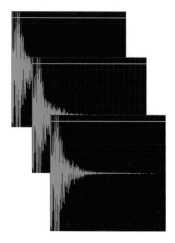

See the UTWeap_GAT_Feedback_Mech.uc script for the system and SoundCue references:

```
WeaponLoadedSnd=SoundCue'A_Weapon_RocketLauncher.Cue.A_Weapon_RL_Load_Cue'
WeaponFireSnd[0]=SoundCue'GATA_Sound.Weapon.WEAPON_FeedbackMech_Fire_Cue'
WeaponFireSnd[1]=SoundCue'A_Weapon_RocketLauncher.Cue.A_Weapon_RL_Fire_Cue'
WeaponEquipSnd=SoundCue'A_Weapon_RocketLauncher.Cue.A_Weapon_RL_Raise_Cue'
AltFireModeChangeSound=SoundCue'A_Weapon_RocketLauncher.Cue.A_Weapon_RL_
AltModeChange_Cue'
RocketLoadedSound=SoundCue'A_Weapon_RocketLauncher.
Cue.A_Weapon_RL_RocketLoaded_Cue'
GrenadeFireSound=SoundCue'A_Weapon_RocketLauncher.
Cue.A_Weapon_RL_GrenadeFire_Cue'
LowAmmoSound=SoundCue'GATA_Sound.Weapon.WEAPON_FeedbackMech_LowAmmo_Cue'
```

Again, try swapping these out for your own **[SoundCue]**s and playing around with the variables (AmmoCount>) within the script to see what they do.

Make a Point

Weapon: Make_a_point

Number 5 on your keyboard will give you the UTWeap_GAT_Make_a_Point weapon. It is based on a principle mentioned earlier in the book, that it can often work well for your sound to "make a point, then go away"—or at least fade out a little. Many retriggered weapons within a confined area during a firefight can quickly combine into less of a "wall of sound" and more of a "wall of mud." In this weapon we've layered in an initial fire sound on top of the normal retriggered sound. This allows us to have the retriggered element slightly lower in volume but still emphasize that the weapon is being fired by having a powerful "crack" at the start.

The script calls a StartFireSound simultaneously with the start of the retriggered element, and it ends with a tail on button release:

(C:\UDK\UDK(***)\Development\Src\MyMod\Classes\UTWeap_GAT_Make_A_Point.uc)

```
StartFireSound=SoundCue'GATA_Sound.WEAPON.MakeapointStartFire_Cue'
EndFireSound=SoundCue'GATA_Sound.WEAPON.MakeapointEndFire_Cue'
WeaponLoadedSnd=SoundCue'A_Weapon_RocketLauncher.Cue.A_Weapon_RL_Load_Cue'
WeaponFireSnd[0]=SoundCue'GATA_Sound.WEAPON.MakeapointFire_Cue'
WeaponFireSnd[1]=SoundCue'A_Weapon_RocketLauncher.Cue.A_Weapon_RL_Fire_Cue'
```

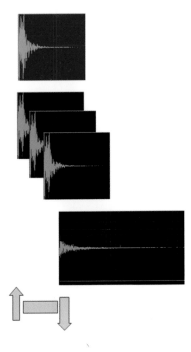

Once we've announced that the weapon has started to be fired, the fact that it is then continuing to be fired is less important as we're already aware of it. This approach can help to thin out an otherwise busy mix (and is applicable to many other audio elements as well as weapon firing).

Looping Mechanical Weapon

Weapon: Looping_Mech_Weapon

The issues mentioned earlier with retriggered weapons become acute with weapons such as miniguns, which have very high fire rates. These weapons can achieve fire rates as high as 6,000 rounds per minute. (This is why they are most often vehicle mounted, as you need the vehicle to carry the weight of all the ammo!)

Let's take a slightly less extreme example of a weapon that fires 3,000 rounds per minute (i.e., one every 0.02 seconds). In the first 0.4 seconds after the player has pressed the fire button, the sound has been triggered 20 times and is therefore taking up 20 of our voices already.

This firing sound sample is actually one second long, and so before it has finished playing you will have 49 voices being used. (See Appendix B for tips on how to monitor your voice count). With such extreme rates of fire, the retriggered approach breaks down and we need to look at a looping solution. By editing the initial transient of the weapon fire sound into a separate file, we can loop this element and then add the tail on the trigger/button release.

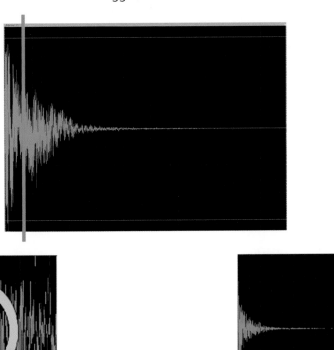

The weapon sound is divided into an initial element to be looped followed by a tail element that will play on release.

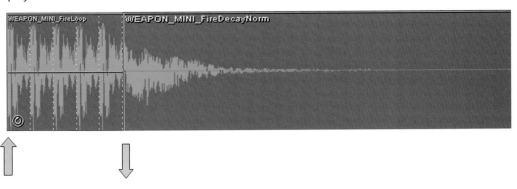

Switch to the UTWeap_GAT_Looping_Mech_Weapon (press number 6 on your keyboard) weapon to hear an example. The two SoundCues referenced are as follows:

```
EndFireSound=SoundCue'GATA_Sound.Weapon.WEAPON_LoopedMechTail_Cue'
FiringLoopCue=SoundCue'GATA_Sound.Weapon.WEAPON_LoopedMechLoop_Cue'
```

You can see from the script (UTWeap_GAT_Looping_Mech_Weapon.uc) that the loop cue is faded in very quickly on fire, held looping, and then the EndFireSound plays the tail on the trigger release. Your **[SoundCue]** for the looping section must have a **[Loop]** node in it:

```
class UTWeap_Looping_Mech_Weapon extends UTWeap_RocketLauncher;
// define sound variables -- AudioComponent used to control looping sound
var AudioComponent FiringLoop;
var SoundCue FiringLoopCue;
var SoundCue EndFireSound;
simulated state WeaponFiring  // things to do when in a "firing" state
{
  simulated function BeginState(Name PreviousStateName)  // what to do when
starting state
  {
    super.BeginState(PreviousStateName);
    if(FiringLoop == none)
    {
    FiringLoop = CreateAudioComponent(FiringLoopCue, false, true);  // creates an
audio component using the looping Cue
    }
    if(FiringLoop != none)
      FiringLoop.FadeIn(0.2f,1.0f);  // fades in firing loop
  }

  simulated function EndState(Name NextStateName)  // what to do when leaving state
  {
    super.EndState(NextStateName);
    if(FiringLoop != none)
    {
      FiringLoop.FadeOut(0.2f,0.0f);  // fades out firing loop
      FiringLoop=none;
      WeaponPlaySound(EndFireSound);  // plays end fire sound
    }
  }
}
```

Exercise 700c_00 Making Your Own Looping Mechanical Weapon

Replace the loop and tail elements of this weapon to create your own.

Tips

1. Find a weapon shot sample that's not too big and booming. Remember, you're going to be looping this quickly so something with more of a top-end element will be more appropriate. (If you listen to real miniguns, they have a very characteristic sound.)

2. Use your audio editor to chop your sample into a loop section and a tail section and make sure the looping section loops smoothly. (See Appendix D for audio editing tips.)
3. Make a copy of UTWeap_GAT_Looping_Mech_Weapon.uc for backup, then replace the references to [**SoundCue**]s in the original script with your own.
4. Close and compile, then try it out in Exercise Room 700_00.

Looping Sci-Fi Weapon

Weapon: GAT_LinkGun

Unlike the repeated transients of looping mechanical based weapons, many Sci-Fi type weapons use loops for more of a constant beam-like quality.

Open the UTWeap_GAT_LinkGun (press number 7 on your keyboard). For now this is an exact replica of the UDKLinkGun. Its primary fire shoots a projectile, but its secondary fire (right mouse) is a beam of plasma, which also has a looping impact sound when it is in contact with a surface or bot.

The beam for AltFire consists of three elements: a starting sound (StartAltFireSound) that is simultaneous with the start of the looping sound (WeaponFireSnd), and finally a sound that plays when you release the AltFire button (EndAltFireSound).

StartAltFireSound		
	WeaponFireSnd	EndAltFireSound

If the beam impacts on a surface or pawn, then an additional loop is layered in.

Looping AltFireImpact

or

Looping AltFireImpactFlesh

the firing and handling sounds are handled by the UTWeap_GAT_LinkGun.uc script:

Sound for the alternative fire mode (right mouse button) (looping):

```
WeaponFireSnd(1)=SoundCue'A_Weapon_Link.Cue.A_Weapon_Link_AltFireCue'
```

Sound for when activating the alternative fire mode (right mouse button):

```
StartAltFireSound=SoundCue'A_Weapon_Link.Cue.A_Weapon_Link_AltFireStartCue'
```

Sound for when deactivating the alternative firing mode (right mouse button):

```
EndAltFireSound=SoundCue'A_Weapon_Link.Cue.A_Weapon_Link_AltFireStopCue'
```

The effect of the beam impact from the link gun is handled by the UTAttachment_GAT_LinkGun.uc script, adding either a normal impact or a flesh impact loop:

```
if (HitActor != None)
  {
    DesiredLinkHitSound = (UTPawn(HitActor) != None && !WorldInfo.GRI.
OnSameTeam(HitActor, Instigator))
  ?
SoundCue'A_Weapon_Link.Cue.A_Weapon_Link_AltFireImpactFleshCue'
  :
SoundCue'A_Weapon_Link.Cue.A_Weapon_Link_AltFireImpactCue';
  if(!bHittingWall)
  {
==================
```

Sound for when alternative fire mode (right mouse button) impacts with player/bots:

```
SoundCue'A_Weapon_Link.Cue.A_Weapon_Link_AltFireImpactFleshCue'
```

Sound for when alternative fire mode (right mouse button) impacts with surface/material.

```
SoundCue'A_Weapon_Link.Cue.A_Weapon_Link_AltFireImpactCue'
```

Exercise 700d_00 Making Your Own Link Gun

So far you have been replacing the **[SoundCue]**s within our existing weapons. Now you are going to make a unique copy of a weapon to call your very own.

Tips

1. Navigate to C:\UDK\UDK(***)\Development\Src\UTGame\Classes and copy the following files:
   UTWeap_LinkGun.uc
   UTAttachment_LinkGun.uc
   UTProj_LinkPlasma.uc
2. Go to C:\UDK\UDK(***)\Development\Src\MyMod\Classes and paste your copies here.
3. Before you edit them you should right-click and select these files' properties in Windows Explorer and then uncheck the "Read only" flag.
4. Give each file a new name like one of these:
   UTWeap_MYLinkGun.uc
   UTAttachment_MYLinkGun.uc
   UTProj_MYLinkPlasma.uc
5. Now you need to open up each of these scripts with Notepad and make sure that all references to itself within the script—that is, all references to UTWeap_LinkGun.uc or UTAttachment_LinkGun.uc, or UTProj_LinkPlasma.uc—are updated with your new name. So you would replace UTWeap_LinkGun.uc in the text with UTWeap_MYLinkGun.uc and so on. The easiest way to do this is with Notepad's Find and Replace function. This is available from the Edit menu.
6. Once this is done, you can replace the **[SoundCue]** references with your own, compile these scripts (UnrealFrontEnd. exe/Script/Compile Scripts), and check for any errors.
7. Now you can restart the UDK Editor and add a weapons locker to exercise room 700d_00.

```
⊖ Categories
    ⊕ Common
    ⊕ Cover
    ⊕ Crowd
    ⊕ Decals
    ⊕ Fluid
    ⊕ Fog
    ⊕ Lights
    ⊕ Navigation
    ⊕ Physics
    ⊖ Pickups
        ⊕ Ammo
        ⊕ Armor
        ⊕ Health
        ⊕ Items
        ⊖ Weapon
            UTWeaponLocker_Content
            UTWeaponPickupFactory
```

8. Within the Weapons Locker properties, you should now see that your new weapon is available from the selection of weapon classes.

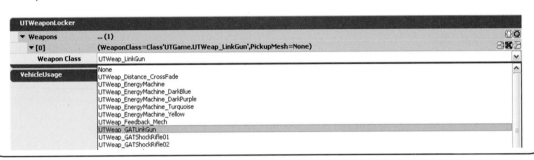

Layers for Weapons

701 Weapons Locker 02

Spatial Layers

Weapon: Spatial_Layers

As you get to the end of the target range, there is another weapons locker that gives you two new weapons. Start with the UTWeap_GAT_Spatial_Layers weapon (press number 1 on your keyboard) and fire it outside, then inside, the blue and orange glowing fields. What you will hear is that different reverb layers are added to the fire sound depending on the location of the player. The reverbs you can enable in a game are often a bit of a blunt instrument so you may want to exclude some weapons from this system and implement a specific imitation reverb system. This is straightforward to do from a programming perspective, but we have provided a slightly less elegant example so that you can clearly see what's going on.

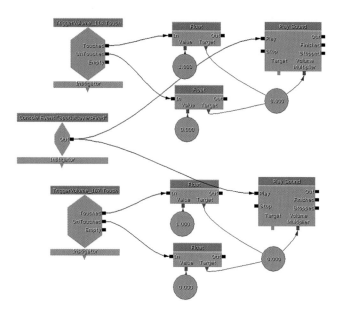

The blue and orange fields are each encapsulated by a **[TriggerVolume]**; these are used as events in Kismet to layer in different reverbs. A line of code has been added to this weapon's script (UTWeap_GAT_Spatial_Layers.uc) so that we get a console event in Kismet every time the weapon is fired:

```
PlayerController(Instigator.Controller).ServerCauseEvent('SpatialLayersFired');
```

This **[Console Event]** leads to two **[PlaySound]**s, one for an outdoor slapback reverb type layer and one for an urban type reverb layer.

Whether or not you hear these layers blended alongside the firing sound (which still originates in the script) depends on whether the player character is inside one of the two **[TriggerVolume]**s, which set the volume multiplier for each sound.

Ideally this would be hard coded and then you would just have to define the areas in the game (probably aligned to **[ReverbVolume]**s) where the different reverbs would be layered in. This would also be possible to do for looped weapons, although you'd need your programmer to be on the ball to manage a perfect sample-level synchronization with the dry loop and the looping layers.

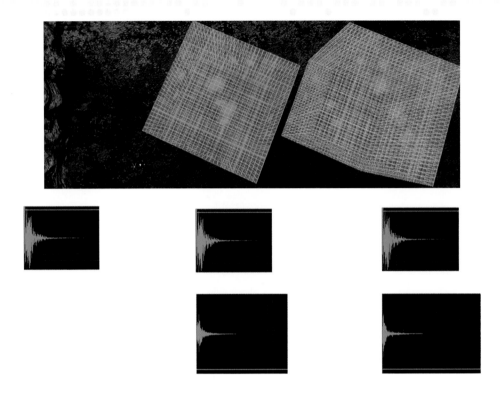

Weapon: Spatial_Tails

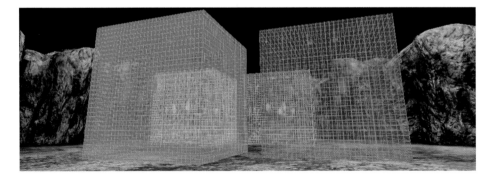

For this area select the UTWeap_GAT_Spatial_Tails weapon (press number 2 on your keyboard). We've looked at how having long samples for retriggered weapons can lead to problems. The difficulty is that the sounds that define larger spaces are by their nature long. In this example, the dry fire sound itself is unaffected but it is the choice of tail that varies according to the player's location.

Here is a retriggered weapon followed by varying tails:

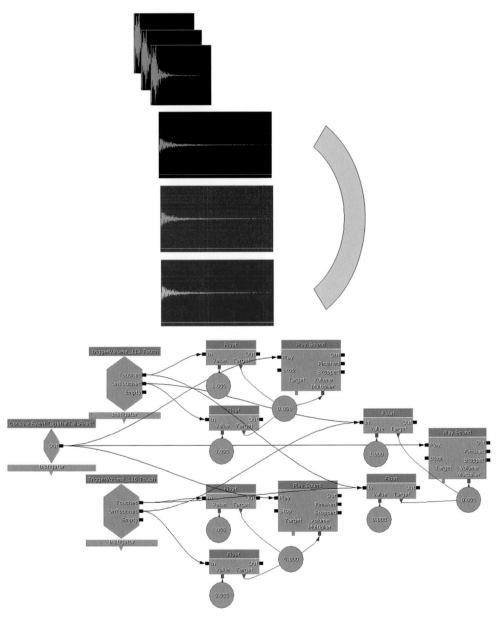

The volume of the three **[PlaySound]**s for the tail samples is controlled by the two **[TriggerVolume]**s surrounding the green and purple fields (and when both are untouched, the volume of the outside tail is at its maximum).

Weapons Sounds: Attenuation and Character Over Distance

702 Weapon: Distance_CrossFade

As weapons are such an important feature of many games, it may also be that the standard spatialization effect of applying a low-pass filter over distance is not satisfactory. The large target on the ground represents the crossfade over distance settings for the weapon that the bot next to the central tower is firing (UTWeap_GAT_Distance_CrossFade). When you approach this area, you can use the H key on your keyboard to teleport to different positions within the target and hear how the sound of the weapon varies according to your distance from it. (We've chosen to teleport you as in the current UDK build there are some issues with the Distance Crossfade function. When you pass a crossfade boundary it incorrectly retriggers the sound.)

Your choices on the character of the weapon over distance will depend on the game type, number of simultaneous weapons, and purpose of the weapon sound. This example is relatively straightforward with the script simply calling the following **[SoundCue]**:

```
WeaponFireSnd[0]=SoundCue'GATA_Sound.Weapon.WEAPON_Distance_CrossFade'
```

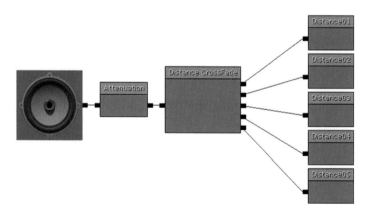

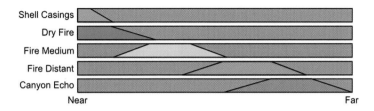

As you can see, there are five versions of the weapon sound depending on your distance from its source. These are governed by the settings within the **[Distance Crossfade]** node. The image above illustrates how the different elements attenuate over distance. (Again, this would be more difficult to achieve with a looping weapon because all the elements would have to be kept perfectly in sync as they crossfaded between each-other.)

Sniper Rifle

703 Weapon: Sniper

After taking the elevator to the top of the tower, you can once again enjoy the simple pleasures of the UTWeap_GAT_Sniper weapon. A right mouse click enables a zoom, but the unsteady breathing causes the view to move up and down. By pressing H on the keyboard, the player can temporarily hold their breath to steady the sights.

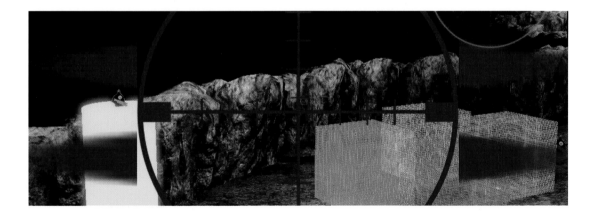

The sniper fire sound and zoom-in looped sound are referenced from the script as normal, but also embedded in the script UTWeap_GAT_SniperBase.uc are two console events that allow us to receive messages in Kismet for the breathing system:

```
PlayerController(Instigator.Controller).ServerCauseEvent('ZoomOn');
PlayerController(Instigator.Controller).ServerCauseEvent('ZoomOff');
```

The ZoomOn console event is received when the zoom is activated by a right mouse button press. This triggers a **[Play Camera Animation]** Action that contains a matinee-based animation for the camera to move up and down. At the same time, it opens a **[Gate]** to allow the H-press keyboard input event through.

The camera animation and associated breathing sounds (produced by the two **[PlaySound]**s on the right) loop around until the H-press event plays a breath hold and stops the animation. The **[Delay]** then lasts for three seconds to enable the player to take a shot before the breath runs out and we return to the swaying camera animation and breathing events. If the player releases the H key during this time, it also restarts the camera animation. (The console event ZoomOff is triggered by the right mouse button being released. This action closes the **[Gate]**s and switches off the zoom view, which is all controlled from within the script itself.)

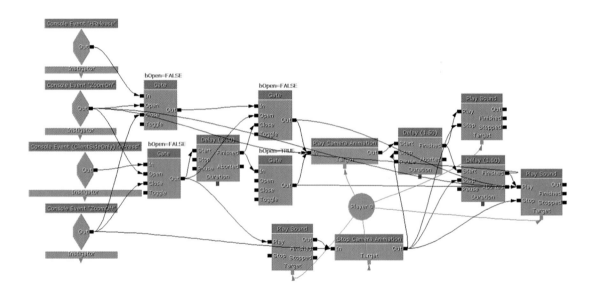

Impact, Whizz-by, and Handling Sounds

Weapon firing sounds do not work in isolation. They are part of a system that includes the whizz-bys, impacts, and ricochets together with the Foley sounds for the weapons handling, reloading, and equipping. In UDK the handling sounds are dealt with within the UTWeap scripts, but impact sounds are handled by the UTAttachment scripts for instant hits weapons (such as the Shock Rifle) or UTProj scripts for projectile weapons (such as the Link Gun LMB Fire).

Weapon Impacts

704 Weapons Locker 03

The weapons in the locker at the second target range have had their impact sounds added back in.

Weapon: Pistol_Surface_Types

You will have seen when you created your own copy of the link gun earlier that the impact sound effects are generated using an additional script for the Weapons named UTAttachment. The first weapon (number 1 on your keyboard) uses the UTWeap_GAT_Pistol_Surface_Types.uc script together with the UTAttachment_GAT_Pistol_Surface_Types.uc script.

The Attachment script detects the Material Type and then references a **[SoundCue]** depending on that type in the same way that the player footsteps worked in Chapter 3. (Parts of the script have been removed for clarity as indicated by ------):

```
defaultproperties
{
  DefaultImpactEffect=(----------Sound=SoundCue'GATA_Sound.Collision.Silence')
  ImpactEffects(0)=(MaterialType=Stone, ----,
Sound=SoundCue'GATA_Sound.Collision.PistolStone_Cue')
  ImpactEffects(1)=(MaterialType=GunShotSurfaces01, ----,
Sound=SoundCue'GATA_Sound.Collision.PistolMetal_Cue')
  ImpactEffects(2)=(MaterialType=GunShotSurfaces02, ----,
Sound=SoundCue'GATA_Sound.Collision.PistolWood_Cue')
  WeaponClass=class'UTWeap_Pistol_Surface_Types'
}
```

The surface material of the shooting range is already set to Physical Material Stone. (You can check the physical material that this uses by right-clicking on the surface and selecting Materials/Find Instance in Content Browser. You can then double-click the material to open the Material editor and see the physical material it references.) You'll remember that this is one of the existing physical materials in UDK along with *Default, Dirt, Energy, Foliage, Glass, Liquid, Metal, Sand, Water, Water_Shallow,* and *Wood.*

In the Attachment script we have added stone as a possible surface type and then referenced our own **[SoundCue]**. You can add your own by simply duplicating the line of script, incrementing the array (the numbers in brackets), defining the material type, and then referencing your **[SoundCue]**. You can see that for the targets themselves we have defined our own new physical material types. For a reminder on how to do this yourself, see the exercise "Custom Materials for Custom Footsteps" in Chapter 3. In this case we've linked GunShotSurfaces01 to a metal impact **[SoundCue]** and GunShotSurfaces02 to a wood impact **[SoundCue].**

Weapon: Machine_Gun_Surface_Types

The second weapon in this area (number 2 on your keyboard) derives from the scripts UTWeap_GAT_MachineGun_Surface_Types.uc and UTAttachment_GAT_MachineGun_Surface_Types.uc. It has the same surface types defined (stone, metal, wood) as the pistol.

With impact sounds that are heard frequently (from a machine gun, for instance), it's obviously important that you try to avoid repetition. Within your **[SoundCue]**s for impacts, you should consider applying some of the techniques covered in Chapter 2 such as modulation of pitch and volume and the randomized recombination of sounds. Bear in mind that, like footsteps, any sounds with a particularly memorable character will stand out, so you should weight them within the **[Random]** object to appear less often. For example, you might want the frequency of a ricochet element within your **[SoundCue]** to be significantly less for a machine gun that fires 2,000 rounds per minute than for a one-shot pistol. You may really like ricochets, but remember that, as well as perhaps getting tiresome after the 700th listening, these relatively long sounds can also contribute significantly to your voice count.

Impacts on NPCs and Player Characters

Another sound you will hear regularly (if you're any good) is the sound of your weapon's impact on the nonplayer characters (NPCs). You can try this out on the poor defenseless bot at the end of the target range.

These are set using the class UTPawnSoundGroup_Liandri.uc from the folder C:\UDK\UDK(***)\ Development\Src\UTGame\Classes:

```
defaultproperties
{
  DodgeSound=SoundCue'A_Character_CorruptEnigma_Cue.
Mean_Efforts.A_Effort_EnigmaMean_Dodge_Cue'
  DoubleJumpSound=SoundCue'A_Character_CorruptEnigma_Cue.
Mean_Efforts.A_Effort_EnigmaMean_DoubleJump_Cue'
  LandSound=SoundCue'A_Character_CorruptEnigma_Cue.
Mean_Efforts.A_Effort_EnigmaMean_LandLight_Cue'
  DefaultFootStepSound=SoundCue'A_Character_Footsteps.
Footsteps.A_Character_Footstep_DefaultCue'
  DyingSound=SoundCue'A_Character_CorruptEnigma_Cue.
Mean_Efforts.A_Effort_EnigmaMean_Death_Cue'
  HitSounds[0]=SoundCue'A_Character_CorruptEnigma_Cue.
Mean_Efforts.A_Effort_EnigmaMean_PainSmall_Cue'
  HitSounds[1]=SoundCue'A_Character_CorruptEnigma_Cue.
Mean_Efforts.A_Effort_EnigmaMean_PainMedium_Cue'
  HitSounds[2]=SoundCue'A_Character_CorruptEnigma_Cue.
Mean_Efforts.A_Effort_EnigmaMean_PainLarge_Cue'
  FallingDamageLandSound=SoundCue'A_Character_CorruptEnigma_Cue.
Mean_Efforts.A_Effort_EnigmaMean_LandHeavy_Cue'
  GibSound=SoundCue'A_Character_CorruptEnigma_Cue.
Mean_Efforts.A_Effort_EnigmaMean_DeathInstant_Cue'
  CrushedSound=SoundCue'A_Character_BodyImpacts.
BodyImpacts.A_Character_RobotImpact_BodyExplosion_Cue'
  BodyExplosionSound=SoundCue'A_Character_BodyImpacts.
BodyImpacts.A_Character_RobotImpact_BodyExplosion_Cue'
  InstaGibSound=SoundCue'A_Character_CorruptEnigma_Cue.
Mean_Efforts.A_Effort_EnigmaMean_DeathInstant_Cue'
}
```

Impacts on the player character are referenced here:

C:\UDK\UDK(***)\Development\Src\UTGame\Classes\GATPawnSoundGroup.uc

```
    BulletImpactSound=SoundCue'A_Character_BodyImpacts.
  BodyImpacts.A_Character_BodyImpact_Bullet_Cue'
```

They are usually heard simultaneously with the Hit, Crushed or Gibbed sounds here:

C:\UDK\UDK(***)\Development\Src\UTGame\Classes\GATPawnSoundGroup_GATCharacter.uc

```
  class GATPawnSoundGroup_GATCharacter extends GATPawnSoundGroup;
  defaultproperties
  {
    DodgeSound=SoundCue'A_Character_CorruptEnigma_Cue.
  Mean_Efforts.A_Effort_EnigmaMean_Dodge_Cue'
    DoubleJumpSound=SoundCue'A_Character_CorruptEnigma_Cue.
  Mean_Efforts.A_Effort_EnigmaMean_DoubleJump_Cue'
    LandSound=SoundCue'A_Character_CorruptEnigma_Cue.
  Mean_Efforts.A_Effort_EnigmaMean_LandLight_Cue'
    DefaultFootstepSound=SoundCue'A_Character_Footsteps.
  FootSteps.A_Character_Footstep_WaterDeepCue'
    DyingSound=SoundCue'A_Character_CorruptEnigma_Cue.
  Mean_Efforts.A_Effort_EnigmaMean_Death_Cue'
    HitSounds[0]=SoundCue'A_Character_CorruptEnigma_Cue.
  Mean_Efforts.A_Effort_EnigmaMean_PainSmall_Cue'
    HitSounds[1]=SoundCue'A_Character_CorruptEnigma_Cue.
  Mean_Efforts.A_Effort_EnigmaMean_PainMedium_Cue'
    HitSounds[2]=SoundCue'A_Character_CorruptEnigma_Cue.
  Mean_Efforts.A_Effort_EnigmaMean_PainLarge_Cue'
    FallingDamageLandSound=SoundCue'A_Character_CorruptEnigma_Cue.
  Mean_Efforts.A_Effort_EnigmaMean_LandHeavy_Cue'
    GibSound=SoundCue'A_Character_CorruptEnigma_Cue.
  Mean_Efforts.A_Effort_EnigmaMean_DeathInstant_Cue'
    CrushedSound=SoundCue'A_Character_BodyImpacts.
  BodyImpacts.A_Character_RobotImpact_BodyExplosion_Cue'
    BodyExplosionSound=SoundCue'A_Character_BodyImpacts.
  BodyImpacts.A_Character_RobotImpact_BodyExplosion_Cue'
    InstaGibSound=SoundCue'A_Character_CorruptEnigma_Cue.
  Mean_Efforts.A_Effort_EnigmaMean_DeathInstant_Cue'
  }
```

You can replace all of these with references to your own **[SoundCue]**s and recompile the scripts in the usual way.

Whizz-Bys

If you're hearing a bullet whizz by your head, then the good news is that you're still alive. As most bullets travel faster than the speed of sound, the usual order of things would be to be hit by the bullet first, then hear the actual shot, and in your dying moments reflect on how you really wish it were easier to get that convincing outdoor tail to the sound that you've been trying to achieve for weeks. Fortunately, most games aren't that cruel and usually give you plenty of opportunity to realize that the distant twinkle you've just been admiring is the reflection off a sniper's sights. The weapon that the bot you just killed was carrying is a shock rifle, and the sound it makes as it whizzes by the player's head is referred to in UDK as a BulletWhip.

The original shock rifle UTWeap_ShockRifle.uc (C:\UDK\UDK(***)\Development\Src\UTGame Content\Classes\) refers to the Attachment class UTAttachment_ShockRifle.uc (in the same folder), which calls the **[SoundCue]** illustrated here:

```
BulletWhip=SoundCue'A_Weapon_ShockRifle.Cue.A_Weapon_SR_WhipCue'
```

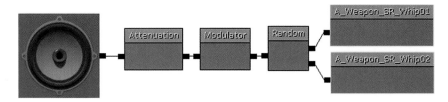

The weapon that the bot was/is using is (Mymod) UTWeap_GAT_BotShockRifle.uc, so you can swap out the BulletWhip here (UTAttachment_GAT_BotShockRifle.uc):

```
BulletWhip=SoundCue'GATA_Sound.Weapon.WEAPON_Bulletwhip_01'
```

Weapon Loading, Handling, and Selecting Sounds

The default weapons in UDK do not have the elaborate reloading animations that are present in many games, but the scripts do reference sounds for when the player picks up the weapon, swaps to, or discards the weapon from use. For example, the shock gun contains the following entries:

(C:\UDK\UDK(***)\Development\Src\UTGameContent\Classes\UTWeap_ShockRifle.uc)

```
WeaponFireSnd[0]=SoundCue'A_Weapon_ShockRifle.Cue.A_Weapon_SR_FireCue'
WeaponFireSnd[1]=SoundCue'A_Weapon_ShockRifle.Cue.A_Weapon_SR_AltFireCue'
WeaponEquipSnd=SoundCue'A_Weapon_ShockRifle.Cue.A_Weapon_SR_RaiseCue'
WeaponPutDownSnd=SoundCue'A_Weapon_ShockRifle.Cue.A_Weapon_SR_LowerCue'
PickupSound=SoundCue'A_Pickups.Weapons.Cue.A_Pickup_Weapons_Shock_Cue'
```

You can swap these out for any of your copied or new weapons in the same way as the other operations you have been doing. If you're working with a team that can supply you with some more sophisticated reloading animations, then you can actually avoid scripts for these items by calling your **[SoundCue]**s directly.

Adding Sound to Animations

Weapon: Animation

If you switch now to the third weapon (UTWeap_GAT_Animation) you picked up at the most recent weapons locker (number 3 on your keyboard), you can see that the right mouse button triggers an Alt Fire mode.

This weapon is based on the rocket launcher and the Alt fire loading sounds are scripted in the UTWeap_GAT_Animation.uc:

```
WeaponLoadedSnd=SoundCue'A_Weapon_RocketLauncher.Cue.A_Weapon_RL_Load_Cue'
WeaponFireSnd[0]=SoundCue'A_Weapon_RocketLauncher.Cue.A_Weapon_RL_Fire_Cue'
WeaponFireSnd[1]=SoundCue'A_Weapon_RocketLauncher.Cue.A_Weapon_RL_Fire_Cue'
WeaponEquipSnd=SoundCue'A_Weapon_RocketLauncher.Cue.A_Weapon_RL_Raise_Cue'
AltFireModeChangeSound=SoundCue'A_Weapon_RocketLauncher.
Cue.A_Weapon_RL_AltModeChange_Cue'
RocketLoadedSound=SoundCue'A_Weapon_RocketLauncher.
Cue.A_Weapon_RL_RocketLoaded_Cue'
GrenadeFireSound=SoundCue'A_Weapon_RocketLauncher.Cue.A_Weapon_RL_GrenadeFire_Cue'
AltFireSndQue(0)=SoundCue'A_Weapon_RocketLauncher.
Cue.A_Weapon_RL_AltFireQueue1_Cue'
AltFireSndQue(1)=SoundCue'A_Weapon_RocketLauncher.
Cue.A_Weapon_RL_AltFireQueue2_Cue'
AltFireSndQue(2)=SoundCue'A_Weapon_RocketLauncher.
Cue.A_Weapon_RL_AltFireQueue3_Cue'
LockAcquiredSound=SoundCue'A_Weapon_RocketLauncher.Cue.A_Weapon_RL_SeekLock_Cue'
LockLostSound=SoundCue'A_Weapon_RocketLauncher.Cue.A_Weapon_RL_SeekLost_Cue'
```

These sounds align to the animations of the weapon, but if you are working with an animator and have a new weapon (or any other kind of animation), you can also call your sounds directly from the animation rather then scripting them. If you're not a scripting expert or are not working with one, then this is a much easier approach.

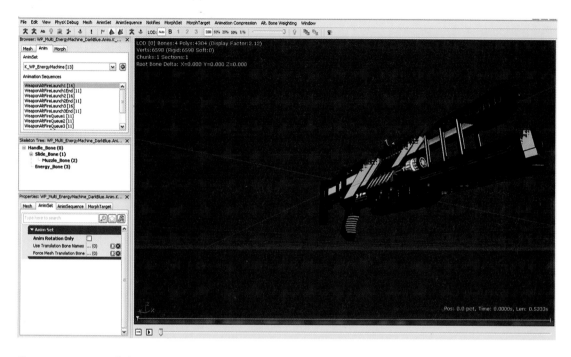

If you open any of the weapons packages you can see that the Anim group contains an AnimSet. Double-click this item to open the AnimSet Editor.

By selecting the Anim tab you can see the individual animations that make up the weapon's movement, and pressing the Play button in the Animation window will allow you to see them in action.

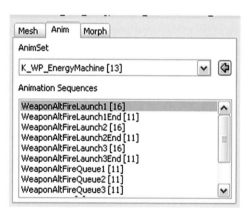

The lower menu in the AnimSequence tab will allow you to add Notifies to this animation at specific time points.

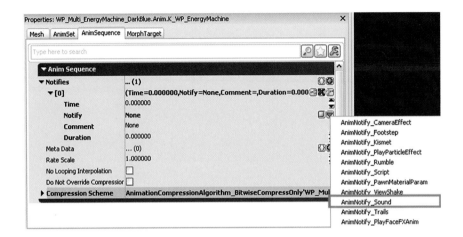

Having added an AnimNotify_Sound, you can reference a **[SoundCue]** from the Content Browser and this will then play every time this animation is used. We've given you a copy of this weapon (UTWeap_GAT_Animation_CLEAR) with no sounds attached so you can use this AnimNotify method of attaching your own sounds to it.

This menu also allows the addition of the AnimNotify_Footstep. This would be attached to new imported characters and creatures to notify the footstep/material types system we were using in Chapter 3—the Footdown variable usually relates to left (0) and right (1) feet. This would be referenced by a script (like the GATPawnSoundGroup.uc we are using for our player character in the tutorial level) to detect the physical material of the surface and then reference the appropriate **[SoundCue]** you've designated for that material.

(An aspect of animation and sound we haven't discussed is matching face animations to dialogue. This is because it's really the job of the animation department—not yours. If you're interested in taking a look into this aspect of animation, then right-click on a skeletal mesh in your Content Browser and choose Create New FaceFX Asset. Doubleclicking on this new asset will open the Face FX Studio editor. From the top menu, select Actor/Animation Manager and click on the Create Animation button. You will be asked to select a **[SoundCue]** and it will then analyze the SoundNodeWave within it and try to match the phonemes in the sound file with the text you have typed in. Getting this right is a complex process, so if you want to pursue this challenge then see the UDK documentation.)

Weapons Summary

Whether you want simple volume attenuation, low-pass filtering over distance, or more advanced crossfading over distance depends entirely on the circumstances in which it will be heard and its importance to the game. We've focused on mechanical and sci-fi-type weapons as these are most common, but all these techniques are equally applicable to everything from melee weapons like axes and swords to magic spells. For a shooter game you would probably combine all of these systems together with whatever real-time acoustic processing systems are available.

To summarize:

- You should first consider the most appropriate system for the nature of the weapon:
  - Single shot
  - Retriggered
  - Looping for speed
  - Looping for consistency
  - Or others
- Decide if it is important that the weapon supplies some kind of feedback to the player.
- Consider adding "prebaked" layers and different tail samples for different types of reverberant environment.
- Consider crossfading between different sounds over distance.
- Consider weapon fire, flybys, impacts, and ricochets together as one inter-related system.
- Consider using AnimNotifies called from the animation itself to get the timing of more complex reload or firing animations in sync.

All of this is, of course, tied into the design of the weapon sounds themselves. For some discussion on this subject, please turn to Appendix E/Example Challenges: Weapons.

As you can see, complex systems such as those for weapons are instances where the roles of sound designer, scripter, and programmer are truly interconnected. We recommend that you learn as much about everything as you can! To learn more about weapon design from the experts, see the bibliography for this chapter.

(If you have an interest in taking scripting further, we'll be discussing some alternative tools in "Scripting" in Appendix C: UDK Tips.)

Vehicle Systems

Simulation of a real car engine is a hugely complex system made of many separate sound sources, each reacting in a different way to the driver input and other physics states on the vehicle. UDK is certainly not the best vehicle (ouch!) for convincing car simulations, but we will try to cover the basic principles. Although we call these "vehicle" systems that you'd associate with a car or motorbike, these principles are equally applicable to vehicles such as skateboards or jet skis, or indeed any other sound that has a complex relationship with in-game variables.

Simple Vehicle: Manta

705a Manta

At the racetrack toward the end of the tutorial level, get into the Manta (vehicle A on the left) by pressing E and fly around to see how it sounds in response to your input and the vehicle's speed.

Each vehicle in UDK is based on three scripts:

This defines how the vehicle behaves

```
UTVehicle_***** (C:\UDK\UDK(***)\Development\Src\UTGame\Classes)
```

This defines the effects and **[SoundCue]**s

```
UTVehicle_Content_****** (C:\UDK\UDK(***)\Development\Src\UTGameContent\Classes)
```

This is the Actor that is created in game. (It refers to the Content script.)

```
UTVehicleFactory_****** (C:\UDK\UDK(***)\Development\Src\UTGameContent\Classes)
```

The Content script references the following sounds.

Engine sound

```
Begin Object Class=AudioComponent Name=MantaEngineSound
  SoundCue=SoundCue'A_Vehicle_Manta_UT3g.SoundCues.A_Vehicle_Manta_EngineLoop'
End Object
```

Collision

```
CollisionSound=SoundCue'A_Vehicle_Manta.SoundCues.A_Vehicle_Manta_Collide'
```

Enter the vehicle

```
EnterVehicleSound=SoundCue'A_Vehicle_Manta.SoundCues.A_Vehicle_Manta_Start'
```

Exit the vehicle

```
ExitVehicleSound=SoundCue'A_Vehicle_Manta.SoundCues.A_Vehicle_Manta_Stop'
```

Scrape

```
Begin Object Class=AudioComponent Name=BaseScrapeSound
  SoundCue=SoundCue'A_Gameplay.A_Gameplay_Onslaught_MetalScrape01Cue'
End Object
```

Jump

    JumpSound=SoundCue'A_Vehicle_Manta.Sounds.A_Vehicle_Manta_JumpCue'

Duck

    DuckSound=SoundCue'A_Vehicle_Manta.Sounds.A_Vehicle_Manta_CrouchCue'

Explosion

    ExplosionSound=SoundCue'A_Vehicle_Manta.SoundCues.A_Vehicle_Manta_Explode'

You can find these **[SoundCue]**s in the Content Browser. If you open the A_Vehicle_Manta_UT3g. SoundCues.A_Vehicle_Manta_EngineLoop **[SoundCue],** you can see that it contains a node that we have not yet fully discussed, the mysterious **[Continuous Modulator].**

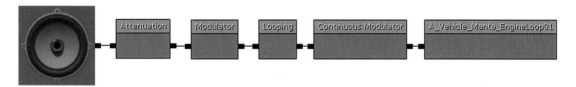

You'll notice in game that the engine loop of the Manta varies depending on the velocity of the vehicle. This velocity (in the range of numbers from 0 to 5,000) is passed to the **[Continuous Modulator]** in the **[SoundCue]** and is used to vary both the volume of the engine loop and its pitch.

You can hear the effect of this input as it is scaled to the ranges 0 to 1 within the **[SoundCue]** by using the arrows on the right hand side to carefully scale the Min Output values up and down. First set the Min Output of the volume modulation to around 1.0, then play the **[SoundCue]** and scale the Min output value of the pitch up and down. You'll hear the same effect as that of the straight-forward (linear) velocity-to-pitch relationship when in the game.

To create your own Manta with your own sounds, use the same method as you did when duplicating the existing weapons. Make a copy of the three script files with your own name and put them in the

C:\UDK\(***)\Development\Src\MyMod\Classes folder. Then make sure that the internal references to the script's name within the script itself are updated to reflect the new name you've given it.

```
UTVehicle_Manta.uc
(C:\UDK\UDK(***)\Development\Src\UTGame\Classes)
UTVehicle_Manta_Content.uc
(C:\UDK\UDK(***)\Development\Src\UTGameContent\Classes)
UTVehicleFactory_Manta.uc
(C:\UDK\UDK(***)\Development\Src\UTGameContent\Classes)
```

Engine-Based Vehicles: Scorpion

705b Scorpion

Now go and use vehicle B in the center. This is UDK's Scorpion.

You'll hear now that the velocity-to-pitch relationship is quite different with a succession of quick rises in pitch to simulate a gear changing effect. Looking at the UTVehicle_Scorpion.uc script(C:\ UDK\UDK(***)\Development\Src\UTGame\Classes), we can see that this uses functionality from the UDKVehicleSimCar class.

(The Scorpion, like the Manta, is also dependent on its UTVehicle_Scorpion_Content.uc and UTVehicleFactory_Scorpion.uc scripts.)

The TorqueVSpeedCurve determines how the vehicle accelerates

```
var() InterpCurveFloat TorqueVSpeedCurve;
```

EngineRPMCurve – maps the vehicles velocity onto an RPM (Revs per Minute) value

```
var() InterpCurveFloat EngineRPMCurve;
```

Looking further in the script you can see that these curves are not linear but have a number of points defined within them:

```
TorqueVSpeedCurve=(Points=((InVal=-600.0,OutVal=0.0),(InVal=-300.0,OutVal=80.0),(I
nVal=0.0,OutVal=130.0),(InVal=950.0,OutVal=130.0),(InVal=1050.0,OutVal=10.0),(InVa
l=1150.0,OutVal=0.0)))
```

```
EngineRPMCurve=(Points=((InVal=-500.0,OutVal=2500.0),(InVal=0.0,OutVal=500.0),(InV
al=549.0,OutVal=3500.0),(InVal=550.0,OutVal=1000.0),(InVal=849.0,OutVal=4500.0),(I
nVal=850.0,OutVal=1500.0),(InVal=1100.0,OutVal=5000.0)))
```

The EngineRPMCurve is the one that is passed to the **[Continuous Modulator]** within the A_
Vehicle_Scorpion_EngineLoop **[SoundCue]** (UDKGame/Content/Sounds/Vehicel/A_Vehicle_Scorpion).

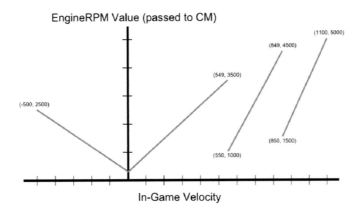

You can see from the diagram that although these values are again scaled between 0.0 and 1.0
within the **[Continuous Modulator]**, the velocity-to-RPM curves for the pitch are significantly
more complex, so we get a more variable RPM-to-pitch relationship, intended to create the impression of the vehicle moving up through gears as its velocity increases.

Because of the acceleration curve (TorqueVSpeedCurve), these actions actually happen very quickly
within the game and the vehicle spends most of its time within the last section of the curve moving
slowly up toward top speed.

You'll appreciate that plotting curves in this way is not the most sound designer—friendly approach and much of the functionality for vehicles is quite inaccessible to non-programmers. Given this fact, and given that there are other things that we want to be able to do, we have had to take an alternative approach to creating our own vehicle, the GATScorpion.

Engine-Based Vehicle with Crossfades: GAT_Scorpion

705c GAT_Scorpion

Go back to the start of the racetrack, enter vehicle C on the right (GAT_Scorpion), and drive it around.

This vehicle is based on the UDK Scorpion and uses the following scripts from the C:\UDK\ UDK(***)\Development\Src\MyMod\Classes folder:

> UTVehicle_GAT_Scorpion.uc
> UTVehicle_GAT_Scorpion_Content.uc
> UTVehicleFactory_GAT_Scorpion.uc

It's unrealistic to expect that a single sound can represent a convincing engine when taken through any significant degree of pitch shift because of the change in timbre that this process produces in a sound. All but the most basic vehicle simulations will instead use several recordings that are taken at different engine speeds and, as the RPM increases, there is often some pitch shift but as importantly, there is a crossfade between these different recordings so that the timbre is maintained or at least is realistic for the vehicle in question. To achieve this state, we've had to create a simulated system in Kismet that allows us to crossfade between samples based on the vehicle's velocity in the game.

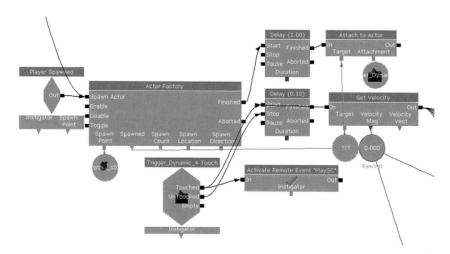

A **[Trigger_Dynamic]** is attached to the vehicle when it is spawned. When it is touched (and sends a **[Remote Event]**), this switches on all the **[SoundCue]**s, which are immediately set to silent.

When the player enters the vehicle (by pressing E), we actually receive an Untouched message so the first output of the switch this is connected to is unused, and when the player does leave the area around the vehicle (and untouches the **[Trigger_Dynamic]**), the sound is turned off.

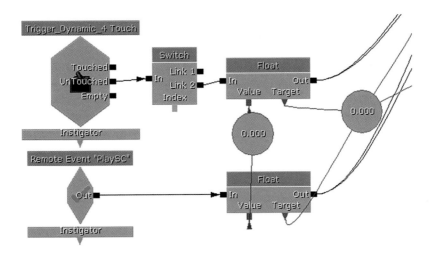

A **[Get Velocity]** action is polled by a **[Delay]** object every 0.1 second, and this velocity value is used to vary the pitch of the sounds, and at the same time to crossfade between four different **[SoundCue]**s:

SoundCue'GATA_Sound.Vehicle.VEHICLE_car_engine_idle_Cue'
SoundCue'GATA_Sound.Vehicle.VEHICLE_car_engine_low_Cue'
SoundCue'GATA_Sound.Vehicle.VEHICLE_car_engine_med_Cue'
SoundCue'GATA_Sound.Vehicle.VEHICLE_car_engine_high_Cue'

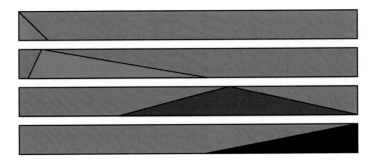

Vehicle velocity to four SoundCue's volumes for the GATScorpion.

The first cue is an engine idle recording (shown in red in the preceding figure). The velocity is scaled using a series of maths actions and then goes to the fade level of a **[GATPlaySound]**. As the vehicle speeds up, the engine idle sounds quickly drop away, as you would expect.

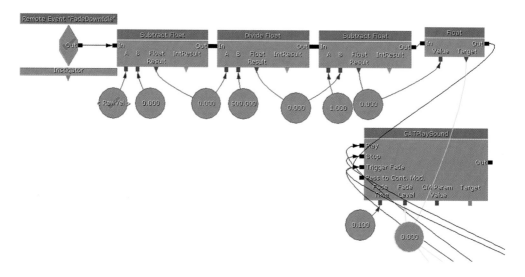

The other elements need their volume scaled both up and down; to make this more straightforward, the velocity values are compared against different ranges to determine which scaling factor should be sent to which **[GATPlaySound]**.

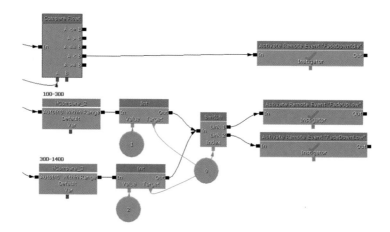

If the velocity falls within a given range of values, then the appropriate **[Remote Event]** receives a trigger to perform the scaling and send the result to the **[GATPlaySound]** fade level to adjust the volume of its **[SoundCue]**.

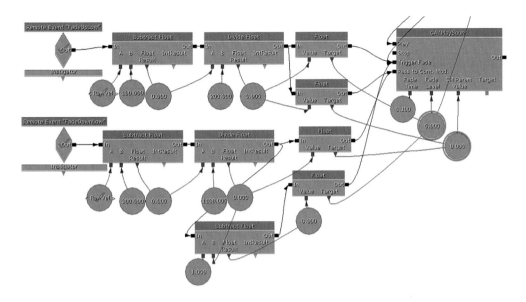

Here is a summary of the compare and scaling operations:

If vel < 500 - - - pass to the "FadeDownIdle" functionality
(This takes the vel and applies it to volume (0 = full vol, 500 = 0 vol))
If vel > 100 & & vel < 300 - - - pass to "FadeUpLow"
(100 = 0 vol, 300 = full vol)
If vel > 300 & & vel < 1400 - - - pass to "FadeDownLow"
(300 = full vol, 1400 = 0 vol)
If vel > 800 & & vel < 1500 - - - pass to "FadeUpMed"
(800 = 0 vol, 1500 = full vol)
If vel > 1500 & & vel < 2000 - - - pass to "FadeDownMed"
(1500 = full vol, 2000 = 0 vol)
If vel > 1100 - - - pass to "FadeUpHigh"
(1100 = 0 vol. 2000 = full vol)

This produces the following volume curves (with each **[SoundCue]** shown in a different color).

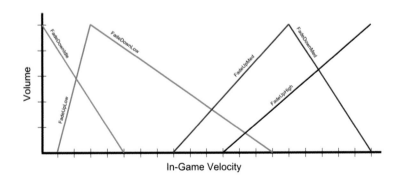

At the same time, this scaled velocity value is also sent to the CM Param value of the **[GATPlaySound].** This aspect of the **[GATPlaySound]** uses the continuous modulator functionality to link into the vehicle's **[SoundCue]**s. Within the **[GATPlaySound]**, you can set a parameter name (such as "Pitch") and then reference this parameter within the **[SoundCue].**

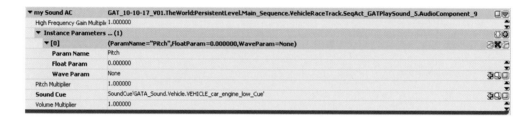

In the figure you can see the **[SoundCue]** for the low engine speed:

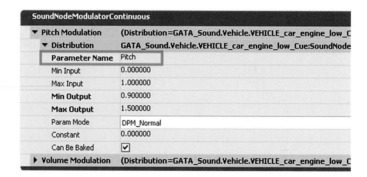

and the properties of its **[Continuous Modulator]:**

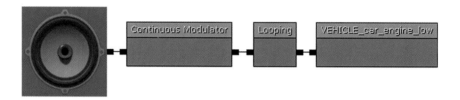

In this instance you can see that the incoming pitch values (derived from the scaled velocity values) are further scaled to produce a range of pitch change between 0.9 and 1.5.

Conclusions

Simulation of various modes of transportation in games is a specialized field often relying on proprietary tools. The component parts of the engine, induction system, and exhaust system, (not forgetting the wheels) would all be modelled not only using crossfade systems but also granular approaches to the sound sources themselves, together with a variety of DSP effects. Within the introductory confines of this book, we can only scratch the surface of what is an area of real expertise and specialism. Play around with the ranges for the GATScorpion vehicle, duplicate it to create your own version, and add your own **[SoundCue]**s to get used to the crossfading principle. If you are feeling particularly masochistic, you could continue to develop this system to layer in other engine elements. As an alternative we'd suggest investigating the middleware options such as FMOD and Wwise, which are both free to download and offer a much more sound designer–friendly environment for this sort of application.

Next Steps

Jobs and Work

Getting work as a sound designer or a composer for games is not easy. Although the industry is big in economic terms and audio teams are expanding along with the size of game projects, it's still a specialized niche. Depending on the size of the project, there could be a full-time audio team of up to six or seven but two to three is more common and the "lone audio guy/gal" is still not unheard of. In addition to the core members, there will be a significant amount of ancillary work or outsourcing, and both the demand for this work and the size of the core team will vary considerably depending on the stage of the project.

We think producing sound and music for games is fun and would hope that you make it part of your life after reading this book. But if you intend to try and earn your living in this field, you need to ask yourself some honest questions.

Do You Have What it Takes?

Sound Designers

- Do you love games?
- Do you understand games?
- Do you love sound?
- Do you carry a portable recorder with you all the time?
- Do you instinctively pick up, tap, rub, scrape, and stroke interesting objects you come across just to see what kind of sound they make?
- Do you stop in the middle of the street when someone knocks against a railing and it makes an interesting noise? Do you come back at 5:30 in the morning when it's quiet and there's no one around to record it?
- When you accidentally break something, is your first thought, "Damn! That's going to be expensive to replace!" or "Damn! I wish my recorder was running for that!"?
- Did you enjoy this book?
- Have you built your own level to try out the ideas in this book?
- Have you made some cool audio systems that we haven't even thought of?
- Have you read every article referred to in the bibliography?
- Have you spent days following the links from the www.thegameaudiotutorial.com website to further your knowledge?

- Have you joined the forums suggested on the site, read through all the past posts, and helped out some newbies?
- Have you downloaded FMOD and Wwise, worked your way through their tutorials, and realized how great they are and what you could do with them if only someone would help you hook them into a real game engine?
- Have you been to GDC? (The Game Developers Conference)
- Have you been to the Develop conference?
- Have you been to an AES conference? (Audio Engineering Society)
- Have you gone to the UDK site and joined a modding team to help them out with the sound for their game?
- Are you an advocate for audio, explaining what you can do to make their game better?
- Are you proactive and self-motivated?
- Do people enjoy working with you?

Composers

- Do you love games?
- Do you understand games?
- Do you love music?
- Do you have a desire to write music that you just can't shake off?
- Do you use this desire to write as much music as you can for any opportunity you find?
- Do you write music for a college band, a local orchestra, a local dance company, student or no-budget films?
- Did you enjoy this book?
- Have you written music to try out the systems in this book?
- Have you played around with these systems so you understand what's going on?
- Have you made some better systems for your music that we haven't even thought of?
- Have you gone to the UDK site and joined a mod team to write music for?
- Are you an advocate for music, explaining what you can do to make their game better?
- Have you read every article referred to in the bibliography?
- Have you spent days following the links from the www.thegameaudiotutorial.com website to further your knowledge?
- Have you joined the forums suggested on the site, read through all the past posts, and helped out some newbies?
- Have you downloaded FMOD and Wwise, worked your way through their tutorials, and realized how great they are and what you could do with them if only someone would help you hook them into a real game engine?
- Can you write music in lots of different genres?
- Can you produce professional-sounding stereo and surround mixes of your music that still sound good when put up against the music in your favorite game?
- Do you understand instruments and how to write for them?
- Can you produce convincing MIDI mockups of that orchestral score you've been working on?
- Have you been to the Develop conference?
- Have you been to GDC? (The Game Developers Conference)

- Have you been to an AES conference? (Audio Engineering Society)
- Are you a member of GANG? (The Game Audio Network Guild)
- Are you proactive and self-motivated?
- Do people enjoy working with you?

These are not exhaustive descriptions of the skills you need but are intended to prompt you to think about whether you have the motivation and commitment to succeed. If you want a better idea of the kind of skills that the different roles require, there are two good places to start looking.

Jobs and Skills

The first place you can get an idea of the skills that employers are after is in the advertisements for jobs themselves. On the website (www.thegameaudiotutorial.com) there are links to the major game recruitment sites and also a link to a document with more than 60 job ads we've collected from the past few years. These descriptions give you a pretty good idea of what people are after.

Here's the list of advertised job titles we've come across:

> Audio director/Audio manager/Audio lead/Audio production director
> Sound designer/Game sound designer/Audio designer/Audio artist/Sound supervisor
> Audio implementer/Audio integrator/Technical sound designer
> Audio engineer
> Audio person
> Audio programmer/Audio software engineer
> Music director
> Composer/Music transcriber/Note tracker
> Voice director

(You'll note that composition work is rarely, if ever, advertised. This is simply because there is no need. Companies will frequently go on word of mouth or with a composer whose work they've heard previously. If these companies want someone new, then there's always the 20 or 30 CDs that arrive daily through their mailbox from budding composers like you.)

In addition, there are many other related roles for people with audio or music skills such as recording engineer, field recordist, music copyist, orchestrator, music editor, dialogue editor, voice-over director, and related casting and localization personnel. As an aside, the one area where the industry is in desperate need for people is audio programming. Knowing about audio, and about programming, is a rare commodity, so if the bit of scripting we've dabbled with has whetted your appetite at all, we'd recommend looking into taking this interest further. Be warned that programming is a unique skill set and a long haul, but it is one of the few areas in the game industry where there's a good chance of a job at the end.

Going back to the job descriptions, you need to read them carefully as there's little consistency in what these titles mean, or what the jobs entail, across the industry. For instance, one person will say that an audio engineer is someone who is chiefly responsible for running the studios and the recording sessions that take place, whereas another will consider this person as an audio programmer or audio software engineer. Getting these requirements wrong can lead to a rather uncomfortable job interview.

In addition to looking at job descriptions, there's another unique resource that should be of great benefit to you when trying to understand what the different roles entail. Read on.

IASIG Game Audio Education Working Group

Author Richard Stevens writes, "I should disclose an interest at this point, as I'm currently chair of this group. Having said that, what follows is, of course, totally unbiased fact."

We hope that by the time you read this book, the snappily titled Interactive Audio Special Interest Group: Game Audio Education Working Group (IASIG–EDUWG) will have published its Game Audio Curriculum Guideline document (a draft version is already available from www.iasig.org/wg/eduwg). This document is the result of several years of work by members of the group in consultation with game audio professionals from around the globe. Although the primary aim of the document is to advise universities and colleges on appropriate topics for courses on sound and music for games, it is also a very useful reference document for people who want to get into the industry.

The initial part of the document describes the variety of sound- and music-related jobs and roles within the industry; this is followed by a list of skills relevant to those roles. This document should be essential reading to anyone wanting to enter the field.

(Richard Stevens writes, "You see. I told you I would be unbiased.")

How to Get Work

Like most industries, some jobs are advertised but actually a significant amount of work is found through personal contacts. Here are some ideas for getting to know people and getting yourself known:

> *Go to conferences.* The Game Developers Conference, Audio Engineering Society Conferences, and the Develop Conference, to name a few, are not only great places to learn but also great opportunities to meet like-minded people. You'll be mixing with game audio professionals and the right attitude, together with a business card with your web address, can sometimes go a long way.
> *Be an active participant in the game audio community.* The community of people involved in all aspects of game audio is unique. As long as you're not wasting people's time with totally newbie questions (which, of course, you won't after reading this book), then you won't find a more supportive and enthusiastic bunch. There are links to the relevant forums on the website and an active community on Twitter. Sign up and join in.
> *Contribute by writing articles and talking about your work.* If the articles are well written, interesting, and informative, then you will have contributed to other people's learning and gotten yourself noticed at the same time.
> *Make sure you have a good friend or influential relative working for a games company.* This always helps.

Making a Demo Reel/Website/Blog

The traditional approach of putting a demo reel together on a CD or DVD and sending them off or handing them out has been pretty much superseded by the web. Your website is your showcase of who you are and what skills you have. Make sure you present yourself in a positive way. The best way to learn what works and what doesn't is to look at other people's sites - to see what works and what doesn't. Having a blog in addition to a site is a good way of getting attention and sharing your work. It's also useful for developing materials in a more informal environment that you can put on your "official" site later.

Here are some tips:

- Avoid sites using Adobe Flash that either (1) have a front page you need to click through to get to the main site, (2) take more than three seconds to load up, or (3) use Adobe Flash. This is number one because if you don't get this right, most people won't even bother to go to your site in the first place.
- Make your best work the most visible, and if it isn't your best work, don't put it on. Too often good work is diluted by having less strong work around it, so you have to resist the temptation to put up everything you've ever done.
- Show that you have a passion for what you do. This doesn't mean saying, "I've always loved music since I was a young child" or "I have a real passion for ....." It means that you show that you're informed by the latest articles, that you're aware of the latest game with great audio, and that you're full of ideas about how to continue to develop great game audio. One way to show your knowledge and enthusiasm for the subject is to write about your process, how you went about things, techniques you used, and why you made the choices you made. This not only demonstrates that you know your stuff but also makes a contribution. (See 'How to get work' above.)

Sound design demos should typically contain some or all of the following:

- Linear videos with re-created soundtracks. This will tell people immediately whether you have a good ear or not.
- Specific sound design examples
  - Atmospheres
  - Weapons
  - Creatures
  - Spells
- Sound implementation examples. Demonstrate your implementation skills by showing off a game level.
  - UDK
  - Crytek Sandbox engine
  - Valve Source engine
  - Unity game engine
- Audio middleware. Show that you can apply game audio principles for any platform by learning one or both of these audio middleware packages.
  - FMOD
  - Wwise
- Location and studio recording techniques
  - Demonstrate your studio and location techniques with a number of clean recordings. Perhaps do a video diary of your recording session. Then combine this with a demo showing how you've layered these up to create an effective sound designed scene or level.
- Speech
  - Show that you can record speech well, get good performances out of actors, and effectively process the files to suit the needs of the game.

Music demos should contain both linear and interactive music demos:

- Styles
  - Show that you are adaptable by composing in a number of styles. Having said that, remember the caveat about not including weaker work. If you can't write up to your usual standards in certain genres then don't put it in. Many people make a career despite being specialized.
- Formats
  - 5.1 Music mixes are becoming very common, particularly for cut-scenes. Demonstrate your ability to produce a good music mix in both stereo and 5.1.
- Interactive demo
  - Produce a video walk-through of a level including your interactive music. Show and discuss (using subtitles) how the music interacts with the game actions and game variables. Record a few versions of the scene that is played in different ways to demonstrate how your music would react.
- Be critical
  - Judge your music side by side with your favorite game or movie scores. If it sounds weak in comparison then (1) don't include it and (2) write some more music.

How to Keep Working

Be extremely good at what you do.
Be nice to work with.

Every game industry person we've ever spoken to (and that's quite a few) has always said these two things about the type of people they're looking for:

1. Yes, we want people to have the technical skills, but to be honest we mostly use our in-house tools anyway, so being flexible and able to learn new things fast is more important than specific skills on a particular piece of software (they change all the time anyway).
2. What they're like is more important than what they know. They need to get on with people, be able to communicate, and put across their ideas in a way that's a discussion—not an argument.

People skills are important in any job, but when you're around people who have been working 16-hour days and eating pizza at their desk for the last month—even more so. Learning to speak and understand the language of other people's disciplines will not only improve communication but will allow you to understand problems from other points of view and bring you closer to finding joint solutions. Be part of the team; go to as many meetings as you can. Partly because of the nature of our work environment in closed-off studios (and closed back headphones) and partly because of the perennial underdog status of audio, it can be easy to develop a siege mentality. This isn't going to help.

Don't assume that everyone's an idiot; they just don't have the same knowledge about what great sound and music can do. Don't get tetchy. Rehearse your arguments well and put them across in a reasonable and reasoned manner. Don't forget sometimes to win the war you've got to be prepared to lose the battle (see what we mean about a siege mentality?).

In conclusion; be really good at what you do, but don't forget to be nice too.

Conclusions

By the time this book is published, the technology and tools will have improved and a new game will have been released that raises the bar or attempts something radically different that no one had thought of doing before. In the field of game audio, there is new research being done and new ideas emerging all the time. This book is your introduction to game audio. This is the beginning, not the end. Get informed, try things out, learn more, surprise us.

And remember—don't just make great audio, help make great games.

Dave Raybould

Richard Stevens

www.thegameaudiotutorial.com

Appendix A
Organization Tips

There are several other books that cover the planning and process of game development and game audio development (see the Bibliography), so we will not cover those subjects in detail here. Instead we will offer a few tips that we hope will make your life easier.

Finding and Seeing What's Going On

Being able to navigate quickly around your level and find the item you're looking for, and remembering what it does when you get there, is the key to working efficiently and productively.

At the very start of the book we mentioned the use of bookmarks within your level to jump to specific areas. After pressing Ctrl and a number key on your keyboard to set these up, you can press this number to immediately move to that position in the level. What's less well known is that you can also use these within Kismet in exactly the same way.

Don't forget the Scene Manager from the very start of the book (Scene Tab). Here you can see all the Actors in your level and double clicking on them will snap all the viewports to focus on them.

If you can't see something that you think you should then check the Show menu (click on Use defaults if in doubt). To more clearly see where your Sound Actors are you can toggle off various items using keyboard shortcuts.

>Toggle BSP – Q
>Toggle Static Meshes – W
>Toggle Terrain – T
>Hide selected Actors – H
>Hide all unselected Actors – Shift + H
>Unhide all Actors – Ctrl + H

Below is the tutorial level showing just the sound and light Actors – pretty isn't it ?

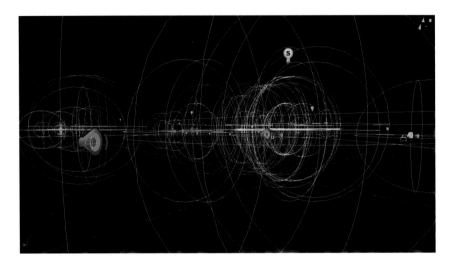

What Does That Do Again?

Adding short text notes to some of the objects within your level can be very useful in keeping track of what you are doing. You can do this for Static Meshes and InterpActors using the 'Tag' within their Properties/Object menu, and you can also add Notes from the Actor classes tab. Enabling Actor Tags within the Show menu will make these visible in your level. Within Kismet there is a comments field within the Properties/Sequence Object menus that also serve a similar function, appearing as text above the objects within Kismet. You can also create comment boxes (and shade them different colors) around groups of objects within Kismet from the right click menu/New comment.

To aid communication in your team it's useful to provide visual examples of what you're talking about. Holding F9 and clicking in a Viewport or Kismet window will capture a screenshot of that Viewport or Kismet system (Stored here C:\UDK\(***)\UDKGame\ScreenShots). This, combined with Actor Tags and the use of Comments within your Kismet systems, can be helpful to you in remembering what it was that you were doing!

Audio File Finder Utilities

As you develop a large sound or music library, you'll need to be able to find things quickly. In addition to a sensible file naming policy (see the following discussion), you may also find some of these utilities useful.

Free/Donation Ware

Foobar (Windows)
www.foobar2000.org
SoundLog (Mac only)

www.soundlog.com/top/products/soundlog/index.htm
iTunes (Mac/Windows)
www.apple.com/itunes

Commercial

Soundminer (Windows/Mac)
http://store.soundminer.com
Basehead (Windows/Mac)
www.baseheadinc.com/basehead-feature-overview
Netmix
www.prosoundeffects.com/p1024/Net-Mix-Pro/product_info.html
Snapper (Mac)
www.audioease.com/Pages/Snapper/SnapperMain.html
AudioFinder (Mac)
www.icedaudio.com
Mtools (Mac)
www.gallery.co.uk/mtools/mtoolsmainframe.html

Naming Conventions

A game might have 100,000+ audio assets. You have to be disciplined about how you name your files if you are going to avoid this becoming a nightmare. At the start of a project you should establish a convention for naming your sound files. This may be the same as the one you use for your ever expanding Sound and Music library or it may be specific to the project. (Some platforms have a limit on the number of characters permitted within the filenames used, so you may also need to develop some meaningful abbreviations.)

In our Sound Library we've organized and labeled our sounds under the following categories:

- Air
- Alarm
- Ambience
- Animal
- Collisions and Destruction
- Dialogue and Vocal
- Electric and Electronic
- Explosive
- Feedback
- Fire
- Foley
- Liquid
- Mechanical
- Movement
- Spooky

- Vehicle
- Weapon
- Weather

Not only do the sounds themselves need to maintain a meaningful naming system, but so do your packages, and the groups within those packages. You'll have seen that in UDK packages relating to sounds or music have the prefix A_ and the assets themselves (mostly) use the following convention:

```
A_Character_
A_Door_
A_Pickups_
A_Vehicle_
A_Music_
A_Powerup_
```

You will have to find a convention that is meaningful to you (people think about sounds in different ways and under different categories) or negotiate one among the team. The important thing is not the convention itself but sticking to it.

In a game consisting of several maps you might consider having a separate package per map. This would be for map specific items such as unique events, music, and location specific ambience. Alongside this you may have other items such as weapon sounds, impact sounds, and character foley in their own separate packages as they are used across all maps.

Batch Renaming Utilities

For a variety of reasons (one of which might be a change in the naming conventions; see the preceding discussion), you will find yourself at one time or another with the unenviable task or having to rename large numbers of files. Don't do it all by hand. This sort of task is what computers are good at:

Total Commander
www.ghisler.com
Better file rename
www.publicspace.net/windows/BetterFileRename/index.html

Appendix B
Troubleshooting and Optimization

Crashes

We can pretty much guarantee that at some point the game will crash. This will usually happen while you are building the level, and specifically during the lighting build phase. Always save your game before building. (See Appendix C: Building.)

If you've lost work, don't despair. Unless you've turned it off, UDK will have auto-saved a backup level. These are found at C:\UDK\UDK-2010-08\UDKGame\Autosaves. You won't be able to open the UEDPIE versions, but the other ones should mean you haven't lost too much.

Version Control

If you find yourself working on a commercial game you'll have to quickly get used to the idea of version control. Obviously in a multimillion Pound/Dollar business you cannot rely on the 'I think Johnny has a copy of it on his pen drive' approach to file management. Typically you will be using a version control software (such as AlienBrain or Perforce) that provides a networked system for backing up and tracking changes of all the game and development related data.

If you're working by yourself or in a small team it is no less important to have your own version control system so that you don't lose hours of work.

Incremental Naming

Don't call your level 'MyLevel' and then keep saving your work over the top of the previous version. If something goes wrong or this file becomes corrupt you are back to square one. Every time you save a level (which should be often) use the date and an incremented file name, for example:

Mylevel _ 2011_ 01_ 01_ V01

Twenty minutes later:

Mylevel _ 2011_ 01_ 01_ V02

You'll notice that we're using Year_Month_Date_ as this makes it easy in Windows to sort by filename to see a historical record of your versions in order of date.

Do the same with your audio files and DAW sessions.

Backup

Once a day, back up your work to several locations. In addition to using different hard drives, this includes physical locations. Offices burn down/get flooded, so keep a copy in more than one place. Consider Cloud (online) storage so you can access your files from anywhere and also be (relatively) safe in the knowledge that the data is secure.

Author Richard Stevens writes:

> *I've had two serious (unrecoverable) hard drive failures. The first lost all the music I had written in the previous 18 months, the second destroyed all the family pictures I had taken in the last five years. Fortunately, I'd learned my lesson from the first experience and had a backup of the pictures online!*

Hearing What's Going On

Pressing the Tab key will bring up the console. (This varies on different language keyboards and can cause some confusion. On some the Tab key will bring down the console window. This will take up approximately half the screen. On others it will just bring up the console command line (a single line at the bottom of the screen). This single line is OK for testing but you won't see the results printed to the console window. You may need to use the '@ key to see this.)

While the game is playing, you can enter a number of commands in the console to help you identify any problem areas in the sound. It is useful to set up a number of SoundModes that isolate certain classes of audio. For example, in the SoundClassesandModes package that came with the tutorial level, you should have the following modes:

GATMusicOnly
GATVoiceOnly
GATSFXOnly

In the console type 'Set SoundMode' and then one of these modes and you can isolate these different elements. Set up your own for your particular needs. You can also type ModifySoundClass (enter your soundclass name) vol=enter the volume, to set the volume of a specific class.

Here are some other useful console commands relating to hearing audio:

DISABLELPF: Disables the low pass filter on all sources for testing.
ISOLATEDRYAUDIO: Removes the reverb to isolate the dry audio.
ISOLATEREVERB: Removes the dry audio to isolate the reverb.
PLAYSOUNDCUE: Plays a SoundCue (you'll need the full name).
PLAYSOUNDWAVE: Plays a sound wave (you'll need the full name).
RESETSOUNDSTATE: Resets all volumes to their default values and removes all filtering.
TESTLFEBLEED: Sets the low-frequency effect bleed to maximum on all audio sources.
TESTLPF: Sets the low-pass filter to maximum on all audio sources.
TESTSTEREOBLEED: Sets stereo bleed to maximum on all audio sources.

(See http://udn.epicgames.com/Three/ConsoleCommands.html#Audio%20Commands.)

The quickest way to use the console is to start typing the command you want. A list of matching commands will appear. Use the up/down arrow keys to choose your command, then press the Tab key again to add it to the command line. Now press return.

Audio Optimization and Tracking the RAM Budget

To see some information about the current audio performance, open the console during play (press the Tab or '@ Key) and type:

```
STAT AUDIO
```

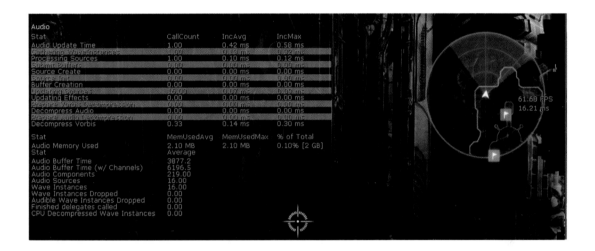

Here's what the terms mean

(http://udn.epicgames.com/Three/StatsDescriptions.html#STAT%20AUDIO):

Audio Update Time: Total time updating all things audio (overall time taken in AudioDevice::Update).

Gathering Wave Instances: Collecting, sorting, and prioritizing all potential audio sources.

Processing Sources: Stopping and starting the sound sources that will be heard.

Source Init: Initialization of all sound sources.

Buffer Creation: Creation of a sound asset (e.g., upload of PCM data to OpenAL).

Updating Sources: Time taken to update the sound sources (position, velocity, volume, pitch, etc.).

Updating Effects: Time taken to apply audio effects (reverb, LPF, EQ).

Prepare Vorbis Decompression: Initializing the vorbis stream for decompression.

Decompress Audio: Time taken to decompress audio (currently, only vorbis).

Prepare Audio Decompression: Initializing of sound decompression in general (currently, only vorbis data).

Decompress Vorbis: Time taken to decompress vorbis data.

Audio Memory Used: Total amount of memory used for all sound assets. Does not include any workspace or internal buffers.

Audio Buffer Time: Number of seconds of stored sound data.

Audio Buffer Time (with channels): Number of seconds of stored mono sound data.

Audio Components: Number of active sounds being maintained for processing (ambient sounds all over the map, player sounds, etc.).

Audio Sources: Number of audio components that are audible and of a high enough priority to hear.

Wave Instances: Number of sound waves being processed.

Wave Instances Dropped: Number of sounds not allocated to a sound source (as they are inaudible).

The ones to pay particular attention to (especially for console development) are the Audio Memory used, which gives the total for the current audio loaded into memory, and audio components, which tell you the number of active sounds at any one time (this relates to the discussion of voice instance limiting in Chapter 6).

There are various other console commands relevant to audio listed here:

(http://udn.epicgames.com/Three/ConsoleCommands.html#Audio%20Commands):

LISTSOUNDCLASSES: Outputs a list of loaded sounds collated by class.

LISTSOUNDCLASSVOLUMES: Outputs a list of all the volume and pitch settings for each sound class.

LISTSOUNDMODES: Outputs a list of all sound modes.

SOUNDTEMPLATEINFO: Outputs information about each unique sound.

LISTAUDIOCOMPONENTS: Outputs a list of all audio components.

LISTSOUNDDURATIONS: Outputs a list of all sounds waves and their durations.

LISTSOUNDS: Outputs a list of all loaded sounds and their memory footprints.

LISTWAVES: Outputs a list of wave instances and whether they have a source.

One useful command that is not listed is STAT SOUNDWAVES. After enabling this in the console window you can actually close the window (press the Tab or '@ key again to exit) and it continues to print a list to the screen of all the sounds that are currently playing.

This is hugely informative, and we'd recommend you spend some time running around various levels with it enabled to get a better idea of what is going on. As an example, the screenshot that follows immediately reinforces the issues we discussed regarding retriggered weapons, the overlap of the tails of their sound, and the subsequent impact on the number of voices used.

As well as what is currently playing we want to know what sounds are loaded into memory, and how much we may have left. The command LISTSOUNDS will show you all the sounds that are currently loaded into memory and their memory footprint (LISTSOUNDCLASSES will collate the list by Sound Class). This is probably your most vital audio troubleshooting tool. We spent some time in Chapter 2 discussing memory issues for game development so we won't repeat these arguments again here but you will remember that, no matter how amazing your sound or music may be, if it doesn't fit into the available memory it simply won't work.

We know it doesn't sound like a particularly exciting prospect but if you're going to create Sound or Music for games you need to learn how to use a spreadsheet. Spreadsheets are your friend and will not only help you manage your projects, by knowing what is done/not done, but are vital in tracking the memory requirements of your assets. For working with our Sound Designer Andrew Quinn on the Sound Library we used the simple GoogleDoc spreadsheet below. With a few formulas you can calculate the size of the sound assets per level (and after different amounts of compression). The advantage of an online spreadsheet is that you all have simultaneous access to it and the version control is automatic (you can always go back to a previous version). You can see who's using the spreadsheet at any time and instant message them directly. After our experience we'd say that if you're not already working this way then it's time to take a serious look!

B	C	D	E	F	G	H	I	J	K	L	M
	GAT Sound Library										
GAT			Total File Size =	117.841796875	mb						
Sound ID	**File Name**	**Format**	**Type**	**Room Details**	**Type**	**M/S**	**Filesize**	**S/R**	**Rec'd**	**Edited**	**Notes**
GAT-0071	ANIMAL_bird_small_tweet_11	.wav	Animal	203 602a	OneShot	Mono	167	44100	y	y	
GAT-0072	ANIMAL_bird_small_tweet_12	.wav	Animal	203 602a	OneShot	Mono	153	44100	y	y	
GAT-0073	ANIMAL_bird_small_tweet_13	.wav	Animal	203 602a	OneShot	Mono	115	44100	y	y	
GAT-0074	ANIMAL_bird_small_tweet_14	.wav	Animal	203 602a	OneShot	Mono	132	44100	y	y	
GAT-0075	ANIMAL_birds_flyaway	.wav	Animal	602a	OneShot	Stereo	304	44100	y	y	
GAT-0076	ANIMAL_birds_flyback	.wav	Animal	602a	OneShot	Stereo	204	44100	y	y	
GAT-0077	ANIMAL_insect_crickets_11k	.wav	Animal	200	Loop	Stereo	167	11000	y	y	
GAT-0078	ANIMAL_insect_crickets_11k_v2	.wav	Animal	200	Loop	Stereo	862	11000	y	y	
GAT-0079	ANIMAL_insect_crickets_22k	.wav	Animal	200	Loop	Stereo	335	22050	y	y	
GAT-0080	ANIMAL_insect_crickets_22k_v2	.wav	Animal	200	Loop	Stereo	1723	22050	y	y	
GAT-0081	ANIMAL_insect_crickets_44k	.wav	Animal	200	Loop	Stereo	669	44100	y	y	
GAT-0082	ANIMAL_insect_crickets_44k_v2	.wav	Animal	200	Loop	Stereo	3446	44100	y	y	
GAT-0083	ANIMAL_insect_crickets_5k	.wav	Animal	200	Loop	Stereo	76	5000	y	y	
GAT-0084	ANIMAL_insect_crickets_5k_v2	.wav	Animal	200	Loop	Stereo	391	5000	y	y	
GAT-0085	ANIMAL_insect_crickets_8k	.wav	Animal	200	Loop	Stereo	122	8000	y	y	
GAT-0086	ANIMAL_insect_crickets_8k_v2	.wav	Animal	200	Loop	Stereo	626	8000	y	y	
GAT-0087	COLLISION_arrow_target_01	.wav	Collision		OneShot	Mono	164	44100	y	y	
GAT-0088	COLLISION_arrow_target_02	.wav	Collision		OneShot	Mono	149	44100	y	y	
GAT-0089	COLLISION_arrow_target_03	.wav	Collision		OneShot	Mono	164	44100	y	y	
GAT-0090	COLLISION_arrow_target_04	.wav	Collision		OneShot	Mono	182	44100	y	y	
GAT-0091	COLLISION_arrow_target_05	.wav	Collision		OneShot	Mono	234	44100	y	y	

Keeping your spreadsheet up to date is vital for tracking your assets and for ensuring that you're not going to be trying to load more sounds into memory than you are allocated. Look at this in conjunction with the in-game tools for tracking audio memory usage (STAT SOUNDWAVES and LISTSOUNDS). Another good way of tracking your success in audio memory management is by noting the number and intensity of angry looking programmers marching towards you.

Streaming

If you are dealing with a large game level or world, then you will need to consider dividing this into separate parts that you can then stream in/out as needed to create the impression of a persistent world.

Run the tutorial level in the Play in Editor window and open the Console Command by pressing the Tab key. Type "Stat Audio" into this command line, and press return. (See the previous section "Audio Optimization" for more.)

If you look at the Audio Memory Used reading, you can see that there's a constant base reading of several MB. This is mainly because of all the music that we are using. The use of this much music within a confined area is obviously a little unusual, as in a game you would be more likely to have music associated with particular levels or areas. Given the nature of the Tutorial level and to avoid confusion, we have not used the Streaming levels in this instance, but it is something you should be aware of, and use, in a more typical game level.

If you were to imagine a large sphere centered around the player as he or she moves through the level, you can appreciate that in many circumstances it is only necessary to load in assets such as music within a given distance from the player. Outside of this sphere would be assets the player simply would not see/hear. Given the fact that you would only need certain music tracks for certain areas, it is inefficient to hold all of it in memory.

In the Levels tab of the Content Browser you can create new levels or export parts of your existing level to a new level. You can still experience the level exactly as you planned, but you can also think of this new level as a layer that you can have or take away. The basic level is referred to as the Persistent level, and this master level controls how the others stream in or out, either through Kismet commands (New Action/Level/Streaming Level), streaming volumes, or distance-based streaming. A common approach to music would be to have the separate music instances in their own streaming levels so that they are only loaded into memory when required.

To put the music for different areas of your level into separate streaming levels, you should select your music actors in the current level, then go to the Levels tab and choose New Level from Selected Actors.

You'll then need to copy across any related Kismet systems by opening the Kismet for your new level using the K symbol.

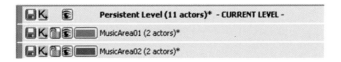

When you've created as many streaming levels as you need (perhaps one for each area of piece of music), you can use the eye symbol to switch them on and off. This way you can see what's included in each level to make sure you have them set up correctly.

You'll now need to set up a system that loads in your music just before the area where it's needed and unloads it outside of this area. This way you can keep the level of audio memory used to a minimum.

Here you can see a simple illustration using two rooms and a corridor. In the center of the corridor is a **[TriggerVolume]** that will control the streaming of the two **[AmbientSound]**s, which are in fact in two different levels.

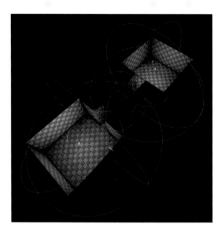

The **[TriggerVolume]** is linked to a looping switch in the Kismet of the Persistent Level. As the player passes, the level (i.e., the music) of the first room is unloaded, and the second level (the music in the second room) is loaded. On the way back the opposite happens.

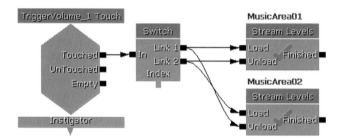

If you run this level in Play in Editor mode or the Start level on this PC mode and run the Stat Audio command, you will note that despite the levels apparently streaming in and out, the audio memory used does not change. Launch the full Game–Unreal Development Kit from your Program Files menu and run the same command. Now you can see that this has actually achieved what we wanted. The music is loaded in and out of memory per area and the audio memory used changes to reflect this. See the GATMusic_Streaming level(s) in the Exercise package for a practical example you can experiment with.

For more on level streaming see the UDK documentation http://udn.epicgames.com/Three/LevelStreamingHowTo.html.

Appendix C
UDK Tips

No doubt you are going to want/need to familiarize yourself with a number of level design techniques in UDK to prototype your own systems. The www.UDK.com website has a huge range of advice and tutorials that will take you through everything you need to know, and there's 1,001 tutorial videos on YouTube. We'd also recommend the *Mastering Unreal Technology* books (Busby, Parrish, Wilson) published by Sams Publishing.

There's little point to replicating this material here, so we're just going to present a few specific examples of techniques used in the book to get you started. The best way to learn is by playing around with the existing systems.

When testing/prototyping mechanisms, it is often a good idea to do this in a small "test" level. This saves on load and build times when you make any changes. You can copy and paste things from your "test" level into the final level very easily. You can't copy both in-game assets (Geometry/Actors/etc.) and Kismet sequences simultaneously, but if you copy the in-game assets and paste these into your final level and then go back for the Kismet, then all references will be maintained and everything will work as it did before.

Running Slowly

UDK is demanding in terms of processing, and demanding on your graphics hardware. If you are building a large level then you may find things slowing down to the point where it becomes difficult to work. In the top menu bar there is a slider called 'Distance to far clipping plane'. If you reduce this you will see that more distant objects are not displayed. As these are no longer taking up memory and processing power you should find that the game runs more smoothly. Rebuilding the lighting regularly will also help (see Building below), as will unloading any packages that are not in use (right click/unload). When working on a large level you should also investigate splitting the level into smaller units. See the 'Streaming' section of Appendix B. If you are still experiencing problems then check the UDK forums for specific advice for your graphics card.

Importing Sounds

When you import a sound using the Import button in the Content Browser, you also have the option of selecting multiple files to import simultaneously and of automatically creating **[SoundCue]**s for each of these sounds.

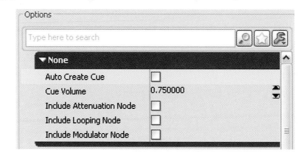

You can see from the check boxes above that you can also add **[Attenuation]**, **[Looping]**, or **[Modulator]** nodes during this process. Most **[SoundCue]**s will probably contain multiple elements, so this is not always appropriate but it can be a real timesaver in some instances.

Bulk Importing of Sounds

From the right-click menu in the Content Browser's Package Tree, you have the option to **Bulk Import Sounds**. If your sounds are stored in a folder structure like the one shown here (obviously you can change the names to suit), then this Bulk Import option will import them and create a corresponding structure of folders, subfolders, packages, and groups for the sounds within UDK. See the Bulk Importer documentation on the UDK.com site for further details if required.

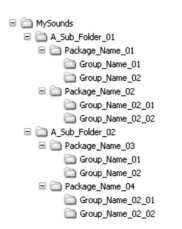

Fast Creation of [SoundCue]s

We've mentioned this in the text but it's so useful that we'll mention it here again. When creating a **[SoundCue]**, most of the time you will probably want it to contain more than one SoundNodeWave. You do not have to add them one at a time. Select all the SoundNodeWaves you want and then by right-clicking in the SoundCue Editor window you can add them all at once. It will appear to only be adding the name of your first sound but in fact does add them all. You can also choose the second option down (Random: (***)), which will add them all preconnected to a **[Random]** node. Very useful.

Basic Folder Guide

The folder structure of UDK is fairly straightforward, and you will probably not need to go into some of them, unless things go terribly wrong!

Here's a brief description of each of the main folders and its content:

- **Binaries**: Contains the game.exe, and the UnRealFrontEnd (used for compiling scripts). You don't need to go in here, other than perhaps to create a shortcut to UnRealFrontEnd to put on your desktop.
- **Development**: Contains all the source code, both those supplied with the engine and your own custom scripts in the Src\MyMod folder.
- **Engine**: Files required by the engine to function correctly.
- **UDKGame**: Files for the game (maps, packages, etc.).
  - **Autosaves**: Contains all automated saves and backups.
  - **Config**: Contains .ini files, which direct the engine to specific files and settings.
  - **Content**: Contains levels and packages.
  - **Localization**: Contains all language-specific files.
  - **Logs**: Contains automated log files, which can be useful for identifying problems.
  - **Movies**: Contains intro movies, loading screens, and so on.
  - **Script**: Contains the compiled UnRealScripts.
  - **Splash**: Contains the splash (loading) image.

Creating Levels

Creating a level allows you to make your own environments to really show off your use of interactive sound and music.

Within your level you will need to create some geometry (this can be rooms, walls, floors, etc.). This is done using binary space partitioning (BSP) and is created using the builder brush (discussed later).

From the CSG menu of the left hand side of the screen; CSG Add is used to create rooms, walls, floors, etc.; CSG Subtract is used to 'punch' holes through the solid geometry for doors, etc. There's lots of documentation on the UDK.com website about building your own levels. It's easier than you think!

Once you've created your level you can then apply materials to it in order to produce richer environments. You will also make use of other placeable Actors such as static meshes and particle systems (discussed later) to flesh out your levels.

When you have created your level using geometry and placeable Actors, you will need to set up your lighting so that you can actually see within your level.

The easiest way to get started is to hold down the 'L' key on your keyboard and left click on the floor of a room with your mouse. This will create a standard light that you can then grab and move up to the correct position using the Blue arrow. (See the Lighting section below for more.)

The Builder Brush for Geometry, Trigger Volumes, and Reverb Volumes

The builder brush is the tool you use to create the geometry of your level. It is depicted by a dark red cube. The idea is that you adjust the dimensions of the builder brush (using the widgets—discussed later) to the correct size and then generate your geometry in its place.

The builder brush can be toggled on and off using the B key. You can select the builder brush by pressing F2 on your keyboard or Ctrl + clicking in an empty space in the viewports. You can then find it by pressing the Home key to snap the viewports to look at your selection.

You can resize the brush using the widgets, or you can also set the builder brush's dimensions manually by right-clicking any of the shape icons (e.g., the cube) on the left-hand screen menu. For creating volumes (such as **[ReverbVolume]**s or **[TriggerVolume]**s), it's often easier to make the builder brush automatically mold to an existing volume or piece of geometry. If you click on an existing volume or piece of geometry and press Ctrl + P, the builder brush will automatically resize itself to the same shape and position itself on top of the selected volume. Again for a good introduction to using the builder brush see the UDK.com website.

Scaling and Other Widgets

If you need to alter the size or rotation of an object within UDK, you need to use one of the three available widgets. With the object selected, the space bar will cycle through these modes:

Translation. Used for moving an Actor within the X, Y, or Z planes.

Rotation: Used for rotating an Actor around the X, Y, or Z planes.

Scaling: Scales an Actor in all three planes simultaneously (maintains scale).

In addition, nonuniform scaling is available from the top toolbar, which scales an Actor in a single plane. Right-clicking directly on one of the widget icons will enable you to directly set values.

There are separate snap values for each of the three widget modes in the bottom right corner of the editor window. The snap values are used to force the amount of movement available to you (depending on your widget) to incremental steps. It is usually a good idea to make use of snap values as they ensure that your world geometry, for example, is aligned correctly. It also ensures that any rotational translation applied is correct.

Saving

We recommend that you save your work often, as any computer program is capable of crashing just as you complete your third hour of consecutive work and usually just after you've solved some fiendishly difficult problem. If you adopt an incremental saving policy (MyWork_V01, MyWork_V02, etc.), then you can always roll back to a previous version should you need to.

It's worth pointing out that UDK has an auto-save function, which will automatically save and back up your work at regular intervals. The time interval can be set in the bottom right-hand corner of the editor window (near the snap values); you can also, if you're feeling brave, turn off the auto-save. If you need to access them, the automatically saved files are in the Auto-saves folder (C:\UDK\(***)\UDKGame\Autosaves). This folder can get pretty full pretty quickly, especially if you're auto-saving every five minutes, so it's worth keeping an eye on the size of the folder and deleting any old files to free up hard disk space.

Lighting

There are two modes of lighting within UDK. By default it uses "Lightmass," which looks great but can take a long time to build out. If you are making lots of changes while building your level and having to re-render your lighting a lot, it might make sense to switch to the older lighting algorithms because they render faster. Once you're finished building and ready to play, you can turn Lightmass back on again.

To turn Lightmass on/off:

View – World Properties – Lightmass – Use Global Illumination = True/False

Alternatively you can uncheck the Lightmass flag in the lighting build options (the bulb icon in the top tool bar).

You can also change the quality of the rendering process by right-clicking on the Light Quality Settings button (within the Build buttons).

It is fairly easy to change the color of any of your lights. Simply access the light's properties and expand the Light Color property and then either enter RGB (red, green, blue) settings directly or double-click and select a color. Various types of light are available, and the type you choose will depend on the light's location and purpose:

[Point light]
[Skylight]
[Directional light]
[Spotlight]

Each type can come in different "flavors": toggleable, movable, and "standard."

It is worth bearing in mind that dynamic Actors (such as InterpActors) require dynamic lighting. This often appears as an error after building your level (discussed later) and can be fixed fairly easily by modifying the light's properties (Light – Force Dynamic Light).

Static Meshes

The majority of the objects that go into making your level will be Static Meshes (walls, rocks, etc.). You can browse available assets using the Content Browser (filter by Static Meshes).

With a static mesh selected you can right-click in the editor and select Add Actor/Add Static Mesh: (name of your static mesh). If the package containing the static mesh is not fully loaded, you may have to load the Actor before you can add it. (You can also drag and drop static meshes from the content browser into your level.)

If you need an InterpActor (for use with a matinee) or a KActor (for physics-based purposes), you can right-click your Static Mesh and use the Convert option.

As all the **[Trigger]**s should be invisible within the game, we've used static meshes to indicate buttons of things to interact with. You might want to add some other graphics to indicate where your triggers are instead of making the actual triggers visible. (For testing purposes, it's often useful to have them visible. In the **[Trigger]** properties, check/uncheck the Hidden option.) Once in the game, you can resize and move these static meshes by using the Widget tool.

Materials

All Static Meshes and Geometry make use of Materials. These are the textures that are applied to your in-game objects. You can browse available Materials using the Content Browser (filter by Materials). The method for assigning a particular Material to an object depends on your object. With the Material selected in the Content Browser, you can right-click an asset and for Geometry select Apply Material, for Static Meshes select Materials/Assign from Content Browser.

Terrain

Terrain is used for outdoor surfaces (e.g., grass) and can be shaped to create hills and valleys. To add a new Terrain, go to the Actor tab of the Content Browser, expand the Info Actor menu, and select Terrain. Then right-click in the editor and select Add Terrain Here. If you want to resize it, you can either use the scaling widget or access the Terrain's properties and under Terrain change the Num Patches X and Num Patches Y values. You need to assign a Layer to the Terrain so that it looks like grass, for example:

- Within the Terrain's properties create a new Layer (green plus icon). Expand the new Layer.
- Find a Terrain Layer in the Content Browser (filter by Terrain Layers [All Types]).
- Move back to the Terrain's properties and assign the selected Layer to the Setup field.
- To create a 3D Terrain, use the Terrain Editing mode (the mountain icon).
- With one of the brushes selected, you can Ctrl + LMB to raise a portion of the Terrain and Ctrl + RMB to lower the terrain. The Tessellation options are used to increase/decrease the size of the grid.

Emitters + Particle Effects

These are useful for adding additional visual effects to your level. Filter the Content Browser by Particle Systems, and then right-click in the editor to add them. Some Emitters are constantly on, whereas others will need to be toggled on/off within Kismet. Use a **[Toggle]** object with the Emitter connected to the target input and then either a trigger or a looping delay to activate the Toggle input.

Weapons

If you don't want the player to have any weapons on startup, you can use the No Default Inventory for Player option within the World Properties. You may need to provide a weapon locker with some weapons depending on your game (Actor Classes Tab/Pickups/Weapon/UTWeaponLocker_ Content). Once your weapon locker has been created go to its properties (F4), use the green + sign to add a weapons slot and then choose the desired weapon from the drop down menu.

Water

Water can be used relatively easily within your level. Create the space you wish to be water (using either the Terrain or Geometry features). Add a plane (using the Builder Brush) and resize it to fit your space.

Find a water Material within the Content Browser (e.g., UN_Liquid package) and assign the Material to the Plane. Add a water volume by setting the Builder Brush to be the size of your water space and creating a **[UTWaterVolume]**. This already has sounds for entry and exit. You can also create a **[PostProcessVolume]** (using the builder brush) to apply visual effects to simulate being underwater. You can also experiment with depth of field (DOF) and its associated settings.

Building

When you make any significant changes to a level, you will need to "build" it. You have various options when building your level and it makes sense to only use the one that is most appropriate at any given time in order to reduce building times:

Build Geometry: Builds all geometry only. (Also used to build **[ReverbVolumes]**).

Build Lighting: Builds all lighting only.

Build Paths: Builds all navigation paths (**[PlayerStart]**, **[WeaponLocker]**, **[PathNode]**, etc.) only.

Build Cover Nodes: Builds all cover nodes only (used for AI).

Build All: Builds everything within the level (can take a while).

Light Quality Settings: Used to determine the quality of the lighting build and therefore the time taken.

After building you will be presented with a dialogue window that displays any error messages generated during the build process. The following link contains some of the more common map errors and probable solutions: http://udn.epicgames.com/Three/MapErrors.html.

Some of the most common errors are the following:

● Only 0 PlayerStarts in this level (you need at least 1). This can be solved by creating a **[PlayerStart]** (Actor Classes Tab/Common/PlayerStart).

- BRUSH_9: Brush has NULL material reference(s). Caused when a geometry brush has been created without a Material assigned. This can be solved by assigning a Material
- Map should have KillZ set. Killz determines the height at which the player will be killed if the player falls off the map. This can be solved by setting the KillZ property (World Property – ZoneInfo – Kill Z).

If you double-click on an error, the editor will jump to the Actor that is causing the error. You can then open its properties and fix the problem. The Refresh button within the Map Check dialogue can then be used to see if the error has been resolved

Kismet Tips

A comprehensive list of all Kismet objects can be found at http://udn.epicgames.com/Three/KismetReference.html.

Kismet System Debugging

Be patient and systematic in tracking systems that do not appear to work. The bad news is that it's almost always your fault. Add **[Log]**s (hold L then click in the Kismet window) to your system in key places and use the Output to screen option within their Sequence Object properties to check that they are receiving a message. You can also expose the variables within a **[Log]** and this will output the values of the variables you attach. The sometimes annoying thing about **[Log]**s is that they output a beep. This can be problematic when you're trying to check audio systems. You can turn this off by editing the utgame.ini file (C:\UDK\(***)\UDKGame\Config). Set the bmessagebeep to false. The other useful thing to do with Kismet systems is to disable links. You don't need to delete your links during testing, just right-click/Toggle Link/Disable.

Sequences/Subsequences

To keep your Kismet sequence tidy and easy to read (a good idea to aid troubleshooting), make use of subsequences. You can create an empty sequence and then start building within it or, if you've been busy creating interesting sequences, you can select a collection of objects and then right-click and select Create New Sequence. This will create a new subsequence containing the selected objects, which can then be given a meaningful name

If the objects selected were passing or receiving signals, these will be preserved automatically. However, variables are not always preserved.

If you need to extend a subsequence so that it is capable of doing the following:

- Receiving a trigger (event) signal – Then use New Event – Sequence Activated
- Passing a trigger (event) signal – Then use New Action – Finish Sequence
- Passing and receiving an external variable – Then use New Variable – External Variable

Copying and Reusing Sequences

All Kismet sequences are essentially just a visual representation of the underlying code. This means that if you select a collection of objects and then paste them into a text editor such as Notepad, you will see the UnRealScript code for those objects and how they are connected. The following code is an example (a **[Player Spawned]** connected to a **[Delay]**):

```
Begin Object Class=SeqEvent_PlayerSpawned Name=SeqEvent_PlayerSpawned_0
MaxWidth=156
OutputLinks(0)=(Links=((LinkedOp=SeqAct_Delay'SeqAct_Delay_0')),DrawY=298)
VariableLinks(0)=(DrawX=-104)
VariableLinks(1)=(DrawX=-34)
ObjInstanceVersion=1
ParentSequence=Sequence'Main_Sequence'
ObjPosX=-152
ObjPosY=232
DrawWidth=98
DrawHeight=144
Name="SeqEvent_PlayerSpawned_0"
ObjectArchetype=SeqEvent_PlayerSpawned'Engine.Default__SeqEvent_PlayerSpawned'
End Object
Begin Object Class=SeqAct_Delay Name=SeqAct_Delay_0
InputLinks(0)=(DrawY=293)
InputLinks(1)=(DrawY=314)
InputLinks(2)=(DrawY=335)
OutputLinks(0)=(Links=((LinkedOp=Sequence'Float')),DrawY=298)
OutputLinks(1)=(DrawY=330)
VariableLinks(0)=(DrawX=124)
ObjInstanceVersion=1
ParentSequence=Sequence'Main_Sequence'
ObjPosX=72
ObjPosY=256
DrawWidth=106
DrawHeight=109
Name="SeqAct_Delay_0"
ObjectArchetype=SeqAct_Delay'Engine.Default__SeqAct_Delay'
End Object
```

This facility allows you to create text files containing Kismet sequences that can be reused at any time by copying and pasting. Doing this via text files is quicker than opening a variety of UDK levels.

Runtime versus Placeable Actors

Within UDK you have placeable Actors, such as **[Trigger]**s and Static Meshes, as well as runtime Actors, such as bots and the player. As you will have seen throughout the book, we can create a variety of events using things like **[TriggerVolumes]**s (such as Touched, UnTouched, etc.). However there is no way of doing this for a runtime Actor as we can't actually select it within the editor because it doesn't yet exist.

If you wanted to create an event based on a runtime Actor, such as the death of a bot, you need to use the **[Attach to Event]** object (New Action – Event). When this object is activated it attaches the Attachee Actor (e.g., the bot that has just been spawned) to the Event connected to the Event input (e.g., Death). See the tutorial level for several examples of this.

Instigators

Anytime an event is activated, it also passes a variable called "Instigator." This is the Actor that caused the event to be activated. So in the case of a **[TriggerVolume]**, the Instigator would be the Actor that walked into the **[TriggerVolume]** and caused the Touched Event to be activated (usually the player). This can be used, for example, to identify whether it was an NPC (bot) or the player that just walked into a **[TriggerVolume]**. You would compare the Instigator variable with a Player variable using a **[Compare Object]** feature.

Take Damage

This provides a trigger if the associated Actor has taken some damage (usually from being shot). As with all events you get the instigator as an output variable. You also get the amount of Damage Taken (as a Float variable). This variable is cumulative, so it increases every time you shoot the Actor.

Within the **[Take Damage]** function, you have the following properties:

Damage Threshold: The amount of damage required to activate the event.
Damage Types: The types of damage/weapon to respond to.
Ignore Damage Types: The types of damage/weapon to ignore.
Max Trigger Count: How many times this event can be activated (0 for infinite).
Retrigger Delay: The time between activations.

Most placeable actors (e.g., static meshes) will work with a **[Take Damage]** event, although you may have to change their collision properties to Block All or Block Weapons in order to get them to respond to being shot. If you want to use a runtime Actor such as a bot to trigger a **[Take Damage]** event, you will need to "attach" the actor to the event using the **[Attach to Actor]** object. You could trigger the **[Attach to Actor]** object using the Finished event from the **[Actor Factory]**.

[TriggerVolume]s and **[DynamicTriggerVolume]**s are slightly more complex to set up as these appear to only respond to certain types of damage by default (e.g., the LinkGun AltFire).

A **[DynamicTriggerVolume]** is easier to set up to take weapon damage. In it's properties make sure it's collision is set to Collide_blockWeapons and the blockrigidbody flag is checked. Then within the Collision Component menu check the flag named Block Complex Collision Trace.

[TriggerVolume]s can be set to generate a Touch event when shot (these need additional properties to be set):

> *Collision − Collision Component − Block Complex Collision Trace = True*
> *Collision − Collision Component − Block Zero Extent = True*
> *CollisionType = TouchAll/TouchWeapons*

Named Variables, and Remote Events

Once you start doing interesting things within Kismet, your sequences will get quite unwieldy with connections all over the place. This can make reading your systems and troubleshooting quite difficult. You can create wireless connections using **[Named Variables]**s, which can really help tidy things up.

Create a "normal" variable of any type and then within its properties change its Var Name to something meaningful (remember, no spaces). This is your wireless "send." Then where you want to receive your variable, create a **[Named Variable]** (new Variable – Named Variable), and within its properties change the Find Var Name to be the same as the Var Name of your "send" variable. You should also set the Expected Type property to be the type of variable you are sending (Float, Object, etc.). Using **[Remote Event]**s can also help avoid a spiders web of connections. Set the Event name within their properties to be the same and you can pass a signal from an **[Activate Remote Event]** Action (New Action/Event/Activate Remote Event) to a **[Remote Event]** Event (New Event/Remote Event) without the need for connecting cables.

Spawning and Controlling Bots

The default AI behavior of the bots is a little unreliable, so we tend to just set up basic movements and "force" their actions using Kismet commands.

Bots are created using the Kismet **[Actor Factory]** Action. Within this object you need to expand the Seq Act_Actor Factory properties and select a Factory type. To spawn Bots you use the UTActorFactoryAI. Once you have selected your Factory type, you can then expand the Factory properties field and start setting up how you want your bot to behave.

The Controller Class field determines whether or not the Bot is spawned with a particular AI. If you want the Bot to be able to move around independently then choose AI Controller, if you want to have full control over the bots movements then choose None. If you want the Bot to have Deathmatch AI, which means that it will move around independently and attack any other bots and/or the player, then you can over-ride AI settings by selecting the Force Deathmatch AI option. (Obviously you will need to give the Bot a weapon of some sort for this to be useful.)

In terms of weapons, you have two choices, you can either use the Give Default Inventory to spawn the Bot with the default LinkGun weapon, or you can use the Inventory List to give the Bot a specific weapon or set of weapons.

You can experiment with the other property fields (such as Pawn Name) but they can be left as their default settings.

Once you have set up the **[Actor Factory]**'s properties you need to set up your Kismet system. You need to connect an Actor to the Spawn Point variable input so that the engine knows where to spawn your Bot. This can be any Actor, but it makes sense to use **[PathNode]**s as these are used by Bots to navigate around a level.

It is useful to connect an empty Object variable to the Spawned variable output as this will enable you to use the ID of the spawned Bot in other sections of your Kismet systems.

You will need to connect some form of Event trigger to the Spawn Actor input of the **[Actor Factory]**, such as a **[TriggerVolume]**'s Touch event.

You can use the Finished output of the **[Actor Factory]** to trigger other actions, such as:

- **[Attach to Event]**: For example, **[Take Damage]**, **[Death]**, **[See Enemy]**
- **[Move To Actor]**: Needs to be used if you want to control the bots movement (ie. Controller Class = None)
- **[Start Firing]**: Needs to be used if you want to control the bots movement (ie. Controller Class = None)

If you want a Bot to automatically move and attack the player, then use:

- Controller Class = None
- Force Deathmatch AI = True

The Bot will then move around a network of **[PathNode]**s shooting at the player.

If you have multiple Bots active at the same time within your level, then you will need to make use of 'forced' actions (Controller Class = None; Force Deathmatch AI = False). (Force Deathmatch AI doesn't work for many situations as the Bots will attack each other as well as the Player.)

To use 'forced actions' to control how the Bot moves use the following Actions within Kismet:

- **[Move To Actor]** (Kismet/Action/AI)
  Used for moving Bots around between **[PathNode]**s
  If you connect multiple **[PathNode]**s to the Destination input the object will randomly select one and route the Bot to that one. A combination of random Destinations and randomly timed **[Move To Actor]**s can give the appearance of self-directed Bots. (You will need to make sure the Interruptable property is set to True.)
- **[Start Firing At]** (Kismet/Action/AI)
- **[Stop Firing]** (Kismet/Action/AI)

See UDK.com for more tutorials and advice regarding Bots and AI.

Key Binding

To create new input keys, you need to edit the UDKInput.ini file (C:\UDK\(***)\UDKGame\Config.) Find the line

```
"Bindings=(Name="E",Command="GBA_Use")"
```

It sets the E key to be the default "Use" key within the game. Add a new line and enter

```
"Bindings=(Name="H",Command="causeevent HPress")"
```

where "H" is the key you want to use and "HPress" is a unique name that will be used to identify the event. If you want a key to do something when it's released, you need to add the "OnRelease" keyword preceded by the pipe operator (|). For example,

```
Bindings=(Name="H",Command="causeevent HPress | OnRelease causeevent HRelease").
```

Save the UDKInput.ini file.

Reopen UDK.

In Kismet create a **[Console Event]** (Event/Misc/Console Event) object. In its properties, do the following:

- Check "Client Side Only."
- Enter the Console Event Name field to the name of your new event (e.g., Hpress).

This event trigger can then be used to trigger any event/action within Kismet.

Scripting

Setting Up UDK for Custom Scripts

To enable UDK to use your custom scripts you will need to make a change to one of its .ini files. Navigate to the Config folder within the UDK folder structure (UDK\(***)\UDKGame\Config).

Right-click the "DefaultEngine.ini" file and access its properties to uncheck the "Read only" option.

Open the "DefaultEngine.ini" file within Notepad. Move down to the "UnRealEd.EditorEngine" section.

Either (1) remove the null pointer (";") from the start of the "ModEditPackages = MyMod" line or, if that line is not present, (2) create a line "ModEditPackages = MyMod" at the bottom of that section. This means that now UDK will also check this folder for scripts in addition to its own. (If you have used the GAT Setup.exe then this should already be done this for you.)

Editing Scripts

Script files consist simply of text, so any basic text editor will do. If you're anticipating doing a significant degree of scripting, you may want to investigate other options.

Free text editors such as Notepad++ or ConText provide add-ons that enable syntax coloring, which can really help with reading scripts. They also provide good search facilities within both single files and folders:

Notepad++: http://notepad-plus-plus.org

Syntax addon: http://notepad-plus.sourceforge.net/commun/userDefinedLang/UnrealScript.zip

ConText: www.contexteditor.org

Syntax addon: http://cdn.contextstatic.org/downloads/highlighters/UEDScript.chl

What's in a Script?

Every script begins with a line that defines the name of the scripts (e.g., class GATPawnSoundGroup extends UTPawnSoundGroup). The class variable (GATPawnSoundGroup) is the name of the script file.

All classes "extend" from a "parent" class; in this case the GATPawnSoundGroup is an extension of the UTPawnSoundGroup class. This system is useful when creating modified classes (such as the GATPawnSoundGroup).

When extending an existing class, you only need to provide references to properties or functions that you want to override. If you are happy with any of the existing properties or functions, then simply leave them out of your custom class and the engine will use the "parent" script.

This idea of "inheriting" properties and functions from parent classes continues all the way up the hierarchy of classes. For example, GATPawnSoundGroup extends UTPawnSoundGroup, which extends Object.

A pretty short hierarchy, for example, would be UTWeap_One_Shot_Pistol extends UTWeap_ShockRifle, which extends UTWeap_ShockRifleBase, which extends UTWeapon, which extends UDKWeapon, which extends Weapon, which extends Inventory, which extends Actor, which extends Object. The Object script is the overall parent of all classes within UDK.

If you look at the GATPawnSoundGroup class, you will see that it only contains a "defaultproperties" section. This is because we did not need to change anything about how the UTPawnSoundGroup functions—we just wanted to be able to define our own sound cues for the various footstep sounds.

The same can be said for the various weapons we have created for the tutorial. Most of their functionality is handled by the parent classes (such as UTWeap_ShockRifle). All we have added to the extension class is a change to some of the default properties (e.g., sounds, firing rates) and some minor tweaks to some of the functions in order to alter how the weapons actually fire or trigger sounds. For example, taken from UTWeap_One_Shot_Pistol:

```
simulated function PlayFiringSound()   // plays back firing sounds
{
  if ( WeaponFireSnd[CurrentFireMode] != None )   // checks to see if we're in a
particular firing mode - primary or alt
  {
    WeaponPlaySound( WeaponFireSnd[CurrentFireMode] );   // sound to play
if enough ammo ---- CurrentFireMode = left/righ mouse button
  }
  ForceEndFire();
}
```

As you can see, the code has been fairly well commented so you can see what is happening within the script. The only modification that has been made to this particular function is the line "ForceEndFire()." This does not appear within this function within the parent class; it has been added here so that the weapon will not continuously re-fire while the mouse button is held down.

Using comments is a really good way of annotating script files. They can be used to remind yourself of things to do. They can also be used to describe what certain parts of your class do.

There are two ways of creating comments. A single line can be done like this:

```
// this is a comment
```

Multiple lines can be done like this:

```
/** This is a comment
 * So is this
```

```
* And this
*/
```

Immediately after the class and parent-class have been defined, you will find any variables that need declaring. There are two ways of doing this:

```
// taken from SeqAct_GATPlaySound.uc
var() name CMParamName;
var float CMParamValue;
```

In the preceding example, you can see that the CMParamName is declared using the var() statement, whereas CMParamValue only uses the var statement. As a result, the var() CMParamName is available for modification by the user from within the editor (right-click properties). The var CMParamValue can only be set or modified by the program itself.

The default properties section of a class is always found at the bottom of the file and is where all references to external files such as materials and sounds are called.

Within the default properties you can also "import" functionality from another class. For example,

```
// taken from SeqAct_GATPlaySound
Begin Object Class=AudioComponent
Name=YourSoundSound //"imports" AudioComponent functionality
End Object
```

In this example, the AudioComponent class has been imported via the "Begin Object Class" statement. This allows us to make use of some of the functionality offered by the AudioComponent class; in this case the ability to apply realtime volume fades to a SoundCue.

You will find that a lot of the more complex classes, such as vehicles, make use of additional imported functionality. This is helpful as it means that a single class (e.g., UTVehicle_Scorpion) doesn't become too unwieldy. Plus it means that if you need to change the behavior of a component element (e.g., the wheels), you can do this in a smaller, more manageable script without affecting the main class script.

If you want to experiment with script files, it is generally better to extend an existing class rather than to modify one of the standard classes as you may make changes that have unseen effects on how the game functions. Plus you may forget what changes you've made and struggle to restore them after you've finished.

If you must modify an existing class rather than extend, make sure you keep backups of the files you modify so can revert easily, or use comments to comment out the line you want to change. For example,

```
// FireInterval(0) = 0.5   // original property
FireInterval(0) = 0.1   // new modified property
```

Don't forget there's lots more on scripting (including a proper introduction) on the UDK.com website.

Bibliography and Further Reading

There are few books written on the subject of game audio. However, there are many web articles and conference presentations that are essential reading. We'll provide links to the latest articles and features on the Game Audio Tutorial website (www.thegameaudiotutorial.com). Here is a selected list from this larger bibliography.

General Texts

These selections are relevant to all chapters.

Collins, K. (2008). *From Pac-Man to Pop Music: Interactive Audio in Games and New Media* (5th ed.). Ashgate.
Collins, K. (2008). *Game Sound: An Introduction to the History, Theory, and Practice of Video Game Music and Sound Design*. MIT Press.
Marks, A. (2008). *Game Development Essentials: Game Audio Development*. Delmar.
Bridgett, R. (2010). *From the Shadows of Film Sound: Cinematic Production & Creative Process in Video Game Audio [Internet]. Available from<"http://www.blurb.com/bookstore/detail/1658613">*

The two books that follow are currently out of print, but they are well worth tracking down in your local library.

Brandon, A. (2004). *Audio for Games: Planning, Process, and Production*. New Riders Games.
Sanger, G. M. (2003). *The Fat Man on Game Audio: Tasty Morsels of Sonic Goodness, (illustrated ed.)*. New Riders.

Chapters 1 and 2

Epic Games, *UDK Documentation* [Internet]. Available from <www.udk.com/documentation>

Chapter 3

Everest, F. A., & Pohlmann, K. C. (2009). *Master Handbook of Acoustics* (5th ed.). Tab Electronics.
Farnell, A. (2010). *Designing Sound*. MIT Press.
Howard, D., & Angus, J. (2009). *Acoustics and Psychoacoustics* (4th ed.). Focal Press.
Miranda, E. (2002). *Computer Sound Design: Synthesis Techniques and Programming* (2nd ed.). Focal Press.
Roads, C. (1996). *The Computer Music Tutorial*. MIT Press.
Rossing, T. D., Moore, R. F., & Wheeler, P. A. (2001). *The Science of Sound* (3rd ed.). Addison Wesley.
Russ, M. (2008). *Sound Synthesis and Sampling* (3rd ed.). Focal Press.

Chapter 4

AudioKinetic. Wwise Documentation. [Internet]. Available from <www.audiokinetic.com/en/products/wwise/introduction>
Davis, R. (2000). *Complete Guide to Film Scoring*. Hal Leonard Corporation.

Donnelly, K. (2001). *Film Music: Critical Approaches*. Edinburgh University Press.

Drescher, P. (2010). *Game Audio in the Cloud*. O'Reilly Broadcast [Internet]. Available from <http://broadcast.oreilly.com/2010/03/game-audio-in-the-cloud.html>

Firelight Technologies. FMod Documentation. [Internet]. Available from <www.fmod.org/index.php/download#FMODDesigner>.

Hayward, P. (2004). *Off the Planet: Music, Sound and Science Fiction Cinema* (illustrated ed.). John Libbey Cinema and Animation.

IASIG, *Interactive XMF: File Format Specification Draft 0.0.1a* Available from <www.iasig.org/wg/ixwg/index.shtml>

Juslin, P., & Sloboda, J. (2001). *Music and Emotion: Theory and Research*. Oxford: OUP.

Larsen, P. (2007). *Film Music* (illustrated ed.). Reaktion Books.

Levitin, D. J. (2008). *This is Your Brain on Music: Understanding a Human Obsession*. Atlantic Books.

Rona, J. (2009). *Reel World: Scoring for Pictures* (2nd ed.). Music Pro Guides.

Veca, D., & Napolitano, J. (2009) Dead Space Sound Design. [Internet]. Available from <http://www.originalsoundversion.com/dead-space-sound-design-in-space-no-one-can-hear-interns-scream-they-are-dead-interview/>

Chapter 5

Beauchamp, R. (2005). *Designing Sound for Animation*. Pap/DVD Focal Press.

Borwick, J. (1996). *Sound Recording Practice* (4th ed.). Oxford: OUP.

Ince, S. (2006). *Writing for Video Games*. Methuen Drama.

Woodhall, W. (2010). *Audio Production and Post-Production*. Pap/Com Jones & Bartlett.

Yewdall, D. L. (2007). *The Practical Art of Motion Picture Sound* (3rd ed.). Focal Press.

Chapter 6

Altman, R. (1992). *Sound Theory/Sound Practice*. Routledge.

Bridgett, R. Gamasutra–Features–*The Future of Game Audio: Is Interactive Mixing the Key?*. [Internet]. Available from <www.gamasutra.com/view/feature/4025/the_future_of_game_audio__is_.php>

Bridgett, R. Gamasutra–Features–*The Game Audio Mixing Revolution*. [Internet]. Available from <www.gamasutra.com/view/feature/4055/the_game_audio_mixing_revolution.php>

Chion, M. (1994). *Audio-Vision: Sound on Screen*. Columbia University Press.

Clerwall, A. (2009). *How high dynamic range audio makes Battlefield: Bad Company go BOOM* Game Developers Conference. [Internet]. Available from <www.slideshare.net/aclerwall/how-high-dynamic-range-audio-makes-battlefield-bad-company-go-boom-1292018>

Jorgensen, K. (2009). *A comprehensive study of sound in computer games: How audio affects player action*. Edwin Mellen Press.

Juul, J. (2005). *Half-Real: Video Games Between Real Rules and Fictional Worlds*. MIT Press.

Katz, B. (2007). *Mastering Audio: The Art and The Science* (2nd ed.). Focal Press.

Salen, K. (2003). *Rules of Play: Game Design Fundamentals* (illustrated ed.). MIT Press.

Sider, L. (2003). *Soundscape: School of Sound Lectures 1998–2001*. Wallflower Press.

Sonnenschein, D. (2001). *Sound Design: The Expressive Power of Music, Voice and Sound Effects in Cinema*. Michael Wiese Productions.

Whittington, W. (2007). *Sound Design and Science Fiction*. University of Texas Press.

Chapter 7

Sweetman, C. *Criterion Games > Black > Behind the Scenes > A Choir of Guns*. [Internet]. Available from <www.criteriongames.com/black/behindthescenes/choirofguns>

Chapter 8

Chandler, H. M. (2008). *Game Production Handbook* (2nd ed.). Infinity Science Press.

Appendix

Ament, V. T. (2009). *The Foley Grail: The Art of Performing Sound for Film, Games, and Animation.* Pap/DVD Focal Press.

Brandon, A. (2004). *Audio for Games: Planning, Process, and Production.* New Riders.

Case, A. (2007). *Sound FX: Unlocking the Creative Potential of Recording Studio Effects.* Focal Press.

Krause, B., & Krause, B. L. (2002). *Wild Soundscapes: Discovering the Voice of the Natural World.* Wilderness Press. [With CD]. Pap/Com

Marks, A. (2008). *The Complete Guide to Game Audio: For Composers, Musicians, Sound Designers, Game Developers* (2nd ed.). Focal Press.

Oltyan, C. Gamasutra–Features–*Game Dev Collaboration: Google Docs Style.* [Internet]. Available from <www.gamasutra.com/view/feature/6112/game_dev_collaboration_google_.php>.

Rinzler, J., & Burtt, B. (2010). *Sounds of Star Wars.* Simon & Schuster.

Rumsey, F., & McCormick, T. (2009). *Sound and Recording* (6th ed.). Focal Press.

Sonnenschein, D. (2001). *Sound Design: The Expressive Power of Music, Voice and Sound Effects in Cinema.* Michael Wiese Productions.

Viers, R. (2008). *The Sound Effects Bible: How to Create and Record Hollywood Style Sound Effects.* Michael Wiese Productions.

Index

Index

Index